DEC 1 3 2002

SEP 1 3 2006

D0085342

MIND
AND
MAZE

Spatial Cognition and Environmental Behavior

ANN SLOAN DEVLIN

Westport, Connecticut
London

Library of Congress Cataloging-in-Publication Data

Devlin, Ann Sloan, 1948–
    Mind and maze : spatial cognition and environmental behavior / Ann Sloan Devlin.
      p. cm.
    Includes bibliographical references.
    ISBN 0–275–96784–0 (alk. paper)
    1. Space perception. 2. Spatial behavior. 3. Spatial ability. 4. Environmental
psychology. I. Title.
    BF469.D45 2001
    153.7'52—dc21   00–052859

British Library Cataloguing in Publication Data is available.

Copyright © 2001 by Ann Sloan Devlin

All rights reserved. No portion of this book may be
reproduced, by any process or technique, without the
express written consent of the publisher.

Library of Congress Catalog Card Number: 00–052859
ISBN: 0–275–96784–0

First published in 2001

Praeger Publishers, 88 Post Road West, Westport, CT 06881
An imprint of Greenwood Publishing Group, Inc.
www.praeger.com

Printed in the United States of America

The paper used in this book complies with the
Permanent Paper Standard issued by the National
Information Standards Organization (Z39.48–1984).

10 9 8 7 6 5 4 3 2 1

Copyright Acknowledgments

The author and publisher gratefully acknowledge permission to reprint the following illustrations:

Figures 3.1 and 3.2 from *Left Brain, Right Brain* by S.P. Springer and G. Deutsch © 1981 by W.H. Freeman and Company. Used with permission.

Figure 4.1 from Levine, M. You-are-here-maps: Psychological considerations. *Environment and Behavior*, 14 (2), pp. 221–237. Copyright © 1982, by Sage Publications. Reprinted by permission of Sage Publications, Inc.

Figure 5.2 adapted from the Map of Soho Design, *Metropolitan Home*, September/October, 1995, p. 128.

Figure 5.5 from *The Modernist City: An Anthropological Critique of Brasilia* by J. Holston, Chicago: The University of Chicago Press. Copyright © 1989 by The University of Chicago Press.

Figures 5.6 and 5.7 from *Great Streets* by A. Jacobs, Cambridge, MA: The MIT Press. Copyright © 1993 by the MIT Press.

ERINDALE
COLLEGE
LIBRARY

This book is dedicated to my parents, my siblings, my husband, and my daughter, all of whom possess a love of learning new things.

Contents

Figures   ix

Preface   xi

Acknowledgments   xiii

Introduction   xv

1   The Development of Spatial Cognition: *Infants and Newcomers*   1

2   Gender Differences in Spatial Cognition: *North by Northwest*   41

3   The Neuropsychology of Spatial Cognition: *In the Mind's Eye*   97

4   Research on Way-finding Tools: *Maps and Minds*   147

5   Spatial Cognition and Urban Design: *Trapped in a Tree*   191

References   233

Index   273

Figures

2.1	A sample item from the Vandenberg and Kuse (1978) Mental Rotation Test	43
3.1	The left hemisphere	98
3.2	The visual field crossover	100
4.1	Levine's YAH example, left map correctly identified with symbols	160
4.2	Westfarms YAH map	160
4.3	Rome subway graphics	163
4.4	Way-finding computer screen in Santa Maria Maggiore	165
4.5	Floor numbering at Westminster Place	173
4.6	Totem poll at the National Zoo	174
4.7	Signs along University of Michigan hospital corridor	178
4.8	Bill Hall west entrance	179
4.9	Bill Hall east entrance	180
4.10	Bill Hall "hidden" stairway to first floor	180
4.11	Shain Library third-floor entrance	181
4.12	Filigree sign	183
4.13	University of Michigan Angell Hall arrow	184

4.14   University of Michigan "LIFT" sign   185
4.15   Office building "wall coverings"   185
4.16   Office building wall index   186
4.17   Philadelphia airport signage   186
4.18   Mystic Community Center signage   187
4.19   Boston City Hall   188
5.1   A strategic node: Union Station in New London   199
5.2   SoHo schematic   204
5.3   SoHo view   205
5.4   Main Street USA, Disneyworld   209
5.5   Brasilia plan   219
5.6   Brasilia city center illustrating voids   221
5.7   Venice, Italy, covering the same area   222
5.8   Roosevelt Island, Main Street, 1978   227
5.9   Roosevelt Island, Main Street, 1991   228
5.10   Celebration, Florida, house types   230
5.11   Market Street in Celebration, Florida   231

Preface

One of the advantages of teaching at a small liberal arts college is that you are often pushed beyond traditional academic boundaries. For those of us who have wide-ranging interests, such a teaching environment provides an opportunity for interdisciplinarity. At a time when knowledge is becoming increasingly specialized with a premium on expertise, a case can still be made for understanding a topic from a variety of perspectives. After all, life is nothing if not interdisciplinary.

This book is an opportunity to examine a fundamental aspect of human behavior, the fact that we are animals for whom functioning in space—moving in space, navigating, or way finding—is essential to our survival. In order to survive, we need to know the "whereness" as well as the "what-ness" of objects in our environment.

All too often, because of the value academia places on expertise with a narrowly defined focus, a book on a topic like spatial cognition would emphasize one particular aspect, like development or neuroscience. This book differs profoundly by approaching a spectrum of topics related to spatial cognition, from developmental psychology to urban planning, from their disciplinary perspectives. Although in all likelihood few urban planners know much about Piaget beyond his basic concepts, the developmental achievements of spatial competence recognized in Piaget's stage of formal operations connect directly to urban planning. The youth in the stage of formal operations finally understands Euclidean principles, and many aspects of urban planning rest on Euclidean concepts. Good urban planning creates an environment where young adults and older individuals can navigate successfully, demonstrating their cognitive competence.

When urban planning fails, or when navigational tools such as maps fail, there is a lack of understanding of fundamental cognitive principles. In particular, if planners and designers knew more about fundamental characteristics of spatial cognition, it might take planning in a new direction or at the very least make practitioners aware of situations to be avoided.

One of the characteristics of this book is that it presents many of the studies in considerable depth—there is a lot of detail about the research. This approach was selected for a number of reasons. First, as with most areas of psychological research, the data often conflict. By presenting the studies in detail, the reader may be better able to see the source of the differences. Spatial cognition is an area where different dependent measures, the way the behavior in question is assessed, are used in studies that examine the same topic. Good examples might be mental rotation or the ever-elusive "way finding." Without a clear grasp of what is being measured and how, conclusions are beyond reach.

Second, the book can serve as a resource of ideas for studies because there is sufficient detail to allow people to decide to pursue particular avenues. Going beyond the kinds of information presented in a typical literature review, the book gives readers a chance to see the kinds of approaches they might consider useful (or practical). The third reason is that the depth of detail allows an evaluation of the ecological validity of the research. If we are to link considerations of development and neuroscience, on the one hand, to urban planning and design, on the other, it is important to use small-scale approaches from development and neuroscience that possess ecological validity. Many times we may be left wondering about the merit of a particular dependent measure in terms of its implications for real-world navigation. The reader here will make judgments for him- or herself. Not every reader will find it necessary or useful to absorb all of the details in each chapter. But for those who want to understand a topic at many levels, information from brain architecture to new town design is provided.

Happy navigating!

Acknowledgments

Although I bitterly complained about attending what I called a "guinea pig" school in my youth, I owe a great debt to my early academic training at the University School (long since closed) in Ann Arbor, Michigan. Whether in art (Mrs. Tejada), German (Miss Trumm), or English (Mr. Shafer), the teachers at the University School fostered a love of learning and interdisciplinarity that is at the heart of my approach to education and research. Who could forget making the nearly life-sized papier-mâché figures (framed over chicken wire) that accompanied our reading of *The Princess and the Goblin* in Mrs. Tipton's class, or constructing the colored paper scenery to create the illusion of rapids on a river for the 4th grade play about Abraham Lincoln written by the class.

In college I was fortunate to find my way into the classes of Steve and Rachel Kaplan, who introduced me to the information processing approach to environmental psychology, a foundation of this book. It would be hard to find better mentors.

In writing this book, my colleagues in the psychology department at Connecticut College were generous with their suggestions, and I owe a particular debt of thanks to Stuart Vyse, who was always encouraging and helpful.

The project would have been far more difficult without a semester's sabbatical from Connecticut College, and without the never-ending support of the Connecticut College library staff, most notably Steven Bustamante. I have little doubt that I pushed the interlibrary loan system to is limits with this project, but my requests were always honored in a timely fashion. Thanks also to Ellen Leiba at Greenwood Publishing Group. She made the production process a very smooth one.

Finally, my research assistants over the past three years, Sara Pikcilingis, Renee Martinez, Linda Najjar, Amy Danna, and Billy Carr, never seemed to tire of tracking down articles for the book. Thank you.

Introduction

Spatial cognition, defined broadly, is the study of knowledge involving the interrelationships among people, objects, and space. We see the manifestations or behavioral correlates of such knowledge in activities ranging from a child's play with miniature farm animals to an architect's rendering of a plan for a new town. The study of spatial cognition interweaves a wide range of topics, from developmental theories and neuropsychology to applications involving architecture and urban planning, and it is one of the central research areas in environmental psychology. While earlier papers exist, Edward Tolman's (1948) classic article, "Cognitive Maps in Rats and Men," is often viewed as piquing psychologists' interests in the isomorphic relationship between the way we navigate in the world and the mental flexibility provided by an internal representation or cognitive map. From the mundane example of the difficulty we have understanding shopping mall "You-are-here" maps to the tragic results for foreign motorists who were murdered after losing their way in Miami, we all face challenges presented by finding our way in the world—using orientation, guidance, and place behaviors (Nadel, 1990).

With the emphasis on cognition in a wide variety of domains within psychology and the mushrooming body of knowledge dealing with brain–behavior relationships, there are fascinating questions to ask about the processes that mediate spatial behavior, and therefore about mind and maze. How do we acquire knowledge about the spatial environment? Do men and women differ in their ability to perform navigational tasks, as has been suggested? Are there different areas of the brain dedicated to different aspects of spatial cognition? How do designed environments facilitate or interfere with our navigational goals? How might maps and other wayfinding aids better guide our navigational efforts? This volume answers these and other questions about spatial cognition, particularly as it applies to navigation in large-scale environments.

One of the challenges facing those who do research on human behavior and those who apply that information is the interdisciplinary nature of knowledge. Seldom is any given subject adequately viewed from a single domain, and the pressure to gain expertise within a domain invariably outweighs the desire to take a more interdisciplinary perspective. Yet the need for interdisciplinary understanding is certainly evident in the field of spatial cognition, a topic that embraces a continuum from basic to applied questions. One of the challenges in this field is that researchers often represent disciplines that have little advanced training in common and share no vocabulary. Those interested in the neuropsychology of spatial cognition concern themselves with neural networks and brain modules, hormonal effects, and, more recently, evolutionary theory, whereas those interested in architectural applications talk about environmental complexity, signage, and legibility. To address the gulf that now exists in this field, this volume presents material generated by cognitive psychologists and neuroscientists, on one end of the continuum, and environmental psychologists, architects, and urban planners, on the other. In between are a diversity of other disciplines, including developmental psychology and behavioral geography. A theme that touches most of the areas and provides at least one context for integration is *scale*.

The primary goal of this volume is interdisciplinary education. Secondarily, the material can suggest new avenues for research and design. Basically, those engaged in cognitive psychology pay little attention to the implications of their work for the designed environment. Similarly, architects and urban planners, with few exceptions, have little understanding of the cognitive and behavioral underpinnings of their designs. A much richer visual environment and one better suited to human needs might emerge if designers and planners knew more about the cognitive capabilities of their users. Conversely, the research agenda of cognitive psychologists might include new questions if they better understood the implications of research on spatial cognition for the designed environment.

The approach taken is a review of the research in detail, with chapters that include laboratory research as well as ecologically oriented studies, in keeping with the emphasis on spatial behavior in the environment.

The chapter topics were selected because they provide a more in-depth look at areas that are of potential interest to people doing research in environment-behavior studies with an emphasis on spatial cognition. The one possible exception to this is the chapter on neuropsychology, which provides a more "molecular" look at the basis of spatial cognition. It is included because even those doing research on such "molar" topics as way finding and navigation may find it helpful to understand more about the neuronal correlates of this behavior, particularly as neuroscience is an area that will become even more dominant as technology improves. Topics such as animal behavior, language and space, or robotics are not included (although there is discussion of computer-assisted navigation systems) because the emphasis is on research judged to be more appealing to environment-behavior researchers.

The first three chapters in this volume emphasize basic research on spatial cognition related to development, gender differences, and neuroscience. Chapter 1, "The Development of Spatial Cognition," begins with an overview of developmental theories in spatial cognition, including Piaget and Siegel and White; reviews criticisms of the theories; and then goes on to discuss research across a variety of scales, with particular emphasis on the ecological validity of the tasks. The research is divided into sections that deal with small-, mid-, and macroenvironmental scales. The next sections of the chapter deal with the contributions made to developmental theory by research in behavioral geography and computational theory. These approaches are noteworthy because, among other aspects, they tend to be interdisciplinary in nature. Golledge's Anchor Point Theory and Garling's Theory of Travel Plans are highlighted. The chapter concludes with a review of navigation in the elderly and in those with visual impairments. It has been argued that the elderly decline in certain cognitive abilities, but the research on spatial cognition in the field with this group suggests that the decline may have been overstated. Research on the spatial cognition of the blind suggests that the blind do, indeed, possess spatial representations that are in many respects functionally similar to those of sighted individuals.

In Chapter 2, "Gender Differences in Spatial Cognition," the issue of whether such differences exist is explored by looking at the traditional spatial tasks (mental rotation, spatial visualization, spatial perception), and the findings of recent meta-analyses of spatial cognition. The chapter also reviews whether these gender differences emerge as a function of age and when the tasks are more ecological, for example, retracing a route across a college campus. Methodological issues are important in sorting out the validity of the claims. The chapter concludes by considering various points of view about these gender differences, including genetic, hormonal, neurological, and psychosocial explanations.

Chapter 3, "The Neuropsychology of Spatial Cognition," explores the data for modules and subsystems dedicated to spatial function and includes the role of vision and mental imagery as they relate to spatial cognition. Lesion and cerebral blood flow data are reviewed, as are the organizational and activational effects of hormones. The data on cerebral lateralization, as well as explanations for such lateralizations, are examined. The role of the hippocampus, both in spatial cognition and in memory, is reviewed. In addition, principles of vision, especially those emerging from the early work of David Marr on primal sketches and edges, is related to principles of architecture and design.

Chapters 4 and 5 focus more specifically on applied issues and the link between the disciplines of psychology and design. Chapter 4 examines research on the "tools" used in way finding, from maps to the building itself. The chapter includes a major section on aspects of cognitive psychology that play a role in the understanding of these tools, including hierarchies, familiarity, and distortions. Individual differences and Gestalt principles are also addressed. Studies from statistical graphics and cartography as well as cognitive psychology are included, with a special emphasis on the role that color and format play in our interpretation of maps and signs. Color has a "checkered" history in terms of its usefulness and the inclusion of color as a way-finding cue is discussed in that context. Issues of format such as the level of detail and the location of labels are also examined. Research on libraries and hospitals is used to demonstrate the intersection between cognition and way-finding behavior.

Chapter 5 examines research on spatial cognition as it relates to principles of urban design, bringing together the work of Kevin Lynch, Christopher Alexander, Donald Appleyard, and other urban-planning theorists. The chapter analyzes their design prescriptions in terms of the cognitive principles that have been described in earlier sections of the book. The basic question to be answered is whether these principles reflect what we know about human cognitive capacities. Lynch's form qualities and five structural elements are discussed with particular emphasis on the role of the street in creating legibility. The schema of "Main Street, USA" is also addressed, as it shows how the schema may shape our perceptions of the environment. After reviewing the effect of the Garden City movement on design, the chapter pays particular attention to the creation of new towns, nationally and internationally, as they offer a special opportunity to examine the planner's intention and the user's way-finding success. Included are the international examples of Chandigarh, India, and Brasilia, Brazil, and the United States examples of Levittown, New Jersey; Roosevelt Island, New York; and Seaside and Celebration, Florida. Because he played a seminal role in the design of Chandigarh, one of the new towns discussed in the chapter, the design philosophy of LeCorbusier is also included.

The Development of Spatial Cognition:
Infants and Newcomers

When we think of way finding, most of us think of adult behavior—the newcomer to the city trying to understand the subway map; the automobile driver who has taken a wrong turn and must redirect his or her efforts— but to fully understand adult spatial behavior, we must first look at the challenges faced by the infant and the young child in forming a representation of the spatial environment. In examining the theoretical formulations and research efforts dealing with the beginnings of spatial cognition, clues will be provided about what is necessary to create an understandable or legible (Lynch, 1960) environment. Two themes highlighted in the research in this chapter are intertwined: the roles of scale and ecological validity. These factors are critical in evaluating the merit of this research and its ability to inform us about spatial competence.

THEORETICAL FRAMEWORKS

Research on spatial cognition and cognitive mapping has generated a number of useful theoretical frameworks, including those of Moore (1976), Siegel and White (1975), Golledge (Couclelis, Golledge, Gale, & Tobler, 1987), and Garling (Garling, Book, & Lindberg, 1984, 1986; Saisa & Garling, 1987). Of these, Moore and Siegel and White have stressed what might be called a traditional developmental approach. The work of Golledge, Couclelis, and others represents a substantial departure from the traditional developmental theories.

While it has been argued that no one theory is dominant in the area of cognitive development (Siegler, 1996), a number of the theories we will consider here rest in large part on the work of Piaget, and it is there we will begin to understand the progression of spatial competence in the child.

Piaget and the Child's Conception of Space

The extent of Piaget's writing and theoretical offerings about the mind of the child is overwhelming. His effect on the area of child psychology has been profound, and no less so in the area of spatial cognition. Whether authors use Piaget as a foundation or not, an evaluation of his work is a good starting point to understand the child's conception of space.

Piaget describes the child's progression through spatial cognition as one involving first topological, then projective, and essentially concurrently, Euclidean or metric relations (Piaget & Inhelder, 1948/1956). Piaget's major developmental periods for intelligence will be familiar to most readers. The periods of development are labeled: sensorimotor (birth–age 2), preoperational (ages 2–7), concrete operations (ages 7–12), and formal operations (ages 11–12 to ages 14–15 and beyond). His spatial sequences are less well known and require some explanation.

In Piaget's view, competence in spatial cognition is not fully developed at birth and emerges gradually, fundamentally through action. As an example, let us look briefly at what he says about the sensorimotor period. Piaget describes three periods of sensorimotor development and their accomplishments in terms of spatial cognition. The first period consists of two stages: pure reflexes and primary habits. The second involves beginning manipulation of objects (secondary circular reactions at 4–5 months of age), the child's "first fully intelligent behaviour" (Piaget & Inhelder, 1948/1956, p. 6). This takes the child through the first year. The third part of this period involves beginning experimentation (tertiary circular reactions) and the child's first "internalized co-ordinations" (p. 6). The reader desiring a good overview of Piaget's equilibration theory in the context of spatial cognition is referred to an excellent chapter by Hart and Moore (1973).

The infant develops a rudimentary spatial competence during the sensorimotor period, which, according to Piaget (Piaget & Inhelder, 1948/1956), consists of relationships that have their foundation in Gestalt concepts. For example, the child has a developing awareness of "nearby-ness" of objects in the same perceptual field. In addition, Piaget talks about the child's awareness of separation, of order (or spatial succession), of enclosure or surrounding, and of continuity. The emphasis in the first period is on topological relationships.

During the second period of sensorimotor development, the major accomplishment is what Piaget (Piaget & Inhelder, 1948/1956) describes as the general coordination of actions. During this time (from age 4–5 months to 10–12 months), the emphasis is on the development of perceptual constancy of shape and size. The child's perspective is fundamentally egocentric and the spatial relationships that are perceived cannot be separated from the child's activity.

During the third period of sensorimotor development, the child begins to manage the relationships of objects to each other. Throughout the sequence Piaget (Piaget & Inhelder, 1948/1956) emphasizes the role of action, of motor activity. Motor activity is the foundation of perceptual activity, the construction of perceptual space, representational images, and, ultimately, how the child represents spatial concepts. This emphasis on motor activity, pervasive through development, is fundamental to way finding, and this is as true for adults as it is for children. Whether we think of examples from adult behavior or from children's experience, the fundamental concept is that acting in the environment will serve the traveler well throughout the lifespan. For adults, consider the difference between route knowledge when we drive a car contrasted with the mental representation that results when we sit as passengers. For children, consider the mental representation of a child that has mastered crawling versus one that cannot yet crawl. For both the adult and the child, the fundamental difference in the examples is the role of action. Even research on the way finding of the elderly indicates a competence in real-world way-finding tasks (i.e., in action) that we do not see in the laboratory environment (Ohta & Kirasic, 1983).

If we concentrate specifically on the content of spatial cognition proposed by Piaget, we have the progressive stages of topological, perspective, and Euclidean relations.

Topological space is defined by Piaget and Inhelder [1948/1956] as encoding relationships of enclosure, touching, order, proximity, and separation within objects. Another way of defining topological space is that it encodes spatial relationships that would be maintained under elastic distortions. It is thus nonmetric. It fails to distinguish between straight lines and curved ones, and between curves and angles. (Newcombe, 1989, pp. 212–213)

When we move on to projective or perspective relations, a major difference is that relationships among objects can be encoded. The self may be one of these objects, and the distinction between the child's view and the viewpoint of others becomes a possibility. The child can thus coordinate views. In Euclidean spatial relationships, the child encodes location with metric information. An abstract system can be used that is an advance over the relation system used in projective space (Newcombe, 1989, p. 214). The similar nature of the projective and Euclidean systems leads to Piaget and

Inhelder's (1948/1956) proposal that they evolve together, but the ultimate equilibrium of Euclidean relations occurs slightly later.

Piaget's Research Paradigm

In developing his theory of spatial cognition, as in other areas, Piaget relied heavily on what must be considered innovative experiments with children. Perhaps the most well-known experiment in the context of space is what is known as the "three mountains" paradigm. In this experiment, the child's task is to indicate what view of the mountainscape would be seen from various vantage points:

A pasteboard model, one metre square and from twelve to thirty centimetres high, was made to represent three mountains. From his initial position in front of the model (A) the child sees a green mountain occupying the foreground a little to his right. The summit of this mountain is topped by a little house. To his left he sees a brown mountain, higher than the green one and slightly to its rear. This mountain is distinguished not only by its colour but also by having a red cross at the summit. In the background stands the highest of the three mountains, a grey pyramid whose peak is covered in snow. (Piaget & Inhelder, 1948/1956, pp. 211–212)

The children view a collection of 10 pictures representing the mountains seen from different viewpoints. They also have three pieces of cardboard, shaped and colored the same as each of the mountains, to be arranged to represent the mountains from a given perspective. The children also use a small wooden doll the face of which is left plain so that the child will focus only on the doll's position. When the doll is put in a number of different places, the child must determine what perspective the doll will "see." The doll, not the child, moves, and here we may have a clue to the child's performance; the child is less an actor than an observer.

Using 100 children from about 4 to 12 years of age, Piaget (Piaget & Inhelder, 1948/1956) found that the preoperational child at Stage II cannot essentially distinguish between his own viewpoint and the viewpoint of others. At Stage III (ages 7–8 to 11–12 years), however, Piaget reports an emergence of discrimination and coordination of perspectives. Piaget says that the children at Stage II cannot rotate their perspective as their viewpoint changes because of their egocentrism. They are unable to shift the relations of the body's axes (left–right, in back–in front). If one word emerges to describe the difficulty the child apparently has, and to serve as a focus of controversy surrounding the child's spatial development, it is the word *egocentrism*.

The Controversy Surrounding Egocentrism

One of the areas of controversy surrounding Piaget's work is the concept of egocentrism and the extent to which the child is able (or unable) to take the perspective of another viewer, as we have seen in the "three mountains" research. In fact, arguments exist about the validity of egocentrism as a construct (Ford, 1979, 1985; Waters & Tinsley, 1985). What has emerged from the considerable literature on this aspect of the child's competence is that the child can, in fact, demonstrate perspective taking under "certain conditions" (see, e.g., Borke, 1975). Generally, those conditions involve familiar materials, and we must keep in mind what that means for the parameters of the child's spatial competence. I have highlighted the phrase "certain conditions" because it is only with a number of specific stimulus changes that the child successfully performs something like the three mountains task.

Both the dimensions of the task and the type of response required influence perceptual role taking in preschool and elementary school children and challenge Piaget's conclusions about the timing of their spatial understanding (Presson, 1982; Somerville & Bryant, 1985). It has been argued that the spatial competence of children is underestimated (Spencer & Darvizeh, 1981); for example, use of the human form (e.g., a doll) can enhance perspective taking (Gzesh & Surber, 1985). Furthermore, Blades and Cooke (1994) argue that by the age of 5, children are able to understand the idea of correspondence between a model of a room and that room, even when the model is not aligned. But 4-year-olds do have trouble with the task when misalignment exists. When the tasks are more abstract (e.g., triangulation, mental rotation), the results seem more in line with Piaget's age sequencing (Hardwick, McIntyre, & Pick, 1976). Generalizations about spatial cognition in the form of a stage theory like Piaget's are likely to underestimate the complexity of spatial behavior. There is an intricate interaction between the task and the response.

How do infants locate objects in space? Presson and Ihrig (1982) examined this question. In particular, they were interested in whether infants demonstrated egocentric responses when their mothers were used as landmarks. In discussing this particular study, I am also introducing a theme we will see throughout the book: the importance of landmarks in way finding. Thirty infants, with a mean age of 9.0 months, were tested in a laboratory situation, a 4×3 meter room with a walker in the middle. Infants were cued to look on a screen to the right or left for a colored slide to appear. After eight training trials, the infant in the walker was rotated 180 degrees. For half the infants, the mothers also moved; for the other half, the mothers remained stationary. The authors predicted that more correct responses would be seen for those infants for whom the mother remained stationary (and hence served as a landmark). More egocentric responses were expected when the mother moved. There was, in fact, a significant effect of the mother's position, with the percentage of objective responders at .80 with stationary mothers and at .43 with moving mothers. The data support the conclusion that 9-month-olds can locate events in relation to the mother-as-landmark. Thus, when egocentric responses are claimed, the errors may result from nonspatial response habits or unreliable spatial cues (the mother who moved). The stimulus (the mother-as-landmark) changed position. This is a clear example of a study in which the egocentrism of the response varies with the stimulus conditions.

Both the stimulus and the response have been demonstrated to matter. Borke (1975) demonstrated the role of both in a study that replicated Piaget and Inhelder's work. But Borke challenged the children with what was viewed as a more age-appropriate task. With 3- and 4-year-olds, Borke exposed the children to three displays; a large, red fire engine; and Grover from *Sesame Street*. The children were told "when Grover stops to look out of his car, I want you to turn the scene that moves so you are looking at it the same way Grover is." The three displays were 1) a landscape with a small lake, a toy sailboat, farm animals, and a model of a house; 2) Piaget and Inhelder's three mountains; and 3) miniature people and animals in a natural setting. The author reports significant differences in performance as a function of the display. All of the children succeeded in predicting what Grover would see for the two scenes involving toy objects, but more errors were made in the Piaget and Inhelder display. Borke suggests that these discrete and easily differentiated objects give more cues for young children to use than they find in the three mountains task, even though it is a similar configuration.

In addition to the nature of the stimuli themselves, the response required of the children is important. Following our theme of the importance of movement, children seem to make fewer errors when they can move, that is, children perform better at these perspective-taking tasks when their response involves moving the display to the other's point of view rather than selecting a picture of that view or building a model of that view. Based on his and other research, Borke questions Piaget's conclusion that young children are incapable of taking others' viewpoints at this age.

Noting that the child passes through the three stages (topological, projective, and Euclidean) with both perceptual and conceptual modes, Blades and Spencer (1994) attempt to explain the inconsistency in data surrounding Piaget's predictions. They do this by pointing to the kinds of tasks (perceptual or conceptual) asked of the child in a given experiment. Perceptual thought is based on the formation of spatial relationships when the information is not directly available. When children perform a task earlier than Piaget's developmental sequence would predict, Blades and Spencer suggest the children were likely to have been given a perceptual as opposed to a conceptual task.

For Newcombe (1989), the failure of perspective taking is not really a matter of being unable to take someone else's view. Perspective taking requires more than simply recognizing that people at different compass points have a perspective different from yours; it requires figuring things out or computing. In discussing egocentrism in infancy and childhood, Newcombe states that beginning by the age of 2 or 3 years, children are aware that people at a different vantage point will have a different view. She reviews the helpful distinctions made by Flavell involving two rules for seeing. At Level 1, children are aware of the existence and general nature of another person's visual experience, but they do not know that experience in great detail. At Level 2, the child has acquired a number of rules with regard to the other person's view. Newcombe goes on to state that, "Absence of Level 1 knowledge is basically the traditional idea of egocentrism. The research of the Flavell group has conclusively demonstrated that egocentrism in this sense simply does not exist, at least not past infancy" (p. 209). Another explanation of the children's seemingly egocentric response is that they may wish to show all the objects they know to be present *as present* and thus are not really demonstrating a deficit:

In summary, a fair conclusion at present is that by age 2 or 3 years, children know that other observers see different objects from those that they see and that these objects can be inferred by looking across a direct line of sight from the observer's eyes. In this sense, toddlers are clearly not egocentric. By age 4 or 5 years, children have mastered a number of additional rules regarding others' visual experience. The relationship of these rules to the computation of the particular nature of that experience is not clear. One hypothesis—that of Piaget and Inhelder as well as others—is that the ability to compute others' views depends on the nature of children's systems for encoding the location of objects in space. In this view, the acquisition of Level 2 rules would bear no necessary relationship to the ability to solve problems requiring computation. (Newcombe, 1989, p. 210)

By the time they are age 4 or 5, Newcombe and others have shown that children can go beyond topological coding. Even in the absence of nearby landmarks, they can encode location well and are able to use a coordinate system provided by the researcher.

Beyond varying explanations of egocentrism, others have pointed to the role of traits (e.g., field dependence, impulsivity) as influencing the performance on perspective-taking tasks. In a longitudinal study (Brodzinsky, 1982), impulsive children were more likely to make egocentric errors and less likely to make adjacent errors than reflective children. Children's cognitive style (reflective versus impulsive) was also assessed in a study of perspective taking in two multiple-object farm scenes, with the use of photographs progressing in 45-degree increments around the scene (Brodzinsky, 1980). As children became more reflective or older, their perspective-taking performance improved.

Summary

Piaget's concept of egocentrism has been questioned by research. It seems that the child in the preoperational stage demonstrates far less egocentrism in the traditional sense than Piaget had described. The child can do a variety of things, some of which are involved in performing successfully on the three mountains task. Certain configurations of stimuli (especially familiarity) and response (particularly movement) will assist the child. However, the *full complement* of fundamental behaviors that Piaget is testing in the three mountains paradigm may take until the child is nearly a decade old to mature. At the same time, one of the contributions of the research on perspective taking is an awareness of other factors that shape the competence of the child, and the ability of the child to perform parts, if not the complete set, of behaviors required by Piaget's experimental conditions. In a helpful article, Rosser (1994) argues that the varying results in such experiments on spatial cognition can be explained by the existence of its multidimensionality. A multidimensional explanation of spatial cognition incorporates the prediction of developmental asynchrony rather than synchrony. "If spatial tasks . . . are mediated by different sorts of representations—propositions versus analogues—then their developmental histories may differ also" (p. 261). In research with four Piagetian-influenced tasks (water level, conservation of area, bead placement, and perspective taking), 100 children participated, ranging in age from 4 to 12. Rosser found evidence for the hypothesis of multidimensionality in terms of variations in age-of-onset, developmental function shape, and intertask correlations.

Alternative Developmental Theories

Piaget's theoretical formulation is set within the framework of the mental life of the child progressing from topological to projective and Euclidean understanding. A variety of other researchers have incorporated a similar developmental progression, but with a different goal—to describe the formation of a cognitive map, an internal representation of our understanding of large spatial arrays, the kind of array that cannot be viewed in a single glance (e.g., a college campus, a city neighborhood). Often these alternative theories stem from the interest of those with more training in geography or environmental psychology than developmental psychology. Although these theories have a different flavor, we often see in them an emphasis on the role of environmental features (i.e., landmarks and routes) in the formation of cognitive maps. This emphasis exists in part because these features can be shaped to create more comprehensible or legible environments (Lynch, 1960).

Moore (1976) proposes that cognitive maps advance from an unorganized form (Level I) through a middle stage stressing more independent clusters of landmarks (Level II) to a third stage characterized by a coordinated frame of reference (Level III). Siegel and White (1975) view the cognitive map as a hierarchical arrangement with the most integrated configurational knowledge dependent upon route knowledge, which is in turn dependent on landmarks. Taylor and Tversky (1992a, 1992b) also state that elements such as landmarks may be remembered within a hierarchical context, with individual elements remembered in the context of smaller regions and those regions, in turn, relative to larger regions.

In the anchor-point hypothesis of spatial cognition, Couclelis and colleagues (1987) also stress the importance of a hierarchical arrangement of features. The properties of maps are to include regionalization, the role of salient cues, and hierarchical arrangement. The anchor concept is central to their explanation; anchors provide a "skeletal hierarchical structure for representing and organizing cognitive information about space" (p. 99).

Saisa and Garling (1987), like Kaplan (1973) and Passini (1984), describe spatial behavior or way finding within a decision-making framework; travel through a large-scale environment can be described as a series of decisions culminating in a travel plan (Saisa & Garling, 1987). Travel plans are postulated to link internal processes (e.g., retrieval of locational information from cognitive maps) to external behavior (i.e., movement). Garling and colleagues (1984) propose three interconnected components that are represented in cognitive maps: places, the spatial relations between places, and travel plans. Like Kaplan (1973), Garling and colleagues (1986) place this cognitive-mapping theory within an information-processing framework, postulating that travelers decide on a destination, identify its location, select a route, and decide on a travel mode.

While the theoretical constructs may differ, these theories have in common an emphasis on progression from a less integrated to a more coordinated spatial framework that develops with experience. There is also an undercurrent of the importance of particular kinds of spatial information. Specifically, *landmarks* emerge as significant sources of information in the theories of Moore (1976), Siegel and White (1975), and, viewed as salient spatial elements, in the work of Couclelis and colleagues (1987). Given the developmental and microgenetic progression hypothesized by a number of these theorists, landmarks appear to be particularly important for the newcomer to an environment. For the newcomer, limited experience has constrained the ability to develop more integrated configurational knowledge (Garling et al., 1986). Thus, these theories place an emphasis on the utility of the environment as a source of information for the way finder.

Siegel and White's Developmental Theory of Spatial Cognition

In their theoretical formulation of spatial cognition, Siegel and White (1975) emphasize the role of landmarks. Routes and paths between landmarks become established with experience. They postulate that spatial knowledge along routes progresses from topological to metric properties, following Piaget's general developmental sequence. Importantly, landmarks and path sets are organized into clusters, where there is a high level of coordination within clusters but only topological information about cluster relations. Finally, an overall coordinated frame of reference develops such that Euclidean properties are available within and across clusters. This theoretical progression is not universally accepted. Spencer, Blades, and Morsely (1989) argue that landmarks may not be prerequisite to route knowledge.

Siegel and White (1975) take a constructivist view, that is, a view that knowledge is a compilation of meaning over time: "Arising from a history of philosophical and neurological analysis, we have the development of an argument that knowledge of extended space is a mental construction. This construction is a kind of temporal integration which man is neurologically predisposed to create" (p. 16).

Much like the view taken by urban planner Kevin Lynch (1960), Siegel and White (1975) see the purpose of spatial representation as supporting movement within the environment to find your way. The model places particular emphasis on the role of landmarks' "unique patterns of perceptual events at a specific location" (p. 23). For adult humans, landmarks tend to be visual; they serve as beginning and end anchors and help maintain orientation along the course of travel. The authors also emphasize the sensorimotor nature of routes. "Routes are nonstereotypic sensorimotor routines for which one has expectations about landmarks and other decision points" (p. 24). What they call configurational knowledge has a Gestalt flavor; the coordination of various perspectives and views to create a whole that would be useful if a new route were required. Configurational knowledge emphasizes clustering or grouping to create a larger representational schema, although they do not discuss configurational knowledge in these specific terms.

Siegel and White (1975) agree with Piaget about the central role of locomotion of motor activity in the development of spatial representations. But their emphasis on the role of landmarks places that environmental feature in a position of greater importance. This emphasis on the role of landmarks in the development of spatial cognition leads them to suggest a "recognition-in-context-memory"; in turn, they make a rather large jump to incorporate Livingston's "Now Print!" mechanism as a player in memory encoding. The "Now Print!" mechanism is most well-known in terms of the flashbulb memory literature; vivid memories of where you were when Kennedy was assassinated are among the best examples (Brown & Kulik, 1977; Neisser, 1982b). Siegel and White argue that ". . . the figurative core of a spatial representation could exist on the basis of a flashbulb going off (an orienting response made, a photograph taken), leading to "recognition-in-context" memory of landmarks. Spatial representations would then develop by organizing a choice-point decision-system between landmarks"

(p. 28). However, it seems unnecessary to postulate the involvement of the "Now Print!" mechanism to explain general locational coding.

For adults, Siegel and White (1975) postulate three kinds of learning systems, starting with landmark knowledge based on a "recognition-in-context" memory. This landmark knowledge is followed by route learning developed through paired association of changes of bearing with landmarks. Finally, routes are integrated into a network-like assembly, which is described as "configurational." In children, the authors suggest a similar progression, which they see in a sufficiently general light to consider a "main sequence." First, landmarks are noticed and remembered with a more iconic emphasis in children than in adults. The authors offer an interesting assertion about cultural variation in that landmarks are thought to vary by culture and would need to be taught to children as distinctive environmental features, following Gibson (1966). Following the use of landmarks as individual references, the child next forms clusters of landmarks and "minimaps." Ultimately, survey maps (configurational knowledge) appear as coordinations of routes within an objective frame of reference. But such survey maps are possible only after both routes and an objective frame of reference are operational.

Despite differences in how iconic the representations of landmarks are, and the speed with which route learning and the objective frame of reference occur, Siegel and White (1975) argue that children's spatial representations conform to the "main sequence" they identified in adult learning. We again see the merit in examining the spatial progression in children because there are so many parallels to adult behavior. The elements of importance to children's way finding (i.e., landmarks) will figure prominently in the success of adult travelers.

Huttenlocher and Newcombe's Location Coding

Huttenlocher and Newcombe propose a slightly different version of the way in which location is coded (Huttenlocher & Newcombe, 1984; Newcombe, 1989). Children are hypothesized to first remember the location of small objects when the objects are coincident with larger fixed landmarks, which the authors explain as a kind of paired-associate learning. By 2 years of age, rough estimates of distances from landmarks are hypothesized to help children encode object location. By age 5 or perhaps earlier, children use more than one landmark to encode location; hence a rudimentary framework or coordinate system may be available to them. By 8 years of age, children are hypothesized to possess a common framework for spatial encoding because they can accomplish spatial transformations that require a common framework, and common frameworks may emerge even earlier.

In summary, coding of single targets may develop from association with single landmarks, to proximity to single landmarks, to distance from frameworks of landmarks, with the third stage possibly including a sequence from local to overall frameworks. Internal coding develops more slowly, and is often not used even by adults and even in situations where it would be helpful. (Newcombe, 1989, p. 217)

THE ISSUE OF SCALE

Scale is a critical variable in the research on spatial development and is to some extent intertwined with the issue of ecological validity. Research in the tradition of Piaget and Inhelder might be described as "small scale," and, in the case of infants, *very* small scale. More often than not, the young child is in a laboratory setting constructing a straight line, drawing shapes, or dealing with the coordination of perspectives, like the three mountains task (see, e.g., Dodwell, 1963). One of the criticisms of this kind of research, as we saw in the discussion of the controversy surrounding egocentrism, is that it underestimates children's abilities. Researchers have been urged to use "techniques of investigation which are appropriate to the interests and real-life activities of young children"(Spencer & Darvizeh, 1981, p. 27).

Researchers in the 1970s and 1980s began to pursue what they called an examination of children's understanding of the "large-scale" environment. This research actually varies widely in terms of the operationalization of "large scale" and in terms of how closely the activities reflect what a child might do in real life. On one end of the spectrum there is research where a child sits in a room and manipulates a map or model that represents an environment not significantly larger than the room itself. On the other end of the spectrum there are studies in which children are retracing paths learned in 12-minute walks in an unfamiliar environment. Within each category of scale, the studies also differ in ecological validity.

The Smallest Scale: The Spatial Competence of Infants

In a developmental progression of spatial competence, we see the human moving from bodily awareness, on one end, to an ability to navigate in a virtually unlimited environment, on the other. There are numerous ways to organize the research about this progression, but one of the most logical choices is environmental scale. The world of the infant presents the smallest scale.

While most of the research dealing with children's spatial cognition focuses on children who are at least preschool age, there is some work dealing with infants. We have already reviewed Presson and Ihrig's (1982) research on infants' responses to their mothers, which emphasized the role of other factors (e.g., landmarks) in the nature of the infant's spatial cognition. The influence of Piaget's theoretical construct of egocentrism is seen in much of this research.

Given the infant's limited mobility, most of the research deals with the nature of the "looking" response. The looking response relative to hidden objects is an indication of where the child thinks the object is at a given point in time. To investigate the response, the child typically sits in an infant chair or is supine. Bremner (1978) examined whether 9-month-olds would take an egocentric or an allocentric (place) view in their search for hidden objects. These children are in the sensorimotor Stage IV period and make what is known as the Stage IV error: when they look for an object, they continue to do so in the "old place," rather than where they have seen it moved by an experimenter. The question Bremner raises is whether more salient cues would enable the 9-month-old to take an allocentric view. Bremner conducted a series of experiments involving infants sitting in baby chairs from which to reach for objects (novel toys) placed in covered wells and varied whether the infant or the object was moved. He also examined the impact of salient cues: differentiating the cover over the well. The results indicated that allocentric responding in searching for a hidden object whose spatial relationship to them has changed was more likely to appear if the infant's movement rather than the object's movement caused the change. The differentiated cover also led to greater allocentric responding. In making a transition from egocentric to allocentric behavior, Bremner and others point to the importance of crawling (beginning at age 8–9 months), which in a sense forces the child to incorporate other perspectives. The multiple perspective taking that crawling involves (seeing objects from a variety of standpoints) may help the child decenter. In addition, salient cues may provide information that helps the child decenter.

Research has even been done with 6-month-olds to determine what kinds of information they use to help guide their visual search for a hidden target after they move to a new position (Rieser, 1979).

In order to use cues from their movement to localize a target after moving, observers must (a) encode the target location egocentrically before moving, relative to the anatomical coordinates of their bodies; (b) keep track of the direction and extent of their movements; and (c) integrate these two and update their initial reactions to the target in conjunction with their movements. (p. 1078)

Rieser suggests that infants possess the first two of these three capabilities—what they lack is the capability to integrate the two. The argument is that infants do not use landmarks to search but rather make reference to their own bodies or instrumental action. In this research, Rieser tested the use of movement, gravity, and landmark cues for spatial orientation. When they were moved to a new position, 6-month-olds were unable to update the spatial position they had learned previously. The data point to at least three different factors guiding 6-month-olds' visual search: 1) learned ego-centric code; 2) learned geocentric code; and 3) distractor influence of any pattern. It is the egocentric code that predominates in 6-month-olds' visual search. While 6-month-olds can encode a location relative to a landmark, their visual search behavior seems controlled by the learned egocentric code in many situations.

Rieser (1979) draws a parallel between the difficulties of infants in new spatial locations and the difficulties adults experience using orientation skills in different circumstances. ". . . infants guide their search for a target earliest by way of gravity as reference information. Next in sequence, they probably use landmarks for spatial orientation. And finally, the ability to keep track of the effects of self-movement on one's spatial relation to a target emerges" (pp. 1086–1087). Rieser's description is also reminiscent of Nadel's (1990; O'Keefe & Nadel, 1978) theory of spatial behavior, involving orientation, guidance, and place systems. Nadel states that the first kind of spatial organization is movement organized with respect to the frame of reference provided by the animal's own body (dead reckoning). The second and more advanced form is spatial behavior with respect to objects and events in the external world. Perhaps we can substitute the term "landmark orientation" for this kind of behavior. The most demanding and mature form of spatial behavior involves the representation of the contingencies in the information (objects and events occur in place and time). This is relational or configurational knowledge, as it is sometimes called. Adults thus may use the same kinds of information in sequence seen in children. Similarly, Baillargeon (1993) made a comparison between the difficulties of infants and adults: " . . . the physical world of infants appears very similar to that of adults: Not only do infants and adults share many of the same beliefs and show many of the same physical reasoning abilities, but these abilities seem limited in the same ways" (p. 311). For both there first is an inability to plan means-end sequences; then there are computation difficulties when they are able to plan search sequences.

The infant's search behavior in these spatial tasks has also been described in terms of a response versus a place strategy (Bremner & Bryant, 1977). When the past actions of the infant lead him/her to repeat the previous movement/searching behavior, we have a *response* strategy. Alternatively, returning to the old position to search may be returning to a particular *place*, unrelated to the actions previously performed. To differentiate between these two strategies, they tested 80 babies (mean age just over 9 months), who sat in a baby chair facing a table, half painted black, half painted white, in which were two wells. Babies had to retrieve an object hidden in the same place. Four conditions varied whether a new response or a new position was involved as a reflection of whether the child or the table moved. One condition served as a control. Results indicated support for the response strategy, " . . . striking vindication of Piaget's suggestion that the original spatial error is based on the infant's actions . . . perseveration is of responses rather than places" (p. 168). As has been the case with a number of other researchers, these authors point to the role of crawling (movement) in the evolution of the child's ability to take different perspectives.

Summary

In their world of restricted scale, infants through their first year demonstrate egocentric behavior in sorting out the environment. Salient landmarks may help infants decenter or respond more in terms of the external environment than in terms of their own bodies. The role of action in the form of crawling may help the child learn to take the perspective of others.

Beyond Limited Scale: Research on Older Children

While the research on preschool children tends to be dominated by Piagetian and neo-Piagetian approaches in terms of the kinds of questions that are asked, other foci emerge when you review the spatial cognition research of those who are school-age and older. As with young children, when the theme is egocentrism, the research on older children to adults generally demonstrates that performance varies as a function of task. Notwithstanding, there are some generalizations that can be made. Typically, judgments improve with the age of the participant and with the familiarity of the environment, although there are some exceptions—female preteens and teenagers appear to know more about their neighborhood than the fathers in the neighborhood (Doherty, Gale, Pellegrino, & Golledge, 1989). For the most part, however, these conclusions about the impact of age and familiarity seem obvious. Less obvious in the research, however, is the role of scale and the ecological validity of the tasks that have been used.

"Small"-Scale Environment Studies

Many of these studies involve more complex activities, use more real-life settings, ask different questions, or challenge the results found in the Piagetian tradition. For example, arguing that not enough attention has been given to real environments, Siegel and Schadler (1977) had kindergartners work with scale models (1" = 2') of their classroom and its contents. Children were to arrange the 40 pieces of scale model furniture "just like it goes in your classroom." They found that increases in familiarity and the availability of significant landmarks (cues that were differentiated) improved the child's performance. The significance of this study is the attempt to use an environment (a model of their classroom) that was familiar and of significance to the children.

More often, an unfamiliar or abstract environment is used to investigate an ability like map reading or understanding the representational aspects of a model (see, e.g., Blades & Cooke, 1994; Scholnick, Fein, & Campbell, 1990). Researchers using this approach are interested in the developmental aspects of abilities like spatial representation. When does the child understand that a model or map "stands for" a larger scale environment? In two experiments, for example, Blades and Cooke (1994) compared the ability of young children to understand the relationship between two models (Experiment 1) or the relationship between a model and a room (Experiment 2). The 3-, 4-, and 5-year-olds in the first experiment used two 30 × 30 × 30-centimeters models (A and B) in which there were four pieces of furniture, including two chairs that were identical. Children participated in placement tasks with aligned and rotated models. They then searched in one model for a toy dog hidden in an analogous location in the other model. Trials varied in terms of whether the dog was hidden in a unique place or under one of the two identical chairs. Three-year-olds in the study could not distinguish between the two hiding places (the two chairs) that were identical. These young children did not understand "the relational attributes of the model" (p. 211). Only 5-year-olds were able to find the toy when it was in a unique location in all alignments. In Experiment 2, 14 children averaging 3 years, 2 months in age, and 14 averaging 4 years, 8 months in age, dealt with a small room (3 meters × 3 meters) and a scale model of the room (30 centimeters × 30 centimeters). There were four pieces of furniture (and scaled furniture): two identical chairs, a cupboard, and a cot. They performed alignment trials as in Experiment 1 and had to find a larger toy dog in the room in a place analogous to the location of the smaller toy dog in the model. There was an effect of age, as 4-year-olds were better at the retrieval than were 3-year-olds. There was also a retrieval effect, as children were better at finding the small toy dog in the model than in the room. Again, 3-year-olds were much poorer at finding the location when the hiding place involved an identical object (one of the chairs). The work of these authors suggests that children by the age of 5 have a sound understanding that the model stands as a representation. They know what information the model provides in relation to the environment it represents. Three-year-olds, on the other hand, are only able to identify the hiding place when it is unique and thus failed when the hiding place involved the two identical chairs. Four-year-olds fall in between. They can distinguish between the identical chairs as hiding places in conditions when the stimuli (Experiment 1: the models; Experiment 2: the room/model) are aligned. The research of this kind often deals with children younger than elementary school age because this is the time when major gains are being made in the understanding of these representational issues.

The importance of exploring children's cartographic understanding has developed into a major research program for Liben and Downs (1989). Their research program at Penn State is called MAPPS (Mapping Project at Penn State). The goal of MAPPS is to explore the development of children's understanding of various properties of maps and their abilities with maps: their conceptualization, identification, and utilization. This research program places an emphasis on cartographic theory. In summarizing their research they recognize children's considerable achievements with regard to mapping, but they also recognize limitations in these abilities. "Our data support the view that maps are *not* transparent and that children's abilities to understand, use, and create maps are linked to their developing representational and spatial skills" (p. 197).

The environmental stimuli in this scale category have some ecological validity in that they often employ miniature furniture or landscape toys with which a child might be familiar. For example, posterboard terrains with representations of roads and railroad tracks have been employed (Anooshian & Wilson, 1977; Scholnick et al., 1990), as have landscape toys (Blaut & Stea, 1974; Borke, 1975). The tasks children are asked to perform in these studies vary in their ecological validity. Some are much closer to the play of children than are others. One of the well-known studies that directly bears on children's play is that of Blaut and Stea (1974). Using toy play materials (houses, buildings, a church, cars, and strips that represented streets), they asked 3-, 4-, and 5–6 1/2-year-olds to "make a street corner" during 10 minutes of free play. They were interested in whether children as young as age 3 could construct a macroenvironmental Gestalt, which they concluded was possible.

While other researchers have used similar materials, the tasks required of children often are at least a step removed from regular play. Placement was one of a series of tasks asked of two groups of children whose mean age was 57 months (48 subjects) and 70 months (46 subjects) (Scholnick et al., 1990). Two identical 35 × 47 centimeters posterboard terrains were used, each of which was divided into 4 unequal quadrants by an intersecting road and track. Each terrain contained five houses that varied in color and size. These houses were distributed across three locations on the terrain. First, with the boards aligned, the children were asked to place a figure as they saw it placed on the researcher's board. There were 12 such placements, 7 classified as near landmarks and 5 as open field positions. Then they were asked to repeat the placements after the researcher's board had been rotated 180 degrees. The distinction between near landmarks and open field placements was important because it was hypothesized to represent the difference between judgments based on isolated cues (landmarks) and on survey knowledge (open field), reflecting a developmental progression. Placement was considered correct if the object was within 2–3 centimeters of its location on the researcher's board. Older children outperformed younger children on these tasks.

In another study using a landscape terrain, Anooshian and Wilson (1977) examined the ability of kindergartners, in contrast to adults, to place objects they had previously seen on a circular "grass"-covered board with train tracks with either direct or indirect routes (looping or elevation of tracks) between objects. The objects were a small tree orchard, a gas station, a log cabin, and a house. Subjects first viewed a training board as the researcher placed each of the four objects at a location as a train moved around the tracks, stopping as each object was placed. The subjects practiced placing the objects on the train board until a criterion was met (when the object was placed with less than a 1.5 centimeter error in any direction). Then, the subject was given the four objects and was told to place them on the test board (which had no tracks). Not surprisingly, adults were faster than children in reaching criterion during training. The study did reveal that children were more affected by the nature of the route (indirect versus direct) and made distance distortions when the routes between objects were indirect.

In terms of understanding what children really do, it is important for researchers to consider the ecological validity not only of the stimulus environment that is used but in terms of the response tasks that are undertaken. The Blaut and Stea (1974) research discussed previously is a good model in terms of capitalizing on children's typical play behavior—making a street corner in a play town is a very common activity. Alternatively, consider measuring errors in centimeters in terms of the way children play in the environment. Is this a reasonable reflection of what children consider important and therefore an area in which they might be expected to demonstrate competence? This concern is reminiscent of the issue raised by Neisser (1982) about the work on memory and experimental research more generally.

Midrange-Scale Environment Studies

In the next category of studies, the children may be asked to perform a task in a small, but real environment. Many of the same questions as we have previously seen are addressed, including the developmental ability of children to use maps and judge distances and the role of environmental familiarity (Acredolo, 1977; Acredolo, Pick, & Olsen, 1975; Blades & Spencer, 1987a, 1987b, 1990; Bluestein & Acredolo, 1979; Cohen, Weatherford, Lomenick, & Koeller, 1979; Dandonoli, Demick, & Wapner, 1990; Golbeck, 1983; Hazen, Lockman, & Pick, 1978; Herman, Norton, & Klein, 1986; Herman & Siegel, 1978; Kahl, Herman, & Klein, 1984; Kosslyn, Pick, & Fariello, 1974; Presson, DeLange, & Hazelrigg, 1989). The following study on the role of motor activity in memory for spatial locations can illustrate some of the major themes and concerns (Herman, Kolker, & Shaw, 1982). In this study, 60 kindergartners and 60 third graders were tested in the gym or recreation hall of their schools. In these spaces, a 4.9 × 6.1 meters section was covered with brown paper (a staple of these kinds of experiments). It was divided into 4 quadrants by a railroad track and a road. There were seven buildings (10 × 17 × 11 centimeters) distributed in this environment in order to build a town. Children were exposed to one of three conditions: 1) they stood at the starting point and looked at the town; 2) they got in a wagon and were pulled through the town by the experimenter; or 3) they walked through the town on the "road" with the experimenter. In each condition, they were required to name each building as the experimenter pointed to it (they had previously practiced naming each building). At the starting point, half in each condition were told to remember the exact location of each building (the intentional condition), and half were told simply to try to name the buildings (the incidental condition). After these exposures, the child returned to the starting point again (the buildings had been removed). The child's task was to put the buildings back in the display in their exact location. Placement was judged to be correct if the building was within 30.5 centimeters of the placement they had seen as they stood, rode, or walked through the town previously. Third graders were better at this than kindergartners; and placement accuracy improved with increasing motor activity but only for kindergartners. The study is illustrative because many studies in this category create room-sized or relatively small environments in which children are asked to perform some task. The spaces are created in a number of ways: with a masking tape outline (see, e.g., Golbeck, 1983; Herman & Siegel, 1978); on the school playground (Blades & Spencer, 1987b, 1990); in a room divided into quadrants by opaque and transparent barriers (Kosslyn, Pick, & Fariello, 1974); by collapsible rooms (Acredolo, 1977; Bluestein & Acredolo, 1979; Hazen, Lockman, & Pick, 1978).

The tasks used in these kinds of small environments tend to have moderate ecological validity, although not to the extent we will see in the studies that truly deal with large-scale environments. As an example of the degree of ecological validity, consider these studies by Acredolo, Pick, and Olsen (1975) that looked at preschoolers' representations of familiar versus unfamiliar environments. In the first experiment, 24 preschoolers (mean age 4 years, 11 months) either took a walk in the nursery school's outdoor playground (familiar environment) or in the hallway of a building next to the nursery school (unfamiliar environment). There was distinctive play equipment on the playground but essentially just a hallway of office doors in the building next to the nursery school. Along the walk, the experimenter dropped a card and the child was asked to pick it up. This was the incidental memory condition. In the intentional condition, children were taken to the spot and told to remember it. After the walk, the child was asked to return to the designated spot. The outcome measure was the distance in feet between the target location and the location selected by the child. Children performed better in the playground than in the hallway and in the intentional than in the incidental condition. In the second experiment with

32 children whose mean age was 4 years, 6 months, incidental and intentional memory were evaluated in four environments. These environments
differed in their degree of familiarity and differentiation. These were: 1) an
unfamiliar hallway; 2) an unfamiliar hallway with two dissimilar chairs
serving as landmarks; 3) a familiar hallway (outside the nursery school
rooms) but undifferentiated because the usual play material was removed;
and 4) the familiar hallway with its usual play equipment. This time, the
experimenter dropped a key ring. There were main effects for differentiation and task, but not familiarity. Memory for location was better in the
differentiated environment and in the intentional condition. In a third experiment, 16 3-year-olds (mean 3 years, 8 months) and 16 children who
were almost age 8 (mean 7 years, 11 months) repeated the tasks in the two
unfamiliar environments from Experiment 2. The 8-year-olds performed
well whether the environment was differentiated or not, unlike the 3-year-
olds (and the 4-year-olds from Experiment 2 whose data were included in
these analyses). The researchers suggest that by the age of 8, metric distance, a Euclidean concept, is more available to the children. They don't
need distinctive environments for these kinds of judgments. On the other
hand, landmarks help children who are still functioning on the basis of
topological relations.

The tasks involved in this study have a certain degree of ecological validity; children go with parents or caretakers into environments that vary
in familiarity, and what happens along the way may be of some consequence (e.g., looking for a lost object). What is less compelling about this
and other studies in this category is the ecological validity of the dependent
measures. Granted, there has to be some way to assess whether the child
has identified the place where the object was dropped. But it may be that
a precise measurement is less important than an indication of whether the
child is in the vicinity or not. Concerns of ecological validity involve how
important such precision is in measuring the child's ability. Humans tend
to operate on the basis of heuristics rather than algorithms (Kahneman &
Tversky, 1983, 1984); our dependent measures should reflect this tendency.

Large-Scale Environment Studies

There are a number of studies that deal with spatial cognition in what
can genuinely be called large-scale environments. These studies do not always take place in the actual environment (they may involve slide presen-
tations, for example), but the environments in question are reasonably
extensive, and certainly require more than a single glance to be perceived.
As such, they are studies that deal with the notion of cognitive mapping as
it is generally discussed in adults. There are a range of questions or concerns
in these kinds of studies, including how people perceive a route in terms
of segments (Allen, 1981), and, more generally, what factors influence route

acquisition (see, Allen, Kirasic, Siegel, & Herman, 1979; Cornell & Hay, 1984; Cousins, Siegel, & Maxwell, 1983).

There are studies that investigate spatial performance in large-scale environments using slides (Allen, 1981; Allen, Kirasic, Siegel, & Herman, 1979; Doherty, Gale, Pellegrino, & Golledge, 1989; Doherty & Pellegrino, 1985; Siegel, Allen, & Kirasic, 1979). There also are studies in the real environment (typically around the home) that use measures, like precise direction estimates, that might be considered of limited ecological validity (Anooshian & Nelson, 1987; Anooshian & Young, 1981; Conning & Byrne, 1984). However, most noteworthy as approaches to the spatial cognition of large-scale environment are the studies of Cornell and Hay (1984), Cornell, Heth, and Broda (1989), Cornell, Heth, and Rowat (1992), and Cousins, Siegel, and Maxwell (1983). These studies demonstrate an ecologically valid approach to the spatial cognition of large-scale environments. In these studies, the participants are in large-scale environments and then are asked to perform a real navigational task, like finding their way back to a starting point.

The study of Cornell and Hay (1984) is particularly noteworthy for these reasons. It also illustrates the importance of the medium in route acquisition. The research of Cornell and Hay contrasted the number of errors made on children's acquisition of a route across a university campus. The route included seven choice points that were highlighted in various ways in each of the exposure conditions. In this study of kindergarten and second graders, children walked the route, saw slides of the route, or saw a video of the route. They were then tested in either the direction they had seen or walked the route during the acquisition phase, or the reverse. At choice points that had been selected in advance, children were asked to point to "where we go next." These points were selected to require a clear left or right turn and thus could be scored easily. As you might expect, the older children performed better in all conditions. Of particular note, children who had the guided walk made fewer errors than those who saw the video. Furthermore, those who were tested in the same direction as in the acquisition phase made fewer errors, and a media by direction interaction indicated that errors were greater for this reversal in the slide and video modes than in the walking mode. These findings are significant for a number of reasons. First, they indicate that the mode of presentation may affect the results. In doing so, they highlight one of the major issues in the developmental literature: the problem of ecological validity. In this study, children in the most effective condition were out walking in a large-scale environment demonstrating spatial behavior (leading the way back on a route). If we are going to reach some understanding of the developmental competence of children's actions in space, more studies of this character are needed.

Summary

As the scale of the environments in the research increases, the ecological validity generally increases as well. The challenge is to incorporate more everyday play behaviors in both the stimulus conditions and the outcome measures in the research that deals with smaller-scale environments.

Spatial Behavior in Children

The review undertaken has highlighted the role of scale and ecological validity rather than reviewing the entire body of literature. Before considering research that is more heavily influenced by information-processing and computational theories, however, it is useful to provide brief summaries of some of the major trends in the developmental literature.

As a very general summary, we can say that familiarity and landmarks play important roles in way finding; that distance judgments, while they improve with age, remain challenging tasks throughout the lifespan; and that children need exposure to a variety of map forms if they are to become competent map users. It is also clear that children can do a variety of cognitive mapping and spatial cognition tasks if experimenters and adults construct situations that capitalize on children's abilities.

In much of the research, familiar environments have been used. Often performance in these familiar environments may be contrasted with novel environments or with less well-known aspects of a familiar environment. Subjects have performed tasks related to their homes (Conning & Byrne, 1984), their neighborhood (Doherty, Gale, Pellegrino, & Golledge, 1989), their school (including nursery school and daycare center) and locations within their school like the library, gym, or playground (Acredolo, Pick, & Olsen, 1975; Biel, 1982; Cohen, Weatherford, Lomenick, & Koeller, 1979; Cousins, Siegel, & Maxwell, 1983; Herman, Kolker, & Shaw, 1982; Kahl, Herman, & Klein, 1984). Camps have also been used (Cohen, Baldwin, & Sherman, 1978). In general, performance on spatial tasks is better around environments that are particularly well known, especially the home.

There are a wide range of tasks that have been used to investigate the spatial cognition of youngsters. One category of tasks involves some aspect of distance or direction. These include directional accuracy (Anooshian & Nelson, 1987), including pointing a telescope toward specific landmarks from different reference sites (Anooshian & Young, 1981) and pointing to out-of-sight targets using a wooden arrow (Conning & Byrne, 1984). Subjects have also made comparisons of distance from two landmarks to a reference site (Biel, 1982), and have provided distance judgments (Doherty et al., 1989). They have judged how many steps it was between locations in novel versus familiar environments (Cohen et al., 1979).

They also have drawn sketch maps (Doherty et al., 1989), identified landmarks and scenes (Cousins et al., 1983; Doherty et al., 1989), demonstrated memory for location (Acredolo et al., 1975), and placed objects in a model of their classroom (Siegel & Schadler, 1977). They also have been asked to return to a place where the experimenter has dropped an object (Acredolo et al., 1975).

The outcomes show somewhat more convergence than the tasks or their settings. A number of studies show that there are significant differences in spatial performance between subjects in grades 2 versus 5, but that fifth graders and college students often do not differ significantly on performance measures (Allen, 1981). The "ability to solve proximity problems by means of computation, that is, the estimation and comparison of metric distances, improves over the course of middle childhood" (p. 129). In a pattern that emerges in the literature, we see that by the time children have reached their preteen years, their performance on many spatial tasks matches that of adults. This correlation between age and performance has been demonstrated repeatedly (see, e.g., Acredolo et al., 1975; Anooshian & Young, 1981; Siegel, Allen, & Kirasic, 1979). We also see that the test environment may have more influence than a child's intellectual stage, at least in terms of directional estimates and response accuracy (Conning & Byrne, 1984).

It is also the case that while age may improve performance on many of these measures, humans are not superior performers when the task is proximity judgments, even in a familiar environment (Doherty et al., 1989). It may very well be that way finding in the environment on a day-to-day basis does not require the kind of precision that is seen in these experiments because we are not that good at these tasks. Changing the tasks to resemble everyday challenges seems an important step in improving this area of research.

As they age, children develop a better sense of what kind of cues the environment provides to help in way finding. If you will, they are learning to better resonate to the invariance of environmental objects (Gibson, 1966), the objects we typically call landmarks. Landmarks are critical in successful way-finding behavior, and children's ability to use them follows a developmental progression. They can use the landmarks others suggest before they are able to identify these on their own. Early on, children may be captivated and misled by the perceptual attractiveness of landmarks. While bright awnings are distinctive in some sense, they may occur along a route rather than at a choice point and thus provide little of the kind of information needed for successful way finding. What children (as well as the rest of us) need, of course, are bright awnings that occur at a choice point, and only at *one* choice point. And that is what making an environment legible (Lynch, 1960) is all about (see Chapter 5, this volume).

INFORMATION PROCESSING AND COMPUTATIONAL
THEORIES OF SPATIAL COGNITION

While Piagetian and neo-Piagetian traditions continue to have their supporters, developments in cognitive science, artificial intelligence, and linguistics, among other fields, have been incorporated into recent research in
spatial cognition, particularly in geography and cognitive psychology. The
tradition of positivism and in turn cognitive-behavioral geography came
under attack in the 1980s, primarily by the Marxist school (Gold, 1992),
which emphasized the importance of social context. However, cognitive-
behavioral geography is a tradition that has contributed new ideas to the
topic of spatial cognition, and it is to these contributions that we now turn.
The theories of Golledge, Couclelis, Garling, and their colleagues figure
prominently in this new wave. The research tends to be focused on adult
subjects, and the "development" to be examined is the adult learner operating in large spaces, the spaces that yield cognitive maps. The spaces of
interest are those that cannot be experienced or seen at a single moment in
time or from a single vantage point: neighborhoods, towns, and cities.

The themes that emerge are the importance of hierarchies in the organization of spatial representations, the similarities between spatial representations and geographical information systems, and the relationship of
such representations to computational process models, neural networks,
and linguistics.

The Anchor Point Theory of Spatial Cognition

One of the foremost researchers in the field of spatial representation from
a geographical perspective is Golledge (Golledge, 1991a, 1992a, 1992b;
Golledge & Stimson, 1997). According to Golledge, Smith, Pellegrino, Doherty, and Marshall (1985), a knowledge structure is a basis for action,
guiding the decisions of the individual that result from the perceptions and
analyses of the self and the environment. This point of view of the knowledge representation is also postulated by Kaplan (1973), who stated that a
cognitive map (a knowledge representation) must make possible recognizing where you are, predicting what will happen next, determining whether
the outcome will be positive or negative, and then taking action. Golledge
and colleagues postulated that:

There is a general progression from landmark to route to configurational knowledge
representing the successive coordination of knowledge units within an external
frame of reference. Similarly, the relational information contained in the individual's representation of the environment progresses from topological to projective
to metric properties. The emergence of these properties also depends upon the availability of referential frameworks that are nonegocentric. (p. 129)

These authors see the child's environmental knowledge as an interaction between cognitive capability and experience in the world. They postulate that the adult's developmental progression parallels that of the child.

The anchor point hypothesis of spatial cognition integrates regionalization, salient cue function, and hierarchical structure—as a theory of the cognitive organization of space. One of the primary organizers of space in this model is the anchor point (like one's home or workplace) (Couclelis, et al., 1987). While similar to landmarks, anchor points are experienced uniquely in individual cognitive maps (whereas landmarks may be experienced collectively, as the Eiffel Tower). The emphasis is on the organizing function of anchor points, which are not merely references. "For any given cognitive environment, and any given individual, a hierarchy of anchor points is postulated. However, this is a hierarchy of *cognitive salience* rather than spatial scale" (p. 103). Couclelis and colleagues draw a parallel with the nodes of semantic networks postulated by Collins and Quillian (1969).

Golledge finds parallels in his own theory and those of Hart and Moore (1973) and Siegel and White (1975), reviewed earlier in this chapter. Golledge's anchor point theory of spatial cognition emphasizes a hierarchical ordering of places in the spatial environment based on the significance of the place to the individual. Primary nodes such as home and work anchor the hierarchy and serve as the foundation from which other secondary and tertiary nodes develop. The importance of the home as a reference landmark has been previously reported (Devlin, 1976).

In summary, a model of the acquisition and representation of spatial knowledge must adequately account for (1) acquisition and representation based on episodic experience and subsequent generalization, (2) different types of knowledge and forms of representation, (3) systematic inaccuracies and distortions in the cognitive representation, and (4) behavioral errors associated with inaccurate and hierarchically organized knowledge. (Golledge et al., 1985, p. 132)

To demonstrate the validity of this anchor point model, Golledge applies the conceptual model to a task environment, in this case a suburban neighborhood. First-level concepts include plots and choice points; a *plot* is a unit of land containing such objects as houses, landscaping, and sidewalks; a *choice point* is any location at which a navigational decision is required (e.g., an intersection). Second-level concepts are data structures called *frames*—organizing knowledge about the characteristics of environmental objects. Golledge is essentially using information-processing theory here, where schemas "represent categorical knowledge according to a *slot* structure, where slots specify values that members of a category have on varying attributes" (Anderson, 2000, p. 155). The frame slots are filled with information about features, properties, and values of the structure in question.

Beyond the description of the environment (which we have through these frames), the second component of the model is the description of the cognitive representations and cognitive control processes of the decision-maker. This information-processing approach includes four major components: (1) feasible actions; (2) procedural and declarative knowledge structures; (3) cognitive processes (perception, storage, retrieval, reorganization); and (4) control processes (the ordering of the cognitive processes) (see also Golledge & Stimson, 1997). This formulation resembles the cognitive map model proposed by Kaplan (1973), described earlier.

Golledge and colleagues' (1985) case study centers on an 11-year-old boy and his neighborhood knowledge. A number of hypotheses generated from the conceptual model were tested during this case study. A sampling of these include: 1) the overall saliency of a plot decreases as the distance of the plot from major choice points increases (i.e., more information is coded near choice points); 2) the more alternative actions that can be taken at a choice point, the more information is coded at that point; and 3) the choice points of a route, at which navigation decisions are made, provide a natural segmentation of the route as represented in long-term memory (LTM).

It is fair to say that the case study provided support for the authors' hypotheses. Of particular significance is the accumulation of knowledge around higher order nodes, and the greater salience of information in the vicinity of choice points. Golledge and colleagues (1985) also talk about the phenomenon of "distance decay" (from geography) and the "spread effect" (from psychology) to describe the concentration of feature knowledge near higher-order nodes. The authors indicate that in geographic theory, this concentration is linked to the development of neighborhoods in the vicinity of major nodes. A place where there is a concentration of activities is likely to provide a good anchor. In some ways, the authors are building on Lynch's (1960) concept of a node as a convergence of activity (see Chapter 5, this volume).

In an illustration of the importance of the home as an anchor point, Schouela, Steinberg, Leveton, and Wapner (1980) explored the development of spatial cognition in first-year college students. Students in the Schouela and colleagues study were told to draw a sketch map of their university and label or identify the parts of the drawing and the order in which the items on the map were added. Their representations were assessed over 6 months, from the first day of residence. As with Devlin's (1976) research on newcomers to Idaho Falls, Idaho, the maps reflected progressive differentiation and integration. Over time, distortion decreased, whereas the number of on-campus buildings, correctly articulated building forms, and streets increased. The authors related this development to the orthogenetic principle. An interesting behavior was the fairly consistent use of the same starting point, or anchor, for the maps, reminding us of the anchor point theory of spatial cognition. Anchors appear as vital elements even when the cognitive maps are constructed from text (Ferguson & Hegarty, 1994).

The hierarchical emphasis prominent in Golledge's theory is also seen in other research (see, e.g., Fotheringham & Curtis, 1992; Stevens & Coupe, 1978). Freundschuh (1992) has also developed a model of spatial knowledge that bears some resemblance to Golledge's. For Freundschuh, the emphasis is the connectedness through time of geographical facts, route knowledge, and configurational knowledge. A number of these authors, including Freundschuh, acknowledge that the existence of errors in people's cognitive representations does not necessarily limit successful way finding in the environment. In fact, Golledge argues that spatial behavior includes a much wider array of behaviors than is typically considered (1992b), and that the current theoretical models do not adequately mirror human behavior (1992a). As Golledge notes, "Humans are notoriously poor path integrators" (1992a, p. 209). He further claims that, "Clear sets of well-authenticated criteria for explaining wayfinding do not exist" (p. 210).

Rather than being limited to Euclidean space, a number of authors suggest that spatial representations are versatile (Franklin, 1992; Franklin, Tversky, & Coon, 1992; McNamara, 1992; Presson, DeLange, & Hazelrigg, 1989), and that the distortions that exist (Freksa, 1992; Tversky, 1992), cast doubt on the assumption that cognitive maps follow metric principles. As Tversky says, ". . . cognitive maps may be impossible figures" (1992, p. 137).

Spatial Cognition Viewed As Travel Plans

Reminiscent of Golledge's theory in its hierarchical emphasis, Garling and colleagues propose a psychological, information-processing model of spatial cognition and way finding. They conceptualize spatial cognition in terms of travel plans with a particular emphasis on the planning process (Garling et al., 1986). Reminiscent of Kaplan (1973), Garling and colleagues (1984) describe the formation of travel plans in terms of hierarchically organized stages: 1) access necessary information; 2) decide upon itinerary (places to visit); 3) determine the order of visits; and 4) ascertain the logistics of achieving that prescribed order. The three interrelated elements in the cognitive maps that travelers form are: places, the spatial relations between them, and travel plans (Garling et al., 1984). "For newcomers the execution of a travel plan requires that close attention be paid to signs, landmarks, and choice points in order to decide when appropriate action should be taken according to the plan (i.e., the observed features of the environment must be 'translated' in terms of the travel plan)" (Garling et al., 1986, p. 57). The task faced by newcomers in a project that emphasized the functional importance of landmarks has also been addressed (Devlin, 1976).

While Garling and colleagues do not emphasize the child as a traveler, this model could apply to children as well. Can children plan? Apparently so. Using 3-, 4-, and 5-year-olds, Wellman, Fabricius, and Sophian (1985) examined the concept of planning in preschoolers. The 4- and 5-year-olds, but not the 3-year-olds, displayed an ability to plan, when judged by the fact that the percentage of children who avoided backtracking on second searches rose above chance level. In another study using 3-, 3½-, 4½-, and 5½-year-olds, the children were told to "go the quick way" in a search task. Going the quick way was really an operational definition of the ability to plan and it was above chance level for children beginning with the 3½-year-olds. The developmental progression is quite clear in that 3-year-olds essentially never planned in these tasks; 3½- and 4½-year-olds showed a combination of sighting and planning; and 5½-year-olds used planning almost exclusively.

Other Theoretical Influences

A number of factors including geographical information systems, computational process models, and linguistic theory, among others, have influenced the shape of research and theory dealing with the development of spatial representations.

Geographical Information Systems

Geographical information systems (GIS) are a class of information systems that deal with spatial data (Medyckyj-Scott & Blades, 1992). They are used for a variety of purposes, including image processing for remotely sensed data and route planning systems. Recently they have entered into the public domain in the form of vehicle navigation aids. Golledge (1992b) questions the relationship between cognitive maps and geographical information systems. His research demonstrates that people have what he calls "commonsense" configurational knowledge of space. The dependent measures that have been used, such as identifying the nearest neighbor location or shortest path, demonstrate that people ordinarily do not possess such information about their surroundings. His conclusion is that current theories embodied in GIS programs do not adequately mirror human behavior in its fuzziness and incompleteness.

Computational Process Models

Perhaps better known in the context of David Marr's (1982) theories of vision, computational process models attempt to explain behavior in terms of the transformations and manipulations that occur toward some goal. In the case of spatial behavior, Gopal and Smith (1990) describe a computational process model called NAVIGATOR, which describes navigation in an environment in terms of the acquisition, representation, storage, and retrieval of spatial knowledge. What is attractive about NAVIGATOR is its psychological orientation. For example, the importance of perceptual information gleaned from each decision point is incorporated into the model. It shapes behavior, and the errors that occur happen where you would expect them: where complex environments create complex decisions.

The neural basis of computational process models has been addressed by a number of researchers, including Portugali (1996), who discusses cognitive maps as interrepresentation networks (IRN). In a delightfully wide-ranging paper, he integrates two theoretical concepts: Bohm's holomovement (similar to the creation of a holographic record where everything is enfolded) and Haken's synergetics (theory of self-organization). The paper includes a discussion of such diverse authors as Christopher Alexander from the field of architecture and planning and Gerald Edelman, who formulated the concept of neural Darwinism. Elsewhere, Portugali states about IRN that "it is an open, complex, and self-organizing system, governed by a complex hierarchy of macroscopic, slowly changing, order parameters, exhibiting phenomena of structural stability and multi-stability, fluctuations, bifurcations, phase transitions, emergent orders, and transformations" (Portugali & Haken, 1992, p. 126). Following Edelman and echoing comments made earlier by others stressing the flexibility of the cognitive map, Portugali and Haken state that "cognitive maps are dynamically created anew, each time . . . by means of learned synaptic connection strengths that govern the cooperation between neurons" (p. 127). Thus, for these researchers, a cognitive map is not a static atlas in the mind. A cognitive map is an IRN that is self-organizing, dynamic, and complexly enfolded. ". . . cognitive maps can be seen as IRN, the elements of which are groups of neurons, brain-maps, maps of maps in different modalities, concepts, categories, patterns, 'ordinary maps' as well as cultural and social human groups. They all exist in people's minds as well as in the outside world" (Portugali, 1996, p. 41). Other articles in Portugali's 1996 edited book also address the neural and connectionist basis of cognitive maps (see e.g., Ghiselli-Crippa, Hirtle, & Munro, 1996).

Another orientation to the understanding of cognitive maps is a linguistic one (Daniel, Carite, & Denis, 1996; Hayward & Tarr, 1995; Landau & Jackendoff, 1993; Schlichtmann, 1991). Daniel and colleagues (1996) raise the question of how language, a one-dimensional linear entity, produces a three-dimensional product: the cognitive map. Subjects in their research used a map of a fictitious island with nine landmarks, and had the task of producing a verbal description of it. The vast majority (89%) produced descriptions that were survey in nature, whereas only 11% produced route descriptions. The authors focus on the linguistic characteristics of the descriptions that were judged to be systematic descriptive systems. Those with such descriptions were more likely to refer to cardinal directions and provided evidence that they were aware of their audience's needs (i.e., they provided an introduction). While we still do not know why these subjects were able to or chose to include such information, the research yields a description of successful communication about spatial locations.

Landau and Jackendoff (1993) pursue the parallels between the "what" and "where" of visual systems and language structure. While objects are typically communicated by concrete nouns, places are identified by prepositions, and the authors focus on the richness in human language of the way in which object nouns as opposed to the place prepositions are represented. In explaining this difference, the authors offer two possibilities: the language design hypothesis and the design of spatial representation hypothesis. The language design hypothesis proposes that spatial representations themselves incorporate information about object shapes; that these are "invisible" to the language faculty; and that they are thus filtered out in the transformation into a linguistic format. The second hypothesis posits that "spatial representation is relatively rich in its possibilities for describing object shape, but relatively limited in the way it can use object shape to encode spatial relations" (p. 234). The authors turn to the neurological evidence of Ungerleider and Mishkin (1982) for support for their hypothesis. While avoiding the suggestion that the "where" system is an internalized map, the authors say ". . . that many of the same design criteria are applicable, in particular, to the need to represent objects as tokens in the representation but to compress their encoding by eliminating most information about their form" (p. 235). What they are suggesting, they say, is a parallel bifurcation in language and in the functional systems of the brain.

Summary

What is frustrating for Golledge and a number of other researchers (see, e.g., Liben, 1991), is that a good deal of research in this area merely describes but does not explain behavior. I am reminded of the important points made by Marr (1982) about the struggle to understand vision. Researchers in that field had essentially put the cart before the horse and had moved to what Marr calls the algorithmic and hardware stages of research before really stating vision's computational mission. People had not figured out the "why" of vision before trying to reproduce it. In the same way, researchers in this area of spatial cognition may have moved too quickly, before stating in simple terms what spatial behavior really accomplishes for humans. The evidence for this criticism rests in the number of researchers who have commented on the differences between the existing theoretical models of spatial behavior and the behavior that humans actually exhibit, with all of its fuzziness and incompleteness.

SPATIAL COMPETENCE IN THE ELDERLY AND VISUALLY IMPAIRED

A final consideration of developmental issues in spatial cognition is how spatial cognition is affected by advancing age and by the constraints of limited vision. Design guidelines that emerge from a consideration of these topics have application beyond these populations.

Spatial Competence in the Elderly

An early field study (Devlin, 1980) focused on the cognitive demands on the elderly created by high-rise versus garden-apartment housing. Oscar Newman's (1973) groundbreaking research on defensible space was one source of interest in this topic, as Newman had recommended placing the elderly in high-rises and families in low-rise structures when land costs dictated the need for greater density and hence at least some high-rise structures on a site. What intrigued Devlin was the issue of the psychological, particularly the cognitive, costs of placing elderly people in high-rise structures. The study did, indeed, reveal that high-rise living for the elderly has cognitive costs.

While living in high rises produced certain kinds of stresses, including fear of being trapped in a fire and of being lost in the building, Devlin (1980) was also struck by the stories of people living in one particular garden-apartment complex that had been "surrounded" by the interstate when new interchanges were created to and from the I-95 corridor. People living in Gordon Court had become "trapped in trees," as Christopher Alexander (1965) would say, and were cut off from what had formerly been major arteries by the cloverleaf configuration of entrance and off ramps. One woman in particular described how the new tangle of streets reminded her of an octopus, and said how confusing she found the new arrangement to be.

The issues of the ease with which the elderly are able to adjust to new environments or changes in their familiar ones are not trivial, and we therefore need to examine the spatial competence of the elderly. Unfortunately, most of the studies done on way finding that include "adult" subjects deal with college students, and the literature on way-finding tasks for the elderly in real-world macroenvironments is sadly limited. The majority of research on the spatial abilities of the elderly has involved laboratory studies of the paper and pencil sort, and it is to that data base that we now turn.

Laboratory Studies of Spatial Cognition in the Elderly

The study of spatial cognition in the elderly is usually set within the context of a larger framework: the issue of the decline of cognitive abilities in general. While the brain "ages," the pattern of loss of neurons is variable, and people in good health may show relatively little loss in performance tests of memory, perception, and language (Selkoe, 1992). At the same time, approximately 5% of the neurons in the hippocampus "disappear with each decade in the second half of life" (p. 135). Thus, some decline in memory function in the elderly would not be surprising.

A common argument seems to be that spatial ability is often mediated by memory, and memory function stereotypically is reported to decline in the elderly; hence, spatial ability will be negatively affected with age (Salthouse, 1991). For example, Salthouse cites more than 20 references indicating significant age differences in the accuracy of recognizing or reproducing geometric designs; more than 10 references indicating older adults perform less well than do young adults on tasks involving memory for spatial location; and another group of studies reporting lower performance for older than younger adults on tasks involving reproducing the positions of target cells in a matrix. Age differences favoring young adults have been found for the following tasks: embedded figures, form board tests, mental rotation tasks, and perspective-taking tasks (Salthouse, 1991). While Salthouse acknowledges that the elderly may be handicapped on these tests because they tend to be timed (speeded), research with time limits removed also indicates differences in these spatial abilities: "most of the age-related decrease in accuracy with multiple operations . . . appears attributable to an inability to preserve the relevant information, and not to difficulties in integrating the products of those operations" (p. 285). In summary, Salthouse says, "Not much can yet be said about the reasons for age differences on measures of spatial ability. Increased age has consistently been found to be associated with poorer performance in tests of spatial memory, and in tests requiring various sorts of spatial manipulations or transformations" (p. 287).

However, there is hope for the elderly and the stereotyping of the elderly as functionally declining has been challenged. There are occasional exceptions to the general laboratory findings that the elderly perform less well than young adults on a variety of spatial tasks. One example is a study assessing the coding of spatial information (on cards) by females (McCormack, 1982). Older adults (mean age 68.3 years) and younger adults (mean age 23.6 years) were exposed to words (nouns) arranged vertically on cards, and then had to distinguish between targets and distractor words. There was no performance effect for age. Perhaps more significant is a longitudinal study by Schaie and Willis (1986), reporting an impressive reversal of decline in intellectual functioning in the elderly using a very limited training procedure. While they acknowledge that age-related decline exists and that it can reach "substantial magnitudes," they also point to the possibility that intellectual stimulation and training can reverse some of that decline. In their study of 229 older adults (mean age 72.8 years) as part of the Seattle Longitudinal Study, subjects took a variety of reasoning and spatial orientation measures and were classified as having remained stable or declined. Subjects were then assigned to Reasoning or Space training programs as a result of their performance status. The training consisted of five 1-hour individually conducted training sessions using practice problems on topics covered in the tests. We will focus on their spatial performance. Using a stringent criterion for performance measures, more women than men were returned to their base level of functioning for spatial behavior; whereas more men than women were returned to the base level for reasoning. In commenting on the moderation of abilities, Schaie and Willis state: "For most individuals the pattern of decline appears to be selective, perhaps even ability specific, rather than global and catastrophic. The considerable stability in intellectual functioning is noteworthy, given that both of the abilities studied (Inductive Reasoning, Spatial Orientation) involve abstract reasoning on speeded measures and would thus be expected to exhibit normative patterns of decline if one were to extrapolate from the widely accepted classical pattern of cognitive aging (Botwinick, 1977)" (p. 228). The training on spatial tasks seems to have been particularly effective for the elderly women in this study, and is all the more impressive given its limited scope and duration.

Despite the hope offered by researchers such as Schaie and Willis and the few exceptions to the general decline in spatial functioning evident in the vast majority of laboratory tasks, it would be possible to reach the conclusion that the elderly are environmentally handicapped because of a decline in spatial abilities. However, when we turn to studies in the macroenvironment, a different and much more positive picture of the spatial capability of the elderly emerges.

Field Studies of Spatial Cognition in the Elderly

Kirasic (1985) raises the important question, "Are elderly adults put at some disadvantage when faced with a new environment or a once-familiar environment that has been changed?" (p. 185). He goes on to cite the general picture drawn by the evidence that perspective-taking problems present difficulties for the elderly. Kirasic reviews the literature and based on that suggests that in all likelihood "elderly adults would encounter difficulties in learning new routes in unfamiliar areas" (p. 190).

However, Kirasic goes on to argue that the laboratory approach to evaluating the spatial abilities of the elderly may have underestimated their competence. In a number of ecologically oriented studies, the elderly have done quite well. In discussing environmental learning in the elderly, Ohta and Kirasic (1983) describe a number of "real-world" examples. For example, in studying the use of detours in a medical center and the requirement to take a different return route from a destination, it was found that the elderly were just as successful as younger subjects in the "real" situation, while doing less well in a number of more typical performance tests, including those of visual acuity, color perception, and road map reading. They also demonstrated a more conservative approach in choosing an acceptable probability level for an alternative route. Interestingly, elderly subjects rated their own sense of direction equivalent to the ratings younger subjects gave themselves with regard to their sense of direction. More importantly, the elderly subjects were just as successful as the younger ones in a way finding task with a real-world spatial problem.

In another study involving the manipulation of spatial arrays, subjects inferred the location of target sites for a novel, experimenter-generated spatial array and for their hometown. Elderly subjects performed with less accuracy than young adults on a variety of measures when the experimenter-generated array was used; but with the hometown as the spatial array, no differences in performance were found between young and older adults (Ohta & Kirasic, 1983). Also, in a study of young, middle-aged, and older adults' sketch maps of the city of Boston, there were no differences across age groups in cognitive errors, Euclidean bias, and superordinate scale bias (Lavoie & Demick, 1995), although the sketch maps of younger and middle-aged adults were more legible than those of older adults, containing fewer nodes and landmarks.

Other research on the elderly has focused not so much on the issue of cognitive decline but on what sources of information would be useful in way finding. Kirasic and Mathes (1990) assessed the effectiveness of different means of providing environmental information by assessing subjects' performance on spatial cognitive tasks of different complexity. Four tasks of increasing difficulty were used: scene recognition, route planning, route execution, and map placement. Forty elderly women with a mean age of 71.8 years participated in laboratory and real-world tasks. The real-world setting was the lower level of a two-level enclosed suburban mall with which the subjects were not familiar. Subjects were in one of four conditions: verbal description, verbal description with imagery instruction, videotape observation, and map study. They also completed tests of imagery, spatial relations, and visual memory as well as a locus of control assessment. Contrary to the authors' hypotheses, the only differences that occurred appeared in the route execution task. The map study and verbal description conditions resulted in greater efficiency in the route execution task than did the other possibilities. They recommend providing information in map/model form or in terms of the sequential mode of presentation (videotape or verbal description) to aid the way finder. As was indicated in the research reviewed by Ohta and Kirasic (1983), the context in which the spatial task is embedded is critical in the likelihood of way-finding success.

In a study with useful design applications for the elderly as well as other age groups, Evans, Brennan, Skorpanich, and Held (1984) investigated the verbal and location memory for urban landmarks of young (mean age 32 years) and older adults (mean age 71 years). Subjects completed a background questionnaire, a recall task, and a spatial location task. The recall task involved having subjects list all the buildings they could remember in a downtown area of Orange, California. In a spatial location task, subjects used a scaled grid to place 13 buildings in spaces corresponding to the location of that building in real space. Using a taxonomy of building characteristics (e.g., size, shape, color, etc.) already developed, subjects also rated the effect of these characteristics on memory. Building characteristics that were particularly salient to older residents were those in which there was: high use intensity, symbolic significance, a natural landscape, direct access siting, and unique style. Buildings lacking these features were recalled more often by young adults, whereas buildings with these characteristics were recalled with equal frequency by the two age groups.

While the recall and spatial location data indicated that the elderly person had less complete knowledge than young adults had of their environments in this study, we might again question the fact that these tasks did not involve *real-time* way finding. In terms of design applications, the authors point to the importance of building access as an important physical characteristic in the older person's environmental knowledge.

Summary

It would be a mistake to let the laboratory findings completely color our view of the spatial competence of the elderly. While the laboratory findings suggest a slowdown in their ability to solve classic mental rotation and perspective-taking tasks, the elderly demonstrate significant competence in real-world way finding.

Spatial Cognition and the Visually Impaired

Despite early claims that blind individuals were unable to form a global conception of space (Von Senden, 1932/1960), evidence has accumulated that refutes that conclusion (Juurmaa, 1973; Klatzky, Golledge, Loomis, Cicinelli, & Pellegrino, 1995; Landau, Spelke, & Gleitman, 1984; Passini, Proulx, & Rainville, 1990). Theoretically, it has been proposed that the visually impaired may construct their spatial knowledge via *different* means and perhaps more slowly than do sighted individuals, but that such representations are still functionally equivalent to those of the sighted (Fletcher, 1980). Similarly, Strelow (1985) proposes a theory of mobility using Gibson's (1966) theory of perception as a starting point, but noting the theory's incompleteness in failing to acknowledge multiple strategies for guiding navigation. Strelow argues that there is no reason that the blind would be unable to understand and that they use nonvisual perceptual stimuli to do so.

Many of the studies that investigate the issue of spatial cognition in the visually impaired use a range of participants: sighted, blindfolded sighted, adventitiously blind, and congenitally blind. To be considered congenitally blind, participants typically are blind at birth or become blind no later than 3 years of age. Studies also employ a range of activities, including those involving manipulatory space (explored by the arm system), and those involving ambulatory space (explored by the leg system or locomotion). Manipulatory space typically involves the use of a single vantage point, whereas ambulatory space may involve a number of vantage points (Barber & Lederman, 1988).

The range of abilities demonstrated by the visually impaired is by no means consistent, and this is one of the challenges in interpreting the literature. Loomis and colleagues (1993) wisely point out that the way in which subjects are selected for these studies as well as the small samples may well explain the range of findings. In their research of blindfolded, adventitiously blind, and congenitally blind subjects performing a range of navigation tasks, they were careful to select individuals who could be considered independent travelers. Similarly, in a study where congenitally blind and partially sighted high school students constructed a tactile map of their environment (Casey, 1978), the author notes that those who constructed more organized maps were more independent travelers.

In the Loomis and colleagues (1993) study, the accuracy and latency responses for congenitally blind subjects in a condition where subjects pointed to targets following locomotion were not significantly different from the sighted and adventitiously blind groups. This finding of Loomis and colleagues does not replicate the data from Rieser, Guth, and Hill (1986) on whose work the navigation task was based. Loomis and colleagues conclude, "Results provide little indication that spatial competence strongly depends on prior visual experience" (p. 73).

Are the spatial representations of the sighted and the visually impaired functionally equivalent, especially if the visually impaired are given sufficient time to perform a task? Given the methodological reservations that have already been highlighted, it is probably impossible to answer that question. But we can consider some data. Rieser and colleagues (1986) emphasize the role of early visual experience in facilitating what they call "perspective sensitivity." The impact of locomoting to a new point of observation to judge perspective had no impact on early-blinded, as opposed to late-blinded and sighted individuals. Using a Gibsonian perspective, the authors take a perceptual learning view and argue that vision can enrich proprioception. Continuing their perceptual learning emphasis, Rieser, Hill, Talor, Bradfield, and Rosen (1992) examined the performance of those with partial vision, congenital blindness, and sight on tasks involving a familiar part of their home town. The subjects with partial vision were further categorized in terms of the onset of visual impairment (early or late) and the range of their visual field (small or broad). Subjects who lost broad field vision early or were congenitally blind performed worse than those with early or late acuity loss and those with late field loss. "The theory is that experience of broad-field vision facilitates the development of nonvisual sensitivity . . ." (p. 217).

In reviewing the use of language and locomotion in the blind, Brambring (1982) reports that, "The linguistic analyses of route descriptions given by blind persons reveals that they use less information from the environment and more information relating to their person" (p. 217). In their route descriptions, the blind also provide twice as much information as do sighted persons, focusing on evaluative comments such as warning of possible dangers.

In a study involving distance and direction estimates in a familiar neighborhood (Byrne & Salter, 1983), congenitally blind subjects and matched sighted controls performed similarly on distance estimations, but the blind subjects had more difficulty with direction estimates, especially if those estimates were given from a location other than their home. The authors discuss the findings in terms of the egocentric orientation they suspect the blind are using in making their judgments. Contrasting vector maps (where geographical information is available in vector form) and network maps (where traversible routes are encoded as strings of nodes), Byrne and Salter (1983) suggest that the restricted experience of the congenitally blind results in less adequate vector maps. When indicating the direction of imaginary locations from a starting point other than home, the authors argue that a vector map is required. Thus, the poorer performance of the blind on this task would indicate a less fully developed vector map system.

This issue of an egocentric reference system has also been raised in a study of school-aged children (Dodds, Howarth, & Carter, 1982). Congenitally and adventitiously blind 11-year-olds performed pointing, map drawing, and spatial reasoning tasks using two simple routes over repeated trials. Individually taken by car to an imaginary friend's house, participants had to then perform the various tasks with the stated goal of getting to that friend's house. In general the adventitiously blind children performed better than the congenitally blind, and 75% of the congenitally blind were described as using a "self-referent" spatial coding strategy. Dodds, Howarth, and Carter (1982) state that none of the coding strategies of the adventitiously blind fit this description. Interestingly, for measurements of object location in the blind, Haber, Haber, Penningroth, Novak, and Radgowski (1993) recommend a pointing response that relies on a body part or an extension of a body part. Such a recommendation may capitalize on the self-referent system the congenitally blind seem to incorporate.

These data suggest some functional differences in the visually impaired when compared to sighted individuals. However, other research has failed to demonstrate such differences or emphasizes an abstract framework for space that is similar for blind and sighted people (Kennedy, Gabias, & Heller, 1992). Using an information-based approach, Kennedy and colleagues (1992) argue that "congenitally blind people are at times more variable or slower than sighted people in solving spatial tasks, but their abstract framework for space may use the same principles" (p. 175). Kennedy and colleagues point to lesion data from the parietal lobe in suggesting that "information-based perception leads to amodal perception of shape and space, in which the parietal lobes may play a vital role" (pp. 187–188).

Klatzky and colleagues (1995) performed a comprehensive study in which congenitally blind, adventitiously blind, and sighted subjects performed manipulatory, simple locomotion, and complex locomotion tasks. Using factor analysis from the data in the range of tasks, three dimensions emerged. One factor involved spatial inference; the second negatively related to performance on tabletop tasks; and the third factor involved locomotor reproduction of simple linear paths and turns. While the authors find no evidence of "general or specific spatial deficits among persons who are blind" (p. 80), they do note some differences with regard to the issue of spatial inference. Both tasks used in a discriminant analysis to classify participants involved multisegment pathways, and there is the suggestion that "people who are blind and people who are sighted differ most on tasks involving spatial inference, rather than proprioceptive memory" (p. 80). Still, the authors argue against any generalizations with regard to spatial cognition and visual status.

Design Implications

The data suggest that the visually impaired are able to form spatial representations, and that independent travel may contribute to spatial competence. Such travel will be facilitated to the extent the environment supports it. Cartographers, planners, and others can provide more travel aids to facilitate independent travel (Golledge, 1991b). The blind can use raised outline drawings (Kennedy, 1983), and in discussing map use more generally, Andrews (1983) describes a variety of maps that the visually impaired can use. These include dot maps (for the densities of mapped phenomena), graduated circle maps (indicating proportions of data), and choropleth maps (where categorical information is indicated by symbols). Just as is the case for real-world navigation, Andrews argues that too few of these kinds of maps are available to the visually impaired. Furthermore, because adults are often reluctant map users (Spencer, Morsley, Ungar, Pike, & Blades, 1992), the ability of blind children to benefit from map use is underestimated (Ungar, Blades, Spencer, & Morsley, 1994). In a study of 23 children who were visually impaired, 8 that were totally blind and 15 with some residual vision, children first explored a room with landmarks and then used a pointer to locate (point to) these landmarks. The authors report a significant interaction of visual status with condition, such that the congenitally blind children had the lowest accuracy when exploring the room, but then were able to perform almost at the level of those with residual vision with the use of a map. For those who are visually impaired, the importance of the map as an aid to way finding must be stressed.

A variety of way-finding strategies are used by the visually impaired (Passini, Dupre, & Langlois, 1986), including cardinal directions, the sun, street systems, and major reference points. Rieser, Guth, and Hill (1982) suggest that the visually impaired are more likely to rely on slower cognitive strategies rather than perceptual updating. Representational aids should also provide a variety of information, given these diverse strategies. Passini and colleagues (1990) stress the need for an environmental information system that is coherent and accessible to all travelers. The visually impaired decision-maker needs cues at appropriate places in the terrain where decisions are made, typically choice points such as intersections and building entrances. Golledge (1991b) has advocated the use of tactual strip maps, similar to the maps used by automobile associations (e.g., a Trip Tik). Each page or segment has a straight-line path, with barriers, locations, and other important navigational information indicated on the strip. NOMAD (Golledge, Parkes, & Dear, 1989; Spencer, Morsley, Ungar, Pike, & Blades, 1992) is another navigational aid that provides auditory and tactile information. Auditory information, corresponding to any graphic in the display, may be placed anywhere on the user's rectangular, touch-sensitive board (Spencer et al., 1992). Another possibility discussed by Spencer and colleagues is REACT, an environmentally based approach in which acoustic beacons located in the environment can be triggered by the user's "smart card." The user could obtain needed way-finding information from these beacons, which would presumably be located at important choice points.

Summary

While more carefully constructed studies are needed to determine whether the spatial representations of the blind are as functionally effective as those of sighted individuals, it seems reasonable to conclude from the literature that they *do* have spatial representations. A fuller understanding of the spatial abilities of the visually impaired will encourage planners to provide more environmental support. The blind *can* travel independently in the environment and will be better able to do so with a greater variety of way-finding aids.

2

Gender Differences in Spatial Cognition: *North by Northwest*

If the only information you have about an individual is her or his sex, you know next to nothing about that individual's cognitive abilities. (Unger & Crawford, 1992, p. 98)

This statement is not uniformly accepted, and three anecdotes will serve to introduce the topic of whether men and women differ in their spatial abilities, with particular reference to way finding. A naval architect who is a friend of the author states with some assurance that he can tell whether directional information has been provided by a man or a woman; he furthermore claims that the information from men is typically superior. His statements may both intrigue and annoy, and because of important implications for way finding and architectural legibility, exploring the nature of gender differences in this area is the focus of this chapter.

The second anecdote relates to a television program broadcast in the summer of 1995 on a PBS station. The program was the *1995 National Geography Bee*, and all 10 young adolescent finalists were boys as were most of the 50 state representatives. Such lopsidedness is also intriguing, inviting questions about the origins of such differences in performance. This dominance is not new. In 1993, about 2 million students in grades 4–8 from 47,000 registered schools took part in the test nationwide. Of the 57 state and territory winners, 55 were boys, as were all 10 finalists (Self & Golledge, 1994). This pattern of dominance by boys in the Geography Bee is being examined by Roger Downs and Lynn Liben in order to better understand this phenomenon (Self & Golledge, 1994).

And finally, there was an article in a Sunday *New York Times* (Schoenstein, 1995) entitled "East is: (a) West (b) North (c) I Don't Know." In the article, the author writes:

As we began a drive from Princeton, N.J., to Portland, Me., one morning last month, my wife, Judy, cheerfully asked,

"On the way, why don't we stop off in Buffalo and see the Whites?"

"If we can arrange an airlift," I replied. "Honey, Buffalo is nowhere near our route to Maine."

. . . And her flair for misdirection has been passed down to our youngest daughter, a highly intelligent college student, who recently said:

"Dad, let's take a vacation in Bermuda. I've never been to the Caribbean."

"Neither has Bermuda," I said. "It's the same latitude as South Carolina."

While the article goes on to decry the lack of geographical knowledge among all Americans, the implication in this opening is that women are somehow less knowledgeable about geography than are men. What are we to conclude from the naval architect's claims, the dominance of teenage boys in the National Geography Bee, and Schoenstein's family anecdotes? At the very least we must question the origins of stereotypes about spatial ability.

There is an abundance of evidence that men are superior at certain spatial tasks, in particular mental rotation (Hyde, 1990; Masters & Sanders, 1993). With regard to way-finding tasks, differences between men and women often appear (Aubrey & Dobbs, 1990; Galea & Kimura, 1993; Holding, 1992; Holding & Holding, 1989; McGuinness & Sparks, 1983; Miller & Santoni, 1986; Ward, Newcombe, & Overton, 1986), but there are instances of no difference as well (Cousins, Siegel, & Maxwell, 1983; Kirasic, Allen, & Siegel, 1984; Sadalla & Montello, 1989; Taylor & Tversky, 1992a, 1992b). The literature on gender differences in spatial ability is not clear-cut; much depends on the kinds of tasks participants are given. To disentangle the findings, it is helpful to look at two general classes of studies: the traditional spatial ability assessments and the more ecologically oriented way-finding studies. In general the traditional studies of spatial ability are paper-and-pencil exercises or at least conducted in the laboratory with isolated stimuli (e.g., 10-block cubes or letters of the alphabet to be rotated). The more ecologically oriented studies sometimes involve real-world way-finding tasks. More often the tasks use slides or videos of the real world about which participants are asked to make judgments (e.g., order a path sequence, make recognition decisions).

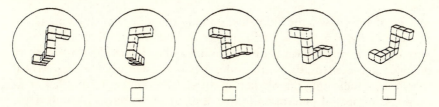

Figure 2.1. A sample item from the Vandenberg and Kuse (1978) Mental Rotation Test.

THE SPATIAL FACTORS

Traditional Tasks

Before trying to dissect the test-dependent factors that influence gender differences, it might be helpful to understand what these tests involve. To group these tests, Linn and Petersen's (1985) categories are used.

Mental Rotation Tests

One of the most widely used tests is the Vandenberg and Kuse (1978) test of mental rotation (see Figure 2.1), an adaptation of the original stimuli used by Shepard and Metzler (1971). In this test, the individual is presented with a drawing of a three-dimensional object composed of a series of 10 connected cubes. Participants must select which two of four choices are the same as the exemplar. The choices include examples that are rotated and flipped images.

Spatial Visualization Tasks

Within the category of spatial visualization, representative tests include the Embedded Figures Test (EFT; Witkin, Oltman, Raskin, & Karp, 1971) and Paper Folding Test (Ekstrom, French, & Harman, 1976). In the EFT, subjects must identify a simpler shape from a drawing of a more complex shape. In the Paper Folding Test, subjects must indicate how a folded piece of paper, marked by a dot through all folds, will look when unfolded.

Other tests that might be included in this category are a number from Thurstone's (1938) test of Primary Mental Abilities (PMA), including Flags (judge whether pairs of American flags in different orientations are the same or different); Cubes (judge whether pairs of three-dimensional cubes with different designs on each face are the same or different after one or more rotations through space), and Hands (judge pictures of hands for left–right discriminations) (Linn & Petersen, 1985).

Spatial Perception Tasks

Spatial perception is another distinguishable factor that is often identified (Linn & Petersen, 1985) and draws heavily on tasks we describe as Piagetian. These tests assess the individual's ability to indicate the horizontal and vertical. In the Water Level Test (Piaget & Inhelder, 1948/1956) or some variation of it, the subject is to draw a line indicating the level of water in a tipped glass; alternatively, the subject may draw a plumb line (vertical assessment) indicating the relation of a tree to a mountain. Another common test of spatial perception is the Rod and Frame Test (Witkin, Dyk, Faterson, Goodenough, & Karp, 1962), in which a subject must place a rod vertically while viewing a frame that is tipped from the upright.

What Are the Factors? How Many Are There?

One of the difficulties in interpreting the literature on gender differences in spatial cognition is the variability in the identification and naming of the factors. In McGee's (1979b) review of the history of factor analytical studies of spatial cognition, he presents the evolution of these factors. In studies by Guilford and Zimmerman based on their test battery (cited in McGee, 1979b), two factors emerged that were called Spatial Visualization (Vz) and Spatial Relations (SR). Vz emphasized imagining the mental rotation of objects and the folding and unfolding of flat objects, whereas SR highlighted the arrangement of elements within a visual stimulus pattern. McGee then goes on to review the factors identified by Thurstone (1950) and those by French (1951). McGee concludes that there is significant support for two distinct spatial abilities: visualization and orientation. Regarding visualization factors, McGee states, "All involve the ability to mentally manipulate, rotate, twist, or invert a pictorially presented stimulus object" (p. 19). Examples of these visualization tests provided by McGee in an appendix include identifying the placement of punched holes when folded paper is unfolded (Thurstone, 1950) and similar paper folding and form board tasks from Ekstrom, French, and Harman (1976). Using the definition he provides, the Vandenberg and Kuse test (1978) would fit in the visualization category.

For spatial orientation, McGee states, "All involve the comprehension of the arrangement of elements within a visual stimulus pattern and the aptitude for remaining unconfused by the changing orientation in which a spatial configuration may be presented" (1979b, p. 19). Example tests include directional orientation (indicate compass directions when rotation has changed) and cube faces (whether two drawings of cubes represent the same cube if a different design is to be on each face). McGee includes no examples of Piagetian verticality and horizontality tasks in this factor.

Meta-Analyses

In moving our understanding of these factors and possible gender differences forward, one central technique is meta-analysis. In early reviews of gender differences in spatial ability (see, e.g., Maccoby & Jacklin, 1974), what is called a narrative review approach was used. This approach involves reviewing the studies in essentially descriptive form in order to reach a conclusion about the data. Meta-analysis has changed the approach taken to this and other areas of psychology. While the phrase "garbage in, garbage out" in describing the data is always relevant, meta-analysis allows us to gather together all of the research on a given topic (e.g., all studies done using the Vandenberg and Kuse [1978] mental rotation test with participants who fall within a particular age range [e.g., over 14]) and then assess the consistency and power of the data. The mathematical technique allows one to calculate a mean effect size (typically d) that takes into account not only mean differences between men and women on this test, but also the variability involved in the scores. The mean effect size, d, is in standard deviation units. Thus, an effect size of .45 represents a difference between means of .45 standard deviations.

When Hyde (1981) performed her meta-analysis of gender differences in cognitive ability, she used the studies cited in Maccoby and Jacklin's (1974) narrative review. With regard to the spatial ability studies, there were 10 studies that were classified as involving visual-spatial ability (with an effect size of $d = .45$ and just over 4% of the variance explained), centering on mental rotation/spatial visualization tasks. Another 20 studies involved field articulation (Rod and Frame Test), similar to a spatial orientation or spatial perception factor, yielding an effect size of $d = .51$. This factor explained 2.5% of the variance. Hyde points out that these gender differences are small and account for very little of the population variance.

Linn and Petersen (1985) moved our understanding of the spatial ability factors further, conducting a meta-analysis of 172 studies done since Maccoby and Jacklin (1974) through June 1982. Linn and Petersen approached their meta-analysis from what they call a differential perspective—comparing the spatial ability of different populations. But to create clusters or groupings of studies to examine, they used rationales that represented both psychometric and cognitive perspectives. Furthermore, variations in performance on the *same* task were interpreted from a strategic perspective. With this approach, Linn and Petersen argue for the existence of *three factors*: 1) spatial perception (determining spatial relations with respect to one's own body; a gravitational kinesthetic process); 2) mental rotation (a Gestalt-like analogue process); and 3) spatial visualization (multistep manipulation of spatially presented information). What Linn and Petersen argue is that spatial visualization involves multiple steps and as such may include aspects of the other two factors (mental rotation and spatial perception). In McGee's two-factor presentation, mental rotation is part of spatial visualization. Linn and Petersen argue that the psychometric data support a *separate* category for mental rotation. Examples of tests for their three spatial factors are as follows: Spatial perception (Rod and Frame; water level); Mental Rotation (Vandenberg and Kuse's [1978] adaptation of Shepard and Metzler's original stimuli; Flags; Cards; Primary Mental Abilities [PMA] Space); Spatial Visualization (Embedded Figures; Paper Folding).

Additional classifications within the three factors were made after an assessment of homogeneity. Age clustering was determined to best explain differences in performance on the spatial perception factor (for all ages, d = .44; under 13, d = .37; between 13–18, d = .37; over age 18, d = .64). For the mental rotation factor, the task itself provided the best clustering (overall d = .73; Vandenberg test, d = .94; PMA test, d = .26). Performance on the spatial visualization factor was homogeneous and did not require subdivisions (d = .13). One might wonder whether the small effect size for gender differences in spatial visualization, as the factor is defined by Linn and Petersen (1985), is related to the hypothesized multistep aspect. Gender differences seem less likely to occur in a multistep process where variable strategies may operate. But the mental rotation evidence is particularly strong, with gender differences reported as soon as they can be measured in children. When meta-analysis is used to review research on spatial abilities, a consistent finding is that the largest gender differences occur on these tests of mental rotation, most notably the Vandenberg and Kuse (1978) test.

When Hyde (1990) discussed the work of Linn and Petersen (1985), she described spatial perception as a sense of verticality/horizontality; mental rotation as the ability to mentally rotate three-dimensional objects pictured in two dimensions; and spatial visualization as spatial disembedding, the ability to extract a visually simpler form from a more complex form. Others (Lohman, cited in Horan & Rosser, 1984) have also discussed three spatial factors from a process perspective: spatial relations (e.g., mental rotation tests), spatial orientation (Piagetian perspective tasks), and spatial visualization (reproduction of visual displays or mental unfolding of geometric shapes). Here, the factors are labeled somewhat differently. It is confusing when researchers adopt the *same* terminology (e.g., spatial relations) to describe different phenomena (see McGee, 1979a, 1979b). The discussion of gender differences in spatial ability is hampered by the inconsistent terminology that has been adopted.

While the findings regarding gender differences in mental rotation are strong, there have been some arguments that gender differences in spatial ability might be shrinking (Feingold, 1988). In reaching that conclusion, Feingold used the Space Relations subtest of the Differential Aptitude Test (DAT), which includes stimuli like unfolded boxes that must be matched against their "folded" version. To examine whether the magnitude of the gender difference in spatial ability has remained robust, Masters and Sanders (1993) conducted a meta-analysis on 14 mental rotation studies (using the Vandenberg test) appearing between 1975 and 1992. They found that men performed better than women in all the studies, with differences at the $p < .001$ level. Moreover, the magnitude of the differences had not decreased over that time frame; 16% of the variability in test performance could be attributed to gender. Again, one of the explanations for the differences in results can be tied to the test used. One conclusion is that the spatial ability measured by the Vandenberg test produces gender differences that are not transitory and do not appear to be decreasing. The interesting questions are why these differences exist and what they tell us about the factors that influence spatial cognition.

Summary

There is disagreement about the existence of two versus three spatial factors. It may be prudent at this point to postulate two factors, and the author proposes using the terms Mental Rotation (covering the Vandenberg and Kuse kinds of tasks) and Spatial Orientation (covering Piagetian Water Level tasks and Rod and Frame tasks) to describe the factors. If a third factor is warranted, covering tasks where a visually simpler form is extracted from a more complex one, Hyde's (1990) language, Spatial Disembedding, is a good choice. Terms such as spatial visualization and spatial relations have been used inconsistently and should be avoided.

Traditional Laboratory Tasks of Spatial Ability

What have we learned about gender differences in spatial cognition from these traditional laboratory tasks?

One of the reasons laboratory studies of spatial ability do not yield consistent results is that spatial ability is not unidimensional. For example, some people claim that they have a good sense of direction and yet have difficulty with the mental rotation often involved in transforming information on a map. Others may describe their strengths and weaknesses as the reverse. Still others claim skill at both kinds of tasks, and there are certainly people who claim they can do neither. As has been discussed, there are a great many tests that measure these various aspects (Linn & Petersen, 1985; McGee, 1979b), and the major point is that these tests tap different aspects of spatial behavior.

As we have seen, the overwhelming majority of studies and reviews indicate that men have a superior ability at mental rotation (see, e.g., Corballis, 1982; Gladue, Beatty, Larson, & Staton, 1990; Halpern, 1986; Harris, 1981; Herman & Bruce, 1983; Lohman, 1986; Sanders & Soares, 1986; Sanders, Soares, & D'Aquila, 1982; Tapley & Bryden, 1977), although there is no agreement about the sources of these differences, which include evolutionary, neurological, hormonal, and sociocultural explanations (Buss, 1995; Halpern, 1986; Hassler, 1993; Geschwind & Galaburda,

1985, 1987; McGee, 1979a, 1982; Neisser et al., 1996; Richardson, 1994; Thomas & Kail, 1991). A fuller discussion of the evolutionary, neurological, and hormonal theories is taken up in Chapter 3. While some do not agree (see, e.g., Berg, Hertzog, & Hunt, 1982; Teng & Lee, 1982; Uecker & Obrzut, 1993; Voyer & Bryden, 1990), even the most skeptical researchers must deal with the preponderance of evidence supporting the superiority of men in mental rotation studies.

What is the nature of the difference in performance on these tasks? Answers to this question include speed, strategy, or a combination of these variables. A number of studies show that women tend to be slower and less accurate in doing these mental rotation tasks (see, e.g., Birenbaum, Kelly, & Levi-Keren, 1994; Blough & Slavin, 1987; Bryden, George, & Inch, 1990). Birenbaum and colleagues (1994) wanted to examine gender differences with more attention to the features of the stimuli used in the task. The stimuli that were used were two-dimensional multipointed objects in which prongs were of different lengths and created different angles with respect to the center mass (the spatial test of the Comprehensive Ability Battery; Hakstian & Cattell, 1975). The authors differentiated between features they labeled structural and those they labeled superficial. Structural features, like symmetry, were those in which their removal fundamentally changed the nature of the shape. Superficial features involved markings (e.g., spots). In the test, an exemplar was followed on the same line by six choices, each of which was rotated or both flipped and rotated. The subject's task was to indicate for each option whether it was rotated or flipped. There were 12 sets of six options each. Dependent measures included accuracy (scores from 0–72) and speed.

Although women were less accurate and slower on this mental rotation task, Birenbaum and colleagues' (1994) research with 410 subjects indicated that both men and women have difficulty with the same kinds of stimulus components. The stimuli that proved most challenging were those with longer rotation trajectories (greater than 90 degrees) and those with greater complexity (more than 7 points, multiple spots, no internal symmetry). The differences between men and women are interpreted in terms of a model offered by Just and Carpenter (1985), which proposes three stages in this kind of activity: 1) stimulus search; 2) initial rotation; and 3) confirmation. Birenbaum and colleagues speculate that the difference between men and women comes in the confirmation stage, with women expressing greater cautiousness about making a judgment, which leads to greater response time. Essentially, with complex objects rotated to greater trajectories, there is simply more for women to "check," and this may slow down their performance. Similarly, Bryden and colleagues (1990) argue that for women the longer response times related to configural complexity merely reflect a slower use of the same strategies as those used by men. Recent research (Loring-Meier & Halpern, 1999) has looked at the role of visuospatial working memory in mental rotation tasks. Results indicate greater speed for men than women but similar accuracy on a number of component processes.

The issue of the slower reaction times of women and the potential effect of cautiousness on their performance has led some authors to question whether the mental rotation differences might be an effect of time limits. Using the Vandenberg test, Goldstein, Haldane, and Mitchell (1990) demonstrated that men did not score higher in an untimed condition or when performance was assessed in terms of ratio-scores (number correct/number attempted). They point to the need to consider the "how" of testing in interpreting gender differences that vary. However, Resnick (1993) also used a procedure that incorporated testing *without* time limits, and found differences on the Vandenberg and Kuse task of the same strength as those using time limits. She concluded that the speed of problem solving could not explain the gender differences in mental rotation performance and questioned whether their problem-solving strategies might differ in other ways as well. In explaining the differences in results between her study and that of Goldstein and colleagues, Resnick points to her use of a larger sample and one with a less restricted range of ability. Resnick's 182 subjects came from a large midwestern university, whereas Goldstein and colleagues' 46 participants in the untimed portion of the study were from a highly selective private university.

Related to the current discussion, one cognitive test in which women do outperform men is Cognitive Persistence (Tanaka, Panter, & Winborne, 1988). In factor-analyzing the Need for Cognition Scale (Cacioppo & Petty, 1982), Tanaka and colleagues found three factors: cognitive persistence, cognitive complexity, and cognitive confidence. There were gender differences only for the Cognitive Persistence subscale, which includes items like the following (published in paraphrased form in the study): "Prefer intellectual task to one that doesn't require much thought," "Appreciate discovering the strength/weaknesses of my thinking," and "I don't care how a job gets done" (reverse scored). About Cognitive Persistence, the authors state that it appears to describe someone "who demonstrates a preference toward evaluating and processing all aspects of the given information deliberately and completely (i.e., a tendency toward a multidimensional as opposed to a unidimensional focus) . . ." (p. 47). It is possible that this aspect of women's approach to cognitive tasks may manifest itself in situations like the Vandenberg and Kuse task which are complex and multidimensional. Use of a deliberate and complete approach may explain why women tend to be slower on these tasks.

Some researchers suggest that a difference in strategy as well as speed may play a role. Kail, Carter, and Pellegrino (1979) suggest that the sizable minority of women (30%) in their study who rotated stimuli more slowly than did men used a different strategy to do so. In their research, subjects were exposed to eight alphanumeric characters and eight characters from the PMA (that looked like hieroglyphics). Choices were compared to a standard, and they could be identical but rotated from 0–150 degrees, or mirror images (rotated in one of three different positions). Subjects had to judge when the comparisons were identical and when they were mirror images. Men and women performed similarly in many aspects of the task, with one exception: "The single significant sex difference in performance was that men mentally rotated stimuli more rapidly than women" (p. 185). The bimodal distribution in performance by women suggested that there might be two groups. Kail and colleagues differentiated between "holistic" mental rotation, in which the "entire comparison stimulus is rotated simultaneously into congruence with the target" and a second strategy in which "individual features of the comparison stimulus are rotated separately" (p. 185). Their suggestion was that the women who rotated the stimuli significantly more slowly were rotating these features separately, leading to increased response time. These authors stress the variability in performance within each gender, rather than the average level of ability, in considering gender differences in mental rotation.

In a similar perspective on strategy, Blough and Slavin (1987) suggest that women may have a bias toward accuracy and perhaps use an analytic strategy as opposed to a holistic strategy. Their research used a variety of tasks (figural choice task; a mental rotation task using letter-like characters from the PMA; box-folding problems from the DAT; static mental imagery task involving shape comparison). In the choice, mental rotation and shape comparison tasks, women took significantly longer, but they were also significantly more accurate than men in the choice task, and there were no gender differences in accuracy on the mental rotation task. The authors suggest that in tasks like mental rotation, women may use an analytic feature-by-feature comparison process, which takes more time to execute.

Similarly, Cochran and Wheatley (1989) discuss strategy differences and suggest that these differences between men and women come into play only on more challenging visualization tasks (presumably like the Vandenberg and Kuse task). They distinguish between verbal/analytic strategies that are sequential and involve breaking apart the stimulus object and nonverbal/holistic strategies involving parallel processing and frequently occurring with visualization. Although men scored higher on the Visualization of Rotations subtest (ROT) of the Purdue Spatial Visualization Test in this study, there was no gender difference in performance on the other spatial task, the Space Relations subtest of the DAT. Further, there were no gender differences on their Spatial Strategy Questionnaire, which measured the frequency of use and difficulty of the strategies employed. Cochran and Wheatley suggest that there may be considerable variability in strategy use, even within subjects, and that the most difficult tasks are likely to produce greater variability in strategy use. Other studies comment on the issue of strategy use as well. For example, Freedman and Rovegno (1981) indicate that men reported using their hands less, counting blocks less, and picturing the stimuli in their minds more than did the women in this study using the Vandenberg and Kuse (1978) test.

Beyond strategy, the different cognitive correlates of spatial rotation performance were examined in a fascinating longitudinal study examining personality, intelligence, and spatial visualization (Ozer, 1987). The study used participants who were recruited at age 3 and followed them through high school, involving them in repeated intelligence tests, field dependence, and embedded figures tests, as well as the California Q-sorts (100 statements describing personality, cognitive, and social characteristics). Then, at age 18, participants were given the Vandenberg Mental Rotations test. There was a large gender difference favoring men on the Vandenberg ($d = .70$), but the more interesting story from the study was in the cognitive correlates of mental rotation. For men, there was a strong correlation (.42) between Performance IQ at age 4 and scores on the mental rotations test at age 18, but there was no correlation with Verbal IQ at any age. Although the Performance IQ of women was also correlated with mental rotation at ages 11 and 18, there was also a significant correlation (.32) with Verbal IQ at age 18. Thus, there is a relationship between verbal skill and mental rotation performance in women that does not exist for men. In attempting to explain why he thinks spatial visualization is related to verbal ability in women but not in men, Ozer suggests that women may employ a verbal strategy and that different sources may explain the individual differences in spatial visualization in men and women. ". . . in females, there may be overlap among the factors causing variability in spatial visualization and verbal ability" (p. 133). Furthermore, for women who scored high on the Vandenberg test at the age of 18, their "intellectual gifts" were visible in terms of test scores and teacher ratings of intelligence early on. The same was not true for boys. Ozer states, "It is as if spatial visualization ability in males was invisible in the social world of the observer, despite its strong implications in the domain of tested cognitive abilities" (p. 132). For women, 12 personality characteristics correlated with mental rotation scores, whereas for men, there were but 2. These distinct profiles may suggest a different approach taken by men and women to cognitive tasks in general and to mental rotation in particular.

In addition to strategy differences and cognitive correlates, researchers have also questioned the effect of the sociocultural labeling of spatial tasks. For example, Richardson (1994) used a task with a mannequin, which had been adapted by Ratcliff (1979), to assess the impact of labeling the activity in terms of gender (man vs. woman). One version of the task was called the "Ratcliff Test of Spatial Ability" and the parallel version was called the "Ratcliff Test of Personal Empathy." The paper-and-pencil task used drawings of a figure that was either a man or a woman with one hand marked by a black disc and the other by a white disc. The figure was either seen from the front or back, upright or inverted, with the black disc marking either the left or the right hand. Random orderings of these eight configurations were presented in a booklet, and the subject's task was to indicate whether the black disc was in the left or right hand. Educational level was also involved in this study, comparing the performance of underclassmen with advanced undergraduates and postgraduates on this task. Results indicated that the gender-typing of the task did not significantly affect performance. However, whereas undergraduate men were better than undergraduate women, there were no differences in performance between men and women in the advanced undergraduate and postgraduate age groups. These findings might argue for an effect of education in ameliorating gender differences on this task. But a second study used a task based on the Shepard and Metzler (1971) stimuli, and found the typical gender difference pattern (superiority of men) independent of educational level. Sociocultural labeling will not necessarily eliminate gender differences on spatial tasks, nor will educational level, in all cases.

Summary

The picture involving gender differences in spatial ability is not simple. Explanations for the differences fundamentally involve the tests themselves. When mentally rotating three-dimensional stimuli, women may be slower at rotation and may use an approach that is analytic in terms of focusing on particular components rather than the whole figure. It is also possible that women's cognitive persistence affects the thoroughness with which they approach a task, in turn affecting response latency. A number of researchers in this field (see, e.g., Hyde, 1990), stress the importance of precision when talking about differences in spatial abilities. Performance is not consistent across tasks. Although women do not appear to be equal to men in terms of their speed of performance, there are tasks on which their accuracy is as good or better.

THE ISSUE OF AGE

One of the controversies surrounding the understanding of gender differences in spatial ability is the age at which such differences emerge. When such differences occur may tell us something about the influential factors. A good many studies point to the emergence of such differences at adolescence (see, e.g., Waber, 1976, 1977), and in fact, some of the meta-analyses on the topic of spatial ability differences between men and women have limited themselves to studies with at least adolescent-aged participants (Hyde, 1981). The studies that stress the emergence of differences at puberty tend to emphasize the effect of hormones. A fuller examination of these effects is undertaken in Chapter 3, this volume.

Another difficulty, of course, is that the studies looking at the emergence of gender differences in spatial ability have not all used the same tasks, which, as we have seen before, is related to the inconsistent findings. For example, Horan and Rosser (1984) did a series of eight studies with 3- to 11-year-olds. Tasks 1–4 involved low-level Euclidean spatial visualization; tasks 5–7 involved high-level Euclidean and projective spatial orientation; and task 8 involved high-level Euclidean and projective spatial visualization. There were a number of noteworthy findings. First, there were essentially no significant gender differences when overall spatial problem-solving ability was considered. However, a meta-analysis of the eight studies showed that the match between the dimensionality of the stimulus verses that of the response items made a difference. Girls had a significant advantage ($d = .54$) when the presentation and response mode were constant (e.g., both involving items presented two dimensionally). However, when the dimensionality of the presentation and response mode differed (e.g., three-dimensional in presentation but two-dimensional in response), boys had an advantage ($d = .40$). Among other things, this research demonstrates that the analysis of tasks may require even more sophistication than simple factor categorization (i.e., just whether a task involved spatial visualization or orientation).

When slightly older children tackle Piagetian-type tasks, some differences have been noted. Liben and Golbeck (1980) used participants from grades 3, 5, 7, 9, and 11 to carry out two Piagetian horizontality and verticality tasks (water levels and plumb lines) and found that in general boys were superior to girls on these tasks. On the other hand, Thomas and Lohaus (1993) examined the performance of German children ages 7–16 on two Piagetian style horizontal (water level) and vertical (plumb line) tasks. They argue that within subject differences regarding performance level on these kinds of tasks is much more significant than between subject differences in gender. After controlling for subgroup performance differences in their study, the gender effect disappeared.

Some support for the contention that spatial ability differences may emerge on the cusp of adolescence is a mental rotation study by Merriman, Keating, and List (1985). The study used 9 ½-year-olds, 14-year-olds, and adults on tasks that required differentiation of left-right orientations of rotated cartoon-like facial profiles. There were four basic profiles, which were upright and rotated (60, 120, 180, 240, and 300 degrees) and their mirror images. Subjects had to indicate whether each face presented was normal or backward. In every age group, women were slower, on average, than were men. However, the variability for the rate of rotation for women was about 50% greater than that for men, suggesting that women are not uniformly slow in this kind of task. This differential performance of women was also noted by Kail and colleagues (1979). An important finding of the study, according to Merriman and colleagues, was that the gender-related mean and variance differences in mental rotation rate previously reported in adults could be extended to children ages 9 1/2 and 14.

However, in a study by Pezaris and Casey (1991) with eighth graders (mean age 13.10 years), significant differences between boys and girls did not emerge on mental rotation tasks using Shepard and Metzler (1971) stimuli. The authors comment that proficiency at mental rotation tasks may not have fully developed by this time and note that boys of this age try less hard and focus less well than older students. At the same time, the study, which also looked at the role of interference tasks on performance, revealed that boys showed less verbal interference to tasks while demonstrating greater visuospatial interference to tasks than did girls. As the issue of strategy differences was also being assessed in this study, the interference results suggested that girls may be more likely to use verbal strategies to solve mental rotation problems, whereas boys may be more inclined to use visuospatial strategies (producing the significant interference differences that emerged). A verbal strategy might involve saying something like, "If I move the image three blocks to the right . . . ," whereas a visuospatial strategy might involve imagining the figure rotated to a new angle. The authors also comment that the difficulty of mental rotation tasks makes their assessment virtually impossible prior to age 11. It should be noted that there were supplemental instructions given to subjects in this study. They were told that the incorrect choices were mirror images of the standard, information which may have improved performance. Whether this modification may have differentially influenced boys versus girls is unclear.

Furthermore, no gender differences emerged in a study of 6- to 11-year-olds involving mental rotation matching (Snow & Strope, 1990), although older children were better at the task. The stimuli used in the untimed task were items (e.g., letters, figures) from the card task of the PMA (Thurstone, 1938). An upright standard was presented on one line with three rotated options (two mirror, one correct standard) beneath. The data support a general developmental increase in performance, with 6-year-olds poorer than all other age groups; and 11-year-olds better than all others except for the 10-year-olds. Additionally, there were no gender differences in a study using 160 high school students (mean age 14.7 years) that included a differentiation between left and right versions of hands, and a route test that involved walking a route on a floor after seeing it depicted on a 3 × 3 grid with black dots (Teng & Lee, 1982). Nor did any gender differences emerge in a study of fifth and seventh graders (Waber, Carlson, & Mann, 1982) that involved the rotation of the uppercase letters R, F, G, and J. There were main effects for grade (seventh graders were better than fifth graders), condition (no information or information in advance), and degree of rotation. It is worth noting that the scoring procedures in this study were atypical in that after a period of 4 seconds without a response, an item was scored as incorrect. Furthermore, although the authors argue that pilot testing indicated no evidence of practice effects, all subjects received the information in the same order (the "No Information" condition preceding the "Advance Information" condition). Thus, the presentation and scoring procedures in this study invite questions about the validity of the data.

Countering studies where no gender differences in spatial rotation emerge prior to adolescence is a large study (over 1,800 participants) of children ages 6–18 (Johnson & Meade, 1987). In this study, seven tests of spatial ability used with adults were adapted for use with children. Tasks in this study incorporated a variety of stimuli, from cubes, hands, flags, blocks, and hidden figures to traditional mental rotation stimuli. General trends included improvement with grade level and an advantage for boys in spatial performance. This advantage emerged reliably by the age of 10 and was maintained through age 18. In their analyses, Johnson and Meade (1987) used a composite measure of spatial ability but also examined performance on individual tasks. The ability of the researchers to fully evaluate spatial ability in young children was somewhat hampered by the difficulty in some of the measures. Although the authors argue that these tests can be used with young children, some of the tests like Mental Rotation and Cubes, the most difficult in their judgment, are not recommended for students younger than fifth or sixth grade. In the Cubes test, subjects saw pairs of three-dimensional cubes with different designs on each face. The task was to indicate whether they were the same, through one or more rotations. In the Mental Rotation task, the stimuli were figures from Shepard and Metzler (1971), but the task required rotation in only the picture plane (to determine a match) rather than in three dimensions. The finding that gender differences in spatial ability appear reliably around the age of 10 (rather than before) may be related to the difficulty of using some of the tests with children below middle-school age. The sample size of this study and its range of stimuli provide persuasive evidence for the existence of gender differences in spatial ability early on.

Other support for differences prior to adolescence comes from a study by Kerns and Berenbaum (1991) that used less frequently seen tests, including two developed by the authors. The four tests were: 1) Geometric Forms—selection (from four choices) of how a taped cube would look when laid out flat; 2) House Plans—the construction of a house with blocks after seeing aerial and frontal views; 3) Mirror Images—identifying a mirror image of a two-dimensional stimulus from four choices; and 4) Mental Rotation—stimuli similar to the Vandenberg and Kuse items, but using actual three-dimensional objects in which the subjects had to compare two block constructions and indicate "same" or "different" without moving the blocks or themselves in relation to the blocks. The first two tests (Geometric Forms and House Plans) were from Tuddenham (1970). Using children ages 9–12, boys scored significantly higher on the House Plans, Mirror Images, and Mental Rotation tasks. In a second phase with modified versions of the tasks to address ceiling effects in the first phase, boys scored significantly higher on the Geometric Forms, Mirror Images, and Mental Rotation tasks. The difference on the House Plans test approached significance. Using different stimuli, this study builds on the findings of Johnson and Meade (1987) to suggest gender differences in spatial ability in preadolescent samples.

Although the major question surrounding the issue of age and spatial ability has focused on emergence, researchers have also been interested in the issue of decline. The issue of the speed with which mental rotation tasks are done with advancing age has been a focus of research (Berg, Hertzog, & Hunt, 1982). Berg and colleagues (1982) used four age groups (mean age roughly 21, 32, 51, and 63 years) to examine speed of performance on a mental rotation task with two-dimensional line drawings. Pairs of stimuli were to be judged identical or mirror images, presented in up to 180 degrees of clockwise rotation from the standard. Subjects were told the comparison stimuli always would be rotated to the right and no more than 180 degrees. Results indicated an increase in reaction time with advancing age. Although there was no main effect for gender, a gender by age interaction indicated that older women had much slower reaction times than did older men. Error rates indicated no effect for age or gender, but there was a linear effect for error rates over days. The tasks were done for four consecutive days, and this kind of practice resulted in a decline in error rates, particularly for Day 1 to Day 2. In contrast, a study by Herman and Bruce (1983) comparing young (mean age 25.3 years) and older (mean age 65.3 years) individuals on a shortened version of the Vandenberg mental rotations test did show an advantage in the number of correct choices of men over women as well as younger adults over older adults. Thus, the nature of the task continues to be a fundamental question in evaluating the research on spatial ability.

In a longitudinal study of elderly individuals (Schaie & Willis, 1986; Willis & Schaie, 1988), both men and women demonstrated an age-related reduction in mental rotation ability across a period of 14 years, but men's scores were higher on both ends of the time frame than were women's, so that the gender differences favoring men were maintained. The authors also note that men and women differ in the nature of the change they experience over time, with women showing less accuracy and men slowing down. It should also be noted that the task involved rotation in the picture plane, not three dimensions, and as such may not have fully evaluated the question of gender differences on such tasks in an aging population. The hopeful aspect of the Willis and Schaie (1988) study was that the training on mental rotation tasks ameliorated the decline in performance, although gender differences favoring men were maintained. Like the Berg and colleagues (1982) study, this research indicates that practice can make a difference in performance and certainly highlights the extent to which the influence of practice (e.g., time spent with computer games) should be assessed in research in spatial ability.

Summary

The data related to the age at which gender differences in spatial ability appear seem very much tied to the particular kinds of tasks used. When Piagetian tasks are involved, typically with elementary school-aged children, significant differences in boys and girls are often absent. There are more likely to be gender differences by middle-school age, when mental rotation tasks are employed. The difficulty of test items, especially those for mental rotation, continues to be one of the barriers to understanding whether gender differences in spatial ability exist in young children. At the other end of the age spectrum, gender differences in spatial ability may well exist, but the more prominent finding is the general decline in spatial ability, in comparison to younger adults.

TASKS RESEMBLING "REAL-WORLD" WAY FINDING

As we saw in the chapter on development, when you examine tasks with greater ecological validity than the ones usually employed to assess spatial ability, there is a great deal more variability in the tasks themselves and in the results. We also saw that for the elderly, performance was not necessarily impoverished when assessed with real-world way-finding tasks, as had typically been the case in laboratory tasks.

When we move out of the laboratory per se and away from tasks involving the manipulation of entities like 10-block cubes, we encounter studies that involve activities such as actual way finding or map drawing in familiar (e.g., schools, neighborhoods) and novel environments (e.g., fictitious towns depicted by maps, nearby but unexplored neighborhoods). Gender differences do not always emerge in these ecological studies, and in a few cases women outperform men.

Even when more ecologically valid tasks are considered, one of the issues that always complicates the interpretation of the research is the variability of the tasks. Many different kinds of performance measures have been used, from pointing to a target to actually walking a route. A fairly commonly used task involves giving information about a familiar environment like a college campus. Subjects draw maps, are guided through unfamiliar campus buildings, give directions, make judgments based on slides, and a host of other activities. Let's start with a typical task—giving building information about a college campus.

Consider the following example. In a study (Holding, 1992) based on the anchor-point theory of cognition (Couclelis et al., 1987), 22 undergraduates were given 3 minutes to write down as many campus buildings as they could recall and were asked to reproduce their lists six more times, starting with a different building for each list, in order to generate the variability needed to assess cluster analysis. The thrust of the anchor point theory is that reference points are thought to anchor distinct regions in the cognitive maps of any given environment. These anchors then create a basic hierarchical structure to organize the individual's knowledge of that space. Cluster analysis allows you to examine what items are likely to be stored together to be recalled as a unit and emphasizes the role of chunking (Miller, 1956) as a means to understand related groupings. The role of reference points in this process can also be examined. It is thought that judgments made about distances that *cross* clusters will be larger than those made *within* clusters.

In this study, subjects were also asked to provide a number of ratings for these buildings using nine-point scales (degree of familiarity with each, each building's visibility from a distance, each building's dominance of nearby structures, each building's cultural impact). These scores were then added to create a total reference point score. A week later, participants made a series of distance judgments dealing with the campus buildings they had listed. Semicircular grids were used to generate a number of distance judgments. A series of 11 concentric semicircular lines were divided into 20 wedges of 9 degrees each. The name of a building was placed at the center of the grid, with a second building name at the top of the page. Subjects were to place an X on the grid at the point that represented the distance between the two structures. To provide a sense of scale, subjects were told that the outermost circle indicated the farthest boundary of campus.

A variety of other tasks were used. These included grid placement (using a grid divided into 225 equal squares on which had been placed three of the subject's building choices in their relative locations; subjects had to locate four other buildings on the grid while maintaining the correct relative relationship to the initial three). There was also a building location task in which subjects were given a campus map on which the buildings were labeled only with numbers; they were also given a sheet of paper with the list of buildings they had generated. With reference to the map, their job was to write the correct number of each building beside its name on the sheet.

Results indicated a main effect for gender, with women providing larger distance estimates than did men, and making more errors in the grid placement task and also in the building location task than did men. These dependent measures are focused on accuracy. Another series of questions examined self-reported abilities. Using seven-point scales, men rated themselves significantly higher in their ability to read maps (mean = 6.36; women, mean = 4.84) and for their sense of direction (men's mean = 6.27; women's mean = 4.21). Although women gave higher ratings in their ability to judge time, the difference was not significant. With regard to the anchor-point theory of cognition, the data indicate that women may be more inclined to use clustering and reference points than are men. Although the study dealt with a real environment (the college campus), the behavioral measures essentially were still limited to laboratory assessment (the accuracy indicators). The emphasis was chiefly theoretical in nature, exploring the role of clustering and reference points in spatial representation. There is no indication in these data that actual way-finding behavior is in any way affected by or related to these representational differences in accuracy.

In contrast, consider the following study (Lawton, Charleston, & Zieles, 1996) that includes an assessment of actual way finding. In this study, women had poorer performance on a direction pointing task but were just as effective as men in retracing a route they had taken. In this research, students with no prior experience with the basement hallways of a university building were led on a route through four connecting hallways as well as through two related interior corridors. At the end of the route, before being asked to find their way back, subjects were given a diagram that depicted the room at the end of the route. Their task was to place an X on a circle drawn around this endpoint. Their placement of the X on the circle would indicate the direction of the starting point. When they actually traveled back to the starting point, subjects were timed and also spoke into a hand-held tape recorder to document what they were thinking about in terms of their route selection. These verbal protocols were analyzed in terms of landmarks and comments related to the route decisions subjects had made.

With regard to gender, there were no significant differences with the way-finding pattern selected, with the time to complete the return trip, nor in the verbal protocol categories. However, there was a sizable difference in accuracy on the pointing task, with women making significantly larger errors (mean = 89.07 degrees) than men (mean = 47.72 degrees). Women also reported significantly more uncertainty about the task. But as the Lawton and colleagues (1996) state, ". . . even if initially less sure of the exact direction of the destination than men, women were equally as efficient in finding their way back" (p. 216). Interpreting these results, the authors note that the environment was not terribly challenging and hypothesize that you might see gender differences in actual way-finding performance in a more difficult environment. At the very least, these results should prompt us to question the nature of the dependent variables used (e.g., pointing measures) in tasks involving macroenvironmental spatial cognition. What is the relationship between being able to point accurately from a destination back to an origin, on the one hand, and actually finding your way back, on the other? These results indicate that there may be no necessary connection.

Other studies have also reported no gender differences on a variety of indicators dealing with cognitive maps of a college campus (Kirasic, Allen, & Siegel, 1984). This study used a familiar environment (a college campus) with a variety of direction and distance estimation tasks based on the concept of projective convergence. What this means operationally is that a number of sighting locations are chosen, and from these locations direction and distance estimates are then made to specified target locations. This process yields a number of direct measures (angular error, distance correlation) and a number of derived measures (locational consistency, locational accuracy, and configurational accuracy).

A template with a clear plastic overlay with a small circle and arrow in the center, a wood stylus, and an unmarked plastic straightedge were used to record the direction and distance selected by the subject. Carbon paper beneath the top layer recorded the judgments. Results indicated that men and women had different patterns of angular error. Men had less angular error on some targets (the gym and stadium); women had less on others (the chapel and biology building). However, there were no gender differences in the estimated to actual distance correlations. In the derived measures, men were more consistent in their estimates of location, but there were no differences in the accuracy of the configurational knowledge. Kirasic and colleagues (1984) conclude that "the present findings do not indicate superior macrospatial cognitive abilities for males" (p. 701). Both men and women "had their moments" in terms of superior performance. In a second experiment, the tasks were essentially repeated in terms of perspective taking or imagery. Subjects were to imagine themselves in various locations and then indicate direction and distance estimates as in Study 1. Prior task performance was used as a covariate in this study. Again, there was very little evidence of gender differences in macrospatial task performance. One of the most useful comments in this paper relates to the appreciation of differences in methodology:

the cognitive operations required by a macrospatial task (i.e., any means used to externalize cognitive maps) affect significantly the assessment of an individual's macrospatial knowledge. Any research methodology for externalizing cognitive maps involves a test of a subject's knowledge base, as well as a test of that subject's ability to manipulate that knowledge base in accordance with task demands. Different task demands placed on the same knowledge base can yield significantly different results. . . . (Kirasic et al., 1984, pp. 710–711)

One of the important questions is how ecologically valid the different task demands are. As has been argued at some length in other areas of psychology (see, e.g., Banaji & Crowder, 1989; Neisser, 1982a), the goal of research should be high generalizability and high ecological validity.

Representational Issues

When way-finding studies involve maps, not only accuracy but representational content and style are issues. We must consider what the maps represent, and in response, what men and women include *on* maps and the information they choose to share *about* maps in giving directions. For example, Ward, Newcombe, and Overton (1986) examined aspects of spontaneous direction giving, including use of landmarks, relational terms, cardinal directions, mileage estimates, and errors of omission and commission. The focus of the study was the verbal directions men and women would give from a map of an unfamiliar environment (covering a distance of about 9 miles). These directions were tape-recorded. The design included a condition with the map present, another from memory, and a third after being prompted to use cardinality in a memory condition. After studying the map for 3 minutes, subjects were asked to give directions (in a condition where the map was still visible). This was done for two different maps. In the memory conditions, subjects had 5 minutes to study each map. The third condition differed only in that subjects were prompted about cardinality *before* beginning the task.

Results indicated that men made significantly more references to the cardinal directions, gave more mileage indicators, and committed fewer errors of omission and commission than did women. While gender differences occurred when maps were both available and in a memory condition, women made more omission and commission errors only when memory was involved. This suggests that when a map of an unfamiliar environment is available, women are as able as men to use it to provide information, neither omitting necessary information nor including substantively incorrect information. Similarly, in a study that involved subjects who were asked to provide written directions for prospective students going from an admissions building to a particular destination on campus, Devlin (1999) also found no gender differences in the number of errors of omission or commission.

As Ward and colleagues (1986) predicted, there were no significant differences in the use of landmarks and relational terms. They expected no differences in these elements because they viewed them as basic building blocks, necessary for effective directions whether the direction-giver was a man or a woman. Stylistically, the authors suggest that while women do not choose to include cardinal directions, they can do so when prompted. They doubt that these differences reflect how information is, in actuality, represented.

Representationally, the use of landmarks and relational turns predominate for both men and women. Very little use is made of mileage estimates and cardinal directions relative to the opportunities to use them. This is hardly surprising given the maps used in the study. The landmarks (which were each outlined by a box) seem much more visually prominent in the map than does the mileage legend. Also, the maps covered a very small area, and it may be that our schema for giving distance estimates is engaged when we are talking about 10s or 100s of miles as opposed to less than 10 miles. Furthermore, because the landmarks were so apparent, it makes more sense to rely on them than to invoke a more abstract orientation system (cardinal directions).

Beyond giving directions from maps, a good deal of work has examined how men and women differ in the elements they actually place on maps. In a map drawing study with a familiar terrain (their college campus), men included significantly more roads and paths and misplaced fewer buildings than did women (McGuinness & Sparks, 1983). Interestingly, women included more extra items on their maps and were more accurate in assessing the relative deviation to a central target point (were more accurate in their sense of distance) than were men. For men, the mean number of major roads and paths was 11.39, whereas for women it was 6.11; for men the number of spatial errors was 4.39, for women it was 6.22. Women included an average of 7.44 extra items, whereas the average for men was 4.33.

Because women had spontaneously included so few roads and paths in their initial maps, a second study was carried out in which subjects were specifically instructed to include all possible routes to three campus buildings and to include all paths, bridges, and steps. Under these conditions, there were still gender differences, with men including significantly more roads and bridges than did women, and demonstrating more accuracy in their placements than did women. "For females, it appears that connectors, especially roads, are not only not relevant in maps, but are also less memorable" (McGuinness & Sparks, 1983, p. 98). The authors suggest that women may operate more in terms of grouping way-finding information, a theme picked up in the work of Holding (1992). The authors discuss what they see as the different approaches taken by women versus men: women use a bottom-up approach, moving from part to whole, whereas men use a top-down approach with a coordinate system, which the authors suggest is more similar to the approach taken by "good cartographers." McGuinness and Sparks suggest that "the female's approach to organizing topographic space operates from principles of grouping (proximity) whereas the male approach is to establish a set of coordinates, for example, the road system, along which efficient motion is maximized" (p. 99). Putting together the studies by Ward and colleagues (1986) and McGuinness and Sparks (1983), it appears that there are differences between men and women in how they choose to represent the environment. Men are more likely to use cardinal directions and route indicators, whereas women are more likely to use landmarks.

Many of these studies take place on college campuses and thus incorporate familiar terrains. In familiar terrains, the superiority of men for what has been called Euclidean, geometric, or configurational knowledge has not always been found. For that reason, Galea and Kimura (1993) chose to use a fictional town on a map as a purer test of this kind of knowledge. The study attempted to relate accuracy scores to landmark and Euclidean-based performance. The task itself involved studying route learning to criterion and controlled for visual item memory. Controlling for this factor was important because women had been reported to have superior visual item memory, which might then influence their performance on map recall tasks. A map was drawn on a 20 × 26-inch sheet of paper with roads, street names, and pictorial representations of landmarks such as houses, apartment buildings, shops, and natural features. Subjects were told that they were taking an imaginary Sunday drive and were to try to remember this drive as best they could. The learning criterion was retracing the route on two successive trials. The time to criterion, the total number of errors to criterion, and the total number of trials to criterion were all used as dependent measures. Subjects were then asked a series of questions without the map in view. These questions were of two sorts: 1) those that assessed knowledge of the landmarks on the map; and 2) those that demanded knowledge of the Euclidean or geometric properties of the map. Other tasks involved landmark recognition and the extrapolation of information from a series of overlapping maps. A number of cognitive tests were also administered (vocabulary, visual memory, mental rotation, perceptual speed), as was a driving history questionnaire.

There was a significant effect for gender in this study, with men outperforming women on all three measures of route learning (time to reach criterion, number of errors, number of trials to criterion) and on a composite score derived from these measures. However, in the landmark *recall* test, women recalled significantly more landmarks, both on and off the route, than did men and recalled significantly more street names than did men. The visual memory test score was used as a covariate in the analysis to control for the influence of visual-item memory in the landmark recall task. In the landmark *recognition* task, women recalled more landmarks both on and off the route (but not significantly so). However, women were significantly higher on a landmark composite score comprised of landmark recall on and off the route and street name recall. The geometric/Euclidean tests (direction, distance, map extrapolation) revealed that men were significantly better at direction questions that appeared to require cardinal directions (e.g., "Where is the bridge from the zoo?" [Galea & Kimura, 1993, p. 57]), but were not significantly better in the distance estimates that asked for a nearer/farther comparison between locations (e.g., "Which is closer to the drive-in theatre: (a) the bridge or (b) the church green?") (p. 57). There was a tendency for men to place the maps more accurately in the map extrapolation task, and the composite of these three tasks showed men to be significantly better.

The results were summarized as follows: 1) men were more adept at learning the route than were women; 2) men were also better than women in terms of the Composite Euclidean measure; and 3) women recalled more landmarks than did men, and this could not be explained in terms of time spent learning the route. Nor could it be explained in terms of better de-layed recognition of visual items demonstrated by women in a separate test. The authors argue that men and women still seemed to be using the same kind of spatial strategy to learn the route. But what seems to differ is the effectiveness with which they are able to apply the strategy. This same kind of argument (use by women of the same strategy but more slowly or less effectively) has been advanced by other authors in discussing the mental rotation findings (Birenbaum et al., 1994; Bryden et al., 1990).

How much does Galea and Kimura's (1993) map learning task resemble behavior in the real world? Even the authors point out that environments are usually learned piece-meal, rather than in one study session, as they employed. Also, when people use maps, they generally refer to them in hand, rather than from memory. Does it really make sense to use *unfamiliar* environments represented in map form, and then to collect dependent mea-sures without the map in view? It seems more ecologically valid to use familiar environments for these kinds of representational tasks.

The predilection for women to use landmarks (see also Miller & Santoni, 1986) has led to an interesting evolutionary discussion. Galea and Kimura (1993) interpret women's proclivity for landmarks in an evolutionary framework in which they argue that landmarks may have been useful to our female ancestors at near distances, where they were likely to spend time (as opposed to the greater distances involved with male hunters). In a similar vein, Buss (1995) discusses the fact that the abilities of men and women will have been differentially influenced to the extent that they faced different types of adaptive challenges in evolutionary history. In explaining the large size effect for mental rotation, he says, "This ability is essential for successful hunting, in which the trajectory and velocity of a spear must anticipate correctly the trajectory of an animal as each moves with different speeds through space and time" (p. 166).

This evolutionary explanation has been extended to anthropological studies of primitive peoples. Documenting the foraging behavior patterns of the Ache of Paraguay (a native population of nomadic foragers in eastern Paraguay), Hill and Hurtado (1989) describe the different foraging roles of men and women. The median size of a band was 48 members, and on foraging trips for food, the men move ahead with bows and arrows while the women and children follow. New paths are blazed through the forest each day. After starting out together and walking for about an hour, the men separate, walking farther and faster than the women as they search for game. At the end of the day, camp members come together again. Men are reported to spend on the average of 6.7 hours/day in subsistence activities, whereas women devote approximately 1.9 hours/day to this same kind of activity. Women spend the majority of their time (8 hours/day) doing light work and child care. Hill and Hurtado suggest that this division of labor by men and women may have begun when women began to ignore the opportunities to secure new foods because this resulted in high child mortality.

The superior performance of women in landmark memory and its relationship to evolution has led to a discussion of the role of location memory (Eals & Silverman, 1994; James & Kimura, 1997; Silverman & Eals, 1992). Eals and Silverman (1994) pursue the hunter-gatherer theory of gender differences in spatial cognition in a series of studies using arrays of familiar and unfamiliar objects. They question whether verbal proclivities could account for the advantage women have in spatial object memory (i.e., women may do better because they use a naming strategy to encode the objects and their locations). Building on research with familiar objects, subjects were told to examine an array of drawings of *uncommon* objects for one minute. These objects looked like components of tools or machine parts. Subjects were then given a second array, with the original objects in the same location but with additional objects added. Subjects had to put an *X* through the "new" objects and were given one minute to do so. This produced an object memory score. Then, in a third array, some of the original objects from the first array were moved to new locations. Subjects were to put an *X* through objects that had new locations and to circle the objects that remained in place. This produced a location memory score. The results indicated that women were better, though not significantly, in object memory and significantly better in location memory.

In a second study, actual unfamiliar objects were displayed and subjects (40 undergraduate men and 40 undergraduate women) were involved in either an intentional or an incidental learning condition. The subjects were taken to a graduate student office, where uncommon objects had been added to commonly found objects in a 6 × 8-foot cubicle. The intentional and incidental conditions involved being told that they had 2 minutes to memorize and remember the locations of the objects in the room, or wait 2 minutes in the room for the experimenter, respectively. At the end of 2 minutes, subjects took object and location memory tests. From a series of cards with either the names of common objects or drawings of uncommon objects, they were to indicate which had been in the room. This was the object memory task. For location memory, they were given a schematic drawing of the room segmented into seven numbered areas. Shown a series of cards of uncommon or common objects, but only those that had been in the room, they were to put the number of the locational area for each object on its respective card.

For *common* objects, results indicated a trend for higher women's object memory scores in both the intentional and incidental learning conditions. For location memory, women were significantly better in both conditions. For the *uncommon* objects, there were no main effects for either object or location memory but there were interaction effects ($p = .07$ for object memory and $p < .05$ for location memory). Specifically, men were significantly better in object memory when the task was *intentional*; women were significantly better in location memory when the task was *incidental*. Eals and Silverman (1994) emphasize that the gender differences in location memory performance are more likely to be related to perceptual style than to actual learning ability. Relating these data to an evolutionary perspective, they go on to state:

Based on their ancestral roles as food gatherers, keepers of the habitat, and caretakers of the young, the attentional styles of females may have evolved as more inclusive of the environment than males. Further, the capacity of females to recall locations of objects without verbal references may suggest that they continuously record details of their environments through some imaging process akin to eidetic imagery. Thus, they are able to retrieve a comprehensive image of a previous physical surrounding without having attempted to remember it or even given it particular conscious attention. (p. 103)

Thus, by using uncommon objects without an easily accessible verbal label in this research, they are able to argue that the advantage of women in location memory occurs independently of verbal skills.

James and Kimura (1997) replicate, extend, and challenge the interpretation of Silverman and Eals (1992; Eals & Silverman, 1994) by examining the difference between what they call a location-exchange task (where the locations of objects are switched) and a location-shift task (where objects are moved to what was formerly empty space). The array used in their research was identical to the one in the original (1992) Silverman and Eals task. In the location-exchange task, subjects (43 men and 41 women) were given one minute to study the array and were then told to put an X around objects that had been moved (changed places with other objects) on the original array and to circle those that had not moved. In the location-shift task, subjects (44 men and 46 women) again studied the array for one minute, and then examined a response array in which about half of the objects had been moved to empty space. The marking procedure was the same.

Results indicated that women were better than men on the location-exchange task, as had been the case for Silverman and Eals (1992). In the location-shift task, there were no gender differences. A final 2 × 2 (gender × task) analysis yielded a gender by task interaction. Men were better at the location-shift than the location-exchange task; women's scores on these two tasks were not significantly different. What the authors suggest is that the location exchange task emphasizes object identity (because no new locations are used in this task). The location-shift task, however, emphasizes location information more heavily (patterns of filled and empty space). Rather than having superior location memory, James and Kimura (1997) argue that women do better when the task emphasizes object memory or object identity. They then go on to review the suggestion that women might have an integrated object and location information system that would be advantageous on a location-exchange type of task. But for location-shift, where the pattern of empty and filled space would provide the clues, object identity information would be less critical. This might explain why women were not superior on the location-shift task. James and Kimura suggest the following:

Prehistoric women are assumed to have predominantly gathered small, immobile food items and would usually have navigated through familiar territory. Successful foraging would require the ability to remember the locations of specific (i.e., edible) plants and efficient navigation would likely favor a strategy that involved recognition of familiar landmarks. These types of selection pressures might have led to the development of a memory system in women that is highly capable of associating an object with a particular location. (p. 162)

James and Kimura (1997) go on to argue that the large home ranges of men who were doing big game hunting would have rendered reliance on landmarks unwise. For these hunters, the use of global coordinates and distance and direction cues for route learning made more sense. These pressures might have resulted in a cognitive system that was different from the one developed by women. "Men would benefit from a higher capacity for location information relative to object information, and the ability to remember the association between an object and a particular location might be less well developed" (p. 162).

These kinds of explanations are provocative, but not all studies demonstrate this superiority of women in landmark recall, and one must ask why. Herman, Kail, and Siegel (1979) studied cognitive maps of a college campus. Their research was set within the framework of Siegel and White's (1975) theory on the developmental sequence of cognitive map formation, from landmarks, to route, to configurational knowledge. Results indicated that it was *men* who demonstrated greater knowledge of landmarks; there were no gender differences on the knowledge of routes. In this study, freshmen at the University of Pittsburgh were tested after 3 weeks, after 3 months, and after 6 months. The testing was designed to assess landmark, route, and configurational knowledge. Testing involved two days for each period. The first day focused on landmark assessment. For landmark recall, subjects were given unlimited time to recall as many campus buildings as possible. For recognition, they then saw 34 slides of university buildings at a duration of 15 seconds each, and were asked to write down the name of each building. The third landmark task was to view the same slides again and match the building in the slide with its appropriate name from a list.

The second day of testing (with an interval of two days in between) involved only those buildings that had been identified by at least 80% of the participants on the first day (because the tasks required knowledge of the buildings). Using this criterion, 10 buildings (in September), 14 buildings (in November), or 18 buildings (in March) qualified for inclusion over the three time periods. Tasks covered route and configurational knowledge. The route task was to generate written directions between a number of pairs of buildings as if the directions were being given to a campus visitor. Subjects were instructed to be as specific as possible. For configurational knowledge, subjects were each given a sheet that included the 10 (14, 18) buildings. For each building, they had to list the N-1 buildings below the identified building in order of increasing distance from that building.

For the landmark assessment, results indicated that men were superior to women on all three tests: recall, recognition, and matching. There were no gender differences in the route knowledge assessment, in which each subject's description had been scored by two raters (from 0 indicating it was not usable, to 6, indicating a perfect description). Subjects seemed to reach a plateau on this task and were quite accurate (75%) after just three weeks. The assessment of configurational knowledge involved multidimensional scaling, and again there were no gender differences. After only three weeks on campus, the students' maps were quite accurate, and appeared to become more finely tuned over time rather than change in any dramatic structural sense. This kind of developmental sequence has been reported in the literature (Devlin, 1976).

Given the trend in the literature for women to use more landmarks than do men, why are the Herman and colleagues (1979) findings inconsistent with the work of Galea and Kimura (1993) and McGuinness and Sparks (1983)? A good way to answer that question is to compare what the participants actually did. One major difference between the Herman and colleagues and McGuinness and Sparks research is that the latter study involved drawing maps. It appears that women in the McGuinness and Sparks research used landmarks as a source of information to structure the environment (the task was to provide a map for a friend who was coming to visit), whereas men concentrated more on routes. The Herman and colleagues task did not involve providing information for anyone else. It was, in a sense, a straightforward performance task (recall as many campus buildings as possible). It may be that women are more sensitive to landmarks when they can be used to provide information for other people, as in the map drawing task of McGuinness and Sparks. Furthermore, as was seen earlier in the research of Kirasic and colleagues (1984), men and women tended to differ in the buildings they placed more accurately, presumably related to frequency of exposure differences (e.g., men were better with the gym, women with the chapel). It is possible that in the Herman and colleagues study, men were simply more familiar with more buildings on campus because of their daily activities. This factor was not really assessed in the study. The studies involving direction giving where no gender differences in the use of landmarks have been found (e.g., Devlin, 1999; Ward et al., 1986), should be considered separately because the demand characteristics of the task are so different. In giving directions, not every landmark is equally useful, and parsimony is valued when people are providing verbal directions.

The studies emphasizing an evolutionary explanation for gender differences in the use of landmarks (Eals & Silverman, 1994; Galea & Kimura, 1993; James & Kimura, 1997; Silverman & Eals, 1992) are provocative. Although there are some inconsistent findings (e.g., Herman et al., 1979), the data are still sufficiently convincing to consider this a viable working hypothesis.

Almost Being There: Slide and Computer Simulation Studies

In addition to drawing maps, giving directions from maps, and making various kinds of judgments based on maps or environmental knowledge, researchers have been drawn to the use of simulated environments, particularly slides, to test representational knowledge. It has been argued that judgments based on slides can parallel those made in real environments (Shuttleworth, 1980; Ulrich et al., 1991), and slide studies provide a different kind of opportunity to assess macrospatial cognition. There are a number of advantages to this kind of simulation, including greater experimental control and easier administration of measures.

Given the trend we have seen for fewer gender differences to emerge when actual way-finding tests are employed, the same pattern might be expected for simulation studies. There are a number of studies that are consistent with this idea. Pearson and Ferguson (1989) combined assessment of traditional tests (Embedded Figures, a short version of the Vandenberg and Kuse test of mental rotation; Differential Aptitude Spatial Relations subtest) with a test of environmental cognition (a slide-simulated walk through a commercial urban area of Windsor, Ontario). Participants (undergraduates) were to watch the slides in order to be able to retrace the steps of the person who took them; after a second viewing, subjects used a city block map to draw the route they had seen. There were no significant gender differences on the macroenvironmental cognition test. Scores were summed for the number of correct corners crossed (or not, as appropriate) and distances. In this study, gender explained only 1% of the variability in performance on that test. This finding is similar to the Lawton, Charleston, and Zieles (1996) retracing steps study discussed earlier, where students had to find their way back through the hallways of a campus building.

In addition to the finding of no gender differences on the macrospatial task, there are a number of other noteworthy findings in this study. Of all the standardized tests, the largest variance attributable to gender was on the mental rotation task (12%), where men were superior. The variance shared by the macrospatial tests and gender was only on the order of 1%. For men, the standardized test math scores significantly predicted spatial ability, whereas for the women, both math and English scores predicted spatial ability. This difference may be suggestive of lateralization differences between the hemispheres of men and women, an issue that will be discussed more fully in Chapter 3.

One of the patterns that seems to emerge in the literature on gender differences is the trend for similar performance by men and women when the task is ecologically related to way finding, that is, when people actually find their way back to a destination or demonstrate that knowledge through slide identification. When the task becomes more abstract and less directly related (e.g., angular judgments about origins and destinations), women more often than not perform less well than men. A slide task with measures that range in terms of their ecological validity nicely illustrates this pattern (Holding & Holding, 1989). The authors used slides depicting pairs of intersections along suburban routes in Frankfort, Kentucky. Each route consisted of three block-long segments that were connected by two turns. Test pairs of slides (consisting of old or never-seen-before slides) were employed for distance and direction judgments. Subjects also gave verbal estimates of the travel distance between scenes and performed map placement by locating dots on a street plan map to correspond to the location of each slide they viewed. The subjects (12 undergraduate men and 12 undergraduate women) also completed the Hidden Figures test as a measure of spatial ability.

When you look at the distance and direction tasks more closely, the abstract components become more obvious. Subjects were given multiple answer sheets, each with a circle with a radius of 2 centimeters drawn in the center. An arrow 3 centimeters in length projected from a dot in the center of the circle toward the top of the page. Subjects were told that the circle represented the standard distance (which had been drawn to the subjects' attention in a slide), and that the dot represented where the photographer had stood while taking the slide projected on the left in the pairing. The arrow represented the direction the photographer faced while taking the slide. For each slide pair, on a separate circle, the subject had to draw an arrow to indicate the direction (the arrow's angle) and the straight line distance (the arrow's length) from the starting slide to the target slide.

In terms of findings related to gender differences, men outperformed women in terms of making angular judgments (they were significantly more accurate by about 5 degrees) and women tended to increasingly underestimate wider angles. Men were also more accurate than women in their verbal estimations of travel distances. There were no main effects for gender in the direct distance errors (from the circle task). Furthermore, when you look at the results of the map placement task (using a street map to locate the particular target scene being projected), there were no gender differences. Regarding ecological validity, you have to question the meaningfulness of the angular error task for way-finding performance, particularly in light of the fact that women did as well on the map placement task and on the direct distance judgments. Although men were better on the Hidden Figures test (a measure of spatial ability) in this study, those scores were not correlated with any of the measures of spatial cognition. Holding and Holding (1989) argue that the data provide "positive evidence for sex differences on several measures of route learning and spatial cognition" (p. 39). This may be an overstatement of the findings, particularly when viewed in terms of their ecological meaningfulness.

With advances in technology, visual material like that used by Holding and Holding (1989) is more frequently being presented via computers than by slide projectors. Two studies by Devlin and Bernstein will serve as examples of the technology and of the gender differences that have emerged. In a study using interactive computer technology (Devlin & Bernstein, 1995), the effectiveness of seven different kinds of way-finding information used by 126 men and 151 women who were first-time visitors to a college campus was examined. The participants were randomly assigned to one of seven different types of cue information presented in the form of a computer simulation of a campus tour. Participants then took a computer "test" using the same touch-screen monitor. Reminiscent of the findings of Kozlowski and Bryant (1977), men (mean = 2.68) were more confident that they could find their way than were women (mean = 3.17) on a scale where 1 equaled very confident and 5 equaled not at all confident, and men made fewer errors (mean = 6.62) than did women (mean = 7.97). Men also generally preferred the use of visual-spatial cues more than women did. Overall, participants who were exposed to textual directions (with or without reference to landmarks) or a plain map made significantly more errors than those who had photos supplementing the text or landmarks supplementing the map.

In terms of men's versus women's preferences in the study for using map, written, visual, or verbal instructions when traveling to a new destination, analyses revealed that significantly more women (67.5%) than men (45.2%) preferred using written directions (alone or with other sources), and significantly more women (29.1%) than men (18.2%) preferred using verbal instructions (alone or with other sources). When the cue sources were considered individually, there was a significant difference in the "map alone" choice, with men (27%) selecting that choice significantly more often than did women (13. 9%). Significantly more men than women also chose the "map plus visual tour of the route" combination, 13.5% to 4.0%, respectively. And significantly more women than men selected the "map + written + visual" combination, 11.3% to 1.6%, respectively. This greater preference for the use of maps by men is in some ways consistent with the findings of Beatty and Troster (1987) regarding the seemingly greater familiarity with geography demonstrated by men on the Fargo Map Test (Beatty, 1988).

Thus, consistent with previous research on the superior spatial ability of men (Hyde, 1990; Masters & Sanders, 1993) and with research on way finding demonstrating a range of tasks in which men make fewer errors than do women (Aubrey & Dobbs, 1990; Galea & Kimura, 1993; Holding, 1992; Ward et al., 1986), men in this computer simulation study made significantly fewer errors in a simulated way-finding task than did women. Men were also significantly more confident in their ability to find their way in the way-finding test than were women. This is also consistent with previous literature that shows men to be more confident about their sense of direction (Kozlowski & Bryant, 1977; Streeter & Vitello, 1986). However, contrary to what might be expected from the literature on women's use of landmarks (Kimura, 1992; McGuinness & Sparks, 1983; Miller & Santoni, 1986), there was no gender by tour type interaction in terms of the number of errors made; women did not perform better than men in three conditions highlighting landmarks.

This research on way finding simulated by computer technology (Devlin & Bernstein, 1995), and a study that followed (Devlin & Bernstein, 1997), also highlight the fact that women tend to be less confident in real-world way-finding tasks. Men in the simulated way-finding study in 1995 were significantly more confident that they could find their way. In the 1997 study that dealt with the effects of label placement, level of detail, and color on map usefulness, women judged the computer way finding-related tasks to be significantly more frustrating than did the men in the study. Women in this study also demonstrated less confidence and more caution in the sense that they took longer to make their decisions by touching the computer screens (response time was summed across the 14 screens), effectively recording their decision about what path to pursue next in the way-finding task.

Other Ecological Concerns

Issues of anxiety related to way-finding tasks have been pursued more directly by Lawton (1994). She developed scales that measured self-reported spatial anxiety and way-finding strategy. The way-finding strategy scale differentiates between a route strategy and an orientation strategy. In the route strategy, the emphasis is on specific steps for how to get from one place to another. An example of one of the items reflecting this strategy: "Before starting, I asked for directions telling me whether to turn right or left at particular streets or landmarks" (p. 769). In contrast, in the orientation strategy, the person's position is monitored relative to specific points in the environment. An example of an item from this strategy is, "I kept track of the direction (north, south, east, or west) in which I was going" (p. 769). Generally speaking, the route strategy items seem to emphasize the role of turns, whereas the orientation strategy places more emphasis on cardinal directions and mileage. The spatial anxiety scale deals with a number of situations in which one might feel anxiety related to navigation. An example of an item on this scale: "Trying a new route that you think will be a shortcut without the benefit of a map" (p. 770). Results in Lawton's study indicated that women were more likely to use a route strategy and were higher in spatial anxiety, whereas men were more likely to report using an orientation strategy. There is also related work that shows that women rate way finding while driving more difficult than do men and also report encountering problems in way finding while driving more frequently than do men (Burns, 1998).

Further scale development by Lawton (1996) on strategies used in way finding produced an indoor way-finding scale, which in many ways parallels the outdoor way-finding scale discussed previously. The indoor scale includes an orientation component (emphasizing orientation to direction cues), a route component (stressing the importance of route information), and a building configuration component (stressing the regularity of building configuration). In this research, which included an indoor way-finding task on the third floor of a campus building, subjects also had to perform a pointing task. They used a compass to indicate the direction of four landmarks in outer corridors of the floor. Results indicated that women were significantly more likely to report using the indoor route strategy, whereas men were more likely to rely on the indoor orientation strategy. Furthermore, women showed significantly larger pointing errors on the compass task, and were significantly less confident about their answers. However, controlling for pointing accuracy eliminated this difference in confidence. Women's confidence in this task is thus specifically related to the pointing task, not to way-finding confidence in general.

Geographical knowledge is another ecological topic where gender differences have been noted. Two of the anecdotes at the beginning of this chapter were related to women's ostensibly inferior working knowledge of geography. Beyond the anecdotal level, geographical knowledge has been assessed with a standardized instrument (Beatty, 1988). In a series of studies with more than 1,800 undergraduates, Beatty and Troster (1987) assessed the geographical knowledge of these students using the Fargo Map

Test. The primary purpose of the test is to assess remote memory for spatial knowledge. The task requires that subjects indicate large geographical features of the United States as well as a number of cities. The authors also added components to the task, including asking subjects to indicate a number of cities in a tristate area that reflected the subjects' residential history. Men located more geographical features more accurately in all segments of this test than did women, even when possible explanatory variables such as age, education, or the number of regions of the country in which subjects had lived were controlled. The authors then introduced a new map with hypothetical towns to examine subjects' ability to *acquire* geographical knowledge. While there was a significant trials effect (a difference in how many trials it took to reach criterion) favoring men, there was no main effect for gender once criterion had been reached. The authors comment that men and women are unlikely to differ in their *capacity* to learn maps, and thus that issues of acquisition cannot really explain the superior performance of men on the standard task. Although this small but generalized difference in performance exists, none of the variables assessed appear to explain the reasons for this difference. The most viable explanation the authors offer is that men have typically been more responsible for making decisions about travel plans, and in particular for route selection as reflected in maps. Beatty and Troster argue that with the changing gender roles in society, women are more likely to be on equal footing with regard to these kinds of decisions, and the kind of differences seen in this study should disappear over time. Echoing a theme in this section, the authors also note that, "poor performance on map tests of the sort used in the present study does not necessarily imply deficits in wayfinding ability" (p. 588).

Summary

What real-world tasks tend to reveal is that men have a greater confidence than women in their abilities to read maps and in their sense of direction. Women tend to be more uncertain about their spatial abilities, and this caution is often manifested in longer reaction times to complete the tasks in question. There is also some indication that women do, in fact, make more errors in particular kinds of tasks, such as directional estimates. At the same time, there is evidence that women may have better memory for landmarks and that men and women are similar in their ability to acquire map knowledge.

Ecological Studies and Developmental Effects

When we move away from college students and deal with either older or younger participants within an ecological framework, developmental issues are generally emphasized. Chapter 1 provides an extensive examination of developmental issues in spatial cognition; for that reason, the following section focuses on the trends related to gender.

Overall, it is fair to say that relatively few gender differences emerge when dealing with macroenvironmental tests that address developmental issues. In some cases, researchers have not examined gender differences at all and simply have balanced the number of men and women across conditions (see, e.g., Allen, Kirasic, Siegel, & Herman, 1979; Anooshian & Nelson, 1987; Cornell & Hay, 1984; Magliano, Cohen, Allen, & Rodrigue, 1995; Siegel, Allen, & Kirasic, 1979). In other studies, when preliminary analyses indicated no gender differences, considerations of gender were then dropped from subsequent analyses or nonsignificant findings were not presented (see, e.g., Cousins, Siegel, & Maxwell, 1983; Doherty & Pellegrino, 1985). While there are macrospatial studies that reveal some gender differences (see, e.g., Anooshian & Young, 1981; Webley, 1981; Webley & Whalley, 1987), the thrust of the findings in these large-scale studies is gender parity.

Gender Parity in Macrospatial Tasks

In these developmental studies, what are the kinds of tasks in which the performance of men and women is essentially comparable? Tasks on which no differences occur include straightforward judgments such as recognition made on the basis of slides in unfamiliar or familiar environments, as well as way-finding activities in restricted and more far-ranging environments.

For the most part, the tasks in these studies reveal no gender differences. However, some multipart studies will be discussed in which parity occurs in one experiment and difference in another. The tasks in which no differences occur tend to stress relative judgments or straightforward recognition rather the angular accuracy or precise measurement. For example, across age groups, boys/men and girls/women (second grade, fifth grade, and college students) perform similarly when making proximity judgments about the location of subdivision boundaries based on slides that represent a walk through different types of scenery, including a park and a university campus (Allen, 1981). In this study, the focus was the effect that perception of subdivisions might have on the processing of route information. The unfamiliar environment was depicted through 60 color slides, and subjects performed a recognition task that involved ordering five probe photographs as they would be encountered along the walk. Subjects then grouped color photos of the slides into categories representing what they considered different segments of the walk. No analyses by gender differences were reported for this part of the study. In a second experiment, subjects performed a series of proximity judgments based on the same walk. Triads of scenes (a reference scene and two choices) were used to create combinations for subdivision and distance ratio judgments. These tasks revealed no gender differences. Unlike many of the studies we have considered in this chapter, these tasks do not require judgments about absolute distances. Rather, the subjects are required to indicate which photograph is closer to the reference target. In these tasks, girls and women perform as well as boys and men.

Boys and men and girls and women also perform comparably when they are identifying scenes with high landmark potential, another task in which relative judgments are required. Subjects from three grade levels (second, fifth, and college) viewed a slide presentation of 52 shots taken of a walk through a commercial area (Allen, Kirasic, Siegel, & Herman, 1979). After viewing the slides, subjects were to use photographs based on the slides to select the nine scenes that would help them remember where they were along the walk (i.e., the scenes with high landmark potential). Performance improved with age, as is typically the case in these studies, and gender differences do not appear to have been addressed. A second study was done with the same age groups and subjects were asked to take each of the nine scenes from the first study (in turn) and rank each of the remaining eight in terms of the increasing distance from the starting point. The children were tested with a somewhat simpler procedure. The study revealed a developmental progression in the ability to employ the landmark information in the context of a real-world setting (as represented by the slide array). But there were no gender differences in the preliminary analyses and that variable was not included for further examination. The task in this second study of placing photographs in order of increasing distance from an origin is similar to the task in the Allen (1981) study in which subjects indicated which of two choices was closer to a reference point. When these kinds of relative judgments are made, there do not appear to be significant differences in the way men and women perform.

Other studies involving judgments based on slides similarly show an absence of gender differences. For example, Doherty and Pellegrino (1985) took subjects who had been residents of a suburban neighborhood for at least a year, and divided them into four age groups: 7- and 8-year-olds; 9- and 10-year-olds; 11- and 12-year-olds, and 13-, 14-, and 15-year-olds. Subjects were to identify target versus distractor shots of the neighborhood, which varied in terms of whether they showed an intersection or not, and whether they were straight-ahead views or plots (a frontal view while facing the house). In a slide recognition test, subjects had to decide whether a scene was familiar. The results indicated no main effects or interactions involving gender. The study basically pointed to a greater accuracy for scenes at intersections, for those of plots over views, and for an effect of age in that the youngest group was less accurate than the other groups.

While there are a number of studies using slides, there are very few developmental studies of actual navigation tasks in a reasonably large environment (an environment where the boundaries are not visible). One of these macroenvironmental studies is an experiment in which 6- and 12-year-olds were to lead the way back after taking a walk with an experimenter across a university campus (Cornell, Heth, & Broda, 1989). Dependent measures included the distance traveled (measured against the prescribed path) and the children's behavior at each of 20 designated choice points along the route. No gender effects emerged in any of the analyses. As is the case with most of these studies, older children generally perform better on the tasks. In a related study (Cornell, Heth, & Rowat, 1992), the experimenters focused on specific kinds of strategies that might consolidate way-finding knowledge. The authors examined the difference between instructions to look back, instructions to retrace, or lack of instructions on subjects' ability to find their way back after a campus walk. The study used 6-year-olds, 12-year-olds, and adults (median age 22 years). There were few gender differences, and only one that reflected spatial performance. A gender by age interaction revealed that 6-year-old boys traveled on the correct path the least (as most first-grade teachers might have predicted!). Furthermore, there was a gender effect with regard to prompts. Girls accepted help more often than did boys. In general, the 6-year-olds did less well than the 12-year-olds and adults, who essentially did not differ from each other. The fact that girls asked for more help than did boys is reminiscent of a number of studies discussed earlier in which women had greater spatial anxiety (Lawton, 1994) and were less confident about their way-finding abilities (Burns, 1998; Devlin & Bernstein, 1995; Kozlowski & Bryant, 1977).

The idea of controlled exposure to an unfamiliar environment was also pursued in a study of 8- to 11-year-olds (Matthews, 1987). The children were taken to an unfamiliar residential environment similar to their own and were told that the main purpose was to be able to draw a map of this area. They were divided into groups. Group A used a complete map of the area for reference as it traversed a standardized hour-long walk of the residential area with the experimenter. Group B also traversed this area, but was interrupted halfway through for about 30 minutes and then continued. Subjects in Group B were given the first half of the map before interruption and the second after interruption. These changes were argued to add complexity to the task. Maps were handed in after the tour was completed and the children were then returned to their school where they drew their sketch maps.

The maps were evaluated in terms of content (e.g., number of items, type of information) and structure (e.g., spatial orientation, accuracy). Generally speaking, boys and girls performed quite similarly in Group A, and the only remarkable difference was that boys drew more roads and girls drew more landmarks (reminiscent of the results for females in Galea & Kimura, 1993). In Group B, however, boys were better at spatial orientation (a method by gender interaction) and at spatial accuracy. Matthews (1987) suggests that controlling the participants' exposure to the environment (as in a novel setting) will moderate gender differences in performance, but that they become apparent in a more challenging task as in the interrupted cognitive processing experienced by Group B. Like McGuinness and Sparks (1983), Matthews suggests that boys take a more Euclidean approach to such tasks and have a greater tendency to create spatial hierarchies, which contributes to their performance in terms of spatial orientation and accuracy. Within a sociocultural context, Matthews suggests that boys have greater freedom to roam and will consequently develop more route knowledge, whereas girls will be more likely to produce stylized and regular maps, regardless of the effects of such strategies on accuracy. Webley (1981), Webley and Whalley (1987), and Van Vliet (1983) also have explored the issue of gender differences in home range. Their studies will be discussed in the section titled "Gender Differences: Developmental Studies of Macrospatial Environments."

More Constrained Environments

When we turn our attention to behavior in more circumscribed environments such as school interiors and playgrounds, we often see a similar pattern of gender parity. There were no gender differences when second, fourth, and sixth graders made distance estimates and time (to travel a distance) estimates after walking through a hallway with various angles that had been built within the school recreation room (Herman, Norton, & Klein, 1986). The focus of this study was the effect of route angularity on a variety of judgments. When participants in the Herman and colleagues study were tested in a more natural environment (their own school rather than a constructed hallway), and then provided the same kinds of estimates, no gender differences emerged either.

Looking more closely at how motor behavior affects cognition, Herman and Siegel (1978) had children in the kindergarten, second, and fifth grades walk through a miniature town created in a school gymnasium. The floor was divided into quadrants, with 19 buildings of different colors and shapes distributed throughout the "town." Eight buildings were then removed and three distractors added, and the children had to then place each building in its previous location. Fifth graders were better than second graders and kindergartners on the task but the two younger grades did not differ significantly from each other. In a second experiment, the authors examined the effect of walking and looking at the town versus just looking at it. Under these conditions, boys were more accurate than girls (in second and fifth grades but not in kindergarten) and on the first and second trials, but not on the third and final construction. Herman and Siegel suggest that the lack of gender differences in the first experiment may have been due to the ease of the task. Continuing to explore the role of motor activity, Herman, Kolker, and Shaw (1982) looked at the difference between standing, riding in a wagon, or walking through a large model town with kindergartners and third graders. While the older children were more accurate, there were no gender differences in this task. Thus, in these more restricted environments with tasks that do not require actual distance judgments (these tasks involved object placement), boys and girls perform comparably.

Moving away from a circumscribed model town and into a larger school environment (Cousins, Siegel, & Maxwell, 1983), children in first, fourth, and seventh grade were asked to take an adult to specific locations on the campus of a large private school. This was done for three routes. They also performed a variety of other tasks: identifying landmarks that would be seen along the route(s), ordering landmarks in the sequence they would be encountered along the route(s), placing the landmarks for each route along a strip of paper to represent the distance between each landmark, and performing configuration tests. The configuration tests involved four sighting locations, and from the sighting location the child was to point to a visible target and to one that was occluded. This was accomplished using an arrow attached to a compass, both of which were mounted on a tripod. Distance estimates for the sighting tasks were made with a box containing a lever, which, when moved along a slot, lighted one of 20 lights spaced about 1 centimeter apart. The distance estimate was the point at which the lever was placed (and its corresponding light, from 1–20). Again, there were no effects of gender on these tasks and the variable was removed from further analyses. As is the pattern in these studies, the task results indicated increasing competence with age. Other studies with elementary school students who gave distance estimates in school environments similarly have reported no gender differences (Cohen, Weatherford, Lomenick, & Koeller, 1979).

Even when we look at younger children, there are any number of studies that fail to demonstrate a gender difference in spatial performance. In fact, many studies dealing with some aspect of spatial cognition in young children do not address the issue of gender differences (see, e.g., Bremner & Andreasen, 1998; Darvizeh & Spencer, 1984). A selected few studies that do discuss gender differences are included here to give some sense of the tasks and of the findings. With the young ages involved, these studies tend to be in restricted environments and may not really qualify as macroenvironmental, although the plea for more research with young children in macroenvironments so that their abilities will not be underestimated is long-standing (Spencer & Darvizeh, 1981).

As an example of research in somewhat restricted macroenvironments, consider two studies dealing with the use of maps (Blades & Spencer, 1987a, 1987b). In one study, they investigated children's understanding of map use with ambiguous landmarks (Blades & Spencer, 1987b). The researchers drew an octagonal layout of paths with chalk on the playground floor of students who were roughly 4, 6, or 7 1/2 years of age. There were landmarks (boxes that contained colored circles) at the end of each vertex. The children were given maps (scale 1:50) for navigation. These maps included the depiction of "road blocks" for seven of the eight possible paths. Children had to use a map (different maps corresponded to different layouts) to navigate successfully through the road blocks. Although there were age effects, there were no differences in performance related to gender.

Pursuing the same theme of map use under different conditions, Blades and Spencer (1987a) constructed a maze 25 meters long in the school playground. The maze was drawn with chalk on the playground and screening was used to restrict views. There were 120 children, approximately 4 to 6 years of age, who represented five age groups, with six boys and six girls in each group. The task was to walk through the maze, making correct directional choices at junctions. For half of the subjects, landmarks were indicated on the maps that corresponded to those in the maze. Over six different routes, the child carried the corresponding map through the maze. Gender had no effect on performance, and the main finding was one of age, with 4-year-olds scoring lower than the other groups.

Similarly, Hazen, Lockman, and Pick (1978) tested the ability of 3-, 4-, and 5-year-olds to navigate their way through four collapsible rooms with opaque curtain doors located in the center of each wall. Different toy animals (landmarks) were located in each room. The children were taken on either a U-shaped route or a zigzag route and had to perform a series of tasks related to these routes: route reversal (pointing to the appropriate door along the reverse route), landmark reversal (stating in advance which animal they would next see), and inference (stating which animals were in other rooms along the route that they had never entered). There were no gender differences in performance on these tasks. When the same tests were done with 5- and 6-year-olds in a six-room collapsible room environment, there was a main effect for gender as well as a gender by condition interaction on the route reversal task. However, the authors do not discuss these findings as they state that they are difficult to interpret because of a ceiling effect on performance. Children in the study were also asked to construct a model of the environment they had traversed using small boxes (4 or 6 as appropriate for the condition) and small toy animals. No gender differences were found for the model construction task in either the 4- or 6-room conditions.

A potential component of map use, the ability to use a coordinate reference system, has also been examined in 4- to 6-year-olds (Blades & Spencer, 1989). Children used a 4 × 4 grid on a wooden board that was labeled with numbers on one axis and letters on the other. The task was to use 16 grid-referenced cards to identify the corresponding location on the board. No gender differences in performance emerged on this task. Age differences indicated that the 6-year-olds were significantly better than the 4-year-olds but not the 5-year-olds. In a second study, the basic task was repeated, but with colored circles to represent the locations in the grid. Again, no gender differences emerged. In a third variation, a 3×3 grid was used with the colored circles as axis markers either with (condition 1) or without (condition 2) grid lines to define the axes. Again, girls and boys performed comparably. Taken together, these studies with young children indicate comparable performance by boys and girls on a variety of spatial activities, from map reading to model construction. These indicate comparability in the ability to use mental representations to solve relatively straightforward spatial problems.

In closing this section, two studies are reviewed that relate to an entirely different domain: computer and video game use. These are included because of a growing body of literature that indicates more involvement by boys than girls in this kind of "virtual" reality (see, e.g., Brown, Hall, Holtzer, Brown, & Brown, 1997; Cassell & Jenkins, 1998; Passig & Levin, 1999) and argues that such experience affects spatial ability. For that reason, it may be surprising that although practice on two computer games related to spatial cognition improved performance, there were no treatment effects of gender (McClurg & Chaille, 1987). Students in fifth, seventh, and ninth grade played two computer games, *The Factory* and *Stellar 7*. The task in *The Factory* is to reproduce what was called a "challenge product," which requires the mental manipulation of objects through an assembly line with different kinds of machines. To reproduce the product, the player must visualize how such things as stripes would look rotated in space. The other game, *Stellar 7*, challenges people to navigate the *Raven* spacecraft through seven star systems, in order to locate and destroy an enemy flagship. This task requires the recognition of three-dimensional objects that appear at different distances, moving at varying speeds and with changing orientations. Thus, both of these games require some ability at three-dimensional manipulation in order to succeed. The dependent measure used in this study was the Vandenberg and Kuse (1978) Mental Rotation Test (MRT). In terms of the *treatment* effects, there were no significant interaction or main effects for gender, and the study demonstrated that playing these games over a number of weeks helped both boys and girls, resulting in significantly better scores on the MRT for those in the treatment condition than in the control group.

Experience also appeared to be a stronger predictor of performance than gender in a study in which computer game use was used to predict performance on a related spatial cognition task. Law, Pellegrino, and Hunt (1993) assessed boys' and girls' routine experience with computer games, and the relationship of such computer experience to a target detection task. Using a dynamic display, with targets moving across a screen under three different velocity ratios, boys emerged more sensitive to relative velocity than did girls. Although there was this gender difference in this study, 60% of the boys and 20% of the girls reported playing video games, and video game playing experience predicted much more of the variance in task performance than did gender.

Summary

There is a significant body of developmental literature demonstrating considerable parity between boys and girls and continuing chronologically on a variety of macroenvironmental tasks. This is true of straightforward slide recognition, judgments about the value of a scene as a landmark, and finding your way along an unfamiliar route in children 6 years old and older. Another body of literature dealing with the use of maps in relatively small environments for children as young as age 4 also shows equivalent performance by boys and girls.

Gender Differences in Developmental Studies of Macrospatial Environments

Where do we see gender differences in developmental studies in macrospatial environments? Perhaps not surprisingly, given the research that has been reviewed in this chapter, there are studies that reveal gender differences where the dependent measures involve precise measurements such as angular judgments. Anooshian and Young (1981) tested first and second graders, fourth and fifth graders, and seventh and eighth graders who lived in a residential neighborhood. Their task was to use the kind of pointing device we have seen employed in other studies, a nonfunctional telescope (nothing could be seen through it) with a compass attached, to point to landmarks in the neighborhood. After performing the judgments by walking through the neighborhood, subjects stood in front of their houses and made pointings from the imagined sites. Not only were there the expected effects of age for absolute accuracy, but boys also had significantly better absolute accuracy scores from imagined reference sites than did girls, as well as higher point consistency scores. Point consistency scores, derived when the experimenters created maps from the children's pointing behavior, were "designed to reflect the degree to which lines from different reference sites (to the same landmark) actually merged and intersected" (Anooshian & Young, 1981, p. 345). The authors stress the dynamic nature of the pointing task (mental transformation related to large perspective changes) as a contributor to the gender differences that emerged.

In something of a reversal of the pattern of advantage by boys, there was a marginal gender difference ($p < 09$) favoring girls in a study that looked at scene recognition and distance judgments for children and adults in a residential neighborhood (Doherty, Gale, Pellegrino, & Golledge, 1989).

In this study, children who were preteens (ages 8–12) created sketch maps and made scene recognition and distance judgments involving target versus distractor shots, intersection versus nonintersection locations, and plot versus view vantage points (discussed also in Doherty & Pellegrino, 1985). What was somewhat amusing about this study was that the best performance (recognition sensitivity) was by preteen girls, and the worst by adult men, presumably reflecting the intensity of exposure each had to wanderings in the neighborhood. The implication is that preteen girls may spend a lot of time in the neighborhood and their recognition memory is thus superior.

A related finding, with a slightly different emphasis, is the work of Webley (1981; Webley & Whalley, 1987). Webley (1981) looked at the home ranges of 8-year-olds, asking them to perform a variety of activities related to their residential environment. They used a road construction kit (with something like the materials you might use on a train board: strips of road, colored plastic houses) to build a model of the area around their school. In this task, children were also asked to name all of the roads that they had constructed. In the Photographic Recognition test, subjects saw 35 slides with landmarks from the area around their school. For the Home Range Map, subjects were shown an aerial photograph of the area around the school and had to indicate the places they had been. The children also completed a standardized cognitive assessment, Raven's Progressive Matrices (Raven, 1960). The major finding regarding gender was that the maps boys constructed represented an area approximately 40% larger than the area represented by girls. Boys also claimed to recognize about 40% more of the photographs than did girls. Boys also reported having been to about 50% more of the area around the school than had girls. There were no effects of gender on embedding (whether the child's cognitive map of the area around his/her home was part of a wider area) or detail (the number of roads and road names and the number of building elements depicted).

However, results were quite different in a second study where children were asked to use the road construction kit to construct maps after touring a *new area unknown to them*. Analysis of the maps revealed that there was only one significant gender difference: girls had better recollection of road names than did boys. What one might argue from these two studies is that experience in terms of more widely roaming the area, rather than some basic spatial ability differences, led to the more extensive knowledge that boys demonstrated in the first study. Similarly, Matthews (1987) claims: "From the age of eight onwards boys . . . roam and play at distances significantly further from their home than girls" (p. 79). This argument might be made because when the advantage of experience in the environment was eliminated in Webley's (1981) second study, that gender difference disappeared. Similarly, you might argue that in the Doherty and colleagues (1989) study in which preteen girls demonstrated superior recognition knowledge, it is precisely because they spend time in that environment, rather than in a broader environment, that their knowledge was superior.

However, this interpretation is somewhat clouded by a study in which Webley and Whalley (1987) took 8-year-olds to an unknown town and had them walk two routes. Without the benefit of experience, the performance of girls and boys presumably should be similar. Inferences about cognitive maps were made via the process of triangulation. On an individual basis, subjects pointed to five landmarks from three reference points. The following day, they constructed a map using the road construction kit discussed previously. In this study, the maps drawn by boys were about three times larger and included more details (road junctions and buildings) than did the maps drawn by girls. Boys were also superior on the triangulation technique. Boys located about 92% of the sites correctly, whereas for girls the total was about 60%. Also, the average distance error from triangulated points for boys was about 67 meters; for girls it was about 103 meters. How can we explain these differences from the earlier study? In the earlier study (Webley, 1981), the children toured the area by car before beginning their walking tour. They also were quizzed about the sites they had seen in order to facilitate recall because some of the children did not draw their maps immediately after the trip. In the Webley and Whalley study, the children walked two different routes around the town, and then the following day all the children constructed their maps. It is not clear whether these changes in procedure, especially the technique that may have enhanced encoding (the quizzing), affected the outcome. Either we should question the reliability of the findings of the two studies, or point to the differences in procedure to explain the inconsistency.

Work on teenagers by Van Vliet (1983) is related. Van Vliet's subjects were 148 high school students ages 14–16 who lived in Toronto or in surrounding suburban areas. They filled out a checklist to indicate the activities in which they participated. They were then asked to locate the site of these activities on a map, and distances from the origin (home) were calculated. For boys who lived in the city, the distance to activities was not significantly greater than it was for girls. In the suburbs, however, the girls did have a slightly more limited home range ($p < .06$). Thus, there is some indication that boys are more likely to have larger home ranges than girls. This experience with a broader environment may enhance cognitive activities of a spatial nature.

Finally, there is a study with young children in which the performance of boys was clearly superior to that of girls (Siegel & Schadler, 1977). Although the task in the study is not really macroenvironmental, it is included here because of its emphasis on the accuracy of measurement in the dependent variable. Siegel and Schadler had kindergartners construct a model of their classroom in September and again in June. Forty scaled items that represented the objects in the classroom were to be placed in the model "just like it goes in your classroom" (p. 389). Boys demonstrated greater absolute accuracy than girls by placing .40 of the items within 2 inches of the correct position in the model, whereas girls' accuracy was .27. The authors comment about the young age at which gender differences in spatial ability appeared in this study and also interpret the girls' performance as failure: "under stress, the relatively less powerful spatial representational system of the girls became 'overloaded,' producing poorer performance" (p. 393). This kind of description unnecessarily seems to portray difference as deficit. What is important about this study is that it once again illustrates the kind of task in which girls do less well. The majority of these tasks seem to require precise judgments, or at least the researchers in these studies use precise measurement as the criterion of success.

Summary

In general, these studies involving children from kindergarten through middle school and early high school show differences in performance almost always related to age, and only occasionally to gender. When gender differences do emerge, boys generally show greater accuracy on tasks that emphasize accuracy, such as placing items in a model and pointing to imagined sites.

Studies with the Elderly

Studies with the elderly generally follow the pattern that few gender differences emerge in macrospatial tasks. For example, Kirasic, Allen, and Haggerty (1992) used color slides of a walk through an urban neighborhood to contrast the performance of young adults (mean age 26.7 years) and older adults (mean age 69.6 years). Subjects performed a landmark selection task (selected scenes that were highest in potential landmark value) and a scrambled route task (made distance estimates for points along the walk, using any scale they chose). There were also a number of psychometric tests (the Identical Pictures Test from the Kit of Factor-Referenced Cognitive Tests and the Picture Arrangement Test from the WAIS-R). Additionally, subjects provided self-report ratings of their way-finding skill and their distance estimation skill. While there were significant effects of age on a number of tasks, there were no gender differences on the proportion scores of the Landmark Selection Task nor on the Distance Estimation judgments. Women and men were equivalent in their ability to identify scenes that were high in landmark potential and to give estimates of distance. The only areas where gender differences occurred involved the standardized tests, where there was a main effect for gender and an age by gender interaction. On the Picture Arrangement Test, young women were better than both young and old men (who did not differ from each other), and each of these groups was better than the elderly women. Furthermore, for the self-rating involving way-finding skill, there was only an age effect, with older subjects rating their skills as significantly *better* than did younger adults. However, on the distance estimation self-rating, in addition to the higher ratings older adults gave themselves, men rated themselves significantly higher for this skill than did women. It may be that women are less comfortable and less practiced in giving estimates based on distance scales. That argument makes sense if women are more likely to think of the environment in terms of its landmark value.

Following the pattern of age rather than gender differences, a test of knowledge of a familiar environment (Orange, California) showed an advantage of age but not of gender (Evans, Brennan, Skorpanich, & Held, 1984). In this study, young adults (mean age 32) were contrasted with older adults (mean age 71) about their knowledge of Orange, California, where they had resided for a minimum of 10 years. Subjects performed a recall task (to list all of the buildings in downtown Orange that fell within four well-known boundaries), and a spatial location grid task in which they were to locate 13 familiar buildings, listed above the grid, in their proper placements on the grid. There were no gender differences in performance, although age effects were reported. In general, younger adults performed better than older adults.

Furthermore, in a large study (over 500 participants) examining the role of age in topographic memory failure, which the authors state is "getting lost when traveling alone," gender explained very little of the variance in performance (Crook, Youngjohn, & Larrabee, 1993). Topographic memory failure is frequently used as an assessment for dementia and is a condition in which individuals either do not recognize landmarks or are unable to use them for navigation. While there is a standardized task to assess sense of direction (Money, Alexander, & Walker, 1965), it contains no memory component. Crook and colleagues addressed this gap in their study. In their research, subjects had to indicate the direction of paths that had previously been traced by a moving dot that appeared on the screen. Four conditions were created crossing the way the dot information was displayed and whether landmarks were included. For the dot variable, the dot disappeared after it had traced the path or, in a second version, a dotted line remained on the screen indicating the path that had been traveled by the dot. For the symbol variable, international symbols were present to emphasize cue use, or were absent. Furthermore, there was a 12-turn trial and an 18-turn trial. Participants ranged in age from 17–70 years and were divided into five age groups. In the 12-turn trial, the major finding was decreasing performance with age across versions. Although men were somewhat better than women, the effect size for gender was only .02, whereas for age it was .18. In the 18-turn trial, performance also decreased with age and there were no effects of gender.

Many of the studies with the elderly emphasize laboratory tasks (see, e.g., Willis & Schaie, 1988), but there are a few that assess cognition in a true macrospatial sense. Older women were identified as particularly deficient in a study (Aubrey & Dobbs, 1990) examining the role of age and gender in understanding the mental realignment of maps. The study compared young (mean = 35.3 years) and older (mean = 67.8 years) adults with equal numbers of men and women in each age group. The task required subjects to use a map approximately 30 square centimeters in size on which had been placed 9 location dots in a 3 × 3 matrix. Paths with turns were drawn connecting these dots, with the number of turns increasing over the course of six maps (6–11 total turns). In the experimental room, nine 15-centimeter red disks were glued to the floor about 150 centimeters apart to reproduce the 3 × 3 arrangement from the map. The subject's task was to "walk" the route depicted on each map. Two conditions were created. In one condition, the subject had to hold the small map with the north (which was indicated on the map) farthest from him/her throughout (stationary position). In a second condition, the subject was to turn the map so that the north edge of the map was always aligned with the north wall of the test room. Both accuracy and time to complete the route were dependent measures.

Results indicated that older people were slower, as were women. With regard to accuracy, younger people made more correct choices before committing an error, as did men. Overall, there were more correct choices prior to error in the map condition in which subjects were to turn their maps in alignment with the room; this finding has implications for the way in which maps are presented in the real world. Aubrey and Dobbs (1990) comment on what most of us have experienced in large malls for the first time: ". . . most people, particularly those who are elderly, are more likely to have difficulty when the map is not or cannot be turned, as in the case of stationary you-are-here maps" (p. 138).

On all measures, women did less well than men, although this gender effect was largely due to the particularly poor performance of older women. Interestingly, in contrast to the Kirasic, Allen, and Haggerty (1992) study discussed earlier in this section, elderly people in this study rated their sense of direction as poorer than did young people, but there were no significant gender differences. Kirasic and colleagues had asked people to rate their way-finding skill and their distance estimation skill; in both cases, elderly adults self-reported their skills in these areas as higher than did younger adults. In addition, men had rated their distance estimation skill better than had women. It appears that sense of direction is a variable distinct in people's minds from general way-finding skill or distance estimation.

Reminiscent of Webley's (1981; Webley & Whalley, 1987) emphasis on home range, there has been some research assessing the extent of one's perceived neighborhood size (the area you describe as your own personal neighborhood) in the elderly. Almost 1,000 residents over 65 years of age in 18 small towns of populations less than 2,500 were involved in this study. Both men and those scoring higher on a mental health index indicated larger personal neighborhoods (Windley & Vandeventer, 1982). The authors suggest that men and women may use different definitions of a neighborhood, or that men are more mobile, leading to an estimation that their neighborhoods are larger.

Summary

In macrospatial research, age tends to be a better predictor of spatial performance than does gender. Whether we are dealing with young children or the elderly, the findings from research involving macroenvironments for the most part reflect reasonably comparable performance for men and women. While exceptions to this generalization occur (see, e.g., Aubrey & Dobbs, 1990), they may be in situations that are somewhat artificial and abstract and fail to reflect the kind of richness of cues that is available in the real world.

POINTS OF VIEW

Despite the gender differences in spatial ability that have been discussed in this chapter, some authors dismiss the findings as having no practical impact (Caplan, MacPherson, & Tobin, 1985; Fairweather, 1976). Caplan and colleagues (1985) emphasize the very small nature of the differences that have emerged, and criticize the lack of precision in the use of the term "spatial ability." They also find fault with the various theories that have been proposed (including genetic and brain lateralization explanations), and comment that possible strategy differences in the approach to the tasks may influence the outcome, clearly a different scenario than concluding actual ability differences exist.

Other researchers question whether research on the differences between men and women should be done at all (Hare-Mustin & Marecek, 1994), and a number of feminists have written about the topic in a cautionary vein (see, e.g., Eagly, 1994, 1995; Hyde, 1981, 1994). The majority of researchers view the undertaking as worthwhile, but see the need to offer guidelines for such examination. One of the themes that emerges is that general statements about the superiority of men in spatial tasks obscure the complexity of the data (Clear, 1978). This is a point well taken, as we have seen that the inconsistency in outcome is in part a function of the kinds of tests that are given. Others have concerns about the importance of specifying the particular spatial ability involved in a given task, about what spatial factor was assessed, the specific task demands, the type of spatial information, the processing mode, and the response mode (Horan & Rosser, 1984).

Still others point not so much to the tasks themselves as to the interpretation of the data (Eagly, 1994; Halpern, 1994; Hyde, 1981, 1994; Hyde & Plant, 1995). Eagly (1995) provides a historical perspective on the science and politics of comparing women and men and discusses two general approaches that have been presented by Hare-Mustin and Marecek (1988), those involving an alpha bias (exaggerate differences) versus a beta bias (minimize differences). Eagly essentially supports the validity of the data that have emerged, evaluating the flaws in four counterpoints made by critics of the data. She critiques the arguments that differences regarding gender essentially can be disregarded because they represent 1) small findings; 2) inconsistent findings; 3) artificial findings; and 4) findings inconsistent with gender stereotyping.

Hyde (1994) has her own set of guidelines for research on cognitive gender differences, convinced that it will continue. The guidelines are based on addressing what she sees as the problems in this area of research, including: 1) a publication bias against reports when the null hypothesis is not rejected; 2) the plethora of unreplicated findings of gender differences; 3) the failure to report effect sizes; and 4) the interpretation of difference as female deficiency. Newcombe (1982) has outlined some additional problems in the literature, including the developmental issues surrounding the emergence of difference, the correlational nature of the data, and the lack of theoretical models that address the complexity of the behavior. Unger and Crawford (1992) express a similar concern with the lack of precision in the definition of spatial ability. They plead for sensitivity in the reporting of findings about gender differences in ability, noting that such reports in popular news magazines have profound effects on parents' communications with and decisions about their children (e.g., steering females away from advanced mathematics courses because females have been reported to have less ability in this area). An article in a local newspaper with the following headline "Parents can help children, especially daughters, succeed at math" (McGee, 1996) illustrates the problem.

Explanations for Gender Differences in Spatial Abilities

A number of different influences have been identified to explain the gender differences in spatial ability seen in the kinds of research discussed in this chapter. Among the contenders—none of which has proven completely satisfactory (Caplan et al., 1985)—are an X-linked recessive gene, chromosomal and metabolic effects, brain lateralization, and psychosocial influences. A cursory look will provide a sense of the theories.

Genetic Theory

One hypothesis is that spatial ability is recessive and is carried on the X chromosome (Harris, 1978). In the X-linked recessive situation, a trait such as high spatial ability will appear only if the corresponding gene on the other member of the chromosome pairs also carries the recessive trait (Halpern, 1986). Thus, high spatial ability in this scenario would occur more frequently in men because they have only one X chromosome, limiting the frequency opportunities for other genetic combinations. Some authors find support for more general hypotheses generated by the theory (see, e.g., Thomas & Kail, 1991). However, the specific predictions made by the theory concerning the familial correlations that should arise in an X-linked recessive gene scenario (i.e., that mother–son correlations should be greater than mother–daughter correlations; that some degree of mother–daughter correlation should exist; that no correlation between fathers and sons should emerge) have found little support (Caplan et al., 1985; McGee, 1982). Halpern (1986) states that this theory was based on misguided assumptions because, "All of the sex differentiated cognitive abilities are composed of multiple components, and it is unlikely that there is a single gene that controls the expression of any of these abilities" (p.73).

Hormonal Influences

In considering whether hormonal influences might play a role in gender differences in spatial ability, McGee (1982) points to developmental studies, studies where chromosomal-hormonal abnormalities exist, and studies involving physical-somatic androgenicity. Research related to fetal adrogenization with both human and infrahuman species suggests that prenatal sex hormones influence sex differentiation in cerebral organization (Halpern, 1986; Reinisch, 1981). One of the critical issues in evaluating the role of hormonal influences is finding a difference at puberty (that is maintained) that failed to emerge earlier (McGee, 1982). For example, some research has focused on the difference between early and late maturers and their patterns of verbal and spatial abilities, with late maturers hypothesized to be more lateralized (Petersen & Crockett, 1985; Waber, 1976, 1977). Of course one of the difficulties with this emphasis on the role of hormones at puberty in the development of spatial ability is the finding of gender differences in certain spatial tasks prior to puberty. The evidence for gender differences in mental rotation tasks of the sort typified by the Vandenberg and Kuse test is that differences are found as soon as they can be measured (Linn & Petersen, 1985). Such early differences thus challenge the hypothesis that hormonal effects at puberty are related to the emergence of gender differences in spatial abilities.

Hassler (1993) built upon a theory by Geschwind and Galaburda (1985, 1987) that increased prenatal testosterone results in anomalous dominance, with more slowly growing parts of the left hemisphere coupled with the faster growth of homologous regions of the right hemisphere (see a fuller description in Chapter 3, this volume). Structures connected with the immune system are also hypothesized to form deficiently as a result of the slowed left cerebral hemisphere growth. In a longitudinal study of healthy men and women (mean age just over 19 years) involving assessments of handedness, lateralization for verbal and spatial materials, spatial and verbal ability, and immune functions (through blood serum assessments), Hassler reports some support, but only for men, for the hypothesis that spatial giftedness is connected to anomalous dominance. A number of immune parameters also showed correlations to anomalous dominance again for men. Support for the Geschwind and Galaburda theory comes from a cross-cultural study of Japanese and American high school students (Mann, Sasanuma, Sakuma, & Masaki, 1990), which showed higher performance by men on a mental rotation task and higher performance by women on story recall and a digit-symbol tasks (interpreted as verbal tasks). Here, culture is a less likely explanation of these cross-cultural patterns of ability. Yet it is reasonable to say that while there may be some hormonal effects on the development of spatial ability, we are far from understanding the nature of the effects or their distribution.

Neurological Differences

Another working hypothesis is that men have greater hemispheric specialization than do women, arguably because they have slower rates of maturation, which provides the time for greater hemispheric differentiation. Theories of sex-differentiated asymmetries have included those of Buffery and Gray (1972) and Levy (1976), which ironically predicted opposite patterns of lateralization. Based on the differences in maturation rates of boys and girls, Buffery and Gray predicted that men's brains would be less lateralized, whereas women's would be more strongly lateralized for both verbal and spatial abilities. Because spatial skills were hypothesized to benefit from bilateral representation, women would be handicapped with regard to their spatial but not their verbal abilities. On the other hand, Levy (1969, 1976) hypothesized that spatial ability was enhanced when strongly lateralized (directly contradicting the optimal spatial ability scenario from Buffery and Gray), and suggested that women were less lateralized due to sex-related differences in their maturation pattern. While not without its critics (Caplan et al., 1985), Levy's theory has demonstrated more empirical support (see, e.g., Voyer & Bryden, 1990). And while Halpern (1986) acknowledges that not all the research supports the relationship between gender differences in spatial ability and brain lateralization, she says, "What is most compelling is that when they are found, they are almost always in the same direction—females less lateralized than males. If these were spurious findings, then you would expect the results to go in either direction about equally often" (p. 83).

A view of the necessary constellation of genetic potential and spatial experiences for women to excel at the mental rotation task has been offered by Casey and Brabeck (1989). In their view, those individuals likely to succeed are right-handed women majoring in math-science fields who have non-right-handed relatives. Handedness is hypothesized to play a role, according to these researchers, with its potential to explain differences in brain organization. And in fact, in their study of 314 women and 119 men in college, they found a significant family handedness by major by gender interaction, with the familial non-right-handed math-science women performing significantly better than either the familial right-handed math-science majors or the non-right-handed group. "The critical role of family handedness on the Vandenberg test supports the view that a genetic factor may be responsible, at least in part, for the performance of women in this mental rotation task" (Casey & Brabeck, 1989, pp. 694–695). The authors subscribe to what has been called the Bent Twig explanation, the suggestion that if you have abilities in a given area, you will tend to develop them, thereby reinforcing the potential. "A subset of women with the genetic predisposition for mental rotation ability may be attracted to masculine sex-typed spatial visualization activities and college majors where this potential would be used and developed" (p. 695).

While the literature consistently implicates a larger role of the right hemisphere and the influence of greater lateralization among men in spatial performance, not all research supports that right hemisphere emphasis. For example, Uecker and Obrzut (1993) found no main effect for gender or visual field in a study that involved deciding on which side of a stick figure stimulus a ball was held. At the same time, the task in this particular study may have been too easy to elicit differences. Van Strien and Bouma (1990) also question the role of the right hemisphere in spatial tasks after finding no visual field differences in the rotation rate on a mental rotation task. Furthermore, Herman and Bruce (1983) found no relationship between preferred hemisphere for processing (as indicated by lateral eye movement, or LEM) and accuracy on a mental rotation task, but the authors themselves question the validity of the LEM technique as an index of hemispheric engagement.

Psychosocial Hypotheses

Anyone who has or has worked with young children can certainly provide anecdotes about the role of our culture in the development of various kinds of preferences and abilities. While we may attempt to give our children exposure to a wide array of toys that might appeal to boys, girls, or both, it is difficult to ignore what might be called the "Barbie and My Little Pony syndrome." Using the criteria of Unger and Crawford (1992), our home had toys that were oriented toward boys (tinker toys, tricycles, drums, dump trucks, a doctor's kit, and blocks) and toys that were neutral (e.g., a rocking horse, finger paints, chalk, clay, Etch-a-Sketch). We also had our share of toys oriented toward girls (Raggedy Anns, coloring books, a doll stroller, puppets, jump ropes, and a shopping basket). But birthday parties provide ample opportunities for the influx of My Little Pony and

Barbie paraphernalia (the outfits and accessories). Furthermore, once the exposure to television moves beyond *Sesame Street* and *Mr. Rogers*, the influence of a more wide-ranging popular culture is overwhelming. There is no question that boys and girls live different lives, and the list of toys (Unger & Crawford, 1992) is but a single indication of that difference.

Boys are given vehicles and building equipment, encouraged to build models from diagrams, construct forts and playhouses, and take apart and reassemble objects. They are more likely to be provided with science-related toys such as microscopes and puzzles. These toys may help them learn more about manipulating movement and space than the dolls and miniature housekeeping equipment provided for girls. (Unger & Crawford, 1992, p. 84)

Does this cultural exposure have an effect on spatial ability? Most certainly. Serbin and Connor (1979) showed that girls and boys who engage in climbing, block building, and vehicle play score higher on a spatial ability test than those using dolls and housekeeping items. In a population of 3- to 5-year olds, Connor and Serbin (1977) demonstrated that even in nursery school children may avoid opposite-gender activities, and that the development of visual-spatial abilities in boys is related to participation in masculine-typed activities. We know that when young children (3½ to 4 years of age) are exposed to training on toys described as boys' (blocks, tinker toys), it can increase their spatial ability scores (Sprafkin, Serbin, Denier, & Connor, cited in Unger & Crawford, 1992), and that spatial ability as measured by mental rotation tasks has implications for science achievement scores (Tracy, 1990). Furthermore, we have already seen that specific training on spatial ability tasks at the other end of the life spectrum (Schaie & Willis, 1986; Willis & Schaie, 1988) can improve spatial ability. We have also seen that while boys and girls differ in their exposure to video games and the relationship of this experience to spatial performance (Law, Pellegrino, & Hunt, 1993), training on new video games improves the ability of both boys and girls, leading to similar performance (McClurg & Chaille, 1987). In a study of adolescents, a list of activities judged as either traditionally feminine or masculine and as either involving spatial ability or not was given to subjects who indicated their involvement in these activities (Newcombe, Bandura, & Taylor, 1983). More spatial activities were considered more masculine, and the activity scale correlated with spatial ability in a college population asked to indicate their degree of participation in the activities. Thus, it is exceedingly difficult to reach conclusions about the causes of gender differences in spatial ability because at the very least they are multiply determined.

Concluding Remarks

Given the evidence for multiple determination of gender differences in spatial ability and the role of learning, it is important to consider the guidelines about the interpretation of gender difference data suggested by Hyde (1994) and others. As has already been pointed out, press coverage of research on gender-related differences can have powerful effects. As Unger and Crawford (1992) state, such interpretations are not "value-neutral" (p. 91), and Hare-Mustin and Marecek (1988) discuss the construction of gender. The gender difference spatial ability research that we pursue can have positive outcomes, but understanding the causes of the differences is important if we are to provide equal opportunities for both women and men (Eagly, 1995).

Moreover, beyond the implications of such data on possible career paths (e.g., engineering, architecture), there are practical implications of these data for the way we live our lives. Devlin and Bernstein (1995) have argued that the fact that men and women differ in their preference for the kinds of cue sources they would select when traveling to a new destination has implications for the formats available in computer-aided way-finding kiosks. As technology increasingly finds a home on the dashboards of our automobiles, such as navigation aids like computer-generated maps, we may want to incorporate what we know about the strategies men and women use for such spatial tasks as way finding to create choices when they approach such information-processing tasks.

The preponderance of the evidence seems to suggest a robust difference between men and women in their ability to mentally manipulate stimuli of the sort used in tasks like the Vandenberg and Kuse (1978) Mental Rotation Test. At the same time, the studies that take people out of the laboratory and into the real way-finding world do not paint as clear a picture of the differences between men and women. And there may be areas, such as the recollection of landmarks, where women are superior to men.

But the gender differences in mental rotation may have implications in the real world. In particular, women who apply for jobs where they cross gender-role boundaries (e.g., applying for jobs that are traditionally dominated by men, such as in architecture) have experienced discrimination. Even with increases in the percentages of women entering the profession of architecture (Nadelson, 1989), men continue to dominate professional practice; women constitute only 15% of those working in the field professionally (Ahrentzen & Groat, 1992). Architect Denise Scott Brown writes of her own experience of sexism and discrimination as the spouse and collaborator of architect Robert Venturi: "In the last twenty years, I cannot recall one major article by a high-priest critic about a woman architect" (1989, pp. 244–245). Exploring this issue, Devlin (1997) conducted a resumé study in which 204 architects licensed in the state of Connecticut participated in a 2 (job level) by 2 (gender) between-subjects design. The architects rated applicant potential on the basis of one-page resumés. Results indicated that architects who were men were more likely to hire as senior architects applicants who were men than applicants who were women. There thus seemed to be discrimination against women as they rose in the profession. The social construction of gender thus has a reality in practice. " . . . assertions about male–female differences and similarities do not have a single, fixed meaning; instead, they serve as raw material for constructing a variety of contested interpretations, cultural meanings and political agendas" (Hare-Mustin & Marecek, 1994, p. 532).

3

The Neuropsychology of Spatial Cognition:
In the Mind's Eye

The direction of cognitive psychology has changed dramatically over the last decade. For that reason, it seems important to provide some sense of this new path—the neuropsychology of spatial cognition—even in a book that concentrates on the molar aspects of behavior. The challenge is to provide a reasonably current and understandable perspective, as new findings about brain function change the field almost daily. It is necessary that the "scale" examined in this chapter be small. Almost all of the tasks that subjects perform confine them to the laboratory. The question is whether the data produced in these studies can be generalized to performance in the extended environment.

While an extensive review of the role of the brain in spatial cognition is beyond the scope of this book, it is important to try to relate the mechanisms of the brain to the legibility of architecture and design. Kosslyn (1994a) has tried to do something similar, but on a limited scale, in his book dealing with the design of graphs. We are animals that can perform particular kinds of cognitive tasks more easily than others. Certain aspects of the environment (like suburban developments with repetitious elements) can confuse us. It is one premise of this book that more attention in design to our biological predilections and brain processes can help create environments that are functional as well as pleasing.

New technologies (Begley, 1995) have permitted us to examine the brain at an entirely different level of analysis than heretofore possible, and it may

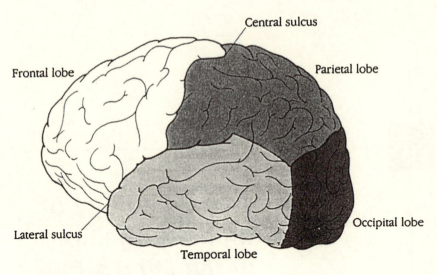

Figure 3.1. The left hemisphere.

now be feasible to examine the loci of spatial cognition on the level of brain function. To better understand spatial cognition on this level, this chapter will provide an overview of the functional asymmetry of the brain and related sex differences in laterality. The influence of hormones, the role of mental imagery in spatial cognition, and the fundamentals of vision will also be considered. Plaut and Farah (1990) have emphasized the importance of connecting computational and neuroscience approaches, and O'Neill (1991a) has developed a biologically based model of spatial cognition and way finding. In this chapter, we will see how the brain affects our ability to navigate in the environment. In following one of the approaches of this book, the methodologies and operational tasks presented in the research in this chapter are typically discussed in detail. This approach enables the reader to better understand the kind of spatial behavior that is involved and make some assessment of the ecological validity of the task as well as its centrality to way finding.

THE BRAIN AND FUNCTIONAL ASYMMETRY

The brain is an impressive apparatus, the equivalent of 100 billion interacting "neuronal" computers (Anderson, 2000). Each hemisphere resembles a boxing glove; looking at the left hemisphere is like looking at the thumb-side of a right-hand glove (see Figure 3.1). The neocortex of the brain consists of right and left hemispheres, each of which has four lobes: frontal (planning and motor functions); occipital (primary visual areas); parietal (sensory functions including spatial processing); temporal (primary auditory areas and object recognition). The two hemispheres are connected by a series of fiber bundles, of which the corpus callosum is the primary conduit. The hippocampus, central to memory function and implicated in spatial cognition, is nestled in the temporal lobe (Anderson, 2000). Its name derives from its resemblance to the shape of a seahorse, and its prolonged postnatal development has been linked to a sensitivity to environmental stimuli (Spreen, Tupper, Risser, Tuokko, & Edgell, 1984).

Although localizations in brain function can be studied in subjects who have suffered brain damage (e.g., lesions), the organization of the brain and its relationship to the visual system make it possible to study the hemispheres in "isolation" in people both with and without brain damage. When the optic nerves meet at the optic chiasma, those from the nasal side of the retina cross over and continue to the other side of the brain. Those from the outside of the retina go to the same side of the brain as that eye. Each visual hemifield thus connects to the contralateral hemisphere (Anderson, 2000). Researchers can thus restrict information to one of the hemispheres when information is flashed to a single hemifield, as long as the subject maintains fixation (Corballis, 1995b). The information is subsequently transmitted to the other hemisphere via the corpus callosum or other commissures. Thus, if a subject fixates on a point and does not move his head, information in the left or right visual field is initially registered in the opposite hemisphere (see Figure 3.2).

While the hemispheres may look essentially the same to the naked eye, over the last 100 years the discovery and subsequent examination of their functional asymmetry has generated considerable research. A simplistic overview of the "responsibilities" of the two hemispheres has given the left hemisphere the major or dominant label, localizing language and analytical functions there. Corballis (1991, 1994) locates a generative assembling device (GAD) in the left hemisphere, suggesting that "the generative, rule-governed nature of human thought and representation may be largely left-hemispheric and uniquely human" (1991, p. 241). He also argues that the left hemisphere may be dominant in temporal processing (Corballis, 1996). The right hemisphere has sometimes been called the minor hemisphere, and it is on the right side that spatial function has been claimed to reside. The left hemisphere has been viewed by Levy-Agresti and Sperry as " 'logical, analytic computer-like' and the right hemisphere a 'synthesist in dealing with informational input' " (quoted in Goldberg & Costa, 1981, p. 155). The left hemisphere has been cited as managing "verbal learning and memory, phonetic analysis, deductive reasoning, serial processing, verbal IQ, and symbolic thinking," whereas the right has been associated with "imagistic learning and memory, perceptual synthesis, analogical reasoning, parallel processing, performance IQ, and concrete thinking" (Levy & Reid, 1978, p. 120).

Even the advertising industry has propagated a simplistic view of discrete

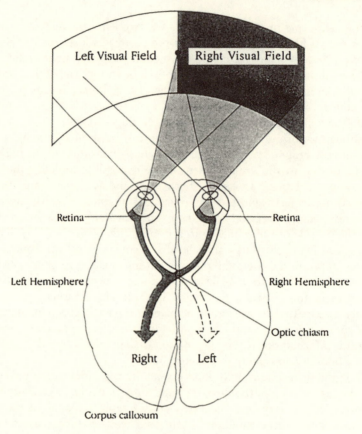

Figure 3.2. The visual field crossover.

hemispheric function. A print ad for United Airlines announces "Coast to coast. Arranged with both your brains in mind" and lists the functions of the left brain and right brain, a sampling of which for the left brain is to "Plan the fax" and "Fax the plan" and for the right brain to "Balance silverware on nose" and "Count the clouds." But just as some aspects of language in the right hemisphere have been demonstrated (Gazzaniga, 1983; Gazzaniga & Miller, 1989), this discrete approach leads to a less than complete understanding of the complexity of interactions that produce behavior. Evidence of interhemispheric integration has already been demonstrated with lower order information (Corballis & Trudel, 1993), and will continue to emerge as technology becomes more sophisticated. A simplistic overview hardly does justice to the complexity of brain function.

While modularity seems to be receiving the majority of attention in theory development, Goldman-Rakic (1988) points out the importance of an integrated rather than a segregated approach to understanding function. Based on work with monkeys, she postulates that there may be parallel cortical networks serving as subdivisions for spatial and nonspatial information processing. "The picture that emerges from the new anatomy is that of a highly integrated but distributed machinery whose resources are allocated to several basic parallel functional systems that bridge all major subdivisions of the cerebrum" (p. 152). Goldman-Rakic (1992) points to the prefrontal cortex, in particular to an area near the principal sulcus (a large groove in the prefrontal cortex) as central for visual and spatial working memory functions. "I think the prefrontal cortex is divided into multiple memory domains, each specialized for encoding a different kind of information, such as the location of objects, the features of objects (color, size, and shape) and additionally, in humans, semantic and mathematical knowledge" (1992, p. 115). Goldman-Rakic's and others' work has also emphasized the interconnectedness and one-to-one correspondence of neurons in the prefrontal cortex with neurons in the occipital cortex and the importance of both for various outputs of visuospatial function.

A Closer Look at Hemispheric Lateralization

Recent research has identified subtle hemispheric differences of function. Claims have been made that the right hemisphere operates more literally and concretely, better than the left hemisphere at rejecting distractors similar to materials presented earlier (Metcalfe, Funnell, & Gazzaniga, 1995). The left hemisphere has been associated with what have been called more advanced cognitive processes, such as the ability to limit search to a particular subgroup of a visual display (Kingstone, Enns, Mangun, & Gazzaniga, 1995). The left hemisphere has also been touted as superior in interpretation and inference (Phelps & Gazzaniga, 1992).

It has also been argued that the right hemisphere may contribute differentially to visuospatial functioning, with a larger role when the behaviors required are more complex than simple (Young & Ratcliff, 1983). At the same time, the left hemisphere has been implicated in more complex processing (Mehta & Newcombe, 1991). One of the difficulties with this line of argument is the labeling of cognitive functions as more or less sophisticated or complex. It is also the case that a right hemisphere advantage for visuospatial processing is not always found (see, e.g., Mayes, 1982).

The right hemisphere is said to perform better when stimuli easily follow Gestalt laws of organization, whereas the left hemisphere may better handle stimuli whose organization violates Gestalt principles (VanKleeck & Kosslyn, 1989). Similarly, it has been hypothesized that the left hemisphere should be better than the right at identifying novel views of nonrigid objects whereas the right hemisphere should be better able to identify familiar views of objects (Laeng, Shah, & Kosslyn, 1999). This difference is posited because the right hemisphere is thought to have a superior facility to store visual appearances of specific shape. The left hemisphere is thought to analyze component parts of novel images or contorted positions, whereas the right is thought to be better if it can make a match to an overall shape. Laeng and colleagues (1999) state, "global matching would have priority in visual perception, and recognition by parts through structural description would intervene at a later phase, particularly in 'visually challenging' situations" (p. 83). Thus, the right hemispheric superiority might emerge in a variety of perceptual tasks that emphasize familiar objects or when operating in a familiar environment.

Dissociations

With the increasing sophistication of the technology available to study brain function, the field of neuropsychology seems to have shifted to one able to dissect specific areas. This approach results in an emphasis on the modularity of brain operation (Fodor, 1983; Gazzaniga, 1989) and an accompanying assumption of locality—that brain damage effects are localized and encapsulated (Farah, 1994). While these assumptions appear to be widely held, it should be noted that both have been questioned (Farah, 1994), and at least one recent review suggests that a relative specialization model rather than an absolute localization model makes more sense (Chabris & Kosslyn, 1998).

Despite the plea for integration, researchers often examine dissociations, where performance is impaired in some brain areas and preserved in others, leading to hypotheses concerning the functional nature of a module or particular brain area (Ellis & Young, 1988; Young, 1983). For example, of special interest to the topic of spatial cognition, two cortical visual systems have been identified, a ventral system from the primary visual cortex to the inferior temporal lobe, responsible for recognizing "what" objects are, and the dorsal system, running from the occipital lobe to the parietal lobe, implicated in locating "where" objects are (Atkinson, 1993; Brown & Kosslyn, 1995; Constantinidis & Steinmetz, 1996; Findlay, Ashton, & McFarland, 1994; Hellige & Michimota, 1989; Jacobs & Kosslyn, 1994; Koenig, Reiss, & Kosslyn, 1990; Kosslyn, 1987, 1991; Kosslyn, Anderson, Hillger, & Hamilton, 1994; Kosslyn, Chabris, Marsolek, & Koenig, 1992; Kosslyn, Maljkovic, Hamilton, Horwitz, & Thompson, 1995; Kosslyn, Sokolov, & Chen, 1989; Morrow & Ratcliff, 1988; Ratcliff, 1991; Rueckl, Cave, & Kosslyn, 1989; Ungerleider & Mishkin, 1982). Corballis (1995b) has also postulated two visual systems: one for the analysis of form, the other for movement and location.

Why is this important? The organization of our visual and imaginal systems tells us a great deal about what is important to an animal that is designed to navigate successfully. In discussing low-level vision, David Marr (covered in more depth later in the chapter) asks us to figure out what vision is about, what problems it solves (Marr, 1982). For Marr, the quintessential aspect of human vision is that "it tells about shape and space and spatial arrangement" (1982, p. 36). If humans are animals that have "what" and "where" systems, this reflects the way in which we subdivide the world and the aspects of the world we need to emphasize in order to make the environment legible.

Much of the evidence for the existence of the "what" and "where" systems comes from research on patients with brain damage. Balint's syndrome (difficulty with locating objects) results from bilateral damage to parieto-occipital areas, whereas Klüver-Bucy syndrome (trouble with what something is or object recognition) results from bilateral temporal lobe damage (Kosslyn, 1987). Here again we see the notion of dissociations, with lesions in these cortical-visual systems leading to distinctly different kinds of impairments. Inferior temporal lobe damage leads to identification difficulties but preserves maze learning behavior, whereas parietal cortex lesions lead to depressed maze learning but preserve the ability to recognize objects such as faces (Morrow & Ratcliff, 1988). Andersen (1988) also argues that the inferior parietal lobes operate in a number of ways related to spatial analysis, including encoding position relative to the observer and extracting spatial information from motion. The inferior parietal lobes are also linked to aspects of spatial behavior related to attention. Differences in the ability of the two hemispheres to handle categorical and coordinate spatial relations also have been postulated (Laeng, 1994; Kosslyn et al., 1989), with the left generally better at handling categorical judgments (e.g., top/bottom, on/off), whereas the right is generally better at coordinate relations (e.g., evaluations of distance).

With regard to the processing of images, there may be hemispheric lateralization as well. Using categorical spatial relations, the left hemisphere may be better at generating images through arranging parts according to descriptions. The right hemisphere, on the other hand, may depend on coordinate spatial relationships to more effectively generate images by positioning parts in exact locations in space (Chabris & Kosslyn, 1998; Kosslyn et al., 1995). The conditions under which the two hemispheres excel at these tasks is being refined as new data emerge (Rybash & Hoyer, 1992).

Receptive field differences also have been linked to hemispheric differences. One theory (Chabris & Kosslyn, 1998) posits that the left hemisphere is biased to attend to smaller regions of space than the right. The left hemisphere is thought to be more involved in monitoring the outputs of neurons with smaller receptive fields whereas the right hemisphere may focus on receptive fields that are relatively larger (Jacobs & Kosslyn, 1994), although both hemispheres are capable of handling a range of receptive field sizes. These biases are thought to be under attentional control, with implications that the nature of the task can affect the way the hemispheres deal with spatial information. In explaining why the left hemisphere may encode small patterns better than large ones and the right hemisphere the reverse, Kosslyn, Anderson, Hillger, and Hamilton (1994) emphasize the concept of attention. As the hemispheres resonate to neurons with receptive fields of different sizes, the authors argue that it is attention that is adjusted according to task demands. The left hemisphere is postulated to handle the more difficult aspects of encoding and the right the (relatively) less difficult aspects. In this study where subjects judged whether two successive line segments were oriented in the same manner, Kosslyn and colleagues state that the results are "most consistent with the view that attention is adjusted so that the hemispheres tend to monitor outputs from neurons with different-size receptive fields" (p. 146). Not the receptive field size, but the difficulty of encoding is the driving factor.

As with the flexibility demonstrated by the hemispheres in handling receptive field sizes, depending on task, it is important to note that both hemispheres can handle categorical and coordinate tasks, although not equally well (Kosslyn et al., 1992). Kosslyn and colleagues (1992) place this flexibility within the context of what they call weak modularity. Thus, while it may be appealing to argue that the left hemisphere handles particular functions and the right hemisphere handles others, such a line of argument underestimates the flexibility of information processing in the human brain.

Summary

Despite the specificity of information like the *what* and *where* processes, we need to think broadly about spatial behavior, as it has been argued that it is modality independent (Kritchevsky, 1988). Furthermore, the dissociation of asymmetry (some processes occurring only in the left hemisphere, others just in the right) has been challenged by recent findings. Additionally, some processes such as mental imagery are sufficiently complex and involve so many components that aspects of both hemispheres are engaged (Kosslyn, 1987). Goldberg and Costa (1981) propose that as cognitive processes become more practiced, there is a right-to-left shift in hemispheric control. Research on deaf and hearing ASL signers also challenges the notion of strong modularity (Emmorey, Kosslyn, & Bellugi, 1993). Thus, the conceptualization of a straightforward left–right dichotomy of hemispheric function is misleading.

A more integrative perspective about the relationship between and within the hemispheres makes sense given the limitations of some of the methodologies that have been used to generate the data (e.g., lesion studies and cerebral blood flow studies). Recent research is assessing functional connectedness at more precise levels, for example, Witelson, Kigar, and McKanna (1992). Goldman-Rakic's work (e.g., Schwartz & Goldman-

Rakic, 1982), some of which is done neuron by neuron, would be an impossibility without the present technology. Ultimately, what may emerge from these newer studies is a map of the interconnectedness of brain areas already implicated in spatial cognition. Other brain areas that discretely control aspects of way finding or are at least implicated may also emerge.

SPATIAL COGNITION AND RIGHT HEMISPHERE FUNCTION

Despite the interconnectivity of the hemispheres and the importance (to say nothing of the challenge) of trying to understand integrated brain function, researchers understandably will try to identify what processes occur in which hemispheres when those data present themselves. Because the right hemisphere is so closely identified with spatial behavior, it is important to more closely examine some of that literature. The headings suggest a general emphasis within a given section, but it is difficult to present data about one hemisphere without implicating the other, as many studies deal with both. The right hemisphere has been implicated in such behaviors as perceptual matching, dealing with task novelty, route finding, spatial exploration, and memory for spatial locations, among others (Dimond & Beaumont, 1974; Goldberg & Costa, 1981; Kimura & Durnford, 1974; Levy, 1976; Morrow & Ratcliff, 1988; Semmes, 1968; Smith et al., 1995). Witelson's early work (1974) supported the hypothesis that the right hemisphere was superior in perceiving nonlinguistic somesthetic stimuli (those involving proprioceptive and tactile sensation), which she observed in young school-aged children. The right hemisphere may have a greater role when a visual pattern deviates from its conventional view in a task like mental rotation (Sergent & Corballis, 1989). In fact, the greater role of the right hemisphere in mental rotation is a strong theme in the literature (Corballis & Manalo, 1993; Corballis & Sidney, 1993), although here again its dominance may be a relational one. Right hemisphere processing of mental rotation may be more pronounced when the left hemisphere is less involved, and its specialization is unlikely to be absolute (Corballis, 1991).

Lesion Data

A sample of research dealing first with lesions and then with cerebral blood flow data will be presented to show both the approach and the general nature of the findings pointing to the role of the right posterior cerebral cortex in spatial function. There are, however, some disadvantages to research using lesions. Lesions are discrete and destroy both connections and cell bodies. Furthermore, in humans the precise boundaries are known only through surgery or autopsy. Despite these limitations, the approach has been helpful in adding to our knowledge of the locus of function.

An early study will help to introduce the kinds of challenges faced by researchers in this area and the kinds of tasks that are used to assess damage related to spatial behavior. In most of the tasks in this literature, the scale of the environment is severely limited, often to a tabletop maze or paper-and-pencil exercises. Almost none of the tasks involves navigating in a real environment. A study by DeRenzi, Faglioni, and Villa (1977) is typical of the tasks used. They reported a diminished ability to reach criterion in a visually guided stylus maze task in patients with right posterior cerebral injury, in comparison to controls and those with hemisphere damage in other locations. The authors were studying topographical amnesia, the criterion for which they stated was losing your bearings in a *well-known* environment. They differentiated this from cases in which people were unable to form representations of *new* routes. Their term for this distinguishable problem was defective route finding.

In their paper, DeRenzi and colleagues (1977) also discuss the many difficulties in pinpointing the locus (or loci) of spatial behavior. There are any number of ways in which people might be unable to find their way. These include loss of awareness of the position, both absolute and relative, of objects. When this happens in more than one hemifield, the individual will be unable to navigate with respect to the object. You might also ignore the left side of space (and consequently ignore left turns) if you have a right hemisphere lesion. Furthermore, you might suffer from visual object agnosia, which in some forms curtails your ability to recognize your surroundings. Or you might be unable to retrieve geographical knowledge and associated visual memories about familiar routes and locales, even though these memories are well established.

In their research, DeRenzi and colleagues (1977) used 51 patients with right hemisphere damage and 54 with left hemisphere damage. These groups were further subdivided in terms of whether there was a visual field defect associated with the hemispheric damage, generating four groups (left or right hemisphere; with or without defect). In roughly 70% of the cases, damage was caused by vascular disease. They employed a visual maze apparatus (modeled after Milner, 1965) that had 23 choice points and implied 6 turns. Using a stylus and moving from bolthead to bolthead, subjects were to discover the correct route, practicing until they reached a criterion of three successive errorless runs. They were signaled with an auditory click when an error was made. Subjects with right hemisphere damage and visual defects were inferior to the control group and to the three other brain damaged groups. In the study, DeRenzi and colleagues also reviewed two case studies in which there were difficulties related to spatial behavior. From these case studies and their stylus maze data, they claim support for the role of the right hemisphere (retroRolandic area) in topographical memory.

The specific characteristics of topographic memory loss were also reviewed in a case study by Hecaen, Tzortzis, and Rondot (1980). The authors provide a clear description of the navigational difficulties of individuals who suffer from this rare disorder. "Topographic memory loss essentially consists of an inability to use landmarks for the purpose of orientation. Patients with this disorder are able to identify and describe various places, buildings, or monuments, however, these landmarks fail to evoke a sense of familiarity for these patients and no longer function to help them arrive at their destination" (pp. 535–536). The authors report on the case of A.R., who had damage near the midline in the right occipital region. A.R. was given an extensive battery of cognitive tests, including those with perceptual and spatial content. Among the spatial tests were a route finding test (requiring him to retrace a particular path sequence in a large room), and the visual maze learning test described above in the DeRenzi and colleagues (1977) research. Although A.R. did not do well on the route finding test, his performance was abysmal on the visual maze learning task. He could not reach the performance criterion even after 100 trials. However, he could do the route test if he verbalized the landmarks. It is possible that the stylus maze task produced such difficulties precisely because it is hard to supplement with verbal description (to work around the landmarkless nature of the task, in other words). The authors argue that most of the evidence seems to point to the relationship between right hemisphere lesions and spatial deficits. But while the parieto-occipital cortex is actively involved in spatial functions, it is not clear to the authors whether it is specifically the hippocampus. Other regions might be involved, given the memory-based aspect of disorders such as topographic memory loss.

But the right hemisphere may not be exclusively responsible for spatial behavior. Using similar tasks, Ratcliff and Newcombe (1973) studied 75 men with missile wounds in the left, right, or bilateral posterior and nonposterior areas, as well as 20 controls. It is worth noting that in addition to vascular disease and tumors, individuals with head wounds from war comprise a sizable population of research subjects for this kind of work. The men performed two tasks: a visually guided stylus maze and a locomotor map-reading task. As we saw in the case study of A.R., stylus maze learning performance was worse for those with lesions in the posterior right cerebral hemisphere. For the locomotor task, it was those with bilateral posterior cerebral lesions who performed poorly, not true of those with unilateral lesions (on either side) or with bilateral frontal lesions. Areas beyond the right hemisphere appear to be involved in spatial behavior. As the authors point out, the stylus maze and locomotor mapping tasks are quite different. The visually guided maze involves running a stylus along a groove for a given number of paths, using 6 or 10 choice points, and measuring the number of trials to criterion in learning the path(s). For the locomotor task, subjects walk from point to point on the floor of a large room, tracing a path shown on a map. These two tasks almost produced a kind of dissociative response, that is, quite different results emerged depending on the locus of the subject's lesion. Bilateral lesions were required to perform poorly on the locomotor task, whereas right posterior lesions were responsible for the worst performance on the stylus-maze task. What Ratcliff and Newcombe argue is that the locomotor task involves an external frame of reference whereas in the stylus maze task it is the body that is the reference. Maintaining orientation during change seems to require bilateral involvement. ". . . it is clear from our results that the designation of either hemisphere as dominant for 'spatial' function would be premature" (p. 453).

Summary

Findings from lesion studies indicate that damage to the right posterior cortex impairs various aspects of spatial functioning, including map reading, geographical knowledge, visuospatial and topographic memory, and mental rotation. Although converging data from different lesion studies support the involvement of the right posterior cortex, one must be cautious in relying solely on lesion studies because of the problems inherent in interpreting the data from such studies. Lesion studies are limited because they cannot confer a one-to-one correspondence between a brain area and a behavior. Lesions are not localized to a single brain area. Lesions destroy cell bodies as well as neurons passing through a brain area, and in people precise boundaries of lesions can be learned only upon autopsy. Therefore, a multimethod approach to studying spatial behavior is necessary.

Cerebral Blood Flow Studies

The measurement of cerebral blood flow (rCBF) is another technique used to examine brain function (Roland & Friberg, 1985) and will be considered to further investigate the role of the right posterior cerebral cortex in spatial behavior. The advantage of the rCBF studies is that the importance of particular regions of the cortex in fully functioning (as opposed to lesioned) individuals may be examined. The disadvantage is that rCBF studies are hampered by less than ideal resolution. Yet the technique enables identification of brain areas that are activated during a cognitive task. In the Roland and Friberg study, they used carotid angiography. In this procedure, the isotope ^{133}Xe was injected as a bolus through a catheter into the carotid artery in order to monitor 254 cortical regions. "Thinking" consumes metabolic energy that will be seen in increases in rCBF. In this study, three different tasks were used (subtraction by 3s beginning with 50; jumping every second word in a 9-word jingle; imagining walking out the front door of one's house and alternating left and right turns at each corner). Because the focus of this book is spatial cognition, our interest here is in the route task. In the test, the 11 subjects were trained before the actual task. They practiced imagining the route out their front door, turning at every second corner, and alternating turns to the right and left. There was no particular destination, it appears. The task simply involved carrying out these alternating turns in a familiar environment. In the actual monitored task, they imagined walking out the front door and alternating left and right turns at every corner or road intersection. Results indicated that the route task involved the greatest rCBF increase in the posterior superior parietal cortex. Some areas, specifically the middle and posterior superior prefrontal cortex, involved high rCBF values across tasks. Although the technique enables you to examine functioning in an intact brain, the route finding task is still so complex that you cannot tease apart the specific components and their associated cerebral areas.

Using spatial tasks exclusively, rCBF has also been employed to examine visual spatial processing (Wendt & Risberg, 1994). In the context of this research, the authors mention that the "dichotomania" of the 1970s and early 1980s, in which the discrete functions of the two hemispheres was emphasized, has been supplanted with a more balanced view. Still, they acknowledge that researchers continue to debate the mechanisms that underlie functional specialization. The authors lean toward the description of the right hemisphere as " 'more spatial than verbal' and the left as 'more verbal than spatial' " (p. 88). Wendt and Risberg (1994) looked at 9 men and 10 women, all healthy volunteers, doing three visuospatial tasks while their cortical flow was measured. In their procedure, one minute of ^{133}Xe was inhaled, followed by normal air for 10 minutes. Flow was measured under four conditions: (1) at rest with closed eyes; (2) while silently counting the number of rectangular shapes of 50 items displayed with the sum reported aloud; (3) doing mental rotation of figures of the Shepard and Metzler (1971) variety (complex cubes extending in three-dimensional space); and (4) doing cube analysis. In the mental rotation task, there were 80 items and 2 figures presented in each trial. The subject's task was to indicate whether the figures were the same ("yes") or mirror images ("no"). In the cube analysis, originally used by Binet, there were complex three-dimensional clusters of cubes; some cubes in the cluster were visible and others were not. The subject had to count (silently) and then verbally report the total number of cubes on each trial. This calculation required inference.

There was activation in the most posterior portion of the cortex during the visuospatial tests. Asymmetries involving the right hemisphere occurred in all conditions. The main finding was that during cube analysis there was a highly significant asymmetry in a region they call the classical posterior association cortices: inferior parietal lobule, angular gyrus, supramarginal gyrus, and visual association area of posterior temporal cortex. In discussing the cube analysis task, Wendt and Risberg (1994) comment that "subjects utilizing a right hemisphere strategy when solving spatial tasks are superior to subjects with more bilateral involvement" (p. 98). They suggest that left hemisphere involvement with cube analysis (presumably this would be a verbal component) may hinder performance. They further state that there is a likely relation between "cognitive strategy, asymmetric activation, and spatial performance" (p. 99).

Design Implications

The study by Wendt and Risberg (1994) highlights some of the challenges faced by designers. In a sense, environmental designers are faced with a double-edged sword. Humans are animals that not only have brains designed to perform verbal and spatial analyses, but they also have brains that permit multiple ways to solve problems. In way-finding tasks, some people may rely more heavily on spatial strategies, others on verbal strategies, and still others, probably the vast majority, on some combination of the two. While this multiplicity may give designers some breathing room, it also means that both the verbal and spatial components of any way-finding system are fundamentally important. An intriguing question is whether there are significant gender differences in preferences for different kinds of cues used in way finding and to what extent the designer should consider these in any plan (see Chapter 2, this volume).

THE RIGHT VIS-À-VIS THE LEFT HEMISPHERE

While emphasis on spatial cognition and to some extent visual imagery has centered on the right hemisphere, the left hemisphere has been implicated in certain aspects of visual imagery (Farah, 1984, 1988b; Farah, Gazzaniga, Holtzman, & Kosslyn, 1985). Specifically, the left hemisphere has a possible role in the image generation process. Given this hypothesized role, questions have been raised about whether spatial functions are dominant in one hemisphere (the right) or are bilaterally represented. In the following section, a number of articles will be reviewed, many of which implicate the left hemisphere in studies that had expected to find the "typical" right hemisphere dominance in spatial tasks. The articles will be covered in some detail to demonstrate the variability in the tasks used and the populations employed in this research.

In reviewing the literature, Morrow and Ratcliff (1988) state that route learning difficulties involving *new surroundings* are related to posterior unilateral right hemisphere lesions, whereas bilateral lesions have been observed in patients who become lost in surroundings *they know*. The role of the right parietal lobe seems more obvious in examples of disturbances of extrapersonal than personal space. Similarly, Kritchevsky (1988) speaks of exocentric object localization as most likely being the function of the right parietal lobe. Personal space involves aspects of one's body in space, as distinguishing between left and right and identifying specific parts of the body. Extrapersonal space thus goes beyond the individual.

Morrow and Ratcliff (1988) suggest that the deficit related to those with bilateral lesions may be memory-based, rather than specifically spatially oriented. As with other investigators, they point to the role of task demands in predicting how involved each hemisphere will be. They review research on the analysis of drawings of bicycles by patients with various lesions. In summarizing this work by others, Morrow and Ratcliff state that those with right hemisphere lesions may have a "scanning or attentional deficit" and may be unable to arrange the elements into a "coherent spatial framework" (p. 12). Problems on the left side may be due to intellectual impairments, motor programming, or practic (movement, action) difficulties. In discussing an unpublished doctoral dissertation by Green, they indicate that "The ability to integrate stimuli into wholes, and to manipulate or transform complex visual stimuli, is a function of the right hemisphere" (p. 14). Green reached his conclusions based on the right hemisphere group's lower scores on tests involving perceptual integration and visualization.

The role of the left hemisphere in spatial processing may involve a variety of functions, according to Mehta and Newcombe (1991). These functions include: (1) managing extraneous and/or distracting visual informations; (2) generating visual images; (3) handling more sophisticated spatial analysis; and (4) understanding Euclidean geometric principles. In their research, men (25 with right and 25 with left hemisphere lesions from military service, and 32 controls) were given five tasks: two kinds of line orientation, two kinds of mental rotation, and a shape matching task. The mental rotation and shape matching tasks all used stimuli based on the Shepard and Metzler 3-dimensional cubes (see Vandenberg and Kuse, 1978). There was the standard mental rotation task; a modification where two of these shapes were shown, one above the other, and the subject's task was to indicate whether they were the same in their rotated form or different; and a shape matching task in which two 3-dimensional cube shapes had to be judged identical or not. For the second and third mental rotation tasks, help was given to the subjects by explaining the structure of the cubes and suggesting a strategy for analysis.

Mehta and Newcombe (1991) argue that the role of the right hemisphere in spatial activity is reserved for the "purest" kind of tasks, without any extraneous or distracting visual information. Both line orientation and angle matching are generally described as pure (Mehta, Newcombe, & Damasio, 1987) because there are no confounding variables such as color, texture, or shape. In this research by Mehta and Newcombe, an even finer distinction is made that angle matching is "purer" than line orientation because angle matching does not have the visual distraction of the multiple lines that occur in the line orientation task. In angle matching, two lines are arrayed in reference to an imaginary horizontal—one above, one below. The subject must determine whether the two lines form the same, or a different, angle with the imaginary horizontal. In the standard line orientation task, 11 lines are arrayed radially in a half circle; each line is numbered in a clockwise fashion with 1 (the first) and 11 (the last) both on the horizontal. Two lines are arrayed above these 11; the subject's task is to indicate to which numbered lines each of the two corresponds in terms of the angle each portends. Results indicated that the left hemisphere group performed significantly worse than the controls on the line orientation task but did not significantly differ from the performance of the right hemisphere group. On the angle matching task, the right hemisphere group was significantly worse (more errors) than the controls and was significantly slower than both the left hemisphere group and controls. Additional analyses revealed that the right hemisphere group's performance on these two tasks did not differ significantly, whereas the left hemisphere group was significantly worse on the line orientation task.

On the standard mental rotation task, the two lesion groups were not significantly different from each other, although the left hemisphere group with above average intelligence was significantly worse than the controls with above average intelligence. Because the scores for this task appeared to be bimodal, groups had been subdivided into those with above and below average intelligence. The left hemisphere group was also significantly worse than the controls on the 3-D cube shape rotation task, in which helpful explanations had been provided. On the simple 3-D cube shape matching task, both groups were significantly worse than the controls.

In considering the poorer performance of the left hemisphere group on the line orientation task, Mehta and Newcombe (1991) point to potentially distracting stimuli inherent in the display. Thus, the left hemisphere may have a role in dealing with distracting or extraneous visual information. When they consider the mental rotation findings, they use Kosslyn and Farah's work as a base and suggest that the left hemisphere may have a role in both image generation and transformation (rotation). This might explain the poorer performance of the left hemisphere on the 3-D shape rotation task.

In conclusion, the salient finding of the current study was that of an important LH [left hemisphere] involvement in spatial processing. Critical intervention of the LH seems necessary to suppress distracting visuospatial material, to understand Euclidean geometry and to perform mental rotations. In contrast, RH [right hemisphere] superiority emerged only for the "purest" of spatial operations. (Mehta & Newcombe, 1991, p. 165)

Thus, we see an emphasis on the right hemisphere as more literal, handling purer spatial functions, and more involved with coordinate relations, with less emphasis on a contribution to higher cognitive processes. The left hemisphere seems to serve more analytical functions, which have been described as more complex.

We have almost exclusively emphasized the role of the left hemisphere for language in cognitive psychology, and have only recently looked at the range of capabilities of right hemisphere language (Gazzaniga, 1983). Similarly, Mehta, Newcombe, and Damasio (1987) point out that little attention has been paid to the *nonverbal* aspects of the left hemisphere. Using 25 left-lesioned and 20 right-lesioned men with missile wounds from World War II, and 22 controls, they examined two visuoperceptual (closure and face recognition) and two visuospatial (line orientation and shape rotation) tasks. The closure task used drawings of human faces with shadows in black and highlights in white. Subjects were to indicate whether they perceived a face, and if so, whether it was a boy or girl, or an old man or an old woman. For the facial recognition task, they were to indicate the identical view of a face from five possibilities in the first six trials (there were variations in the next 16 trials). The standard line orientation involved matching to a sample task (described previously) while shape rotation was the Vandenberg version of the Shepard and Metzler stimuli. They were to match a shape to two rotated versions of that shape plus two distracters.

The results revealed a significant interaction between task and group, with greater right hemisphere impairment on the visuoperceptual tasks and greater left hemisphere difficulty on the spatial tasks. The data present an interesting pattern of dissociation, with more perceptual than spatial information maintained in the left hemisphere and more spatial than perceptual in the right hemisphere following lesions. Mehta and colleagues (1987) note that this outcome is not the typical picture of the dominance of the right hemisphere in spatial processing and state, "The LH deficit on spatial tasks raises the question as to whether there are significant qualitative differences and therefore different mechanisms implicated in the contribution of left and right hemisphere to visuospatial processing" (p. 455). Outcomes such as these point to the differential involvement of both hemispheres in visuospatial processing, with the involvement of the right hemisphere in perceptual processing and the left hemisphere in some aspects of spatial tasks. Because the generation of images has been proposed as a function of the left hemisphere, it is possible that the mental rotation task was tapping that aspect.

Left hemisphere involvement has been postulated in mental rotation tasks by others as well (Fischer & Pellegrino, 1988). Twenty right-handed men in college were shown rotated alphanumeric and unfamiliar characters in either the left or right visual field and had to decide whether they were identical or a mirror image. The stimuli were eight uppercase alphanumeric characters (two numbers, six letters) and eight two-dimensional figures from the Primary Mental Abilities Tests. These unfamiliar characters essentially look like hieroglyphics. These stimuli had been used in earlier research, and Fischer and Pellegrino (1988) questioned how stimulus characteristics influenced the outcome in this kind of research.

Each trial consisted of the presentation of two stimuli: an upright version and a rotated comparison. These two were either the same or mirror images. To ensure that the comparison was presented to the contralateral hemisphere, the upright standard was always presented in the center of the screen (for 1.8 seconds) and then was joined by a comparison about 8 centimeters away (for 200 milli-seconds); then both went off together. The rotated figure could appear in the following rotations: 0, 50, 100, or 150 degrees. Beyond results consistent with earlier literature (latency increases linearly with degree of rotation), only the visual field effect occurred with regard to lateralization. The latency data revealed an advantage for the right visual field (left hemisphere), whereas the error data showed that the left hemisphere was better when the stimuli were alphanumeric, with no hemisphere differences for unfamiliar characters. This finding challenges the role of the right hemisphere in spatial rotation and adds further data for considering the contribution of the left hemisphere. Fischer and Pellegrino (1988) suggest that some aspect of the process of mental rotation is functional in the left hemisphere, and that nonspatial aspects of the task may have yielded the right visual field (left hemisphere) advantage. "The current instantiation of a mental rotation task produced a 'left hemisphere' performance superiority, suggesting that one or more components of task performance may be differentially processed by the hemispheres. Their combined lateralization effects most likely determine the overall performance asymmetry" (p. 13).

Corballis and Sergent (1989a) have also found left hemisphere involvement in mental rotation tasks. They examined mental rotation in normals (133 college students) as well as one commissurotomized subject, L.B., who had a complete forebrain commissurotomy for epilepsy at age 13. The task was to judge whether rotated letters (F, P, or R), shown to either the left or right visual hemifield, were normal or mirror images. This task is similar to the one used by Fischer and Pellegrino, but instead of using comparisons, just a single stimulus had to be judged on each trial. The study yielded an array of unexpected results, in that there were more errors to normal than backward letters, and a significant right hemifield advantage for reaction time (faster to normal than backward stimuli). For L.B., there was a significant left hemifield advantage in reaction time, confirming earlier data on the left hemifield advantage for mental rotation stimuli for L.B. (Corballis & Sergent, 1988, 1989b). "Perhaps the major conclusion to be drawn from this result is that visual-hemifield differences should not be interpreted too readily in terms of hemispheric specialization" (1989a, p. 21). Corballis and Sergent suggest that the task of identification (these were letters) may be processed more readily in the left hemisphere whereas the actual mental rotation aspect is right-hemispheric. The authors also speculate that we do not detect the mental rotation component in the right hemisphere in normals in visual-hemifield research because the left hemisphere's advantage in identification overrides it. This is an important point and argues for more research that uses both lesioned and normal subjects. Each category of subjects tells us something different about the complexity of spatial processing. Although it is tempting to conclude that the data from lesioned subjects give us the veridical or true picture of hemispheric processing, we have no way of knowing about integrated processing without using normal subjects. On the other hand, the processing in normal subjects is difficult to tease apart because of multiple approaches that may be used to solve problems that we have traditionally labeled "spatial" or "verbal."

It is also important for us to keep track of the kinds of tasks used in these studies. While a good number of studies have employed stimuli based on the Shepard and Metzler three-dimensional cubes, there are exceptions. Using notably different tasks, Butters and Barton (1970) examined the effect of parietal lobe damage on the ability to perform reversible operations in space. They used 50 patients from the Boston VA Hospital, 31 with left hemisphere damage, 4 with right hemisphere damage, and 15 with no cerebral injury. Neurological evaluation led them to create two groups based on the degree of impairment: severe and moderate. All of the right hemisphere damage subjects fell into the severe group. Subjects performed three tests that stressed reversible operations or transformations: a stick test; a village scene test; and a pool reflection test. The stick test used four wooden sticks 5½ inches long, of which the top ½ inch was painted black (like a long fireplace match). The subjects had to copy the examiner's pattern of sticks under conditions of rotation or straightforward matching. In the rotation condition, the subjects were told to " 'make your pattern look to you like mine looks to me' " (Butters & Barton, 1970, p. 207). The 10 patterns each used from 2–4 sticks. The village scene test used a three-dimensional scale model of a village with three mountains, a gas station, a church, a house, a barn, and trees, cows, and cars. The model was somewhat reminiscent of Piaget's three mountains array. Three color photos of each of the four sides of the village were taken; of these, one picture was accurate; the other two had errors. In a variety of perspective tasks, the subject always had to select the correct view from a group of six photos that represented the village perspective about which he was being asked. In the pool reflection task, items were drawn on 5 × 7-inch cards. These objects look like geometric figures with some modification (e.g., a triangle with one darkened angle). There was a standard object in the first row, and four comparisons in the row beneath it. Subjects were to select from the four comparisons which one was identical to the figure in the first row except that it was rotated 180 degrees in the same plane.

Those with severe left or right parietal damage performed more poorly on the village scene (familiar objects) and stick construction test (unfamiliar objects) than those with mild parietal damage or controls. Those with right parietal damage (all in the category had injuries judged severe) were worse on the village scene test than those with severe damage in the left hemisphere. Butters and Barton (1970) suggest that a general inability to incorporate different perspectives may result from parietal lobe injury. This study introduces yet another cluster of tasks and also points to the importance of trying to quantify the degree of cerebral damage in reaching conclusions about spatial abilities. Those with severe right parietal damage were worse on the village scene test, a test that emphasized mental rotation more than the others in this research. However, it should be pointed out that the lack of a right hemisphere group with mild damage limits the comparisons of performance that can be made in this study.

In an often quoted study because of its anomalous findings, Ornstein, Johnstone, Herron, and Swencionis (1980) explored the role of the hemispheres in visuospatial and verbal tasks using EEG recordings. Also, they used normal subjects (20 right-handed subjects; 10 men, 10 women) in a field where the early work pointing to the role of the right hemisphere in spatial behavior typically came from individuals with brain injury (missile wounds, lesions). They state that EEG readings are less restrictive than other methods such as reaction time, dichotic listening, or taschistoscopic recognition.

There were seven tasks (six spatial tasks and one verbal-analytic task). In each task, subjects had a target provided on the left side of the page and a series of five potential matches on the right side. Subjects were informed that any of the choices might be correct. The first task was the Nebes arc–circle matching. In this task, a circle is presented followed by arcs (portions of circles) that could be possible matches. The second task was the Nebes circle–circle matching, in which a circle is presented followed by five other circles of various circumferences, any of which could be a match. The third task was modified from the Minnesota Paper Form Board test. A complex figure is presented in sections. Then the subject is to select from five assembled or constructed figures that could have been made from the sectioned target. The fourth task was picture completion, in which a silhouette of an object, animal, or human was partly degraded to make it difficult to recognize. Subjects were told to match the degraded target against other nonidentical versions (also degraded) of the target. The fifth task was a mental rotation task modified from Shepard and Metzler. A target (a 10 sequence three-d cube) was to be matched to choices that were either the same figure rotated in three-dimensional space or a different figure. The last spatial task was face recognition. The subject had to match a target photo of a face to possibilities that were rotated slightly or lighted differently. The last task, selecting the correct definition, involved verbal-analytic analysis. Subjects had to match a target word to a synonym in a series of possibilities.

Based on earlier research, greater left hemisphere involvement was expected for the verbal definitions whereas greater right hemisphere involvement was expected for the spatial tasks. Surprisingly, the mental rotation task primarily engaged the *left* hemisphere. The part–whole portion of Nebes's (arc–circle) test also primarily involved the left hemisphere, whereas the whole–whole portion of the task (circle–circle) primarily involved the right hemisphere. In explaining the results, Ornstein and colleagues (1980) point to DeRenzi's claim that the left hemisphere is involved when you go beyond the perceptual level and the spatial processing increases in complexity. Regarding the Nebes circle–circle matching task, they claim that this comes closest to a pure spatial task in the sense that it cannot be done with an analytic strategy. In showing the lowest alpha power in both the central and parietal areas, they state that it is the one that most involves the right hemisphere. Their explanation is presented here at some length because of its theoretical value:

One explanation which fits the findings seen here is that it is not spatial tasks themselves which engage the RH, but approaching the tasks with simultaneous-synthetic strategies which the RH is specialized to use. A spatial task lends itself to this type of solution, particularly if it is simple, and this bias could account for the greater competence of the RH typically found in spatial tasks. However, when the task becomes more complex, such as Mental Rotation, an analytic strategy may become more appealing, as the problem is verbally analyzed and coded, regardless of whether the problem is verbal or not. Similarly, the RH capacity for simple language . . . may employ a simultaneous-synthetic understanding, while the normally observed LH bias in language tasks could be due to the ordinarily more complex characteristics of natural language tasks. (p. 61)

Summary

The relationship between the two cerebral hemispheres is complex. Our understanding of it is changing rapidly as data emerge that redefine the hemispheres' abilities with increasing sophistication and precision. A sense is emerging that the nature of the task will influence the involvement of the hemispheres, and not simply in a left-takes-language and right-takes-space manner. The left hemisphere appears to contribute more significantly to tasks that involve greater analysis of stimuli, whereas the right seems to adopt a "fresh" approach, with a predilection for novel and "pure" stimuli.

A picture is also emerging that different results occur depending on the use of normal versus lesioned subjects. It seems that a left hemisphere involvement in spatial tasks is more likely to be seen in normal subjects. This may reflect the multiple strategies available to normal subjects, perhaps with a heavier emphasis on verbal encoding and analysis. The right hemisphere, particularly the parietal lobe, may well be critical to spatial behavior, but again the variability in the research points to the flexibility of strategies humans can employ. Designers must create environments that are rich in cues and that cover multiple possibilities for encoding and analysis.

Let us now briefly focus our attention on a specific brain component, the hippocampus, that has been implicated in spatial behavior.

THE ROLE OF THE HIPPOCAMPUS

No discussion of the cognitive architecture of spatial behavior would be complete without a look at the hippocampus. In terms of brain function, much of the early focus on spatial behavior centered on the specific role of the hippocampus (Milner, 1965; Muller, Kubie, Bostock, Taube, & Quirk, 1991; O'Keefe, 1991; O'Keefe & Nadel, 1978; Thinus-Blanc, Save, Buhot, & Poucet, 1991; VanPraag, Dreyfus, & Black, 1994). More recently, the view of the hippocampus has broadened to include a spectrum of memory functions, some of which relate to spatial behavior (Squire, 1987, 1992, 1993; Squire & Knowlton, 1995; Suzuki, Zola-Morgan, Squire, & Amaral, 1993; Zola-Morgan & Squire, 1990; Zola-Morgan, Squire, & Ramus, 1994). For example, Muller and colleagues (1991) suggest that the context sensitivity noted in neural firings in rat brains is a subcomponent of a more general information-handling process and indicates great flexibility for the role of the hippocampus. Sholl (1992) argues that a variety of mind-brain systems contribute to different aspects of spatial orientation. So, not only has the view of hippocampal functioning broadened, but the functional architecture of spatial behavior may not be exclusively tied to the hippocampus.

Some of the emphasis on the special role of the hippocampus in spatial cognition can be linked to the early work of O'Keefe and Nadel (1978) and Milner (1965). In Milner's early study of patients with unilateral cortical lesions, removal of the hippocampus after right temporal lobectomy critically influenced performance in a visually guided stylus maze task (discussed earlier in this chapter). What O'Keefe and Nadel argued in their seminal book *The Hippocampus As a Cognitive Map* was that "the hippocampus is the core of a neural memory system providing an objective spatial framework within which the items and events of an organism's experience are located and interrelated" (p. 1). Rather than view the cognitive map as a model or picture that looks like what it represents, they argue that it is "an information structure from which map-like images can be reconstructed and from which behaviour dependent upon place information can be generated" (p. 78). O'Keefe and Nadel discuss place and misplace systems, with place systems providing information about places in the observer's environment, their spatial relations, and specific objects in specific places, whereas the misplace system signals changes in a particular place. Egocentric spatial systems are referred to as taxon systems, whereas systems that are observer-independent or Euclidean-based are referred to as locate space. They are trying to provide a neural model for a spatial map, with the mapping system containing three sections, one for each part of the hippocampus (fascia dentata, CA3, CA1). O'Keefe (1993) has argued that the anatomical and physiological aspects of the hippocampus create a spatial mapping system and that neuronal elements themselves create a vector space, predisposing them to register place information. The hippo-campus is postulated to deal with space in an absolute rather than an ego-centric manner. Humans suffering hippocampal damage were hypothesized to perform poorly when the task involved knowledge or representation of the integrated or total environment, integrated in an absolute rather than a relative (egocentric) sense. Others have also discussed this kind of abso-lute knowledge, some using geographical language (Lieblich & Arbib, 1982).

Nadel (1990) provides a useful overview of three kinds of spatial systems postulated to exist in animals: (1) dead reckoning—recording the speed and direction of one's movements; (2) landmarks—making frequent sightings on individual landmarks; and (3) relational landmark use—using land-marks relationally or in what we might call a cognitive map. These func-tions, progressively more sophisticated, are also called orientation, guidance, and place systems. In reviewing the literature, Nadel notes that damage to the hippocampus may make use of relational knowledge im-possible; it is the place system with which the hippocampus is involved.

Not all researchers are content with this spatial emphasis for the hip-pocampus. Squire (1987, 1992) has directed our attention more toward the memory than the spatial components of hippocampal functioning. Dis-cussing the patient R.B. who had a lesion in area CA1 of the hippocampus Squire (1987) outlines this memory component: "Indeed, the fact that the CA1 lesion resulted in amnesia shows that the hippocampus must perform some computation upon newly processed information, if that information is to be stored in an enduring and useful form" (p. 194). On the other hand, the hippocampus is not solely responsible for memory, as the cortex adjacent to the hippocampal region has also been implicated (Alvarez, Zola-Morgan, & Squire, 1995). While Squire, as well as others, has noted that varieties of memory (e.g., procedural, declarative) exist, he argues that it is declarative memory that is impaired when medial temporal and dien-cephalic structures are affected in amnesia.

Pointing out the limitation in the O'Keefe and Nadel approach to the hippocampus, Squire states that,

a literally spatial hypothesis about hippocampal function does not fit well with the findings from the human cases. The human cases have a memory impairment, not an impairment restricted to spatial operations. Patients with right medial temporal resections do have difficulty remembering the spatial location of objects (Smith and

Milner, 1981). But they also have difficulty in image-mediated verbal learning (Jones-Gotman and Milner, 1978) and facial recognition (Milner, 1968). Similarly, H.M.'s amnesia includes the spatial dimension but is not limited to it. (1987, pp. 221–222)

While Squire acknowledges the difficulty in separating a discussion of space from a discussion of memory, he argues that our greater understanding of the varieties of memory function have helped us to form a new interpretation of the tasks that remain unimpaired after hippocampal damage. It is not that they are nonspatial, but that they are nondeclarative memory functions.

Squire (1992) describes the role of the hippocampus in memory as time limited. The data indicate that very remote memories are typically preserved in patients with hippocampal damage. When affected, these memories tend to be temporally graded, with the more recent memories being more severely affected. "Memory is initially dependent on the hippocampus formation, but its role diminishes as a more permanent memory is gradually established elsewhere, probably in neocortex" (p. 196). If you have ever seen the striking videotape of Clive Waring (from the PBS series *The Mind*), the British composer and conductor who suffered severe hippocampal damage, the role of the hippocampus that Squire outlines is strikingly evident. Waring lives in the moment, with no ability to consolidate or transfer declarative memory to a permanent store; Clive suffers profound anterograde amnesia (forgetfulness for new information).

Despite the more broadly defined role of the hippocampus outlined by Squire and others, there are researchers whose work gives greater emphasis to the spatial role of the hippocampus, and the debate is far from over. For example, in discussing a model of hippocampal functioning, Burgess, Recce, and O'Keefe (1994) state, "The popularly held view that the hippocampus is a more general store for declarative memories is undergoing revision because much of the deficit in short-term memory tasks appears to be accounted for by lesions of the perirhinal cortex rather than the hippocampus . . ." (p. 1065). Sherry and Healy (1998) point to differences in procedure (i.e., lesioning vs. other cell destruction techniques) and anatomical specification (i.e., how researchers actually define the hippocampus) as possible explanations for the varying results regarding the role of the hippocampus. They also state that the larger hippocampal size in animals that are brood parasites, search widely for mates, and have caches of food is evidence that is better explained by the spatial memory hypothesis than the declarative memory hypothesis.

Among the strongest proponents of the role of the hippocampus in spatial behavior is Maguire (see, e.g., Maguire et al., 1998; Maguire, Frackowiak, & Frith, 1996, 1997). Maguire (1997, pp. 1479–1480) states,

Most human spatial behaviour takes place in large-scale, spatially extended environments. This requires the ability to recall points in space that cannot be perceived simultaneously in one field of view. This ability, common to most animals, is subserved in humans by a network of brain regions involving the hippocampus. The brain regions developed for this phylogenetically old ability, particularly the hippocampus, have undoubtedly now also been recruited for other non-topographical functions with similar processing requirements. The exact kind of processing mechanisms extant in this domain remain to be specified.

In one of the experiments that leads Maguire to her emphasis on the spatial role of the hippocampus (Maguire et al., 1998), positron emission tomography (PET) scans are used to examine subjects' behavior with a virtual reality town made familiar through earlier computer exploration. In different conditions, subjects could navigate toward the goal directly, or they confronted detours. This performance was compared to a task where they followed arrows through the town (which thus did not necessitate an internal cognitive map). Performance was also assessed in a static condition where feature identification was required. The results indicated that there was higher activity in the right hippocampus when subjects were navigating toward the unseen goal. More noteworthy, the more accurate the way finding, the higher the activation in this area. Research by Maguire, Frackowiak, and Frith (1996) and by Ghaem and colleagues (1997) also supports a primary role of the hippocampus in handling topographical information, whether in encoding or in retrieval.

One final study will serve to illustrate this line of research that emphasizes the role of the hippocampus in spatial cognition. In an innovative study, Maguire, Frackowiak, and Frith (1997) examined the PET scans of experienced taxi drivers in London. Their primary spatial task was to describe the shortest legal route between an origin and a destination. There were also tasks involving landmarks, and a number of nontopographical tasks. Of particular note, the results indicated that "both retrieval of landmark knowledge and retrieval of complex route information activate many similar brain regions, but the right hippocampus is activated only during routes recall" (p. 7105).

Summary

Again what we see in information about the hippocampus is that a strict modularity view (i.e., that the hippocampus deals with space) may not represent the array of functions handled there. A dynamic debate continues to be waged about the role(s) of the hippocampus. Certainly the point of view represented by Squire must be acknowledged, but Maguire's research demonstrating the role of the right hippocampus, in particular, in spatial cognition in real-world and complex environments is convincing.

Nadel's three spatial systems (orientation, guidance, and place) are particularly useful in thinking about the requirements for way finding. Relational landmark use requires a number of landmarks, and their arrangement may or may not facilitate cognitive map formation. As we will see in Chapter 5, there are design principles for the macroenvironment that facilitate cognitive map formation. Many of these principles focus on the role of landmarks.

EXPLANATIONS FOR CEREBRAL LATERALIZATION

Given the complex relationship between the hemispheres that has been reviewed in some detail in this chapter, it is natural to wonder about the reasons for their differences. It is not the purpose of this chapter to explain the causes of cerebral lateralization and functional asymmetry (the causes remain under debate). At the same time, a brief examination of some of the more viable explanations may help the reader better understand the major issues. The biological underpinnings of most of these theoretical candidates also may become clearer in the process.

Geschwind and Galaburda's Theory

One of the better known theories of cerebral lateralization has been developed by Geschwind and Galaburda (Geschwind, 1974, 1980; Geschwind & Galaburda, 1985, 1987; McManus & Bryden, 1991). A variety of factors (in fact, Geschwind & Galaburda, 1985, list over 10 of them) contribute to the foundation of cerebral lateralization, from the asymmetry of the brain and laterality in developmental disorders, to hormonal influences on the brain and genetic studies of handedness. Their theory of lateralization centers on the concepts of standard and anomalous dominance and fundamentally on the effects of testosterone. The standard pattern is a strong left hemisphere dominance for both language and handedness (and thus right-handedness), with a right hemisphere dominance for other functions. The definition of anomalous dominance is quite straightforward: a pattern that differs from the standard. Geschwind and Galaburda postulate an innate propensity for left hemisphere dominance for both language and handedness and the possibility that influences during fetal development can attenuate this innate bias, creating random dominance. Their theory can be (and often is) contrasted with Annett's (1980, 1985) theory of handedness. In Annett's theory, it is hypothesized that some people carry a right-shift gene that increases the probability of the left hemisphere's dominance for language; lack of this gene leads to a random determination of laterality (see the section on handedness in this chapter for a description of Annett's theory),

Whereas Annett argues for right-shift influences, which can drive the system from randomness to left-dominance, we argue for left-shift influences (as proposed by Corballis and Morgan), which drive the system to symmetry. Reverse asymmetry is uncommon. An important reason for our formation is the fact that fetal brains at very early stages typically show asymmetry favoring the left side. (Geschwind & Galaburda, 1987, p. 236)

The theory is a comprehensive one and includes a discussion of the role of testosterone levels on the brain and immune system and its relationship to the occurrence of anomalous dominance (McManus & Bryden, 1991).

Sex Differences in Brain Lateralization

It has been argued that cognitive functions are represented more bilaterally in women than they are in men. This situation is hypothesized to occur either through less specific assignment of function to one hemisphere in women or through stronger interhemispheric commissural connections in women (Kimura & Hampson, 1993), although there is disagreement about the validity of these hypotheses. Some researchers criticize the discussion of sex differences in cognitive ability and the concept that there are biological underpinnings (Sherman, 1967, 1978; Sherman & Denmark, 1978). They further note "the flimsy quality of the theories of biological influence" (Sherman, 1978, p. 172). Numerous researchers present arguments to proceed slowly in this area because of ambiguous support for sexual dimorphism in the brain (Janowsky, 1989), inconsistent mental rotation differences (Jones & Anuza, 1982), response strategy rather than spatial ability differences (Bryden, 1980), publication bias (Richardson, 1991), or questions concerning the clinical significance of sex differences in sexual dimorphism (Hier & Kaplan, 1980). However, the majority of the literature points to the validity of dimorphism.

Although some of this material was outlined in Chapter 2 on gender differences, for example, that in general men score higher on tests of mental rotation (Hyde, Geiringer, & Yen, 1975; Linn & Peterson, 1986; Wilson & Vandenberg, 1978), this section will provide more neuropsychological detail about these differences. Those interested in such topics as the differences between early and late maturers (Waber, 1976, 1977), the effects of toy play (Tracy, 1987, 1990; Unger & Crawford, 1990), and the effect size of gender differences in cognitive abilities (Hyde, 1981, 1990) are directed to Chapter 2.

DeVries, DeBruin, Uylings, and Corner (1984) devote an entire volume of *Progress in Brain Research* to sex differences in brain lateralization.

Findings that are discussed in this volume include the fact that extent of exposure to testicular hormones determines brain organization (Gorski, 1984), that sex differences exist in the size of the cortex and hippocampus, and in particular that dendritic structure varies by sex (Juraska, 1984), that sexual dimorphism in spatial behavior exists (Beatty, 1984), and that visual field asymmetry differences indicate women possess less asymmetry in perceptual tasks than do men (Kimura & Harshman, 1984). Findings are also presented that there are biological correlates of individuals who are extremely gifted in mathematics, that these people are predominantly men, and that there are correlates with left-handedness, immune disorders, and myopia (Benbow & Benbow, 1984). The DeVries and colleagues volume is but one compilation of research (another is Wittig and Petersen, 1979) on the topic of the neuropsychological aspects of sex differences in cognitive functioning.

Given the biological emphasis in discussing brain lateralization, a number of researchers have begun to incorporate evolutionary perspectives in their discussions of sex differences and laterality. Harris (1978) outlines the types of activities in which the performance of men is superior to that of women, pointing to support for the hypothesis that there is greater lateralization in men. Tying this to an evolutionary perspective, Harris states that it is "reasonable to suppose that spatial visualization and an ability to anticipate the results of a given blow would have high survival value in such practices and, therefore, would be selected for the practitioners" (p. 484).

One of the major proponents of the biological bases of cerebral lateralization is Kimura (1983, 1987), who reports on data from a clinical population of 81 patients (1983) with lesions restricted to anterior or posterior regions. Kimura argues that sex differences in speech and praxic organization exist in the left hemisphere, and that it is not merely the case that women have language represented more bilaterally than men. The impressive data were that in men, of the 41% who were aphasic, 70% had posterior lesions. In the women patients, of the 31% who were aphasic, 80% had lesions in the anterior portion. These data produced a three-way interaction between lesion locus, sex, and aphasia. "Thus, there is the possibility that some functions (e.g., linguistic) are more diffusely represented in the female brain, and thus show more duplication between hemispheres (McGlone, 1980), whereas others (e.g., praxic functions) are focally organized" (Kimura, 1983, p. 31).

Kimura (1983) provides a provocative evolutionary explanation of the possible origins of these regional brain differences:

If evolutionary pressures were greater in males for developing the ability to encode certain spatial information (Maccoby & Jacklin, 1974) about the external environment, then there might be some tendency to develop motor skill vis-à-vis the distance receptors, particularly vision. This might account for a 'migration' of certain aspects of motor control to posterior regions in males, whereas in females no such evolutionary pressures operated. Alternatively, one might equally well speculate that praxic function in females migrated anteriorly because it was advantageous for fine motor skills, at which females excel, (Tyler, 1965), or advantageous to be coordinated with speech-articulatory function, at which females also excel (Maccoby, 1966). (p. 32)

Kimura and Hampson (1993) review evidence that supports the greater functional symmetry of women. The kinds of data include evidence of less asymmetry of women on a number of perceptual tests, fewer performance deficits after injury to a given hemisphere, and lower incidence of developmental disorders such as aphasia after left-hemisphere damage. However, the largest difference according to these researchers is related to the ways in which the anterior and posterior regions of the brain contribute to speech, praxic, motor, and constructional behavior. The authors argue that there is greater concentration of these functions in the anterior portion of the brain for women than for men.

Gaulin (1995) also uses an evolutionary approach to explain sex differences in the brain, and specifically those involving the spatial behavior of rodents and birds. Voles have both polygynous (e.g., meadow voles) and monogamous (e.g., pine voles) species. Range sizes that differed statistically by sex in polygynous voles were related to superior performance by males on spatial tests in the laboratory as well as to larger hippocampi. In the reproductive behavior of a polygynous species, it would be advantageous to have a larger range encompassing more females. It would also be important to keep track of their spatial location. Although the work with the spatial abilities of polygynous versus monogamous species suggests the role of biology, Gaulin (and others) point out that *experience* could just as easily lead to the same result: "The experience hypothesis predicts an ontogenetic effect of range size and the sexual selection hypothesis predicts an evolutionary effect of range size" (p. 1219). Gaulin and colleagues addressed this question by trapping voles in the wild and then testing their first-generation offspring who had been reared in small mouse cages since birth. " . . . this extreme manipulation of experience had no effect on maze performance; the spatially deprived group performed just as well as did their wild-caught parents" (p. 1219). This evidence is thus consistent with the evolutionary effect of range size and the sexual selection hypothesis.

Gaulin (1995) also discusses evidence from research on the brown-headed cowbird, a brood parasite in which the females lay eggs in others' nests and their young are consequently reared by other hosts (see also Sherry, Forbes, Khurgel, & Ivy, 1993; Sherry, Jacobs, & Gaulin, 1992). These female cowbirds must search for available and appropriate spots to lay their eggs, whereas the males are not involved in such searches. It is the female in this species that has a larger hippocampus. This points to selection pressures, in this case nest searches and periodic nest visits, rather than to the role of maleness or femaleness per se in shaping spatial ability (Gaulin, 1995). Gaulin argues that sex differences in spatial ability are not a function of maleness or femaleness but rather "evolve in response to the particular reproductive problems and conditions that have faced each sex over the species' evolutionary history" (p. 1220). The brown-headed cowbird thus provides an ideal comparison: a species in which females have greater navigational demands than do males.

Gaulin's analyses suggest an interesting question: What factors would lead to women who have high spatial ability? Casey and Brabeck (1990) combined Sherman's (1978) bent twig hypothesis ("as the twig is bent, so grows the tree") with Annett's (1985) theory of handedness to predict what constellation of factors would result in women who would excel on a spatial task. These would be women who combine the genetic predisposition for spatial ability (which men are postulated to have) and the appropriate experience with spatial activities. Annett proposes that the optimum genotype for mental rotation ability in women is right-handed women who have non-right-handed relatives. Casey and Brabeck add a requirement for the experiential component: these women must have had involvement with activities that emphasize three-dimensional manipulation and visualization. Model building and carpentry are examples that fall into this category. They used the Vandenberg and Kuse (1978) mental rotation task and a shortened form of the Spatial Activities Questionnaire. The form was shortened to include only items that involved mental rotation. The scale consisted of the following items: sketching house plans, carpentry, electrical circuitry, building go-carts, building model planes, and blowing glass. Subjects rated the frequency of experience with each item on a scale where 1 = never to 6 = more than once a week at some point in their lives. Casey and Brabeck made the assumption that mental rotation skills could be developed with considerable experience in any *one* of these activities. Participants were divided into high (at least a "4" on any one activity) and low spatial experience groups based on their scale responses. The target group (mixed family right-handed women with high spatial experience) outperformed the other three combinations of family handedness and spatial experience. When the authors used a more stringent criterion for high spatial experience (a score of at least "5" on any of the activities), even larger effects for the target group emerged. The data thus provided support for Annett's hypotheses that those with mixed family right-handedness (right shift heterozygous constellation) would have better spatial abilities.

But not every study supports sex differences in lateralization. Kingsberg, LaBarba, and Bowers (1987) used an approach infrequently employed in this literature: a dual-task paradigm. The dual task typically involves performing a manual component like finger tapping while simultaneously doing a spatial or verbal task. Because the findings using this paradigm had been mixed, Kingsberg and colleagues decided to look further. They used block design problems with two levels of difficulty (each level to be solved with the left or right hand) and finger tapping with the left or right hand. There were a number of hypotheses: (1) in the easy block condition, both men and women should show right hemisphere dominance, indicated by interference with the rate of tapping with the left hand; and (2) in the difficult condition, they expected right lateralization in men (asymmetrical declines in left hand tapping) and bilateralization in women (symmetrical declines in the tapping of both hands). Furthermore, they explored the role of verbal mediation in visuospatial processing and hypothesized that women were more likely to use a verbal strategy in this kind of visuospatial task (block design) and that women should slow down in solving block problems when verbalizing.

Finger tapping was measured with a telegraph key on a wooden base. The number of finger taps made in 15 seconds was recorded. The block designs came from the WISC-R and the WAIS-R. For baseline measures, the subjects tapped alone with one hand then the other and also did the easy and difficult block designs with each hand. Then there were four conditions involving finger tapping, hand, and difficulty: tapping—left and easy block—right hand; tapping—right and easy block—left hand; tapping—left and difficult block—right hand; tapping—right and difficult block—left hand. In the second portion of the study, vocalizations were done alone and then concurrently with each of the two levels of spatial tasks: easy block—left hand and right hand; difficult block—left hand and right hand. The vocalizations consisted of repeating the phrase "cat, dog, horse" as many times as possible in a 15-second stretch.

Results were analyzed in terms of a change score (baseline performance minus dual task score). Results indicated that both men and women were slower on both levels of block design with right hand tapping. Therefore, there were no differential lateralization patterns in men and women. Furthermore, the level of difficulty had no effect on the rate of tapping. But tapping with the right hand and doing block design with the left was hard for both men and women. When the right hand does the block design and the left the tapping, both sexes seem to benefit in terms of spatial processing speed. Thus, not only do these data fail to indicate differential cerebral lateralization in men and women, they also do not show a right hemisphere advantage for manipulospatial processing.

When the verbal strategies were analyzed, there was a main effect for gender. With vocalization, women were slower in completing the block design than were men. There was also an interaction effect showing that women were more affected solving the difficult block design. Men actually took less time in the dual task condition with reference to baseline measures. It is possible that women are employing a verbal strategy more heavily when faced with the more challenging level of block design. Again, these results show the complex nature of the cerebral patterns underlying spatial behavior. It may be fair to state that there are differences in the nature of the performance of men and women on various tasks, but these differences vary and we are still grasping for adequate explanations for the differences.

Hormonal Effects

Continuing an overview of explanations for cerebral lateralization, we turn to the role of hormones. The question of hormonal effects is intimately related to questions about sexual dimorphism in the brain, as exposure to prenatal hormones has a permanent organizational impact on CNS and gonadal development. In general, exposure to androgens in the first several prenatal months has a masculinizing effect on the brain and gonads and later sexual development, whereas absence of androgens has a feminizing action.

In discussing hormonal influences, it is helpful to make a distinction between their organizational versus activational effects. Providing an excellent review, Weekes (1994) discusses the differences between the organizational and activational effects of hormones. Organizational effects typically occur in the perinatal environment. They result in structural changes that are permanent and are likely to be different in males and females given the availability and activity of specific hormones. Activational effects are linked to temporary changes (most often seen in adulthood). An example is the menstrual cycle. When the hormone underlying the change is reduced or absent, the effects also diminish or disappear. The data generally indicate that neonatal testosterone affects the organization of the brain and is related marginally but consistently to improved spatial ability. The activational effects of hormones on spatial ability are less clear. It is possible that the activational effects of hormones amplify the organizational effects, yielding a greater disparity in the differences between the sexes in how they use environmental cues and how they respond to anxiety (Johnston & File, 1991). Frye (1995) has shown that the activational effects of hormones play a significant role in the performance differences between male and female rats in the acquisition of a novel task (Morris water maze).

Witelson (1991) stresses the role of sex hormones early in development as the trigger for asymmetrical brain development, with the morphology of the corpus callosum differing between the sexes. In men, the callosal and splenial areas have tended to be larger. Witelson has hypothesized that there is a difference between men and women at the histological level, in particular in the number of callosal axons interconnecting the two hemispheres, especially in the temporo-parietal cortex.

I hypothesize that in men, lower levels of testosterone lead to less axon elimination, a larger callosal isthmus and associated temporo-parietal structures, greater left handedness (less consistent-right-hand preference), and greater bihemispheric representation of cognitive skills (less functional asymmetry), and that these same factors are not similarly operative in the development of the female brain. (p. 143)

Witelson discusses the possibility that the process of sexual differentiation in different areas of the brain may be independent. This is referred to as "neural sexual mosaicism." The research reviewed in this article focuses in particular on the temporo-parietal areas as one of those that is independently influenced. "Sexual mosaicism of the brain also may underlie, within each sex, the dissociations among numerous factors including early neuroendocrine events, neuroanatomical features, cognitive abilities, patterns of functional asymmetry, sexual orientation, and sex identity" (pp. 147–148). While there are researchers still discussing behavior on a molar level (see, Sharps, Welton, & Price, 1993; Tanaka, Panter, & Winborne, 1988), evidence supporting functional differences between the sexes is increasingly being presented at neurophysiological levels of analysis.

In reviewing the animal literature, Kimura and Hampson (1993) conclude that androgens, both pre- and perinatally, play a critical role in organizing the brain in terms of sexually dimorphic behaviors, including those based on spatial cognition. They as well as other authors have noted a curvilinear relationship between androgenization and spatial ability, with the optimal level of spatial performance occurring in women when they have a higher level of androgenization than the average woman, whereas for men the optimal pattern occurs when men have a lower level of androgenization than the average man. Kimura and Hampson review evidence of androgenization and tomboyishness, masculine toy preferences, congenital adrenal hyperplasia (CAH), and androgen exposure in women related to higher performance on spatial tasks. They also review evidence of generally superior male than female rodent performance in a radial arm maze (Williams, Barnett, & Meck, 1990). Their assessment will provide an outline for this section. I am selectively reviewing research they cite in their article and elaborating on studies I judge of particular importance. Additional research has also been included.

As Kimura and Hampson (1993) point out, evidence from work with rats has provided important data regarding spatial ability, and the Williams and colleagues (1990) study is one of the more helpful in understanding hormonal effects. Williams and colleagues did a series of experiments involving neonatally castrated (feminized) and control male rats (normals) and female rats treated neonatally with estradiol benzoate (androgenized) and female controls (normals). Regarding their findings, Williams and colleagues state that the data suggest that "early exposure to gonadal steroids (probably estradiol) improves acquisition of spatial tasks by reorganizing and simplifying associational-perceptual processes that guide spatial ability" (p. 84). Essentially, when male rates are neonatally castrated they behave more like normal female rats in terms of performance on a spatial task. Conversely, newborn females perform more like male rats (fewer errors than control females) when exposed to estradiol benzoate for Days 1, 3, 5, 7, and 9 postnatally.

One of the fascinating aspects of this experimental series on the organizational effects of hormones is the information it provides about what kinds of cues these rats employ. Rats with " 'male-type brains' " (female estrogen and male control groups) were more likely to use geometric cues such as the shape of the room than they were to use landmarks (movable objects in the room such as a table, chair, rat cage cart, and experimenter). Alterations to the geometry of the room (by hanging sheets of opaque black fabric to change its shape) significantly affected performance in the male control and female estrogen group. For the female control and male neonatally castrated animals, changes in geometry and landmarks both affected performance.

The general finding . . . is that rats exposed to neonatal hormones solve spatial problems by selecting a single aspect of the environment that is easily, perhaps preattentively, detected. This aspect appears to be a coordinate system defined by the shape of the environment. In contrast, rats exposed neonatally to no or low levels of gonadal steroids use two or more features from different dimensions (e.g., landmarks and geometry) in order to locate a target. (p. 92)

Rats with female-type brains may take longer in the acquisition of tasks because they are learning more than one type of cue. These findings may have implications for human behavior.

The work of Williams and colleagues is reminiscent of the Ames perceptual distorted room paradigm, which shows that humans focus on the overall frame of the room to maintain the perception of parallelism/right angles at the expense of the absolute size of the individuals in the room. In this funhouse room, what we see appears to be a giant and a midget standing at opposite ends of a "regular" room, when in fact it is the room that is irregular, high at the "midget's" end and low at the "giant's" end. This finding may have implications for the design of environments, instructing us to pay attention first and foremost to their overall shape and layout. Studying the effect of good plan configuration, Weisman (1981) demonstrated the importance of the complexity of floor layout in producing wayfinding disorientation. Judged simplicity of floor plan accounted for 56% of the frequency of disorientation, whereas judged familiarity contributed only 9%. From a design standpoint, this suggests that the floor plan is the foundation of a legible structure.

Findings that are similar to Williams and colleagues' (1990) have borne out the organizational effects of testosterone in work with rats tested on various kinds of mazes (Roof, 1993). In a series of three experiments, Roof looked at whether there would be a dose-level effect of testosterone propionate (TP) on performance that might indicate an optimal hormonal level for spatial behavior. A curvilinear relationship between spatial ability and physical androgenization has been postulated, and a dose-level experiment would allow this to be investigated. She also used two kinds of mazes. In one, the radial arm maze (RAM), local cues can be used. Rats were first tested on an eight-arm version of the maze and then on a four-arm version. In the other task, the Morris water maze (MWM), only distal cues are available because the water is cloudy (from powdered milk) to obscure the escape platform.

In the acquisition phase of the RAM, there was a sex by dose interaction. TP treatment decreased the number of trials needed for females to learn the task but increased the number of trials for males. Females with the high dose performed better than those with the low dose. Once the criterion for acquisition had been reached, accuracy was assessed first for the eight-arm and then the four-arm version of the maze. On the eight-arm version, there were no significant effects of TP treatment, although males performed better than females collapsed over dose. Parenthetically, the superior performance of human males to females on the Porteus Maze Test has consistently been reported (see McGee, 1979a). It was thought that the eight-arm version might have produced a ceiling effect, and hence had masked the effects of TP, because the animals generally did well. On the four-arm version, judged to be a more demanding task, TP improved performance in females in contrast to control females, whereas males were negatively affected by TP administration in contrast to control males, although not to the same extent. In the Morris water maze (MWM), control males took less time and took a shorter route than control females. In general, TP administration helped females whereas the opposite effect was seen in males.

In the third experiment, Roof (1993) examined whether these effects would be seen prior to adulthood by using 21-day-old rats on the MWM. If such effects were seen, it would point to the organizational as opposed to the activational effects of testosterone. Again, maze performance was influenced by sex and TP exposure. Control males, treated males, and treated females all improved from trial one to trial two. On the basis of these results, it appears that testosterone influences spatial ability *prior* to puberty because the pattern of performance in young rats (21 days) was basically like that of adults. Comparing these results to the Williams and colleagues research, Roof states, "It may be that testosterone may be converted to estrogen in the brain prior to exerting effects such as those seen in the present experiments" (p. 8). The author concludes that the experiments point to the following findings: (1) males demonstrate better performance on spatial tasks; (2) females exposed to early testosterone treatment perform as well as males on the spatial tasks in question; and (3) the sex difference and the impact of testosterone take hold before puberty.

Although there was no clear support for the hypothesis that there is an optimal hormonal level for spatial behavior, Roof (1993) notes that the doses in the study may not have pushed males out of the optimal range and therefore may not have adequately tested the hypothesis. She further notes that the action of testosterone on male and female performance may be through different mechanisms. The curvilinear relationship has been noted in humans by Petersen (1976), who showed that more physically masculine men were better at fluent production than spatial ability, whereas less physically masculine men showed the reverse pattern of cognitive abilities—the androgynous pattern of the more masculine women and less masculine men performing better on measures of spatial ability. It should be noted that some researchers have found support for the masculine-gender hypothesis—that spatial ability is correlated with masculine-gender identity, regardless of sex (Krasnoff, Walker, & Howard, 1989). The curvilinear relationship is more like what is called the cross-gender hypothesis (Krasnoff et al., 1989), in which spatial performance is negatively correlated with masculine identity in men and with feminine identity in women.

In addition to the organizational masculinizing effects of androgen that influence spatial ability, early androgen exposure programs the CNS to later release gonadal hormones that may have an activational influence on spatial ability. Gouchie and Kimura (1991) examined the effects of testosterone on spatial ability, measuring the concentration of salivary testosterone in humans. Eighty-eight right-handed volunteers (42 men, 46 women) were tested on measures of spatial ability, perceptual speed, mathematical reasoning, and verbal-articulatory ability. The spatial ability tests were paper folding (Ekstrom, French, & Harman, 1976) and the Vandenberg and Kuse mental rotation task (Vandenberg & Kuse, 1978). Radioimmunoassays of saliva were evaluated using samples taken at the beginning and end of the test session. Overall results indicated that men were superior on the tests of mental rotation and mathematical ability and, using a one-tailed test, on paper folding. No other differences emerged. When the impact of the testosterone levels was examined, only the paper folding test showed a significant interaction between sex and hormone level. Low-testosterone level men were superior to high-testosterone level men, and high-testosterone level women were superior to low-testosterone level women (the same pattern, though not significantly so, emerged for the mental rotation and mathematical ability measures). Like Roof, Gouchie and Kimura point to the role of androgens early in development as an influence on spatial behavior. The optimal organization of the mechanisms involved in spatial ability is not known. However, sex hormones are postulated to influence cognitive performance through "the activities of enzymes in brain regions which contain hormone receptors, the modification of uptake of neurotransmitters, and the generalized increase or decrease of neuronal electrical activity (McEwen, 1980)" (Gouchie & Kimura, 1991, p. 331).

While work with infrahuman species provides one mode of investigation for these hormonal effects, so-called "accidents of nature" have provided another avenue. Congenital adrenal hyperplasia (CAH) is an autosomal recessive disorder in which women are masculinized due to elevated prenatal adrenal androgen levels (Resnick, Berenbaum, Gottesman, & Bouchard, 1986). Examining the performance of CAH women on three measures of spatial ability (Hidden Patterns, Card Rotations, and Mental Rotations), Resnick and colleagues found that these women demonstrated higher performance than unaffected women relatives. Moreover, there was no significant correlation between a spatial manipulation activity scale and spatial ability, ruling out environmental variables as a complete explanation, according to the authors. The authors point to the impact of pre- and perinatal androgenizing hormones for spatial ability.

The relationship between CAH and sex-typed toy preference has also been examined (Berenbaum & Hines, 1992). Berenbaum and Hines (1992) suggest that girls with CAH will exhibit behavior that is similar to that exhibited by normal boys, that is, tomboyism, rough outdoor play, preference for traditionally masculine toys and activities, and greater spatial ability. Using children identified from pediatric endocrine clinics, the authors tested 26 girls and 11 boys, with 15 unaffected relatives who were girls and 18 unaffected relatives who were boys serving as controls. Toy preference was assessed by determining the time children played with toys shown to be preferred by girls, boys, or both. "Boy toys" centered on transportation vehicles (helicopters, cars) and construction manipulables (blocks, Lincoln logs), whereas "girl toys" included dolls, kitchen supplies, and art materials. Toys preferred by both sexes were books, board games, and puzzles. Children's play with the materials available in the play area was videotaped. Results indicated that CAH girls were more like control boys than control girls in that they played significantly more with boys' toys than did control girls and more with boys' toys than with girls' toys; they also played less with girls' toys than did the control girls. There were no significant differences between CAH boys and control boys in terms of sex-typed play.

Berenbaum and Hines (1992) wisely note two factors that need to be taken into account. While parents stated that they treated their CAH girls "normally," only direct observation could verify that behavioral interaction. The authors also note that toy play may be indirectly, rather than directly, affected through hormones in terms of activity level, motor skills, abilities, and temperament. The impact of gonadal hormones (synthetic progestins taken by the mother during pregnancy) on aggressive behavior has also been demonstrated (Reinisch, 1981) and has been linked to the development of tomboyish behavior in girls.

Another group of individuals that has been studied with regard to their organizational and activational hormonal abnormalities are men with idiopathic hypogonadotropic hypogonadism (IHH) and those with acquired hypergonadotropic hypogonadism (AHH) developed after puberty (Hier & Crowley, 1982). In idiopathic hypogonadotropic hypogonadism, pubescence fails to occur due to the deficiency of the gonadotropin-releasing factor, leaving these individuals with a pubertal deficiency of androgen. There is little organizational influence from androgens and no activational influence. Hier and Crowley (1982) used three verbal tests (the Vocabulary, Similarities, and Information subtests of the Wechsler) and three tests of spatial ability (Wechsler Block Design; Embedded Figures; Space Relations from the Differential Aptitude Test) to examine the differences between the IHH and AHH groups and the controls. Results indicated that while the groups did not differ on the verbal measures, the IHH group performed less well than did the controls on all spatial measures. The controls and the AHH group did not differ significantly on the spatial measures. Moreover, hormone replacement therapy administered to six of the participants did not significantly change their performance on the spatial measures. The results of the study led Hier and Crowley to suggest that androgens may create a permanent organizing influence on the brains of boys at or before puberty. The authors state, "Our results suggest that androgenization (presumably mediated by testosterone or one of its metabolites) is essential to the full development of spatial ability" (p. 1204). The level of fetal androgens has also been implicated in the relationship between sexual orientation etiology, sex differences in cerebral asymmetry, and consequently sex differences in cognitive abilities (Sanders & Ross-Field, 1986). The message seems to be that early exposure to androgens is critical to the development of spatial ability.

Summary

For the majority of these studies, the implication has been that androgens exert some kind of organizing and activating function on the brain (Dorner, 1977) that leads to the performance differences reported. However, the mechanisms that underlie this relationship are unknown. The masculinizing effects of androgen appear to be fundamental to the development of spatial ability. This seems especially clear when we consider the spatial behavior of individuals with various kinds of chromosomal and hormonal abnormalities.

Handedness

No discussion of brain asymmetry and laterality would be complete without some mention of handedness. With the standard dominance pattern (Geschwind & Galaburda, 1987) consisting of left hemisphere language and right-handedness, there has always been a question about the origin of the relationship between brain asymmetry and handedness (Corballis, 1980, 1995a; Corballis & Beale, 1983). Why are most people (estimates are 90% cross-culturally) right-handed? There is some disagreement about whether the dominant pattern of language and handedness is controlled genetically, with Annett (1985) favoring a more genetic model and Corballis (1980) stressing environmental factors.

The importance of the role of handedness in this discussion is also indicated by the fact that handedness, hand posture in writing, and sex have been used to predict cerebral organization (Levy & Reid, 1978). Left-handers are more bilaterally represented than right-handers and are more heterogeneous with regard to the direction of lateralization; whereas 60% of left-handers are estimated to have left hemisphere language dominance and 40% the reverse, only a small percentage of right-handers are estimated to have right hemisphere language (Levy & Reid, 1978).

Annett's (1980, 1985, 1995) theory of brain structure and handedness is called the right shift theory and has been criticized by a number of authors, including Bryden (1982). Rather than genetic factors, Bryden stresses the role of external variables such as the participant's own strategy in explaining task performance. The fundamentals of Annett's right shift theory are that (1) the human distribution of handedness is shifted to the right of other mammals; (2) the shift is a by-product of a factor that induces speech representation in the left hemisphere; (3) this factor is likely genetic; and (4) in some people the right shift factor (RS+) is missing (RS−). Where this theory differs from Geschwind and Galaburda's (1987) is that the main influence of right–left variation is hypothesized to be accidental, resulting in the hypothesis that all asymmetry in those who are missing the right shift factor is random (due to chance).

Struck by the variability in results of hemispheric laterality and cognitive performance, investigators have assessed the role of abilities as well as handedness in determining the outcome of tasks (Harshman, Hampson, & Berenbaum, 1983). Following Levy's theory (1976), in which individuals developing bilaterally for language will have less space available for spatial development in the right hemisphere, Harshman and colleagues (1983) added reasoning ability (split above or below the median) to help explain performance results. Separate sex by handedness analyses were performed for these two reasoning groups. The Harshman and colleagues study involved three different samples and a variety of measures, making comparisons somewhat difficult. Nevertheless, they argue that introducing the reasoning factor helps to explain the variability in results from numerous earlier studies. Harshman and colleagues' data indicate that factors such as reasoning ability may act as a moderating variable in helping to explain the relationship between handedness, sex, and cerebral organization. "To date, we believe that the most plausible interpretation of these moderator effects is that individuals at different levels on the moderator variable have brains that differ in terms of structural organization" (p. 187).

Handedness has been used to predict a variety of abilities, including mental rotation (Casey, Colon, & Goris, 1992). Working within the context of Annett's (1985) theory, Casey and colleagues (1992) address the issue of the generality of family handedness effects in predicting spatial ability. In this research, they used black and Hispanic high school students from lower to lower-middle income families who were enrolled in a science and technology preparatory training program. With this sample, they wanted to extend their results beyond a college population used in earlier research (Casey & Brabeck, 1989). The relationship between math and spatial ability makes a training program in science and technology a good place to examine the factors underlying gender differences in spatial ability. Examining performance on a mental rotation task where the most robust of the gender differences in spatial ability are found, the data yielded a main effect for gender, with boys superior to girls, and a gender by handedness interaction. Right-handed girls in the program with one or more non-right-handed first degree relatives were superior both to right-handed girls in the program with all right-handed relatives and to non-right-handed girls in the program. It thus appears that there is a constellation of factors in women that make it more likely that they will have high spatial ability. In addition to its relationship to spatial ability, handedness has also been linked to creativity (Burke, Chrisler, & Devlin, 1989; Newland, 1981; Stewart & Clayson, 1980). Also, a higher percentage of left-handers than would be expected by chance have been found in architectural programs (Peterson & Lansky, 1977), again pointing to the relationship between handedness, spatial ability, and, presumably, creativity.

We continue to be intrigued by the fact that most humans are right-handed and left hemisphere dominant for language. Watson and Kimura (1989) argue that right-handedness and speech have a common neural foundation. They suggest that the left hemisphere is chiefly responsible for orchestrating sequential upper limb movements, and thus may be the foundation of right-handedness. Using 48 undergraduates, 24 men and 24 women, whose handedness was determined by assessing preferences on eight tasks, the authors measured both their throwing and intercepting accuracy. While men were significantly better than women on both tasks, there was a task by hand interaction. The right hand was significantly more accurate than the left for the throwing task, but there was no significant hand difference on the intercepting task.

It has been suggested that left hemisphere specialization stems from the evolutionary development of a cerebral timing system, coincidentally vested in the left hemisphere. . . . According to this theory, selection pressures would have favored even faster and more accurate throwing ability, as a hunting technique. A throw capable of bringing down a small game animal would have a small "launch window" in the arc of the overhand delivery. Accurate timing of the release of the projectile within the launch window is claimed to far outstrip the timing capabilities of individual neurons. . . . a large network of parallel timing neurons would be required to provide the necessary precision. Once in place in the left hemisphere, this system might provide a convenient substrate to subsume motor programming and verbal functions. Such a mechanism has been extended recently to explain the right hand advantage in visually-guided reaching. . . . (Watson & Kimura, 1989, p. 1411)

Watson and Kimura point out that hand preference becomes stable with the onset of babbling and that the maturation of the left hemisphere praxis system may be responsible. Corballis (1991) has also emphasized the role of praxis in the development of hemispheric differences: "My own view is that the most likely precursors of hemispheric asymmetry in humans are a right-hemispheric bias for emotion and perhaps for spatial representation and a left-hemispheric bias for praxis" (p. 272). Calvin (1990) as well emphasizes the left-hemispheric bias for action, arguing that the "advantage" of the left hemisphere emerged initially in the role of missiles thrown at a distant target. He argues that speech is likely to have evolved in the left hemisphere because of its similar involvement with precise, rapid timing.

The neuroanatomy of cognitive selection systems has also been argued to depend on sex and handedness (Goldberg, Podell, Harner, Lovell, & Riggio, 1994). Goldberg and colleagues (1994) have done intriguing work relating lesions, laterality, sex, and handedness in a task involving cognitive bias. Rather than viewing language as the fundamental determiner of hemispheric specialization, Goldberg and colleagues point to what they say is a broader organizing principle: cognitive novelty and routinization. The right hemisphere is postulated to play a central role in the evaluation of novel situations. The role of the left is hypothesized to be greater for situations in which a pre-existing approach can be applied. Goldberg and colleagues designed a Cognitive Bias Test (CBT) to evaluate their hypotheses. The test assesses the role of cognitive context in making a visual response. The test is designed to gauge preference as opposed to accuracy.

In the test, there are five binary dimensions: shape, color, number, size, and contour. A target is followed (vertically) by two choices, and subjects are told to pick from the two choices the one they *like* better. The two stimulus choices can range from those that are identical (the same on all 5 dimensions and thus a score of 5) to those that are different on all dimensions (a score of 0). It is thus possible to calculate a similarity index with regard to the target choice on each trial. Over trials, a subject's behavior (the subject's score) can be described as high (context dependent—reflecting similarity as a response bias toward the target); in the middle (indifferent to the target with regard to a selection bias); and low (context independent—expressing diversity with regard to a response bias toward the target). Goldberg and colleagues (1994) point out that a low score also reflects a context awareness, and is context dependent in the sense that the subject chooses what the target *isn't*.

Goldberg and colleagues (1994) initially looked at the responses of healthy right-handed men and women and then went on to examine the response biases in subjects with lesions in one of the four quadrants (frontal left or right hemisphere, posterior left or right hemisphere). To the extent possible (because of the difficulty in finding enough subjects), they also examined the effect of handedness. Although the results reported must be considered preliminary because of the small sample sizes, the findings have fascinating implications. Although a review of all of their findings is beyond the scope of this chapter, a summary is provided: (1) In general, the effects of lesions in the frontal lobes were far stronger than those in the posterior lobes; (2) right frontal lesions produce the same kinds of effects in both men and women—CBT scores increase, reflecting a context-dependent response bias; and (3) handedness has a greater impact on CBT scores for women than men.

In their research, handedness introduces yet another dimension that allows an examination of cortical functional architecture.

CBT allows two kinds of context-dependent response strategies: "similar-to-the-target" constancy-seeking and "away-from-the-target" novelty-seeking. In our right-handed samples the first strategy predominates, and the second is all but absent. In our non-right-handed samples the two strategies are represented in roughly equal proportions. This raises the possibility that cognition in left-handers is characterized by unique features and that their cerebral organization is not just an attenuated direct or mirror image of the right-handed one, but is in some respects qualitatively different. May it be that the two types of context-dependent response strategies are differentially associated with handedness: familiarity-seeking with right and novelty-seeking with left. Could this account for the reported association of left-handedness with creativity . . . ? (Goldberg et al., 1994, p. 291)

This research is important because it continues to delineate the effect of cortical architecture on behavior and does so with a task that de-emphasizes the role of language, thereby creating the possibility for cross-species comparisons.

On an anatomical level, Witelson and Goldsmith (1991) have examined the relationship between handedness and the size of the corpus callosum, noting that research indicates greater bilateral representation of function in left-handers. Examining callosal anatomy and hand preference in men, they determined that those who were nonconsistent right-handers (non-CRH) had a larger midsagittal area of the corpus callosum than those who were consistent right-handers (CRH). The isthmus of non-CRH was 38% larger than that of CRH. Witelson and Goldsmith argue that "callosal morphology is part of the anatomical substrate of functional asymmetry" (p. 180). Their idea is that callosal fibers may be eliminated through axon deterioration, as a result of what they term "naturally occurring regressive events" (p. 180). Witelson (1985) also provided evidence through postmortem assessment that the corpus callosum of left-handed and ambidextrous individuals was 11% larger. "Hand preference is related, although imperfectly, to the pattern of hemispheric specialization. Left-handers as a group have greater bihemispheric representation of cognitive functions than do right handers" (p. 665).

Finally, in looking at six deaf, brain-damaged signers, Poizner, Klima, and Bellugi (1987) are able to broaden our understanding of hemispheric functions because in the case of signing, the modality for language is different. In their book *What the Hands Reveal about the Brain*, the authors argue the following:

the left cerebral hemisphere in humans may have an innate predisposition for the central components of language, independent of language modality. Studies of the effects of brain damage on signing make it clear that accounts of hemispheric specialization are oversimplified if stated simply in terms of a dichotomy between language and visuospatial functioning. Such studies may also permit us to come closer to the real principles underlying the specializations of the two cerebral hemispheres, because in sign language there is interplay between visuospatial and linguistic relations within one and the same system. (p. 212)

Summary

In summary, the literature appears to lean toward evolutionary pressures for lateralization, perhaps mediated by androgens, related to the different tasks of men and women in a hunting-gathering society. The dominant pattern of right-handedness may in fact be related to neural organization in left hemisphere language and speech functions and fine motor control. Although this material may seem far removed from applications to design, what it demonstrates is that evolutionary pressures have produced an animal with a specific hemispheric organization, typically dominant in the left hemisphere for language and right-handedness. These two aspects may very well be related functionally (in terms of timing mechanisms) and point to the importance of understanding "for whom we design." For all of our sophistication, we are still very much bound by the products of evolutionary pressures; designers must understand that we are fundamentally biological creatures. It might be better for designers to concentrate on way-finding cues that mesh with primitive visual categorization rather than sophisticated language use. That would certainly be true in terms of cross-cultural applications. Furthermore, the research on handedness suggests that both cues that are similar to a target versus those that are different might be considered as way-finding aids.

BRAIN FUNCTION, VISION, AND MENTAL IMAGERY: IMPLICATIONS FOR DESIGN

Vision

Let us now move to an examination of principles of vision as they may relate to environmental design. The bias here is that humans are primarily visual animals, and this section will relate vision and mental imagery, as aspects of brain function, to design. One of the individuals who had the most profound effect on our thinking about vision was MIT's David Marr, who died of leukemia in his 30s. Despite his early death, he contributed a perspective that continues to influence our thinking about the visual process (Tye, 1991). Marr pointed out that we need to consider the process of vision on three levels of explanation: computational, representational and algorithmic, and mechanistic (hardware). What is helpful in his view of vision is his emphasis on the need for explanation as opposed to description, an emphasis that has been picked up in evolutionary biology (Cosmides & Tooby, 1995). In discussing low-level vision, what Marr asks us to do is to figure out what vision is about, what problems it solves. The response he gives us is that, "Vision is a process that produces from images of the external world a description that is useful to the viewer and not cluttered with irrelevant information" (1982, p. 31). The "quintessential fact of human vision" is that "it tells about shape and space and spatial arrangement" (p. 36). This emphasis on the representation of shape leads to Marr's theoretical framework that includes the concepts of image, primal sketch, 21/2-D sketch, and 3-D model representation, processes that deal with what has been called low and intermediate vision. These processes emphasize extracting information from the immediate stimulus environment as opposed to dealing with the influence of past visual experience. The essence of what comes out of his model of representation is the importance of intensity changes in the visual array. The emphasis leads to the critical role of edges in our understanding of the world around us. This makes sense if what vision is "about" is shape representation, and shape emerges out of boundaries of objects, from their edges as it were. Others (Kosslyn, Flynn, Amsterdam, & Wang, 1990) have provided more information about high-level vision and interrelated processing subsystems.

Biologically, what kind of world are we prepared to segment? The early work of Hubel and Wiesel demonstrated the specificity of receptors for particular orientations in the striate cortex of the cat (DeValois & De-

Valois, 1988). What followed was a plethora of research, including such findings that there is a movement vector in the motor cortex of rhesus monkeys that resembles a rotated imagined movement vector (Georgopoulos, Lurito, Petrides, Schwartz, & Massey, 1989). From these studies we have begun to understand that humans are designed, presumably in terms of survival, to distinguish or be sensitive to certain aspects of the physical world around us. We are tuned in to spatial, movement, and orientation variables. Evidence of neurons particularly responsive to movement has also been found in the anterior portion of the superior temporal sulcus in the macaque (Bruce, Desimone, & Gross, 1981).

Building on Marr's (1982) work with vision, Plaut and Farah (1990) present a list of requirements for object representation, including scope and uniqueness, stability and sensitivity, and accessibility. In many ways the trade-offs they outline are reminiscent of the earlier work of Ernest Hilgard (1951), who discussed the interaction between stability and definiteness in perceptual learning. Reviewing evidence from brain-damaged humans, lesioned animals, and single-cell recordings, Plaut and Farah suggest that the inferotemporal cortex (IT) has a substantial role in visual object representation, and that this area may provide perceptual constancy. The authors go on to provide a computational interpretation of IT functioning (the representation of shape with either surface or volumetric primitives): "Cells in IT respond selectively to physical properties of distal objects rather than the more variable properties of the proximal image, and damage to this area in humans as well as in monkeys produces systematic deficits in visual recognition and discrimination of objects and disproportionate reliance on proximal cues in visual tasks" (p. 339).

This importance of edges and the ability to distinguish where one entity ends and another begins can inform the designer—Marr's (1982) work points to the importance of what Lynch (1960) has called making the environment "legible." A legible environment is one that makes sense. Certainly an environment that is distinguishable in terms of edges is one that contributes to legibility. Marr was influenced by the work of J. J. Gibson (1950, 1966), who emphasized the role of the structurally invariant properties of objects. For example, what is it that makes a given object a chair? In other words, what is "chairness"? To the extent that we do not live in a solipsistic world, we live in a place where our visual systems have evolved to detect what it is in the world that remains invariant or unchanging—Gibson's structural invariants. Presumably, the essence of "chairness" focuses on the structural invariants common across cases that Marr talks about in terms of intensity changes and edges. Chairs have legs, a seat, a back, and a certain range of widths, heights, and proportions. We resonate or tune in to the properties of a chair that differentiate it from a stool (no back, perhaps three legs), a bar stool (its height), and a love seat (wider than a chair), for example. Perceptual learning involves becoming better at tuning in or resonating to the structural invariants of any category of object.

Researchers continue to be influenced by Marr's and Gibson's ideas (Corballis, 1988; Shepard & Cooper, 1982; Yuille & Ullman, 1990). Humans are remarkable in their ability to understand the correspondences between multiple and varying representations of real objects and those objects themselves, presumably because they are able to resonate to the invariants in those objects. This ability is unlike that of chimpanzees, who have trouble "seeing a correspondence between photos, pictures, TV images, maps, and dollhouses and the real objects and actual spaces they represent for us" (Premack & Premack, 1983, p. 147).

Mental Imagery

A section on mental imagery is included because of its importance in such activities as reading maps, transforming two-dimensional into three-dimensional arrays, and building spatial schemata. One of the aspects of thinking that is fundamentally related to making one's way in the world is mental imagery, and most profoundly, visual imagery. In every situation where we find a detour, a road block, a "what if," we rely on visual imagery and often mental rotation to create a picture or schema. What happens when we take a particular route or path to solve a problem or reach a destination? Mental imagery helps us predict consequences. We rely, in a sense, on what Kaplan (1973) has called a cognitive map, which allows us to recognize where we are, predict what will happen next, evaluate the consequences, and then take action. The presentation of information in the environment (e.g., how it is oriented) is a critical variable in our ability to find our way. Subjects have difficulty consulting a map that is not oriented as they are to the environment (Levine, 1982; Levine, Marchon, & Hanley, 1984; Peruch & Savoyant, 1991). Such misalignments cause difficulty in mental rotation and ultimately in way finding.

Thus, a discussion of mental imagery follows naturally from our overview of vision. Shepard and Cooper provide a link between Marr's work and a discussion of mental imagery. Like Marr, Shepard and Cooper (1982) pay homage to a Gibsonian foundation (Gibson, 1950, 1966) in discussing the parameters that determine transformations of objects in space.

Throughout evolutionary history, rigid structure has been a prominent aspect of the surrounding world and of many of the most significant objects that populate that world. . . . Indeed, even the most flimsy, limp, liquid, insubstantial and evanescent objects tend, in the absence of external disturbance, to preserve their three-dimensional shapes over significant periods of time and, hence, to yield perspective transformations approximating those of rigid objects as we move around them in space. (pp. 2–3)

In the world of cognitive psychology, much of the debate about mental imagery and the role of mental imagery has centered on whether it is merely an epiphenomenon or by-product (Pylyshyn, 1973) versus a process independent of abstract propositional structure—that is, whether it has a life of its own. Theorists such as Paivio (1971, 1986) and Kosslyn (1987) have championed imagery as a process important in its own right and not merely as a by-product of more abstract activity. Kosslyn (1994b) has written a volume that really puts to rest Pylyshyn's claim that mental imagery is merely epiphenomenal, and Pylyshyn's argument seems to hold little sway today (DeVega, Marschark, Intons-Peterson, Johnson-Laird, & Denis, 1996).

More recently, two basic questions have been whether mental imagery overlaps with vision and whether it possesses a spatial format (Farah, 1995). Farah responds with a tentative "yes" to both questions. Neuropsychological work by Farah and others (Farah, 1984, 1988a, 1988b, 1991; Farah, Gazzaniga, Holtzman, & Kosslyn, 1985; Kosslyn & Ochsner, 1994; Roland & Gulyas, 1994) has helped to identify in what ways imagery both overlaps with and is independent of vision. Denis, Goncalves, and Memmi (1995) endorse the position that visual imagery and perception share not only a number of functional properties, but also have some common underlying brain architecture. Others (see, e.g., Holtzman & Kosslyn, 1990; Kosslyn & Shin, 1994) also emphasize the multifaceted nature of imagery and the mechanisms that vision and imagery share.

Early studies of mental imagery and rotation dealt with tasks such as letter rotation, paper folding, or tracing a route on a fictitious island map (see, e.g., Kosslyn, Ball & Reiser, 1978; Shepard, 1988; Shepard & Cooper, 1982; Shepard & Metzler, 1971). Studies have since moved on to include clinical neuropsychological populations as well as rCBF and PET scan studies. In a paper examining the contribution of vision to imagery, Farah (1988a) outlines Pylyshyn's contrasting view (that subjects may rely on "general purpose" cognitive processes, including tacit knowledge of the way in which visual systems behave, to perform the visual tasks presented to them). In the paper, Farah reviews regional blood flow and electrophysiological data indicating activity in the occipital lobe during imagery: "Across a variety of tasks it has been found that imagery engages visual cortex, whereas other tasks, many of which are highly similar save for the absence of visual imagery, do not" (p. 312). To rule out an alternative explanation, that visual area activation is merely a by-product or epiphenomenal with respect to imagery, Farah reviews brain activation after lesion damage. What she concludes is that "imagery is not visual in the sense of necessarily representing information acquired through visual sensory channels. Rather, it is visual in the sense of using some of the same neural representational machinery as vision" (p. 315). Rouw, Kosslyn, and Hamel (1998) argue that the mental image contains relatively "raw" or unprocessed perceptual material rather than simply an overall description. They therefore emphasize imagery's depictive as opposed to its descriptive qualities.

Kosslyn (1987; Kosslyn, Holtzman, Farah, & Gazzaniga, 1985) has proposed an elaborate model of imagining that engages both hemispheres. The evaluation of the abilities of split-brain and other clinical patients leads to the hypothesis that the right hemisphere cannot really generate images and has difficulty accessing and interpreting "categorical representations to arrange parts" (Kosslyn, 1987, p. 158). Posner, Peterson, Fox, and Raichle (1988) also subscribe to the position that the left hemisphere generates complex visual images but that the right hemisphere lacks the mechanisms required for this.

Kosslyn (1987) argues that the categorical function, because it was similar in many respects to language, evolved on the left side. For the right hemisphere, Kosslyn posits a unilateral search controller, whereas the left has a unilateral speech output controller. The left also maintains central bilateral control of the subsystems. He links the search controller in the right hemisphere to fundamental aspects of way finding: "The principle of unilateral control of rapid, bilateral operations, also applies to our control of rapid shifts of attention over a scene. This sort of visual search is used in navigation, when one is systematically examining the environment as one is moving" (p. 162). Kosslyn presents evidence that categorical relations are better processed in the left hemisphere whereas coordinate relationships fare better in the right hemisphere. In many ways this emphasis on coordinate relationships in the right hemisphere sounds like the place system postulated by O'Keefe and Nadel (1978). Imagery is a complicated process involving different areas of the brain and has been interpreted in terms of Marr's idea of natural computation (Kosslyn et al., 1985).

Kosslyn and colleagues (1993) also investigate what brain areas are activated during different perceptual and imaginal tasks. In a series of experiments, subjects were either to view a letter in a grid (perception) or to imagine its presence in an empty grid (imaging): "The most striking aspect of our results is that we found *greater* activation of visual cortex during image generation than during perception" (p. 268). The authors presume that this greater activation stems from the fact that humans have to work harder during imagery than in perception where the visual stimulus is present to provide information in bottom-up processing. Just think about the fact that imagery is hard work for most of us and typically results in poor detail; we are creating our output from information that has already been encoded and refined. Remember Marr's statement that vision produces an image not cluttered with irrelevance. Imaging is at least a step removed from the richness of visual input. Their evidence indicates that mental imagery activates two or three areas of the visual cortex that are topographically organized in the brains of humans. "The finding that even one topographically organized part of cortex is activated during visual mental imagery suggests that image representations are spatially organized" (Kosslyn et al., 1993, p. 280).

Summary

Visual imagery has a life of its own, and one of the strongest pieces of evidence supporting its central rather than epiphenomenal role is the existence of topographically organized areas in the visual cortex that are activated during visual imagery. It is also evident that both hemispheres of the brain are involved in the processes of mental imagery, and we thus see an intersection with the beginning of this chapter—discussing the roles of the hemispheres in brain function. We have come full circle—starting out by looking at the two hemispheres and their properties, and finally dealing with dual hemispheric involvement and integrated brain function in the processes of mental imagery.

In stepping back to consider the additions to our knowledge of spatial cognition, we have to be impressed by the radical transformation in the methodology we employ. Early work on mental rotation was strikingly limited to the "molar" level, with latency and error data unaccompanied by rCBF or PET scans, for example. Now, we see a dramatic shift to the analysis of brain functions when we try to understand what is going on in people's minds when they look at a map that is rotated from their viewpoint or "conjure up" an alternate route to handle a detour. Ironically, the very sophistication and precision of the technology has limited its ecological validity because subjects are confined to the laboratory for precise measurement of brain function. But it is not too far-fetched to imagine headgear that will make similar kinds of measurements as subjects navigate in real-world tasks.

While it seems unlikely that planners and designers would become expert at reading PET scans, what does seem important is developing a greater understanding that the visual system and brain organization influence our ability to deal effectively with a complex world. These brain systems determine how we perceive the environment, created and designed well or poorly by humans. Some attention to the principles that govern visuospatial processing might in fact inform designers that some tasks they require of us (mental rotation of stationary maps, for example) are not only difficult but that the ability to do so may differ by sex.

What might be asked of designers and planners is that they stretch their interdisciplinary understanding of human nature and that cognitive psychologists, on the other side, acquaint themselves with the large body of literature in environmental design from authors like Kevin Lynch (1960,

1981; Banerjee & Southworth, 1990), Donald Appleyard (1969, 1970, 1976), and Christopher Alexander (1965, 1979; Alexander, Ishikawa, & Silverstein, 1977). These authors, as we will see in the next two chapters, employ concepts with striking parallels to the work of Marr, Kosslyn, and others.

4

Research on
Way-finding Tools:
Maps and Minds

Way-finding tools vary in scale. On one end of the continuum, we have the environment itself; elements such as a vista can provide a useful overview of the environment, as can the layout of a building. On the other end of the continuum, we have environmental representations—information about the environment in the form of maps, models, and signage. This chapter focuses on what is traditionally considered the basic way-finding tool: the map. But it will also consider signage and building layout as other cues to navigating in the environment.

There are a number of approaches to learn about the characteristics of these way-finding aids. We can study them directly, as we might if we looked at street or topographical maps, varied their parameters (size, color, complexity, organization), and noted the impact of those changes on simulated or real way finding. Alternatively, we might study cognitive mapping behavior and infer the variables that made a difference in the outcome, even when the way-finding tool is not a focus of study. Yet another approach is to examine research from disciplines that share an interest in graphic display—cartography and statistical graphics—to see what they have to offer. This chapter incorporates all three approaches.

One of the basic questions in these approaches is whether the way-finding aid is the focus of study. With few exceptions, psychology has not focused directly on way-finding tools. In psychology, tools such as maps are usually a means to an end in the study of more fundamental processes like memory.

Thus, to develop a list of recommendations about way-finding aids, we must make inferences from studies that deal with a wide range of variables. Unfortunately, merging the approaches is less than easy, as there is some resistance in cartography to the psychophysical paradigm (Blades & Spencer, 1986). Some cartographers object to the approach because it involves testing variables in isolation, thereby ignoring the effect of the whole map. Cartographers' reactions to experimental data are not necessarily enthusiastic (Phillips, 1979).

MAPS: USERS VERSUS CARTOGRAPHERS

Navigational tools such as maps have all sorts of uses, from way finding itself (e.g., road atlases), to advertising (Fleming, 1984; McDermott, 1969). Maps vary in quality and accuracy; consider Monmonier's book, titled *How to Lie with Maps* (1996, in its second edition). In this book, he explains how to evaluate the quality of the information we see in newspapers, books, political documents, and television displays. Mapmakers are human (a point made by Monmonier, 1996, and Wright, 1942), and we need to understand that different motivations will produce different outcomes.

In addition to a variety of uses, maps produce a variety of comfort levels among users. Muehrcke (1986) comments that people have a distrust of maps as separate from reality, and he recognizes the fallibility of both the mapmaker and the map user:

Mapping, as a communication process, is influenced by human shortcomings throughout. We, map maker and map user alike, are fallible. We crave simplicity; we are strong in some areas and weak in others; we are biased in many ways; and our integrity, judgment, and insight are never beyond question. We are human, and the mapping process is built around this fact. (p. 404)

Arnheim (1976) also notes that mapmakers have to find an appropriate compromise between reality and its representation, stressing "the kind of simplification that facilitates perception" (p. 9). As abstractions, maps are representations of reality, not reality itself. In the process of representing reality, conscious or unconscious biases may occur.

For many, maps are not easily comprehensible, and that result is just as likely to be the fault of the map as it is the user. A fundamental reason people have trouble using maps is their inability to connect two things: the environment and the map it represents. Southworth and Southworth (1982) state, "Maps fail when users cannot find needed information, cannot 'read' the map's language, or cannot relate the map to the real world; the user becomes upset, disoriented, lost" (p. 14). Their comments are reminiscent of what urban planner Kevin Lynch (1960) has to say about way finding and the sense of anxiety that accompanies disorientation (see a discussion of Lynch in Chapter 5, this volume).

Maps really can confuse. Consider the following example: In a study that exposed some junior high school students (and not others) to maps of a natural area they were going to visit, the maps were a liability (Devlin, 1973). The use of modified contour lines in a cloud shape to simultaneously indicate both elevation and foliage proved confusing for students and many adults as well. The students with the map exposure were actually less confident in their way-finding ability in the natural area than were those who had not seen the map. In the study, control participants who had not seen the map were significantly more assured that they knew the park well enough to be a friend's guide than were those who had actually viewed the map. A map that appears complete and relatively detailed and yet in reality is much different from the area it depicts may be more harmful than an incomplete picture. Such maps begin the formation of a cognitive map too far removed from the reality it depicts.

In addition to the fact that the mapmaker is a human whose motivations and skills may vary, the problem of diverse bodies of literature on maps also challenges us. On the one hand, we have cartography texts such as Robinson's on map layout and design (Robinson, Morrison, Muehrcke, Kimerling, & Guptell, 1995), which has little to offer with regard to the behavioral effects of these guidelines. On the other hand, we have studies dealing with cognitive maps and their development and use, which only indirectly address map format and legibility features. Dent (1985) agrees with the assessment that the contributions from cartography have a limited research foundation: "There is a paucity of cartographic research into color meaning and map design" (p. 353), forcing cartographers to use material from psychology and advertising. In general, there is little research to support the guidelines used to create maps. They *may* offer good advice, but how do we know? Remembering that, "Every visual image worth existing is an interpretation of its subject, not a mechanical copy" (Arnheim, 1976, p. 10), we have a situation where we are at least a step removed from reality and must struggle with interpreting its representation. With regard to cartography, Robinson (1982) states "it is certainly an art now in practice because we are forced to employ our structural materials largely on the basis of individual subjective judgment, otherwise called intuition" (pp. 27–28).

The field of cartography contributes few research-based principles to the creation of way-finding tools such as maps. But *advice* emerges from textbooks and treatises on map design (Arnheim, 1976; Bertin, 1983; Chambers, Cleveland, Kleiner, & Tukey, 1983; Dent, 1985; Fisher, 1982; Holmes, 1984; Kosslyn, 1985, 1989, 1994a; Monmonier & Schnell, 1988; Muehrcke, 1986; Robinson, Sale, Morrison, & Muehrcke, 1984; Southworth & Southworth, 1982; Tufte, 1983, 1990; Wood, 1968). With regard to the issues of interest in this book, we see guidelines for such variables as placement and color (Dent, 1985). For example, we are told not to hyphenate names and labels. If lettering is not horizontal, we are to make sure it deviates significantly from the horizontal so that it doesn't pass for a mistake. Letter placement is to be consistent with our normal left-to-right reading pattern.

There are other guidelines about these kinds of stylistic variables (Robinson, 1952). Legibility varies with type styles; the contrast of dark on light background is more legible than the reverse; italics are difficult to read; perceptibility of print increases with increasing thickness to a point and then declines; the use of color is complicated and poorly understood. In creating a map, the cartographer can use simplification, classification, and symbolization (Robinson et al., 1984). Robinson and colleagues (1984) state that in terms of determining what should be kept or discarded, we are guided by (1) the relative importance of the item; (2) its relation as a class of data to the map objective; and (3) the graphic impact of keeping the item. The major graphic elements we use are hue, value, size, shape, spacing, orientation, and location. We have clarity and legibility, visual contrast, figure–ground differentiation; balance, hierarchical structure, color, pattern, typography—these are the graphic constituents of design. Familiarity is argued to facilitate legibility. Another emphasis in good map design for what is called general reference cartography (Fisher, 1982) is the avoidance of clutter. Holmes (1984) gives us the simple rule that maps should have an "ease of reading" (p. 34). Thus, with limited research support, cartography texts such as Robinson and colleagues' *Elements of Cartography* are forced to simply provide a list of guidelines or principles for use of these major graphic elements.

Implicit in some of the map guidelines are aspects of human information processing. Southworth and Southworth (1982) have suggested that unsuccessful maps present too much information. This comment certainly reflects a concern with cognitive capacity. They also state that prominent landmarks should also have prominence in the map (a kind of isomorphism); and that color used for merely decorative purposes can distract or confuse. While such advice is helpful, the specificity of this information is limited, and it is not related to research. More precision about the use of such factors as color and extent and placement of labeling is necessary, and the guidelines need to emerge from scientific inquiry. While the need for empirically based guidelines has been recognized as a priority (Robinson, 1982), these guidelines have not been developed.

Thematic cartography, which highlights quantitative differences through graphic symbolism (Fisher, 1982), has lent itself to a more thorough analysis than has general reference cartography. For example, Kosslyn (1989) provides an information processing approach to analyzing the effectiveness of charts and graphs—allowing us to evaluate what Kosslyn calls acceptability principles. His review of the literature indicates that "marks intended to signify different symbols should be distinguishable, every mark should have an interpretation, and the interpretations should be distinct" (p. 194).

Research on graph perception also offers information relevant to understanding maps and, in turn, spatial cognition. As suggested, potentially useful information comes from research on statistical graphics (Cleveland & McGill, 1984, 1985, 1986, 1987). Cleveland and McGill have ranked what they call elementary codes (e.g., position along a common scale) in terms of subjects' accuracy in making judgments using these codes. Carswell (1992) used the work of Cleveland and Kosslyn and Tufte as theoretical starting points and conducted a meta-analysis on graphical display research. Cleveland's basic tasks model predicted performance fairly well for local comparison and point-reading tasks, particularly if graphs were present rather than recalled. Ironically, in terms of mapping tasks, the model's success was lowest when the task predictions involved position (aligned and misaligned), length, and angle. On the basis of this meta-analysis, Carswell suggests we revise Cleveland's task rank ordering.

Summary

Cartographers recognize the need to provide a research base for their decisions (Robinson, 1982), most of which seem to be based on tradition and intuition. "For 150 years, distinct rules concerning type placement spread among topographers and cartographers by word of mouth" (Imhof, 1975, p. 128). It is also the case that maps used in information processing research (e.g., memory function) may not be realistic or representative of actual maps (Tversky & Schiano, 1989). This failing furthers the need for the field of cartography to generate an empirical base. Some of the guidelines for map layout have reflected Gestalt principles (see, e.g., Dent, 1972) and psychophysics (see, e.g., Spence, 1990; Spence & Lewandowsky, 1991), whereas others have described map and graph interpretation in information-processing terms (Kosslyn, 1989, 1994a; Simkin & Hastie, 1987). Additionally, the increasing use of computer simulation of navigational information raises the important question of how much data should be presented and the form such information should take. The next section of this chapter examines the principles that emerge from cognitive psychology with implications for maps, signs, and building layout as wayfinding aids.

PRINCIPLES AND CONTRIBUTIONS FROM COGNITIVE PSYCHOLOGY

The Roles of Hierarchies, Familiarity, and Distortion

One way to approach way-finding aids is the use of indirect evidence generated by research in spatial cognition. Although some of this research uses maps or map-related variables as stimuli, the focus is generally more basic than applied. Hirtle and Jonides (1985) give us evidence of hierarchies in cognitive maps, and it is thus not surprising that cartographers have been urged to create hierarchies in the maps they create. In a multitask study of students' knowledge of landmarks and distances, Hirtle and Jonides demonstrate this hierarchical organization. The authors took 32 landmarks in Ann Arbor, Michigan, with no apparent clustering that crossed four subjective neighborhoods. Subjects then performed a variety of tasks with these landmarks, including free recall, map drawing, and distance judgments. These participants, who had been on campus over two years, generated subjective cluster membership about landmarks, storing non-Euclidean as well as Euclidean information. The participants overestimated the distances across landmark clusters and underestimated those *within* clusters. Hirtle and Jonides demonstrated that nonspatial information like the subjective landmark clusters can influence spatial judgment. They suggest that it would be a mistake to describe mental representations of space as Euclidean survey maps.

In a related study where subjects were exposed to a slide presentation of a route, they consistently divided the route into discrete segments (Allen & Kirasic, 1985). The authors hypothesize that these segments affect distance judgments, and that route segmentation may be an analog of categorization and could be related to systematic distortion of distance judgments. It is apparent that spatial judgment is influenced by subjective processes like landmark clustering and route segmentation. Mapmakers need a better understanding of the subjective processes that influence people's map interpretation and subsequent way finding.

In terms of hierarchies, something also can be learned from research in education that examines what are called knowledge maps—two-dimensional spatial arrays that present information in a node–link–node pattern (Wiegmann, Dansereau, McCagg, Rewey, & Pitre, 1992). In this research, knowledge maps were presented either in gestalt or web form, with the gestalt arrangement stressing an overall organization of good continuation whereas the web form had no such organization. Students who had the gestalt form generally performed better than those with web forms. Wiegmann and colleagues (1992) also examined performance when students looked at information on a whole map versus on six smaller, interlocked, stacked, and cross-referenced maps. High spatial ability students performed better with the stacked maps, whereas those with low spatial ability did better with the whole maps. The advantage of the stacked map for those with good spatial ability is consistent with the findings of Hirtle and Jonides (1985) discussed earlier. They found that subjects internally chunked or organized spatial information about a town. Thus, geographical maps that emphasize hierarchical structure or facilitate the formation of hierarchies should match our cognitive tendencies.

In addition to hierarchies, landmarks and reference points also play a role in structuring our understanding of the environment. Emphasizing the role of discriminability, Holyoak and Mah (1982) show that reference points may influence distance judgments and the speed of such judgments. In their research, pairs of U.S. cities along an east–west axis (e.g., San Francisco, Denver) were judged in terms of which was closer to the Atlantic (or Pacific) Ocean (the reference point). Judgments of differences between the city pairs were greater when the pairs were closer to the reference point. It seems that reference points may expand and in that sense distort our perception of the nearby landscape.

The studies discussed above are examples of research that links macrospatial behavior and more general cognitive processes. Macrospatial cognitive processes are considered by some to be a fundamental or primitive aspect of cognitive development in humans (see Allen & Kirasic, 1985, for a discussion), because almost all human activities involve spatial relations in some form. As such, macrospatial processes may provide an important route to understanding basic cognitive processes.

Distortions

One of the findings that consistently emerges from macrospatial research is that the cognitive maps of humans may include distortions. Because both map reader and map interact in the perceptual process (Dobson, 1979), distortion is possible. A number of studies demonstrate that cognitive maps contain inconsistencies and distortions (Milgram, 1976; Poulton, 1985; Tversky, 1981). Even for those who know an area well, distortions may emerge (Byrne, 1979; Moeser, 1988). An interesting question is whether and to what extent these distortions actually impede way finding.

Inconsistency in spatial knowledge is not uncommon (Moar & Bower, 1983)—we may get along, but we may do so with internally inconsistent spatial information. Humans tend to simplify and such simplification may very well lead to distortion and inconsistency. Not only can't we store all the information, but we also make inferences from the information we do store. Subjects who were familiar with a city for at least five years judged directions between a triad of locations, producing biases in the direction of 90 degrees. Others made judgments about the direction between pairs of U.S. cities (judged from each city). For more than half the pairs, the judged directions were not consistent (not reversible). Moar and Bower (1983) state that this inconsistent information may be due to either storage or retrieval processes, and that we appear to use simple heuristics (e.g., the bias toward a right angle) in the creation of our cognitive maps. Quite obviously, cognitive maps may contain information that is inconsistent.

Another aspect of distortion involves the pull or power of reference points (Sadalla, Burroughs, & Staplin, 1980). Reference points are important because they provide an organizational structure. The cognitive distance between reference points and nonreference points is asymmetrical; nonreference points are judged nearer to reference points than vice versa. Nelson and Chaiklin (1980) studied memory for spatial location and how it was affected by near and far locations. Subjects had to reproduce the location of one dot, either in view or after an offset of 1 second. Accuracy for the memory group tended to decrease as distance increased between the dot location and the border. The authors suggest that there may be a pull of nearer landmarks. They speculate that there is biological significance in the findings because the organism would tend to put greater weight on nearer landmarks (presumably with greater functional importance) when remembering a spatial location.

When distortions occur, they may be more problematic at small than large distances (McNamara, 1986). McNamara's (1986) goal was to differentiate between three theories of mental representation: nonhierarchical, strong hierarchical, and partially hierarchical. The nonhierarchical representation is a proposition or network where information is represented on the same level rather than hierarchically. The distinction between the strong and partial versions of the hierarchical approach is that the partial allows spatial relations "to be encoded between locations in different regions of an environment" (p. 90). In the strong version, spatial relations at lower levels must be inferred from the higher order encoding. McNamara studied 72 college students, 24 in each of three groups: map, free navigation, and constrained navigation. Students either experienced navigation (free or constrained) of a 20 × 24-foot space that had been subdivided into four regions with eight locations specified in each region, or they learned the layout through a map. Dependent measures included a recognition test, a direction judgment test, and a distance estimation test. The results supported a partial hierarchical theory that involves redundancy in the representation. Although the focus of the research was theoretical differentiation of the mental representation of spatial relations, the results shed some light on the impact of distortions. Discussing direction estimates, McNamara points out that when people make mistakes about position when objects are close together, the changes in relative orientation that occur will be large. When objects are farther apart, the same errors will produce small changes in orientation and thus will be less problematical.

The extent of distortion can also be affected by context. Tversky and Schiano (1989; Schiano & Tversky, 1992) say that strategic factors shape errors in memory, and that there is a bias toward the diagonal on graphs but not maps. In one study (1989), the authors examined memory using graphs and maps as stimuli. Subjects remembered lines in graphs but not maps as closer to an imaginary diagonal. This study provides an exception to the Gestalt principle that memories necessarily tend toward good figure. Thus, memory for visual stimuli is selectively distorted by conceptual factors. People may have a conceptual schema for the components of graphs versus maps. Diagonals are frequently a component of graphs, but not necessarily maps, and that fact may bias subjects toward this presumption of the diagonal on graphs. The tendencies that occur in our interpretation of graphs may not occur when we "read" maps. Thus, we should question our generalizations across stimulus types. Even with a single line segment, errors in memory can be produced by strategic factors that you would not predict simply on the basis of the structure of the stimulus. Simkin and Hastie's (1987) information-processing analysis of graph perception dovetails nicely with Schiano and Tversky because they talk about the schemata people have for graphs, like the strategic factors Schiano and Tversky demonstrated.

Summary

A number of studies demonstrate that what is available from a cognitive map is not necessarily reflective of Euclidean distance but of what subjects actually experience (McNamara, Ratcliff, & McKoon, 1984). These experientially based representations often contain distortions of Euclidean space (Tversky, 1981) but do not necessarily incapacitate the traveler.

While distortions exist in experimental dependent measures (e.g., maps drawn), people can still find their way. Moeser's (1988) study of student nurses in a complex health sciences building is one such example. What we often see is that what are called cognitive distances (the distances that reflect our personal mental maps and may contain distortions) are better predictors of behavior than are "objective" Euclidean distances (MacKay, Olshavsky, & Sentell, 1975). Similarly, travel time may be a better predictor of cognitive distance than real distance (MacEachern, 1980). Therefore, when people talk about cognitive distance, they mean the individual's understanding or estimation of distance as opposed to actual distance. In many instances our own representation of distance is a better predictor of some behavior of interest (e.g., travel time, shopping behavior) than actual distance. In learning artificial road maps (McNamara et al., 1984), subjects encoded locations as closer together when these locations appeared on a single route than when they crossed multiple routes. This may point to the role of Gestalt variables in explaining our perceptual lives and to the fact that distortions exist within the framework of perfectly functional way-finding behavior.

It is possible that current theoretical and methodological approaches bypass more fundamental characteristics of human orientation skills. We do not understand the relationship between distortions and non-Euclidean maps, on the one hand, and way-finding success, on the other. Perhaps we can approach this relationship indirectly. Given differential way-finding success, we might ask about the variables that predict these differences.

Individual Differences: Familiarity and Ability

Familiarity and ability are variables in cognitive psychology with implications for way-finding aids. There will be differences in the levels of familiarity novices and experts have with displays (Lewandowsky & Spence, 1989), just as has been demonstrated in other domains such as chess (DeGroot, 1965; Simon & Gilmartin, 1973).

Those with extensive versus less familiarity with the environment differ in their way-finding approaches (Peruch, Girando, & Garling, 1989). Taxi drivers are argued to have procedural knowledge (knowing how) of paths from A to B, whereas the average user has declarative knowledge (knowing what). This is a case where the familiar taxi driver creates a survey map (a more integrated form) in an environment that is understood. Similarly, Egan and Schwartz (1979) looked at the ability to recall symbolic drawings in experts (electronics technicians) versus novices (college students or lab technicians). This skill is pivotal in such professions as engineering, chemistry, and architecture as well as electronics. Perceptual chunking is usually pointed to in such games as chess and Go (a strategic board game in which two players attempt to cover a checkered board with black or white markers); their research suggests that conceptual as well as perceptual chunking may occur in recalling symbolic drawings. Knowing the conceptual category of a display may lead to grouping in units that are functional, facilitating recall.

Phillips and colleagues (1990) demonstrated the difference between novice and experts in reading map symbols and tried to use perceptual guidelines to develop new symbols to reduce the confusion caused by some symbols. The confusing symbols were those for cutting (where a road or railway passes through an excavation below ground level) and embankment (which raises a road or railway above ground level) from Ordnance Survey topographical maps. The authors tested ninety-nine 11- to 13-year-old girls to see if new symbols for embankment and cutting could be better differentiated than the standards and then did the same with an experienced group at a cartography conference. The "experts" had better performance and were more facile with the new designs: "differences in map symbols do affect performance of less experienced map readers, but their interests are often ignored" (Phillips et al., 1990, p. 497). The research on familiarity suggests that *maps need to be designed for the less experienced user*.

While familiarity typically predicts better performance, there are exceptions (Moeser, 1988). In a series of studies with student nurses who had varying degrees of familiarity with a complex hospital environment, nurses who traveled through the facility for a number of months were actually *worse* at some way-finding tasks than students new to the building who memorized floor plans to criterion and took a short building tour. Another example of the occasional lack of relationship between familiarity and environmental performance occurred with nursing home patients (Weber, Brown, & Weldon, 1978). Their performance in identifying photographs of their nursing home (with from 6 months to 6 ½ years of residence) was worse than the performance of students who had a total of 40 minutes of exposure to the environment. The authors offer no definitive explanation for the patients' poor performance, but suggest that patients may "gate out" information they find unnecessary. This raises a question about the ecological validity of the dependent measures we use in such studies vis-à-vis the ability of residents to get along day to day.

Spatial ability is another variable that affects performance. A study of drivers' map-reading abilities (Streeter & Vitello, 1986) looked at those with self-reported high and low spatial abilities. While the groups differed in their approach to map reading, both groups relied on landmarks for navigation to some extent. Those with low spatial ability were reported to avoid carrying maps, consulting maps, or liking maps. This is all the more reason to think about how to make maps palatable. The authors suggest that navigational guidance systems need to emphasize the voice, given the difficulty maps present to many people. They suggest that one instruction be coupled with each turn. The rapid expansion of navigational tools for automobiles presents an ideal place to expand our understanding of how people use maps and directions—what works and what does not.

Gestalt and Perceptual Principles

An area in cognition with a long history of contributions to spatial understanding is Gestalt psychology. Despite what may seem like unsophisticated principles, Gestalt guidelines still carry explanatory power and have profound implications for way-finding tools. For example, Chen (1982) discussed global topological attributes as fundamental to perceptual organization. When we do something like detect a hole within a circle, we are relying on principles like connectedness-closedness. Not only is this related to Gestalt principles, but also to a Gibsonian (1966) stance—we resonate to the invariant properties of the object. Chen quotes Gibson (1979) that, "The perceptual system simply extracts the invariants from the flowing array; it resonates to the invariant structure or is attuned to it" (p. 700). Maps need to present information in a manner consistent with Gestalt principles.

Imhof (1975) offers useful map-labeling principles that have a foundation in Gestalt psychology. For example, we should avoid covering, overlapping, and concealing information so that other map contents are visible. Rather than being evenly spaced or densely spaced, information should reflect its level of importance. The hierarchical emphasis we saw in research on cognitive mapping emerges here as well. Labels should appear to the right of the object and slightly above it. Quoting W. Schule, Imhof says "Above all, the undesirable impression of chaos, of the crowded anthill, of the dancing type, must be held off" (p. 141).

As in mapping (Imhof, 1975), Gestalt principles play an important role in statistical graphics. For example, grouping plays a role in the perceptual experience of graphs (Coren & Girgus, 1980). Interior distances can be underestimated relative to exterior distances due to this grouping. Their point is that "the perceptual effects are not merely organizational in nature but seem to be accompanied by a distortion in the spatial relationships perceived in the field" (p. 409).

Dent (1972) also talks about the role of visual organization. Discussing thematic map communication, he argues that you want the thematic symbols to emerge as figures and the base map to stay grounded. Figure perception is significantly influenced by heterogeneity, contour, and enclosedness. We are urged to study the perception of the total map, and not just the role of the individual symbols. The map is thus to be understood as a visual hierarchy, with the most important elements emerging for our eyes. Figure–ground differentiation will contribute substantially to this hierarchy. "Each visual level (or plane) can be thought of as distinct from another by virtue of the intellectual importance attached to the visual stimuli of that level" (Dent, 1972, p. 83). For Dent, the most important impact results from the contrast at the edge of figures and their ground. This analysis sounds very much like Marr's (1982) explanation of low-end perception. Marr and Nishihara (1978) emphasize that edges and contours are needed for good figure–ground differentiation. A sharp edge can contribute to a stronger figure; figures are perceived in large part due to contours. Dent uses the work of J. J. Gibson and his theory of direct realism as a basis for his guidelines. Another Gestalt emphasis emerges in the work of Nothdurft (1991), who states that it is the differences that make things pop out or emerge from the ground; it is not the orientation features themselves that are important, but the orientation *differences*.

Summary

In providing way-finding information, we must present the cues in a form understandable at the lowest ability level. While familiarity and high spatial ability enhance our way-finding success, we need to design way-finding aids for those without such characteristics. Furthermore, mapmakers need to understand more about human perceptual preferences that reflect Gestalt principles (e.g., similarity, grouping, good continuation). In their representation of reality, cartographers should be mindful of these perceptual preferences and their impact on the interpretation of map information.

STUDIES OF WAY-FINDING AIDS: MAPS, SIGNS, AND BUILDINGS

Let us now turn our attention to the specific tools that may help us in way finding. When we think of tools or external devices that help us find our way, maps and signs certainly come to mind. But when we consider extensive structures like hospital complexes, we realize that the building itself can play an important role in understanding the environment.

Maps As Tools

Maps are double-edged swords. On the one hand, people view maps as efficacious and select them either alone or in combination as way-finding aids (Devlin & Bernstein, 1995). On the other hand, people may have a kind of map phobia or anxiety, particularly the elderly (Devlin, 1980). We use maps, but we may not be comfortable using them.

While most of the research we will discuss comes from cartography and statistical graphics, there are some studies from psychology that deal directly with maps. Perhaps the most well-known studies dealing directly with way-finding aids are those of Levine (1982; Levine, Marchon, & Hanley, 1984). Levine and colleagues addressed the effectiveness of You-are-here (YAH) maps and suggested ways to improve them. Several useful YAH rules emerge from Levine's (1982) work, including the orientation principle (the map needs to parallel the terrain) and forward-up equivalence (people assume forward movement and "up" on the map are equivalent). Levine recommends that the location for the YAH map is chosen first, ideally near an asymmetrical part of the environment. The YAH map can then be structured to parallel its environmental placement. Levine refers to the importance of the "bipart YAH symbol," by which he means that the symbol (showing where you are standing relative to the map) has to indicate both the orientation of the map within the terrain as well as the side of the map on which the viewer is standing (see Figure 4.1). One study (Levine et al., 1984) looked at YAH maps in 14 shopping centers in the New York City area. People behaved as if the maps were aligned with the environment (which they typically were not), and when given way-finding tasks that involved contraligned maps, very few participants could solve the problems.

One of my favorite local examples of a contraligned map (now corrected) was the YAH map at the Westfarms Mall, outside of Hartford, Connecticut (see Figure 4.2). As you face the pedestal YAH map in Figure 4.2, you have actually exited from Filene's, one of the anchor stores, and are entering the interior of the mall. As you can see from the picture, the map is 180 degrees out of alignment. Assuming forward is up, as Levine says we do, you assume you have exited J.C. Penney's, not Filene's, even though the map

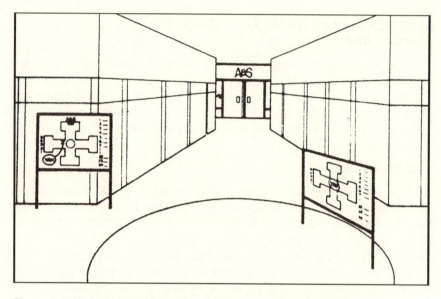

Figure 4.1. Levine's YAH example, left map correctly identified with symbols.

Figure 4.2. Westfarms YAH map.

correctly depicts the YAH location with a red dot outside Filene's. You are challenged to perform spatial rotation to determine where you are.

A study dealing with aspects of cognitive map formation dovetails with Levine's work. The study involved learning a series of landmarks (e.g., farm, church, park, lake, and bridge) using slides of object pairs that subjects needed to integrate into a coherent map (Wall, Karl, & Smigiel, 1986). Participants were exposed to conditions of chaining (viewing the landmarks in the object pairs in a sequence paralleling their array in the actual map), of putting the items in their appropriate location on the slide (spatial condition), or of centering the object pairs on the slide (nonspatial condition). Performance in creating the overall map was enhanced in both the chaining and the spatial conditions. These findings supplement those of Levine (1982; Levine et al., 1984) concerning You-are-here maps. Context is important in forming the cognitive map. Attention to the location of the YAH symbol relative to the immediate surrounding overlaps with the chaining and spatial aspects of the Wall and colleagues (1986) study.

Approaches

Levine's studies of YAH maps are exceptions in the domain of mapping research. Most of the research on maps deals with the manipulation of individual variables, either format-oriented (usually outside psychology) or conceptual (inside psychology). As an example of format-oriented research, consider a study using eye movement measurements to develop recommendations for the location of place labels on maps (Phillips, Noyes, & Audley, 1978). Aspects of type legibility influence search time, and search time can be reduced if map readers know in advance that name coding is keyed by color or point size.

In a study involving issues of complexity (a conceptual example), three levels of complexity and two styles of maps were crossed to yield six map designs that were evaluated when subjects drove to a street address (Kovach, Surrette, & Aamodt, 1988). The levels of complexity were low (direct route with left–right directions); medium (direct route, left–right directions, five adjacent streets, and major mileage estimation); and high (seven landmarks added to the medium complexity variables). The two styles were: (1) written verbatim directions, or (2) illustrated map of the same route. The amount of time driving to the address was the dependent variable. Results indicated that those with written verbatim instructions found the destination faster and that the level of complexity did not significantly affect the time to reach the destination. This study has a couple of important implications. First, we are typically more comfortable, skilled, or facile with verbal information than with map information. Second, way-finding aids, whether written verbatim directions or maps, need not be highly detailed to be effective for a fairly simple task. What we need is an accurate description or depiction of the route to be followed.

In our focus on psychology, let's continue with research on conceptual variables. As you might expect, behavior that reflects principles from human information processing appears in research involving maps. Just as the benefits of chunking and hierarchical organization occur in mainstream research on cognitive psychology (see, e.g., Bower, Clark, Lesgold, & Winzenz, 1969), they also emerge in research on maps. Maps that facilitate chunking and hierarchical organization appear to communicate effectively and assist the map reader. As an example, consider a study by Eastman (1985). Five fictitious maps with different graphic organizations were learned to criterion by 50 students who performed various kinds of tasks with these maps. The maps varied in terms of increasing differentiation, from the simplest (showing just cities), to the most differentiated (showing major and minor cities, county boundaries with color tints, and road connections differentiated into major and minor categories). Eastman focused on measures of learning efficiency. Subjects showed strong evidence of clustering the information into hierarchies, as has been indicated in other research (Hirtle & Jonides, 1985). Eastman was interested in the effects of graphic variability on the formation of chunking and made some observations regarding what constitutes a good map. Commenting on the information maps should communicate, the author states, "Effective communication requires *structure*—a pervading organization of all map elements that naturally binds the many features presented" (p. 18). What emerges as advice is that the graphic aspects of the map should emphasize regions (chunks) and a hierarchy of such chunks, reflecting the fact that humans have a tendency to form hierarchies.

Although chunking and clustering are human tendencies, maps don't always accommodate these tendencies. In a study of subway map use in New York City (using real maps), the participants had considerable difficulty (Bronzaft, Dobrow, & O'Hanlon, 1976). Newcomers to New York City (in residence less than seven months) were given the 1972 subway guide (supposedly superior to its predecessor) and one token to complete a travel route with four connected trip segments. None of the 20 travelers could plan acceptable routes for all the destinations, and Bronzaft and colleagues (1976) recommend a number of modifications, including improved graphics in stations and concourses. Revisiting Rome in 1996 after a 20-year absence, I was struck by the metro system that had miraculously been wedged underneath a city spilling over with historic landmarks. Much less complicated than the NYC subway system, the version in Rome was easy for the newcomer (much easier and far faster, in fact, than the city's bus system). The system has two major routes (red and blue) intersecting at a central switching station. The graphics are clean and bold, clearly directing the traveler at every choice point (see Figure 4.3). Even the Paris Metro system,

Figure 4.3. Rome subway graphics.

although far more complicated than the one in Rome, is easier to follow than the New York City lines. In addition to its increased complexity because of the number of different subway lines, I think one of the reasons for the difficulty of the New York system is the infrequent intersection of lines. This fact makes it difficult to get from one side of Manhattan to another.

Researchers have also examined simulation as a preview to a real environment (Weisman, O'Neill, & Doll, 1987). The responses of those who visited the real environment (an area within a university building) and those who viewed a computer graphic simulation of that environment were similar. Thus, in addition to maps, computer simulations can provide wayfinding orientation. However, from both a theoretical and practical standpoint, there is concern with the comparability of maps and simulations versus real-time environmental experiences as a form of environmental learning. For example, Thorndyke and Hayes-Roth (1982) compared subjects who actually walked through an environment and those who studied maps. Those with the real-world task made more accurate route estimates, whereas those who studied maps made more accurate survey estimates, including Euclidean distances and the relative positions of locations. With experience, the real-time navigators were hypothesized to acquire the survey knowledge that map learners possessed. Therefore, while some outcome measures for simulated versus actual exposure show similar results, others do not. Map use seemed to facilitate success with map-oriented dependent variables (Euclidean distances), whereas those who were in the environment were more accurate on a dependent measure (route estimates) that reflected their experience. Again, we see that the selection of dependent measures is critical in evaluating knowledge. We need to continue to examine the effects of real and simulated experience in order to better understand their comparability.

In terms of simulation, technology now plays a role in many way-finding aids. The advent of computer-based formats for way finding has stimulated research about the effectiveness of navigational information that is presented via computer simulation and interactive means (Devlin & Bernstein, 1995, 1997; Golledge, Smith, Pellegrino, Doherty, & Marshall, 1985; Gopal, Klatzky, & Smith, 1989; Leiser & Zilbershatz, 1989; O'Neill, 1986, 1992; Smith, Pellegrino, & Golledge, 1982; Tlauka & Wilson, 1996; Weisman, O'Neill, & Doll, 1987). Way-finding computer kiosks are proliferating, and I even found one inside the majestic Santa Maria Maggiore basilica in Rome, providing touch-screen information (descriptions and maps) for the major landmarks in the city (see Figure 4.4).

Sometimes technology and reality are misaligned. An ironic moment occurred during the 1996 Summer Olympics Games in Atlanta, where a July 26 *Today Show* segment focused on Hertz Rental Car's NeverLost system, which had been added to 500 rental cars (for $6 more per day) to assist drivers in way finding. The problem was that road blocks and detours were everywhere. A global positioning-based system (GPS) really didn't work for the Atlanta Olympics, not because the paths were incorrect but because they were unavailable! As such way-finding aids as video maps for auto navigation grow in availability (Haavind, 1985; Sloan, 1997), it is important to investigate how to effectively present dynamic information. One such aid, the Etak system for auto navigation, compares the vehicle's movements with stored map data and rotates the map (visible to the driver on the dashboard) to keep the road at the top of the screen (rather than north).

The rotational aspect of the Etak system points to the importance of such factors as map alignment in way finding (Haavind, 1985). Maps misaligned to the environment are likely to cause errors (Rossano & Warren, 1989; Warren, 1994; Warren, Rossano, & Wear, 1990; Warren & Scott, 1993; Warren, Scott, & Medley, 1992). As we have seen, Levine (Levine, 1982; Levine et al., 1984) has also demonstrated that You-are-here maps are not always as helpful as they should be, as they are often misplaced and misaligned. These systems are becoming increasingly available

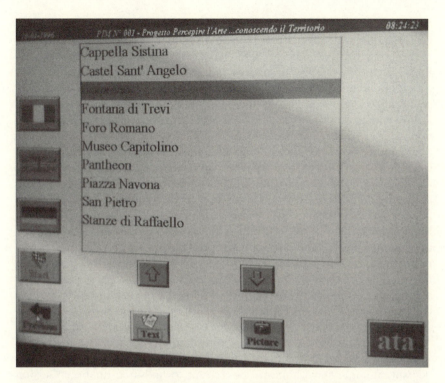

Figure 4.4. Way-finding computer screen in Santa Maria Maggiore.

(as the proliferation of television ads suggests) in a wide price range of automobiles and provide us with the opportunity to ask research questions about alignment, level of detail, mode of presentation, and so on.

Directions

Finally, let us consider the topic of directions. The focus of this chapter is on way-finding aids that are typically experienced without the assistance of additional interpretation (i.e., from another person). At the same time, it is useful to consider briefly what we know about the process of verbally communicating directions—what happens when people give directions? What can we learn about what they think is important (which in turn might tell us something about creating helpful maps)? When 78 people were asked to give directions to a neighborhood landmark (Hill, 1987), they emphasized directness (100% gave directions for the shortest route). Their responses emphasized: (1) geometry and spatial relations—providing verbal descriptions of aspects maps show graphically, such as "straight," "curves around," "across," and "up"; (2) compass directions (objective or relative—e.g., left, right); and (3) distance units—giving an estimation of how far the landmark is, usually in block units. Mileage estimates or standardized metrics occurred infrequently. This again points to a deemphasis on Euclidean properties in our understanding of the world. Direction givers also used street names, route and landmark descriptions, and offered personalizations. Nonverbal aids included pointing to the destination. Hill (1987) emphasizes the following themes of direction giving: accuracy, helpfulness, knowledgeability norms, and simplicity.

In another study involving giving directions (Ward, Newcombe, & Overton, 1986), participants demonstrated a preference for using landmarks and relational terms more than cardinality and mileage. With regard to using the cardinal directions, east–west is harder to differentiate than north–south (Carreiras & Garling, 1990). As an explanation for this difference, Carreiras and Garling (1990) point to a plausible role of body axes, with the up–down or front–behind asymmetry providing more clues than the left–right. It appears that in terms of giving directions, users are unlikely to provide some of the fundamentals of general reference maps like cardinality and mileage estimates. As an adjunct to general reference cartography, perhaps maps can be developed that make more use of features like landmarks. At the very least, maps of the local terrain should reflect this emphasis.

Consider the following example about local way finding. In a field study that varied whether instructions were given (Gordon & Wood, 1970), participants unfamiliar with an area were sent to find a destination. Gordon and Wood (1970) were particularly interested in drivers' way-finding strategies. Some were told to get any information they could in order to get there whereas others were given complete instructions about reaching the destination. The behavior of those without instructions was far more interesting than those with instructions, who found the destination in about half the time. Gasoline station attendants were far and away the most frequently consulted information source, and almost all of those without directions drove as close as they could to the goal in the local area before asking directions to the address. The authors point to local area way finding as a challenge made more difficult because large-scale maps do not contain a sufficient level of detail. To help travelers, Gordon and Wood recommend way-finding aids, such as road signs, that could direct the driver to gasoline stations with local maps. They also recommend visible and systematic house numbering, for example streets arranged with numerical or alphabetical grids.

I think we have a good sense of what people are likely to emphasize in giving directions—brief information, usually in steps, that they think people need to know in order to get from Point A to Point B. Giving directions is something we are able to do at a relatively young age, although our ability to provide the information our listeners need has a developmental progression (Waller & Harris, 1988). Verbal directions may be a source of information people feel comfortable providing.

But with regard to maps, we don't know what difference it makes how they are designed. Furthermore, to some degree people differ in their ability to identify what information is useful in a way-finding task (Hardwick, Woolridge, & Rinalducci, 1983). Maps drawn by 59 college students were scored using Moore's (1976) developmental categories, and then these subjects viewed slides of a simulated walk through an unknown area. They were told to pick nine photos that would be useful in recalling the walk. Those who had drawn maps that reflected the highest level of spatial organization (level III) were significantly better than those at the other two levels in picking scenes showing landmarks where changes in heading occurred (considered critical information). Similarly, people who subjectively describe themselves as having a good or poor sense of direction (Kozlowski & Bryant, 1977) differ in their enjoyment of maps, a kind of self-fulfilling prophecy. People with a self-described good sense of direction were better at such activities as giving and following directions, and remembering routes while in cars.

While we have seen some research on the map as a whole (Levine's YAH studies) and on conceptual issues (e.g., map complexity, simulation research), let us turn our attention to the bulk of the research on individual variables in the visual display. One question that has received some attention in research is the role of stylistic factors in the map display itself. Among the variables of concern to any mapmaker are the use of color and format (e.g., level of detail, location of map information such as labels). While other aspects will be included, we focus on these.

INDIVIDUAL VARIABLES IN MAPS AND DISPLAYS

Color-coding: Reputation and Guidelines

The use of color to transmit information in maps and graphs has a mixed reputation. While the use of color has potential benefits, color has been called a complex symbol for map use (Monmonier & Schnell, 1988), potentially distracting and confusing (Southworth & Southworth, 1982). The ability of color to add information in color displays comes from its potential contribution to clarity, offering a range of possibilities for differentiation (Robinson, Sale, Morrison, & Muehrcke, 1984). Many writers, some of them researchers, offer guidelines about the use of color in maps and graphic displays (Kosslyn, 1994a; Olson, 1987; Travis, 1991). In terms of research, much of what we know about the use of color comes from work in statistical graphics (see, e.g., Cuff, 1973), where color has been called the "most efficient dimension for the labeling of information in visual displays" (Smallman & Boynton, 1990, p. 1985). As we will see, this assessment of the advantage of color is not universally shared.

As one of eight visual variables that can be used in display (Bertin, cited in Olson, 1987), color can be described in terms of certain conventional uses, for example, color has associations with temperature (e.g., blue with coolness); color wavelength produces colors that advance or retreat; and colors covering small areas need to be bright and differentiated from those around them to be noticed (Olson, 1987). Travis (1991) states that colors should be used for one or more of the following reasons: realism, formatting, coding, and aesthetics. It can help by highlighting a target in a dense display; segment an area of the display; warn; help to group or chunk; suggest a physical state (e.g., warmth); and create an aesthetically pleasing display. Travis provides a series of rules, including using color to group and for emphasis, and gives us six principles of color coding—that it be discriminable, detectable, in perceptually equal steps, meaningful, consistent, and aesthetically pleasing. For aesthetics, complementary colors and a logical sequence are recommended.

Color can be disadvantageous as well—it can distract; overload; be ineffective for the color-blind; conflict with cultural conventions; and produce unintended visual effects, such as illusions (Travis, 1991). It should not be employed if there are other means of communicating the information. Travis (1991) states that you don't necessarily turn to color first. It may be redundant. He says that when color coding is used, strive to make it a secondary cue. For Travis, color might involve the following problems: a peripheral visual field, contrast effects, chromatic aberration chromostereopsis, luminance differences, and visual aftereffects. His guideline is *"design for monochrome first"* (p. 117). Olson (1987) differentiates between decorative uses of color on maps (for aesthetic or attentional purposes) and functional uses (to symbolize some component of content). To use color in a functional manner, not only must it represent something, but its presentation monochromatically would have a negative effect on the "amount or accuracy of information or speed of extraction" (p. 208). So before using color, the criterion for the functional purpose must be satisfied.

Research on Color Displays

The effectiveness of color in displays has been studied extensively. Many of these studies involve searching a display for a target. In fact, the effect of color on search time has a long history and has been investigated over the last half-century (Green & Anderson, 1956; Smith, 1962). Green and Anderson (1956) looked at three-digit numbers as symbols, measuring the search time for displays that varied in the number of colors. When the subject knows the color of the target, search time appears proportional to the number of items of the target's color. When the target color is unknown, it is the total number of symbols that seems to influence search time. Moreover, multicolored displays in general seem to produce longer search times than do uniformly colored displays. With a small number of colors (5–8) searching for three digit numbers, neither target nor background color affected search time (Smith, 1962). Search time increased linearly as the display density increased.

The impact of color compared to achromatic display was reviewed in 42 studies conducted between 1953 and 1973 (Christ, 1975). Christ's (1975) general conclusion was that color is helpful in certain circumstances and not in others:

... if the subject's task is to identify some feature of a target, colors can be identified more accurately than sizes, brightnesses, familiar geometric shapes, and other shape or form parameters, but colors are identified with less accuracy than alphanumeric symbols. This is generally true, both when comparisons are made between unidimensional displays and within multidimensional displays, although the differences tend to be larger within multidimensional displays. (p. 560)

The superiority of alphanumeric relative to color target identification is linked to subjects' greater familiarity with alphanumeric than color searches.

One of the indirect findings that emerges is that colors will be more effective in displays if they are *maximally discriminable* (Boynton, Fargo, Olson, & Smallman, 1989). Cahill and Carter (1976) looked at a three-digit search task paradigm, with displays of 10 to 50 items coded in 1 to 10 colors. The number of colors constitutes the code size while the number of data items in the display is called the density. Code sizes larger than five can be effectively employed if discriminable colors are selected. If the display is considered low density (10–20 items), up to 10 colors are possible. Furthermore, in differentiating strata in scatterplots, Lewandowsky and Spence (1989) found that use of colors produced the best performance, then shapes, degree of fill, and lastly confusable letters.

The issue of basic colors and their function in a display was also investigated by Smallman and Boynton (1990), who emphasize the segregation of colors in color space for maximum discriminability. While other researchers had suggested that there was an upper limit of about six to the number of colors that could effectively be used in a display, Smallman and Boynton showed that the use of focal basic colors could expand that number considerably (perhaps double it). The question is not whether they are optimal basic colors, per se, but how separated they are in color space. "The time required to find a critical target of a cued color increased only marginally as up to nine groups of different colors were added to the display" (p. 1985). The more discriminable or separable in color space, the better. Therefore, one of the factors that emerges (with possible implications for way finders and tools) is the discriminability of the colors used. If you want people to notice them, the colors need to be discriminable.

Color similarly has implications for attention. From the theoretical work on attention, it has been suggested that when similarity increases (when the colors become more similar), the subject is forced to shift from a preattentive to an attentional search (Moraglia, Maloney, Fekete, & Al-Basi, 1989). Similarity of colors is hypothesized to put greater attentional processing pressure on people, who must shift from a preattentive to an attentive mode. When the color of the background items is dissimilar to the target, search times are unaffected (Carter, 1982).

Color seems to affect certain aspects of task performance and judgment, including search time and preference (people like color graphs better than monochromatic ones), but often error rates are not among the differences. For example, in a study of point-reading, point-comparison, trend-reading, and trend-comparison tasks, use of color graphics led to lower task completion time, lower rated information-processing load, and higher preference for three of the tasks, but error scores were unaffected when compared to the monochromatic versions (Casali & Gaylin, 1988). However, Casali and Gaylin (1988) point out that the use of color in this study was redundant, that is, the information was available from another source, so it is difficult to evaluate the contribution of color in this study. But in other studies there has been no clear advantage to the use of color. For example, in a study where subjects were asked to understand a display about a computer-based telephone line testing system, color did not contribute significantly to subjects' performance (Tullis, 1981).

In trying to organize the findings from the research on color, one of the strong themes is that the nature of the task affects the viability of color use. For example, using two colors in statistical maps creates certain problems (Trumbo, 1981). There are the issues of order and separation. Wainer and Francollini (1980) also studied how we understand two-variable color maps. The legend scheme for two-variable color maps is difficult to learn, according to these authors. When there are two statistical maps that one wants to display simultaneously, difficulties arise. In reading statistical maps, the advantage of using multiple hues may depend on task complexity (Hastie, Hammerle, Kerwin, Croner, & Hermann, 1996). Thus, the effects of color coding seem to depend on the experimental conditions (Tullis, 1981). Generally, search tasks seem to be enhanced by the use of color (see, e.g., Carter, 1982; Lewandowsky & Spence, 1989; Moraglia et al., 1989) and identification tasks go either way.

Other advice about color use comes indirectly from Tufte. In addition to creating lovely books, Tufte's volumes (1983, 1990) contain good advice (although not presented in a research format). Color creates its own puzzles, according to Tufte, because the "mind's eye does not readily give a visual ordering to colors, except possibly for red to reflect higher levels than other colors" (1983, p. 154). Rather than using color to show quantities, Tufte advises us to use progressive gradations of gray, precisely because they have a visual order.

While people like color displays better than those in black and white (Tullis, 1981), preference is not a compelling reason for adoption. We need more empirical guidelines about the use of color. These guidelines are particularly important for cartography, because most of what is known about the effects of color comes from work in statistical graphics. It is difficult to know about the extension of this work to cartography.

In addition to the work in statistical graphics, some research in psychology and education focuses on color, but typically as only one of a number of variables. For example, in a study involving maps (Garland, Haynes, & Grubb, 1979), the effectiveness of color and street detail on a city bus map for trip planning performance was examined. The study used four different map types: color (version 1) and black and white (version 2) official transit maps; a black and white stick route map (version 3); and a major street and route map (version 4). In the Garland and colleagues (1979) study, 11 different colors were used to indicate 26 separately labeled routes. The authors reported that elimination of small street detail is helpful in the absence of color coding on the map, as there were more errors in the black and white version of the official transit map than in either the color version or the black and white major streets and routes version. They suggested that considerable money can be saved without much loss of usefulness by using black and white maps with a reduced level of street detail. Other research (Devlin & Bernstein, 1997; Wong & Yacoumelos, 1973) also showed no improvement in performance with the use of color over black and white displays. Research in education has been more positive about the potential contribution of color and has indicated that color-enhanced materials can facilitate recall of maps and traditional text (Hall & Sidio-Hall, 1994). There is a role for the use of color in maps, but the extent to which it parallels the role in statistical graphics applications is unknown.

Summary

In summary, color works better as a redundant cue (Shontz, Trumm, & Williams, 1971) and seems to help viewers structure their searches more efficiently, especially where a category label or symbol accompanies each use of the category color. As indicated by Hastie and colleagues (1996), the advantages of using multiple hues may depend on task complexity, and Christ's (1975) summary of the literature does a good job in indicating under what task circumstances color may help or hinder.

Practical Implications

Are there practical implications of color in the larger designed environment as well as in the representational forms of maps and graphics? Certainly designers and planners behave as if color coding plays a useful role in way finding, although its impact is not always known. The practical use of color is particularly evident for signage and on large surfaces (e.g., walls, carpeting). Let me provide a number of examples. In housing projects, I have seen color coding used as an effective, although redundant, way-finding cue. In the Westminster Place housing for the elderly in Providence, Rhode Island, four different colors were used on the door trim of apartments on 11 floors as an aid to way finding. According to the architect, these colors were called chili sauce (floors 1, 5, and 9); bib lettuce (floors 2, 6, and 10); blueberry (floors 3, 7, and 11); and winterberry (floors 4 and 8). Winterberry was a kind of brownish hue. Fortunately for the residents, these names were never associated with the floors. Of course, color served as a redundant cue because each of the floors also had numeric markers, from the elevator to a ceramic floor pad (contrasting figure and ground tiles) placed just off the elevator (see Figure 4.5). With just four colors, residents were able to remember what color their floor was and were likely to notice if they stepped off the elevator on a floor of a different color. The importance of using color as a secondary or redundant cue is reinforced by the fact that age-related changes in the lens of the eye tend to alter the way color is perceived. In turn, this limits the use of color for architectural differentiation.

An ineffective use of color occurred in the Hempstead Street High Rise in New London, Connecticut (Devlin, 1980). All floors were painted the same green color. Residents often complained about stepping off the elevator on a floor, placing their key in "their" lock, and being terribly embarrassed when they realized they were on the wrong floor and were trying to enter someone else's apartment.

Weisman (1987) has indicated that color is not always noticed as a way-finding indicator, as fewer than 20% of the residents of a long-term care facility realized that color was intended as a specific way-finding aid. I also remember a local bank using a colored "carpet path" that contrasted with the rest of the carpeting to indicate where bank patrons were to stand in line as they waited for the next available teller. No one paid any attention to the color path! They may have noticed it but had no idea of its purpose, they may not have noticed it, or they may have thought it was silly. Whatever the reason, the colored carpet path was ineffective for queuing bank patrons.

In discussing the use of color for way finding in libraries (Selfridge, 1979), caution is urged: "it works only when it is repeated clearly enough

Figure 4.5. Floor numbering at Westminister Place.

so that people notice that color is functional and not merely decorative. If different colors identify different major places in the library or different floors in the building, the colors should be used on every direction and identification sign to those major places or floors" (p. 62).

I have seen color used effectively as a redundant cue at the National Zoo in Washington, D.C. At the zoo, color joins a number of other way-finding devices, including the use of international symbols, a painted red path indicating the major spine of the park's pathway system, a series of graphic totem polls, and animal footprints (in color) to indicate a path with a major attraction (see Figure 4.6). Although I visited this zoo many years ago, it remains one of the best examples of supportive way finding I have ever seen.

Format Issues

The issue of format (e.g., detail, label placement) represents another major concern to mapmakers, model makers, and users.

Figure 4.6. Totem poll at the National Zoo.

Level of Detail

An important aspect of format in maps and models is the level of detail represented. We need to provide sufficient information without over-whelming the user, to avoid the chaos about which Imhof (1975) spoke. While greater detail may add realism to a visual display, it does not nec-essarily affect functional variables (i.e., the ability to make judgments based on the information). For example, Kaplan, Kaplan, and Deardorff (1974) demonstrated that subjects could base judgments on the information pre-sented in architectural models with limited detail. They argue that simpli-fication of the display has a number of benefits, from increasing generality to reducing information-processing demand. In the Kaplan and colleagues (1974) study, models of high- or low-detail housing developments were presented to subjects in a between-groups design. The high-detail model had facade and landscaping details such as windows and contour lines. Subjects rated the housing development models in terms of functional as-pects (e.g., how satisfactory they would be for privacy) and concluded that the simple model was as useful as the more detailed one in making these kinds of judgments. When subjects viewed pictures of the actual housing development on which the models were based, participants in both high- and low-detail conditions reported that the model that they had seen was an adequate representation of the actual development. Tufte (1983) is another author who argues for simplification in visual displays, as does Arnheim (1976), who stated that, "A map containing a maximum of detail makes it almost impossible to grasp the essential elements" (p. 9).

Typeface and Label Placement

We do have guidelines for map typeface size, style, and vertical spacing (Poulton, 1972). We also know what lettering size can be discriminated on a map (Shortridge, 1979). Shortridge (1979) examined 253 maps in 26 introductory geography texts. Varying letter size was the most typical way of creating a hierarchy. Testing 21 pairs of letters indicated that, "A size difference of 34 percent or greater generally elicits a correct response by at least 85 percent of the population" (p. 16). According to Shortridge, we are to avoid lettering size differences in the range of 17–22% and never use differences of less than 15% because we cannot differentiate them. Furthermore, sometimes "reality" must be modified in order to be noticed or detected. The aspect ratio may have to be altered to emphasize small changes because the perceptual categories might not otherwise be detected (Simcox, 1984).

We also know that certain number styles may be read faster than others (Smith, 1978) and that the legibility of displayed letters depends on the subtended visual angle at any viewing distance (Smith, 1979). Other factors that influence legibility include brightness, the array or alphabet of letters used, detailed shape features, case (upper or lower), height-to-width ratio, and stroke width: "But it is letter size which most seriously constrains display design" (Smith, 1979, p. 661).

With regard to the legibility of individual symbols, some work has been done on the effectiveness of tactual elements. In testing different forms for blind observers, those with open contours with straight lines and sharp corners were more discriminable as were outline compared to solid tactile map symbols (Lambert & Lederman, 1989). But we don't know what can be carried over to our understanding of two-dimensional graphic arrays for sighted observers. It is important to remember that, "Legible symbols in themselves do not guarantee effective displays" (Smith, 1979, p. 669). It seems wise to reiterate a point that was made earlier in this chapter: Variables examined in isolation do not necessarily tell the whole story nor predict performance.

One of the problems with the cartographic literature is that it has not developed a broad base of empirical research, and it is not clear how generalizable the specific research on isolated variables (e.g., type size, etc.) is to broader scale issues in cartography and ultimately to way finding. There is also a problem with operationally defining legibility, as it has been done in a number of ways (Bartz, 1970). We may know something about the minimum letter size needed for slide displays (Bockemuehl & Wilson, 1976) and whether medium- or bold-faced letters are easier to read than delicate styles or those employing serifs, but how is the overall gestalt perceived and how is performance affected?

Another aspect of format is the legend. DeLucia and Hiller (1982) looked at the use of what was called a natural legend for thematic maps. A natural legend involves the re-creation of a portion of the mapped landscape or surface with appropriate labeling in the legend. A natural legend was hypothesized to be more visually efficient for the map reader. What you are doing is taking a part of the natural format (like contour lines) and creating a legend from that rather than using a standard format (like a graded bar). Using 40 subjects to contrast four different formats, results indicated that the natural legend design produced better performance for accuracy for questions that required them to correctly visualize the landscape. The format did not matter for questions involving elevation. Thus, the advantage to this kind of legend appears to be limited to issues where it overlaps with the content of the question asked.

The question of label placement as well as the notion of the legend has also been of cartographic interest. Research supporting the conjoint retention hypothesis, an extension of Paivio's (1986) dual coding theory, suggests that label information on the map is better recalled when it is presented at appropriate positions, rather than in a separate list of labels (Kulhavy, Caterino, & Melchiori, 1989; Schwartz & Kulhavy, 1981). The dual coding theory proposes that spatial/perceptual information and linguistic/verbal information are coded separately but that the codes lead to connected representations that can be used simultaneously when retrieval cues are provided for each (Kulhavy, Stock, Verdi, & Rittschof, 1993; Kulhavy, Stock, Woodard, & Haygood, 1993; Webb, Saltz, McCarthy, & Kealy, 1994). In a study by Kulhavy and colleagues (1989), verbal material was integrated with the spatial map information (map condition) or presented on the left side of the page (list condition). The participants in the map condition recalled more information than those in the list condition. The authors conclude that, "The economy with which the intact map can be represented in working memory allows a wider search to proceed in a manner significantly more effective than when subjects attempt to use list-presented items in the same fashion" (p. 303). Thus, when labels are included within the spatial structure of a map itself, they are coded as part of an intact unit, facilitating a faster search process on the basis of a more economical memory representation. Kuo (1996) reported that participants in a condition where labels were placed directly on buildings on a campus map learned more from the map than those who used a map where the labels were adjacent to the buildings.

In a study examining how variables affected computer-simulated way-finding ability (Devlin & Bernstein, 1997), participants were randomly assigned to one of eight different map conditions that varied level of detail, color, and label placement. Participants with landmarks identified by number and labeled in a legend (legend condition) took significantly longer than those in conditions where landmark names were listed at the site of the landmarks themselves (labels intact condition) to locate one of the specified landmarks. This evidence of map–label integration supports the hypothesis of Kulhavy and colleagues (1989, 1993) about conjoint retention. The greater economy with which the intact map with focused attention to landmarks can be stored and retrieved presumably facilitates a faster search than for maps with the labels keyed separately by number.

The issue of format also has been of long-standing concern in statistical graphics. Early research (Carter, 1947; Eells, 1926) focused on what kind of format (e.g., circles vs. bars) was superior to represent data, and to some extent the field continues that interest in format. In a study using graphs, it was demonstrated that placing labels directly to the right on the graph function (Milroy & Poulton, 1978) resulted in faster judgments (although not fewer errors) than conditions where the key was on the graph field below the functions or inserted below the graph in the location of the figure caption. This result parallels the advice of Imhof (1975) about the position of labels on maps: generally above and to the right of the item.

Summary

It appears that way-finding detail need not be great in order to be effective. Regarding letter size, there must be a size variation between letters of at least 34% if they are to be understood as signifying difference. Label information integrated as much as possible with the site or destination and placed either on or adjacent to the site will facilitate the retrieval of information.

SIGNS AS WAY-FINDING AIDS

In addition to maps and graphic displays, signs play a critical role in helping us to find our way, in simple to complex environments. In their study of hospital environments, Carpman, Grant, and Simmons (1986) point to the importance of sign placement at key decision points (e.g., a choice of corridors) rather than at some arbitrary distance along the route. The point is to place signs in any situation where a single cue or a series of cues indicate that the way finder is moving (or has the opportunity to

Figure 4.7. Signs along University of Michigan hospital corridor.

move) to a new area. Any kind of change, whether in lighting, materials, or color, as well as corridor openings, doors, and so on, should be accompanied by signage clarifying the choices. However, if there are no key decision points along a route, Carpman and colleagues recommend placing signs every 150–250 feet in order to provide reassurance for the traveler (see Figure 4.7).

A number of the buildings at the college where I teach have a long history of ambiguous way-finding cues and signs. In Bill Hall, home of the Psychology Department, the west (second floor) and east (first floor) building entrances are on different levels (see Figures 4.8 and 4.9). Thus, when you enter the building from Harkness Green, on what looks like the ground level (refer to Figure 4.8), you are actually on the second floor. To make matters more confusing, as you enter the stairwell from Harkness Green, the stairwell to the first floor is immediately to your left as you enter the building (see Figure 4.10), often overlooked. Countless delivery people come to our department office (on the second floor) looking for rooms on the first floor, confused about the entrances and floor numbers. In recent years, large floor numbers on the fire doors and stairwell walls have been added in order to direct people.

Yet another campus building with its own signage problems is the Cummings Art Center. For some reason, floor numbers were never officially added to the stairwells, and over the years a series of hand-lettered signs indicating the first, second, and third floors have been posted. For a while,

Figure 4.8. Bill Hall west entrance.

color was also used ineffectively as a way-finding aid in the stairwells. I say "ineffectively" because the different floors were painted such subtly different colors (shades of peach in one iteration), that floor differentiation by color was impossible.

Libraries present their own signage challenges, and an excellent compendium of information is Pollet and Haskell's (1979) book dealing with library sign systems. Even small libraries may present their own way-finding challenges, as I learned when the Shain Library at Connecticut College first opened. The stairway to the third floor (see Figure 4.11) sends an ambiguous message because of the surrounding light from a skylight (which seems to suggest that there is no third floor because there is light "to the sky"). The fire door also seems to suggest a terminus rather than an opening. Before signs were installed, people confronted the ambiguity, turned around, and enlisted the help of a library staff member to "find the third floor."

Signs in libraries can be located strategically to answer anticipated questions, such as the location of the third floor (Loomis & Parsons, 1979).

Figure 4.9. Bill Hall east entrance.

Figure 4.10. Bill Hall "hidden" stairway to first floor.

Figure 4.11. Shain Library third-floor entrance.

Downs (1979) states that a successful way-finding system will incorporate at least two types of signs: those for direction and those for identification. The two types of signs should differ in color, shape, size, and placement, in order to be perceived as distinct. To the categories of direction and identification, Selfridge (1979) adds those of instruction (for rules, restrictions, special conditions, and procedures).

The key to good signage is, first, to establish a systematic pattern of major and minor identification, direction, and instruction information so that people will rely on it, finding the data they need at the right place as they go to and through the library, and, second, to present the information with different degrees of visual emphasis so that it can be comfortably absorbed. (p. 52)

Good signage requires an orientation to the library plan. It requires a way for people to create an internal map linking where they are and where they want to go. According to Selfridge, signs and maps should first orient people to the overview and then to the specifics.

While graphics may communicate effectively, symbols that are less easily recognized "should be used with explanatory words. Studies have shown that the words should be placed either below or at the right of the symbol" (Wilt & Maienschein, 1979, p. 106). However, research indicates that when arrows are involved (to indicate some location), the arrows should be placed to the left of the other symbols, and they, in turn, should be to the left of the sign's words (Wilt & Maienschein, 1979).

Hospitals and libraries present certain challenges, and so, too, do airports. Using a large metropolitan airport as the field study base, the effectiveness of cues in communicating that areas were nonsmoking was investigated (Gibson & Werner, 1994). The relevance of this study to our current discussion lies in the concept of environmental legibility: could people "read" which areas were designated nonsmoking? Unobtrusively observing over 1,000 users at this airport, Gibson and Werner (1994) determined that smokers do, in fact, comply with clearly labeled regulations but may not when these same regulations are presented in an ambiguous manner (e.g., ashtrays present in areas labeled "No Smoking"). In a second study, the legibility of an area was manipulated by varying the strength of boundaries/edges (i.e., edge distinctiveness created through clear boundary or not) and presence of ashtrays in smoking areas or in both smoking and nonsmoking areas. The ashtray and boundary manipulations increased the clarity of the "No Smoking" rule.

Airport signage has a poor image in the media and has received harsh criticism in the press. In an article entitled "Signs and Blunders: Airport Travelers Share Graphic Tales" (O'Brian, 1995), we hear about the difficulties travelers experience. "U.S. airports are notorious for their baffling and garbled signs, which either give too little information, trailing off after just a few pointers, or overwhelm with an abundance of data" (p. A1). The author explains that while color-coding was popular as a way-finding aid in the 1960s and 1970s, the color-blindness of 12% of the population argued for another (or at least a supplemental) approach. A graphic designer quoted in the article describes a well-designed airport as one that " 'lets you down a slot, like a coin-sorting machine,' " " 'It will get you headed in the right direction and give you just enough information, at reasonable intervals, to get you to your destination' " (p. A5). Of course the challenge is achieving this balance between too little and too much. Because airports are enlarged and renovated over time, earlier signage systems may no longer function effectively (Sullivan, 1996). At Kennedy Airport in New York, names like the International Arrivals Building no longer effectively describe where arrivals occur (not just in this one building), and numbers are now to replace these out-of-date names. At a cost of about $1 million, the terminals are being renamed and 250 signs replaced.

Weisman (1987) has offered a useful distinction between the kinds of cues, such as signs and room numbers, that are intended for way finding and others, such as elevators, potted plants, doors, and so on, that are not so intended but are used as aids nevertheless. Signs and room numbers are called manifest cues, while the unintended aids are called latent cues. In a study of manifest and latent cues in an extended care facility (Weisman, 1987), 18% of the cues mentioned by residents were manifest while 82% were latent! In the Psychology Department at Connecticut College, we have a red bench outside the department office that serves as our major way-finding landmark; clearly this is a latent cue.

Figure 4.12. Filigree sign.

In our attempt to create an attractive and pleasing environment, we sometimes create signage that sacrifices legibility for aesthetics (or what passes as aesthetics). Consider the example of a filigree building address (see Figure 4.12). Not only is it above eye level and thus difficult to notice, but the lack of figure–ground differentiation also renders it less than effective. I have seen supergraphics backfire as well. Consider examples from the University of Michigan some years ago at a time when supergraphics were popular (see Figures 4.13 and 4.14). We have an arrow that is undifferentiable as an arrow, a word for elevator ("lift") that is foreign to our culture, and on its side to boot; and decoration passing as information in an office building (formerly a hospital) that has too much wall space (see Figures 4.15 and 4.16). Another example of modest illegibility is the typeface selected to label terminals at the Philadelphia Airport (see Figure 4.17). We might see "131" rather than "B3."

Not infrequently, signs also violate information-processing limitations (Miller, 1956) by presenting too much information (see Figure 4.18). In this example from the Mystic Community Center, too much information is given in a single sign. It would be preferable to offer fewer labels with greater generality at the origin, providing more specificity in the signage at each subsequent choice point.

Figure 4.13. University of Michigan Angell Hall arrow.

THE BUILDING AS A WAY-FINDING AID

Not only can maps and signs be considered way-finding aids, but often the structure of the building itself can serve that purpose. Ideally, but unrealistically, the building could be "read" or understood to such an extent that no additional aids would be required. However, the complexity of most large buildings where way finding becomes a challenge (e.g., hospitals) necessitates supplemental aids. A number of studies have indicated that the building itself can be a source of disorientation, contributing to way-finding difficulty (Berkeley, 1973; Moeser, 1988). Visitors to Boston's City Hall (see Figure 4.19) have complained about disorientation, perhaps because of the building's lack of symmetry (Berkeley, 1973). Lack of perceptual access or visibility to the outdoors appears to be one of the major contributors to this disorientation in Boston's City Hall. While differentiation is important in memory for building types (Purcell, 1987), it appears possible to exceed what is helpful.

In complex buildings, even familiarity does not always guarantee good

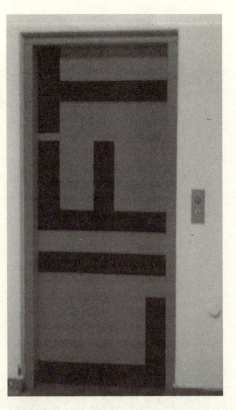

Figure 4.14. University of Michigan "LIFT" sign.

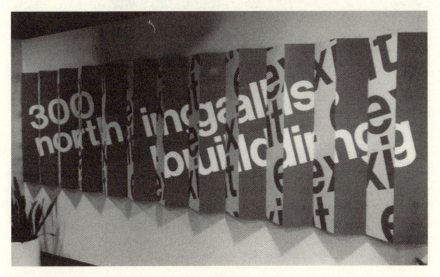

Figure 4.15. Office building "wall coverings."

Figure 4.16. Office building wall index.

Figure 4.17. Philadelphia airport signage.

Figure 4.18. Mystic Community Center signage.

way finding. In a hospital with no main corridors or corridors spanning the length of the facility and rooms that were not rectangular, disorientation developed (Moeser, 1988). In a series of studies with student nurses who had varying degrees of familiarity with the hospital complex, nurses who had traveled through the facility for a number of months were actually worse at some way-finding tasks than students new to the building who memorized floor plans to criterion and took a short building tour. Reminiscent of Levine and colleagues' (1984) work, a number of nurses in the study commented that the floor plans just confused them. The authors recommend that orientation to the environment or way-finding training be provided in such complex environments. They also mention unpublished data that documents the anxiety that may accompany difficult way finding. Being lost is unnerving (Lynch, 1960).

To the extend that the legibility or understandability of a building can be enhanced (Hunt, 1985), it will contribute to way finding. If you use a model to help people preview a building, it is important to incorporate the

Figure 4.19. Boston City Hall.

components people really need in order to make sense of the building. A number of studies point to simplifying models as a strategy to enhance environmental learning (Hunt, 1985; Kaplan, Kaplan, & Deardorff, 1974). Following the work from Weisman's doctoral dissertation (cited in Hunt), Hunt suggests that you need to provide *identification* (through signs and numbers and visual access) and *spatial orientation* (through architectural differentiation of the building's regions and plan configuration—legibility of the building's basic layout). For environmental learning, Hunt recommends giving orientation information before more detailed material is provided. Similarly, Devlin (1976) noted that people learn the basic structure of an environment before the details are incorporated. Weisman (1981) found that familiarity accounted for only 9% of the variance in way-finding scores in university buildings, whereas judged simplicity of the floor plan accounted for 56%. The more complex the floor plan (the greater the number of angles), the greater way-finding difficulty it presented for students.

Using field study and simulation, O'Neill (1991b, 1991c, 1992) has conducted research on signage, floor plan configuration, and legibility. As have others, he points to the difficulty in understanding complex buildings, suggesting that signage may not be able to overcome the challenge presented by plan complexity (1991b). Using a field study with subjects whose rate of travel, backtracking, stopping and looking, and wrong turns were recorded in way-finding tasks, O'Neill found that an increase in plan complexity is related to a decrease in way-finding performance. The addition of signage resulted in a 13% increase in rate of travel, a 50% decrease in wrong turns, and a 62% decrease in backtracking across the five settings. Graphic signage produced the greatest rate of travel in all settings, but textual signage was the most effective in reducing way-finding errors, such as wrong turns and backtracking. He suggests that graphic and textual signage may be applied to optimize different aspects of way finding, depending on the needs of the facility.

In another study related to building complexity in which a simulated study of way finding used a modified version of *Labyrinth* (a computer graphics program), subjects viewed three-dimensional images showing movement through a building's hallways (O'Neill, 1992). As in the field study we just reviewed, as plan complexity increased, way-finding performance dropped, as did cognitive map accuracy. Familiarity attenuated the effects of plan complexity, because way-finding performance improved with familiarity, unlike Moeser's (1988) results in the hospital, where familiarity did not always improve cognitive task performance. Certainly one of the implications of this study is that building design (in terms of plan complexity) and way-finding aids must be structured for the *newcomer*. We cannot depend on familiarity to solve way-finding problems, particularly in environments such as airports and hospitals, where newcomers abound.

To better measure floor plan complexity, O'Neill has developed a measure called InterConnection Density (ICD; 1991c) to indicate "the density of travellable paths between places in the environment" (p. 265). ICD is based on the topological relations between choice points. Research indicates a drop in way-finding performance and cognitive map accuracy with increasing ICD. Using the theory of space syntax, which describes spaces in terms of the configuration of connections between them and bears a resemblance to O'Neill's ICD, Peponis, Zimring, and Choi (1990) also emphasize the importance of the overall pattern or configuration of the building as an aid to way finding. In understanding a large structure like a hospital, for example, it is the configuration of the building as well as what they call the local characteristics, signs and landmarks, that must be considered. The importance of space configuration can also be seen on a much smaller scale in steps that have been taken to reduce disorientation for the elderly (Liebowitz, Lawton, & Waldman, 1979). At the Abram and Helen Weiss Institute for the elderly, a corridor was widened to give residents a lot of perceptual access to other areas, thereby reducing confusion and disorientation. Perceptual access can thus be viewed as a way-finding aid (Garling, Lindberg, & Mantyla, 1983).

Concluding Remarks

We can all think of examples where way finding made a difference in our lives. Often these examples come from auto travel, and many of them involve near-accidents. Some years ago, a colleague and I were returning in separate cars at night from a former student's wedding outside Boston. Leaving an hour apart, we both made the same mistake of entering a highway ramp traveling the wrong direction. Fortunately, we and other people in these separate vehicles realized quickly that we were going the wrong way and avoided a head-on collision with oncoming traffic. The fact that two people made this same error independently suggests there may have been something amiss with the signs. In this case, signs for the north- and southbound entrances were so close that differentiation was difficult.

While most of the examples in this chapter deal with situations far less life-threatening than this story of highway illegibility, signs and maps play important roles in our daily lives. It is clear from the research that has been done in psychology, cartography, and statistical graphics that we know far less than we need to about creating useful tools. In general, we can say that detail is not necessarily desirable, especially when we are gaining an overview of an area; that color should only be used when it contributes information that cannot be gained achromatically; that labels should be placed on or adjacent to the sites they identify; that Miller's magical number seven needs to be heeded for signage; and that map organization should facilitate the formation of hierarchies (e.g., through varying the type sizes). Moreover, buildings need to be designed for the newcomer just as maps need to be designed for people with unremarkable spatial ability.

We also realize that researchers from different disciplines can benefit from a more interdisciplinary perspective, at the very least considering the information contributed by specialists outside their own area. One of the points of this book is that the integration of research on spatial cognition from different disciplines will advance our knowledge. Too often we have little familiarity with contributions outside our own disciplines.

5

Spatial Cognition and Urban Design: *Trapped in a Tree*

Urban design provides the largest context in which to consider the principles of spatial cognition. Perhaps ironically, the use of *human scale* contributes fundamentally to a legible environment, but human scale is difficult to apply over a vast expanse, especially in metropolitan areas where the cost per square foot invariably requires high-rise construction. The predominance of the highway and other concessions to the automobile also lead to environments that are difficult to comprehend.

Consider the following comment: "It's just like an octopus and I don't understand it." This was the view of an elderly resident of a New London, Connecticut, housing project I studied in the late 1970s (Devlin, 1980). What she was describing was the confusing interrelationship of streets and highways that now constitute the I-95 corridor and its entrance and exit ramps near her housing development. Gordon Court, where she lived, existed prior to the I-95 interchange construction, and as a lifelong resident of the city, she not only lived through the construction process, but then had to relearn the new street interrelationships. In some respects, New London has changed little in the half-century since psychologist E. L. Thorndike, better known for his research on learning, used it as one of his comparison cities for a book on 144 smaller cities in America (1940). New London is about 6.6 square miles and has about 30,000 inhabitants, just as it did in the 1940s. But one of the aspects that does seem to have changed in the last 30 years is the proliferation of public housing and the separation of neighborhoods as the result of the highway interchange. Many sections of the city have become what is called "illegible." When you consider environments with many components where the whole cannot be perceived in a single glance, the question of legibility arises. A city that functions well gives choice to its inhabitants (Gruen, 1964), and legibility provides at least one basis for making spatial choices.

Although the precise term may have been unfamiliar to this elderly public housing resident, what she was describing was a street pattern that had become "illegible," a word most closely linked with the writings of urban planner Kevin Lynch (1960, 1976, 1981). When we describe handwriting as legible, we are saying that we can "read" it. When we describe a building, or a neighborhood, or a city as legible, we are saying that we understand its interrelationships, that they make sense, and that they create a pattern that enables us to find our way. According to Lynch, "Orientation in space (and time) is the framework of cognition . . . we take delight in physically distinctive, recognizable locales, and attach our feelings and meanings to them. They make us feel at home, grounded" (1976, p. 23). As Lynch and others have pointed out, there is psychological comfort in knowing where you are and how to reach a particular destination. As has been discussed in earlier chapters, a good cognitive map permits this kind of secure way finding. The particular characteristics of city layout contribute directly to the formation of this cognitive map. Legibility, the conditions that create it and the cognitive principles that underlie it, is the focus of this chapter. Related aspects of city form that provide satisfaction to the resident and visitor also receive some attention.

LEGIBILITY IN THE HISTORY OF URBAN DESIGN

Legibility is an important aspect of city design, and it is obviously related to spatial cognition, and in particular to way finding, but it is not an aspect of city design that you will find frequently mentioned in the history of urban planning. Yet throughout the history of cities, we might apply the *criterion* of legibility to the forms that have emerged and evaluate what humans have created for themselves. What forms have cities taken and what do their structures reflect, if anything, of cognitive principles?

Arguably, aspects of cognition as they relate to survival have shaped environmental design from the beginnings of humankind (Crowe, 1995). If you take Kaplan's (1973) criteria for a cognitive map of recognizing where we are, predicting what will happen next, evaluating whether the consequences will be good or bad, and ultimately taking action, it is evident that aspects of the physical environment can support such activities. Even in early human communities, having a vista or a line of sight was important for survival. Humans craved prospect and refuge, a view and a place of retreat and safety (Appleton, 1975). Sacred places were created on mounds, hence the importance of elevation, and "the sight lines from natural features or standing stories gave rise to the concept of *alignment* (Crosby, 1973, p. 14). I can remember my childhood summer vacations in Marietta, Ohio, the home of my maternal grandmother. Just up Sacra Via, the street on which she lived, was a Native American burial mound, precisely the kind of elevated place one would expect for a sacred site.

The Importance of the Grid: Street, Hierarchy, and Mental Image

The organization of the city has a profound effect on our ability to conceptualize it and navigate within it, in other words, on our ability to form a cognitive map. A brief examination of urban history points to hierarchical organization and the street pattern as fundamental in forming a coherent mental image of the environment. In terms of environmental history, Curran (1983) provides a scenario of the changes that have occurred in city organization. The Middle Ages gave us a closed order (the walled city); the Renaissance provided a structured order, with earlier influences of Greek and Roman culture; and with the Industrial era has come a functional order. Our modern era is said to have an open order.

The importance of hierarchy emerged with the Renaissance, providing clarity that was essentially absent in medieval construction. Rationality begins its domination with the Renaissance, and the plan for Rome developed by Sixtus V is an example in which order was wrested out of chaos (Brett, 1970). The importance of scale was also highlighted in the Renaissance (Churchill, 1962). However, in the modern era, an over- or underreliance on the orderly grid plan often has been perceived as a liability. Overreliance on the grid produces cities that lack vitality; underreliance creates environments that are difficult to visualize (Curran, 1983).

Streets (paths) as grid elements predominate in the modern metropolis, and axiality has dominated since the Renaissance, although streets were secondary to buildings during Greek times. "It is . . . the street endowed with a spiritual significance that has acted most powerfully as a generator of the city plan" (Spreiregen, 1967, p. 26). Whether radiocentric or gridiron, the street began to dominate by the 19th century. However, with the growth of the metropolis, fueled by transportation, many theorists have questioned whether the *whole* of the city can be envisioned, even with the assistance provided by a rational street plan. The modern city has become so extensive that it presents an incredible challenge to conceptualize. The scale has in some sense exceeded our mental framework. "It is evident that the enormous expanse of the modern metropolis can no longer be articulated by streets and plazas. If it can be articulated at all, it can be only as an urban landscape composed of the contrasting elements of built-up and open sections" (Spreiregen, 1967, p. 233). In other words, we need to chunk or cluster the sections of a city in order to manage the scale. This kind of chunking leads to a hierarchy of units.

The size of the metropolis and its relation to mental comprehension also plays a role in the writing of Bacon (1976). In Bacon's mind, the key to city planning involves the street system and a simultaneous movement system. He cites the Greek processional route as an earlier example of a street and movement system that succeeded. But multiply these routes by the scale of modern cities and it is evident that such expansion creates difficulty in conceptualizing the whole.

The dominance of the gridiron pattern is related to a number of factors (Barnett, 1986; Goodman, 1971; Schuyler, 1986). Louis Mumford, according to Barnett (1986), theorizes that long, straight streets proliferated when horse-drawn carriage travel replaced the pedestrian, and a different kind of vista was required to engage the carriage traveler. Another view is that the predominant gridiron pattern of the 19th century with its rectangular street configuration reflected the country's rationalization (Schuyler, 1986). Others stress the role of the grid in expediting land settlement (Kostof, 1987). In the United States, the Land Ordinance of 1785 regularized the pattern of settlement. Regarding the development of our spatial plan, "Regular geometric layouts characterized urban existence by 1800. . . . The simplest way to survey land and divide it for settlement was to use a grid system. It served as an expeditious pattern for fast colonization, and so was uniformly applied to new towns" (Kostof, 1987, p. 151). Goodman (1971) traces the grid to Roman military camps, but says that the real dominance of the form is the result of the industrial expansion of the 1900s. Zucker (1959) relates the gridiron system to orientation, how a structure corresponded to the points of a compass: "Orientation, first applied to the town as a whole, was later on extended to the street layout, which in turn gradually led to the gridiron system" (p. 20).

While legibility may emerge out of a grand scheme like the grid, and often does, it need not (Churchill, 1962; Gallion & Eisner, 1950). Legibility requires attention to topography, variety in types and sizes of streets, promoting a certain degree of homogeneity within small areas but then varying styles from area to area. Churchill (1962) reminds us that the environment is three-dimensional.

The ground plan controls only the great general movements of people and things; the particular development of the particular street or square is what makes the city pleasant or unpleasant, and this means not so much control of the architecture of individual buildings as it does control of bulk, skyline and placing. (pp. 112–114)

In large environments, people tend to cluster or chunk the available information rather than focusing on a particular building (unless its distinctiveness makes it a landmark). So, rather than thinking about a building, people may think about a larger spatial unit, like a neighborhood. Manhattan has frequently been described as a legible environment, not only because of the centrality of its grid, but also because of its distinctive neighborhoods—the Upper West Side, Chelsea, Greenwich Village. When large neighborhood units (e.g., the Upper West Side) are broken down into smaller units (e.g., above and below 96th Street), we see how a hierarchy of spaces can emerge to order our cognitive map.

Consequently, one of the suggestions to increase legibility is the use of a spatial unit like the neighborhood, which is often seen as a natural entity. The sense of neighborhood has its roots in the village and is important in order to maintain a sense of human scale in rapidly developing cities (Mumford, 1961). Zoning should respect topography; natural topographic features can help construct a neighborhood (Churchill, 1962) and in turn facilitate legibility.

But the role of human scale, so critical in legibility, has been challenged by technology, particularly by the use of the elevator. Monumental city design and its general support of legibility through rational street plans, apparent in one way or another since the Renaissance, was changed by the elevator (Barnett, 1986). With the introduction of the elevator, human scale and the relationship to the street was lost. "From the mid 1950s, and for almost twenty years, the idea of an urban area as a large, interconnected building dominated much architectural thinking about cities. The street would become a weather-protected corridor or bridge, the plaza an interior atrium, the building an incident within a larger framework" (Barnett, 1986, p. 157). Among the examples Barnett (1986) cites are those of Habitat, Arconsanti, and Boston's Government Center. With the elevator, the basic principles emphasizing the street that had guided city design for centuries were essentially abandoned.

The loss of contact with the street was developed visually in William Whyte's (1979) delightful film *The Social Life of Small Urban Spaces*. This film graphically illustrates the unwelcoming streetscapes of such cities as Detroit and Los Angeles. Whyte says that the Renaissance Center in downtown Detroit and its lack of relationship to the street proclaim, "Come in and be safe from Detroit!" This kind of inhospitable design is one reason people are now enamored of the neo-traditional approach in such places as Seaside, Florida, and Celebration, the new Disney-built development near Orlando, Florida.

"Although older buildings constructed on street frontages often received deficient amounts of light and air, the street turned out to be the primary mechanism of human interaction in cities. When it was eliminated, no amount of park or plaza could take its place" (Barnett, 1986, p. 189). To create the kinds of environments people will find pleasing as well as legible, Barnett (1986) seems to think we should incorporate these older design approaches. These include traditional spatial relationships, axes, continuity of design, street walls of human scale, and plazas defined as exterior spaces. People want streets and sidewalks (Breines & Dean, 1974), they want neighborhoods (Cassidy, 1980), and they want places with a "sense of place" (Kaplan, 1997). The antisprawl movement, with its emphasis on walking, mass transit, the street, and a compact town center, is a powerful force in planning today (Dunlap, 1999).

Most 20th-century urban planners lament the changes that have occurred in the evolution of the metropolis (Jacobs, 1961; Lynch, 1976; Tunnard, 1951; Tunnard & Pushkarev, 1963), the regional city, or what the British call "conurbation." Most also seem to identify the same problems—the evils of the automobile, the sameness and chaos that have emerged, the speed with which growth occurs. Like the other planners cited here, Tunnard and Pushkarev (1963) want a metropolitan area that has variety, which they believe can be achieved out of a superposition of order based on a hierarchy. A simple gridiron leads to monotony whereas a lack of order leads to chaos. To solve the problem, the gridiron must be differentiated in the third dimension, and this can obviously lead to the kinds of neighborhoods and districts and resulting legibility we have in a city like Manhattan. Jane Jacobs (1961), too, talks about ways to create variety within the grid structure, including adding what she calls "subsidiary irregularity" to the basic grid form. "The combination of a basic, easily understandable grid system, together with purposely irregular streets dropped in where the grid is too large for good city functioning, could be, I think, a distinctive and most valuable American contribution to the tactics of city design" (p. 381).

Groth (1981) seems to think that architectural education devalues the grid with its emphasis on standardization, a standardization that is endemic in modern planning (Benevolo, 1981). When such standardization exists, students are taught that design is limited. Groth does not agree with this negative stance and goes on to list the values of the grid, among which are the possibility that the grid may actually promote organic growth and support a sense of community. Rather than thinking of our cities as single large grids, he suggests we recognize that they are in actuality mixes of mini-grids with ample diversity. A clear theme emerges from the writings of Jacobs, Groth, and others, a theme fundamentally related to principles of spatial cognition. Legibility must combine diversity within order. A grid can contribute to legibility, but a grid without diversifying elements is a recipe for placelessness.

On a smaller scale, the lack of distinctive elements undermines the sense of place in regional shopping districts. We see a kind of cookie-cutter uniformity in the upscale retail/commercial developments that punctuate the eastern shore of the United States, from Boston to Baltimore. In a wonderful, wry article by Calvin Trillin in The New Yorker (1977), he describes "Thoughts Brought on by Prolonged Exposure to Exposed Brick" in such places as Boston's Fanueil Hall. It would be hard to know if you were in Boston or in Baltimore's HarborPlace because of the similarity of offerings, particularly the franchises that are national (e.g., The Gap, Pottery Barn) rather than local. These developments with their sandblasted brick walls and ficus plants promote sameness. And while one might argue that having familiar national retail chains close by is reassuring, what we are really lamenting is the absence of any indication of identity and distinctiveness. The kind of monotony we find troubling in the larger urban layout also emerges in these specific developments.

Summary

This brief history of urban design reveals the importance of ordering principles—in particular the grid, the hierarchy, and the neighborhood— in shaping a legible environment. But what is developed within the grid must possess diversity and variety if legibility and an understanding of the whole is to emerge. The street is the fundamental design element supporting the grid and the hierarchy, and its importance will be developed further in the principles of Kevin Lynch and others.

THE PRINCIPLES OF KEVIN LYNCH

With his seminal book *The Image of the City* (1960), published at the dawn of the field of environmental psychology, Lynch made us aware of the cognitive conceptualizations that underlie making our way through cities. Using Boston, Jersey City, and Los Angeles as his examples, Lynch had residents talk about their understanding of the city and draw maps of these environments. A passing knowledge of these three different urban settings would suggest some differences, and they certainly emerged in Lynch's analysis. Others (e.g., Arnheim, 1966; Canter, 1974; Deasy, 1985; Perin, 1970; Prak, 1968; Tuan, 1974; Walter, 1988) have also stressed the importance of perceptual theory in environmental design, but Lynch has done more to advance the relationship between cognition and urban planning than any other designer.

What most memorably emerged from Lynch's book were some principles about legibility, about the elements that order a city, and about the relationship between these elements and the experience of legibility. About legibility Lynch says, "Nothing is experienced by itself, but always in relation to its surroundings, the sequences of events leading up to it, the memory of past experiences" (1960, p. 1). To Lynch, the legibility or clarity of the city is "the ease with which its parts can be recognized and can be organized into a coherent pattern" (pp. 2–3). Rather than being instinctive, Lynch suggests that our ability to find our way rests on "consistent use and organization of definite sensory cues from the external environment" (p. 3).

What we must do in order to find our way is create an environmental image in our minds, an image that will then "guide us" as we move from a starting point to a destination not now visible. For Lynch, "surprise" in the environment may be welcome, but only if it does not undermine our overall sense of direction and orientation. From a cognitive standpoint, many of Lynch's points relate to principles of Gestalt psychology and the concept of good form.

To create a match between perception and settlement form, there are two basic options Lynch (1981) and others identify: we can change the settlement form or change the mental image we have of that form. While reconstructing a schema through learning is possible, it makes more sense to essentially do it right the first time, that is, to create an environment that facilitates the formation of a coherent mental image. That is the essence of what a legible environment makes possible. The essence of legibility, if we look at what we know from cognitive psychology, is the integration of order and variety.

Lynch has also described the process of environmental perception as one of hypothesis testing, and identifies what he calls "congenial physical characteristics" (Lynch & Hack, 1984, p. 189), which will facilitate the hypothesis formation. These characteristics, "symmetry, order, repetition; continuity and closure; dominance, rhythm, common scale or similarity of form or material" (p. 189) have a good deal in common with Gestalt psychology. Moving away from the atomistic and elemental emphasis of the day, Gestalt psychology (Kohler, 1947) emphasized the concept of force fields, focused on the self-organizing aspects of sensory experience. The Gestalt principles of proximity, similarity, continuity, common motion, closure, and good figure have direct application to urban planning and perception, as we will see again and again. In Lynch's congenial physical characteristics as well as in Gestalt principles, we see that the variation between parts ultimately helps us to create an understanding of the whole. Without differentiation, there is confusion.

Lynch's Five Structural Elements

Lynch (1960) provides us with five structural elements for the city: paths, edges, districts, nodes, and landmarks. There are the linear elements (paths and edges), the point elements (nodes and landmarks), and the two-dimensional elements (districts). Paths are just what you might imagine— streets, boulevards, meandering walkways, and so on. Edges have a linear component, but do not serve the same function as paths; rather, edges are linear elements that create a border or boundary. Examples are walls, shores, divided highways, and railroad cuts. Nodes are point references that serve as junctions or pivotal areas; spaces into which you can enter, where paths may converge or activity is concentrated. In New London, Connect-

Figure 5.1. A strategic node: Union Station in New London.

icut, the primary node is Union Station, where all transportation modes (auto, taxi, bus, rail, ferry, and foot) converge. This spot is the quintessential transportation node (see Figure 5.1). In *The Image of the City*, Lynch uses the example of a shopping node in downtown Boston, where the old major department stores (Filene's and Jordan Marsh) converged at an intersection.

Landmarks are point references that may be unique to the observer but have a singular quality, standing out from the surrounding area, like a mailbox in the shape of a shark in the otherwise uniform expanse of rectangular boxes along a rural route. Finally, districts are somewhat larger components of the city that have a thematic concentration, such as a strip consisting of car dealerships.

Lynch (1960) uses these elements to provide guidelines for creating more legible environments. Some of these guidelines emerged out of interviews with residents of the three cities in Lynch's study, whereas others appear to be long-standing principles of design, occasionally with a cognitive basis.

Designing Paths

Most people seem to rely on paths to structure their mental images, although Lynch (1960) reports that the degree of familiarity people have with a place mediates their use of paths. What he reports about familiarity is that people seem to use a layering process. Those who know the city least well use large regions, districts, or "chunks" to organize their knowledge; those with an intermediate degree of knowledge shift more to paths; and those with the most complete knowledge rely on landmarks. This pattern is similar to one I reported in an early study about newcomers to a small town (Devlin, 1976), where an overall structural framework emerged in advance of detailed knowledge.

Differentiation is important in creating legible paths. Paths that have particular qualities appeared to stand out in people's minds—paths at the extreme of width or narrowness; paths with a thematic quality or an emphasis of use; paths near critical features; or paths that themselves were landmark in quality (consider Manhattan's 5th Avenue). Paths are a critical component in the legibility of the city because, Lynch comments, "Where paths lacked identity, or were easily confused one for the other, the entire city image was in difficulty" (1960, p. 52). Gestalt principles appear to influence our perception of paths; Lynch notes that people have an easier time with perpendicular path crossings than they do with intersections where streets enter from a variety of angles. "Crossings of more than four points almost always gave trouble" (p. 58). Given the research on human information processing by Miller (1956) and others, it is not surprising that this limitation of four points is consistent with what we know about human capacity. Furthermore, as Lynch notes, we humans have trouble understanding our directional movement when many turns are involved. While irregularity can create difficulty, Lynch admits that regularity can cause trouble as well in terms of our ability to keep the elements separate in our minds. We therefore again have the theme of order *and* diversity.

More discussion is devoted to paths than to any other component of the image, and Lynch says, "The paths, the network of habitual or potential lines of movement through the urban complex, are the most potent means by which the whole can be ordered. The key lines should have some singular quality which marks them off from the surrounding channels" (1960, p. 96). For this quality to be effective, it must appear continuously over the length of the path.

Following Lynch's emphasis on streets, Allan Jacobs (1993) has described the physical qualities that he says form the criteria for great streets, streets that are better than others to visit, to be on, to experience. For Jacobs, great streets are entertaining, and joyful as well as utilitarian. The criteria for great streets include: accessibility, physical comfort and safety, participation, publicness, definition, and livability. Some of Jacobs's examples of great streets, such as the Via del Corso in Rome, are familiar. Others, like Roslyn Place in Pittsburgh, are less well known. With regard to the issue of legibility, Jacobs states:

Some streets may be called "ordering streets." They bring comprehension or order to a city or district. . . . They let you know where you are. To a considerable extent, it is the street patterns, by themselves or in relation to each other, that may give an initial order or disorder in relation to which individual streets can play their roles. The street and block patterns are the starting points. (p. 203)

Jacobs's descriptions of ordering streets are consistent with Lynch's principles.

Edges, Districts, and Landmarks

Lynch's studies revealed that the most effective edges will be "visually prominent," "continuous in form," and "impenetrable to cross movement" (1960, p. 62). Of these criteria, continuity and visibility are said to be more crucial. Continuity in edges, as in paths, helps their legibility. An edge, like a path, that "keeps going" and has a specific characteristic (e.g., it follows a river), provides an ordering quality. It is as if you say to yourself, "This is the section that follows the river." Obviously, a view of the river along the edge reinforces its sense of structure or place.

Lynch agrees with me that Manhattan is a legible borough of New York City, in his mind the result of a "number of well-defined characteristic districts, set in an ordered frame of rivers and streets" (1960, p. 67). Districts are defined by their thematic continuities, which can be created by any number of repeated elements, from building type to topography. Definite boundaries also help define a district; think, for example, of a residential area accessed only by a narrow bridge.

Lynch says little about nodes—they are strategic foci: "The node is more defined if it has a sharp, closed boundary, and does not trail off uncertainly on every side . . ." (1960, p. 102). It probably helps the legibility of the city to locate nodes in strategic places—centers of areas or districts that might otherwise lack focus. New London has an effective node in the transportation hub at Union Station, where all modes of transportation converge. In Manhattan, Times Square might be considered a strategic hub. With regard to landmarks, what seems important is a prominent location and good figure–ground contrast. Again, we see the hint of Gestalt principles. Churches on the knolls of New England greens create prominent landmarks rising above their surroundings, as do major buildings located at intersections. "Location at a junction involving path decisions strengthens a landmark" (p. 81). In other writings, Lynch identifies paths, nodes, and special districts as the basics of urban form (1990d).

The landmark has a special role beyond urban planning in another domain where legibility matters: the theme park. Walt Disney employed a variety of principles of urban planning and had his own term for the landmarks in his theme parks; he called them "wienies" (Doss, 1997). All of Disney's theme parks have a similar form—a single entry point at the base of a heart-shaped plan; this hub provides both physical and visual access to the wienies that anchor the park—"the Frontierland stockade, the castle drawbridge to Fantasyland, the Tomorrowland rocket, the bamboo portals of Adventureland" (Marling, 1997, pp. 73–74). Disney was interested in creating a park with inherent organization. Orientation was provided by the hub; rather than a reliance on signage, the structural form of the park provided a sense of security and well-being (Doss, 1997). Disney and those who worked for him seemed to have understood some of the fundamental principles of creating a legible environment.

Lynch, the Grid, and the Hierarchy

While Lynch's main emphasis in his 1960 book is the five structural elements, he addressed the grid and the hierarchy in a variety of writings. Lynch was not a cognitive psychologist, but he recognized the relationship between environmental form and mental structure. One of the intersections between cognition and urban planning is the emphasis on hierarchies. Lynch states, "The idea of hierarchy is persistent in planning. It seems to be a natural way of ordering things, although this may be a consequence of ways in which our minds work" (1981, p. 389). We see this emphasis in his book on site planning (Lynch & Hack, 1984), identifying precisely the variables that are central to schema formation:

A place must not only fit the structure of our bodies. It must fit the way in which our minds work: how we perceive and image and feel . . . there are regularities in these perceptions due to the structure of our senses and our brains. We are all engaged in identifying the features that surround us, organizing them into images, and connecting those images to the other meanings we carry in our heads. Places should have a clear perceptual identity: be recognizable, memorable, vivid, engaging of our attention. It should be possible for the observer to relate the identifiable features one to another, making an understandable pattern of them in time and space. (p. 72)

What Lynch says is that we need to "clarify the circulation system as the key to settlement structure by making understandable street patterns, heightening the identity of streets and destinations, making intersections intelligible, or creating vivid spatial sequences along some important path" (1981, p. 146). The essence of this message is just what we have described: order and diversity. An example of an identifiable street pattern is, of course, the ubiquitous grid. Lynch has highlighted the advantages of this particular form in a variety of papers (see, e.g., 1954/1990b; 1961/1990c). Critics might call this form monotonous, but there are ways to include the necessary variety within this order. Mid-town Manhattan is a favorite example, where the grid is formed from the major avenues and the minor cross streets, which vary in "weight." The avenues (e.g., 5th, Madison, Lexington) are wider and handle more and faster traffic than do the cross streets, and each avenue has its own distinct character, creating the needed diversity. A grid can fail the legibility test when this kind of differentiation is absent. Manhattan provides an example of such failure in SoHo, a street grid of upscale retail stores south of Houston Street (hence SoHo), where the streets bear equal weight, the architecture is fairly similar, and tourists are constantly confused (see Figures 5.2 and 5.3). There is no place to get a real vista in SoHo; the streets are narrow and the height of the buildings often blocks the angle of the sun as a cue. I always carry a small map of SoHo (torn from a magazine) and invariably consult it to get my bearings.

Lynch (1981) endorses the grid when discussing an imaginary model of a city; it is the foundation of the city, with the possibility of differentiation occurring within the structure that the grid defines. In addition to the grid, Lynch (1954/1990b) stresses the relationship between the street and focal centers, "the axial patterns of streets leading to and from important centers" (p. 45). Knowing where you are in such a pattern is easy, according to Lynch, if the number of lines does not become excessive. How many streets can you have in and out of a focal point? Logically we would use George Miller's (1956) magical number seven (plus or minus two), as a gauge. Elsewhere, writing about the cognitive maps of people he studied, Lynch writes that, "Crossings of more than four points almost always gave trouble" (1960, p. 58). This stress on the importance of the circulation system appears in the writings of other planners as well (see, e.g., Tunnard & Pushkarev, 1963). The importance of the road emerges as well in the writings of Kostof (1987): "Always the road came first. Before there were houses, there had to be access. . . . The road brought farmers to market, soldiers to the battlefield. The road served as a vessel of community and bonded us into one nation" (p. 139).

Form Qualities

Form qualities, which can be applied to Lynch's (1960) five structural elements, provide another layer of guidelines to create a legible environment. These form qualities are reminiscent of aspects of Gestalt psychology. Among the vestiges of Gestalt psychology are figure–ground sharpness and contrast; the idea of simplicity; continuity; dominance, clarity of joint (the visibility of joints and seams, like the lakefront in Chicago); directional differentiation (such as asymmetries, so that one side is distinguishable from another—as is not the case in SoHo); visual scope (to broaden a vista); motion awareness (what makes us aware of movement, as traversing hills and valleys—think of walking up 5th Avenue or up and down West End Avenue). Elsewhere, Lynch (1981) talks about related aspects of environmental form that reflect its structure. These aspects include the form or activity of centers (e.g., a town square), sequential linkages (e.g., smaller paths leading to larger ones), landmarks (e.g., a church steeple in the distance), time and distance (e.g., noting how long you have traveled on a particular freeway), path or edge continuities (e.g., observing that a street parallels the river's edge), gradients (e.g., noting the ups and downs along a particular path, like West End Avenue on Manhattan's Upper West Side), and panoramas (e.g., surveying the available view). Our job, of course, is

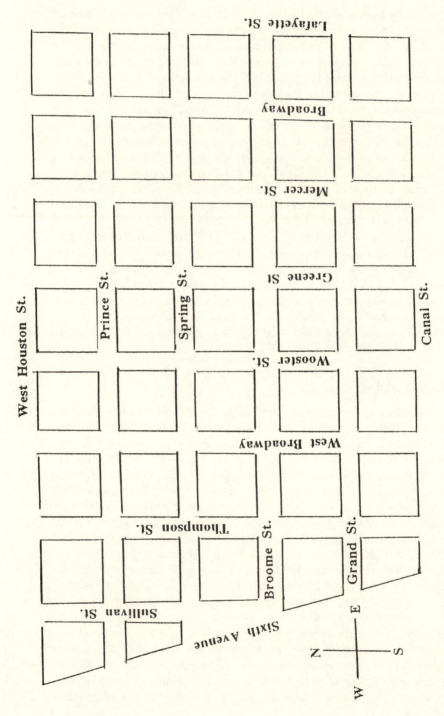

Figure 5.2. SoHo schematic.

Figure 5.3. SoHo view.

to construct a mental image from these elements, creating an understanding of their interrelationships.

Even when the principles are observed, Lynch questions whether you can actually achieve a "pattern of a whole" for a large metropolitan region. "Large-scale imageable environments are rare today. Yet the spatial organization of contemporary life, the speed of movement, and the speed and scale of new construction, all make it possible and necessary to construct such environments by conscious design" (1960, p. 119). Lynch recognizes that the pattern that emerges for the modern metropolis will be complicated, and argues that it must be malleable and plastic. In a fascinating statement from a paper titled "The Visual Shape of the Shapeless Metropolis" (1990d), he denies the need to be able to conceptualize the metropolis as a complete unit. He states, "For many purposes, it is enough if the environment is simply *continuous*, one part linking to the next so that eventually any part can be reached or conceived. . . . To go farther, it is not even necessary that there be any visible organization in the environment at all, as long as there is some unseen organization which can be called up at will, as in the telephone system" (pp. 75–76). There may not be an overall Gestalt or coherent whole, yet there is an underlying system of order.

Throughout Lynch's career, legibility remained an important theme in creating a livable city (1954/1990b, 1960, 1961, 1965/1990a, 1981, 1990d). In *A Theory of Good City Form* (1981), his magnum opus of city design, Lynch talks about legibility in terms of structure or settlement form, the shape of the largely inert physical environment. About settlement form, Lynch, like most planners and environmental observers, comments that what does not work is easier to describe than what does. Lynch even uses the special term "cacotopias" to describe the horrifying worlds of the future. Others view the city with trepidation; for many, it is a nightmare (see, e.g., Doxiadis, 1963).

In *A Theory of Good City Form* (1981), legibility is but one part of the city, and it is discussed in terms of a performance dimension Lynch calls "sense." Performance dimensions are the foundation of Lynch's theory for good city form; they are the building blocks of a normative theory of the city—essentially aspects of the city to consider when evaluating its success. Sense is the "degree to which the settlement can be clearly perceived and mentally differentiated and structured in time and space by its residents and the degree to which that mental structure connects with their values and concepts" (p. 118). What he is talking about is the relationship between perceptual and cognitive processes, on the one hand, and settlement form, on the other, echoing his work in *The Image of the City* (1960). Important among the aspects of sense is orientation. Environmental form fundamentally contributes to orientation, yet as Lynch notes there are alternative sources of information, including maps and people. However, environmental form should be the primary communicator of structure, given the potential unavailability of other sources of information. " . . . the fear and confusion that attend poor orientation, and the security and pleasure evoked by its opposite, connect environmental form to deep psychological levels" (1981, p. 134).

Any number of studies have put Lynch's theories to the test, including those of DeJonge (1962), Milgram (1976), and Orleans (1973). In a paper examining the cognitive schemas of residents of the Netherlands, DeJonge essentially verified Lynch's emphasis on paths and regularity: "Formation of a map image is easiest where there is a street plan with a regular pattern, and a single dominant path, characteristic nodes, and unique landmarks" (p. 274). DeJonge also notes the problem with too much regularity (or regularity without diversity): "It seems that identity is especially difficult to establish where there are more than three elements of the same appearance" (p. 275). Milgram as well as DeJonge documented the tendency for people to regularize that which is almost regular, just as one might expect from

Gestalt predictions. In a different application of Gestalt-like principles, Canter and Tagg (1975) have argued that a relationship exists between spatial configuration and people's distance estimates in a city, with legible environments leading generally to underestimates (as if aspects were grouped together), whereas cities with less apparent structure would lead to overestimates.

Summary

The path emerges from Lynch's principles as the most important element in urban form. A grid pattern that includes a diversity of areas (e.g., in architectural facade or retail function) will help to create a legible environment. Cognitive aspects in Lynch's principles also include limiting the number of streets that cross a major intersection (to no more than four). The Gestalt principle of continuity also plays a role in Lynch's work; paths and edges that have continuity become ordering elements in a mental image.

MAIN STREET, USA

For Lynch, the path was the most important organizing element in a legible environment. In the United States, the organizing value of a single dominant path reaches its apex in Main Street. This concept ties together a number of psychological principles, not the least of which is the importance of hierarchy. Main Street (or its substitute, Broadway, State Street, Market Street, and Front Street) is a hierarchical organizer from which other streets of secondary value may branch. Consider the fiction of John Updike (1997), speaking about a small town in Pennsylvania where a character lived:

They were not necessarily officials—the town was too small to have many of those. . . . But certain local merchants, a clergyman or two, the undertaker whose green-awninged mansion dominated the main intersection, across from a tavern and a drugstore, not to mention the druggist and the supervising principal of the school where my father taught, projected an aura of potential condemnation and banishment. (p. 80)

Updike's prose leads us to envision what the main street of that small town was like, and it could pass for many others.

We have no trouble envisioning and traversing Main Street, and in fact, it is the basis of a number of children's play sets by Fisher-Price, one based on a generic small town, the other with a specific Western theme. The generic small town includes a post office, fire station, bank, market (the modern general store), and an ice cream parlor. The Western version accommodates offices for the sheriff, dentist, and blacksmith, as well as providing a depot and hotel. Just as in the Fisher-Price Western play set, the schema of the small town in America is apparent in locales where the railroad passed.

> The one indispensable element of these fledgling towns, the one that has survived as a fundamental American institution, was Main Street. Main Street, of course, is much more than a place name to Americans. It is a state of mind, a set of values. . . . The general appearance of Main Street is easily conjured. . . . It was usually not more than two or three blocks long, wider than the rest of the town's streets, and open to farmland at either end. (Kostof, 1987, pp. 164–165)

Kostof also sees Disneyland and the modern shopping mall as providing their own version of "Main Street." Francaviglia (1977) as well points to the model of Main Street advanced by Disney. What makes these Disney streets successful, he says, is the arrangement of vistas and the limitation of traffic, turning them into wonderful pedestrian environments. "The amount of control necessary to create this 'mindsetting' pedestrian environment is found in very few real towns today" (p. 22). If we miss these kinds of spaces, Francaviglia would have us look no further than the enclosed mall. Beth Dunlop's (1996) book on Disney architecture also devotes considerable attention to the concept of the Main Street: "Main Street, U.S.A. (Disney edition), is not an official address, but it is nonetheless one of the most influential streets in America" (p. 117). Disney's Main Street, "made Americans yearn once again for the towns and squares they'd abandoned" (p. 117) (see Figure 5. 4).

Rifkind (1977) argues that Main Street is critical in developing a sense of place and identity.

> In one town after another, almost without regard to region or period or community resources, certain elements came to symbolize Main Street structures: the tall church spire; the town hall cupola; the curved and molded bank door; . . . the pillared hotel veranda. Time-honored street-level symbols were the barbershop pole, the jeweler's clock, the cigar store Indian. (p. 64)

Not surprisingly, Rifkind decries the fact that time and again we have lost the essence of Main Street through urban renewal. "Homogeneity replaced diversity. Order obliterated vitality. Space succeeded place" (p. 239). We see this concern with Main Street and the fate of downtown nationwide (Schluntz, Erickson, Blackwell, Shneider, & Peterson, 1973). In a book on revitalizing communities, Kemmis (1995) stresses the importance of Main Street in small-town America; like other theorists such as Christopher Alexander (1965) and Jane Jacobs (1961), he endorses the idea of incremental growth in changing environments.

In terms of our schema or understanding of the city, the concept of Main

Figure 5.4. Main Street USA, Disneyworld.

Street or the dominant path looms large. In addition to appearing in Fisher-Price toys (the Main Street and Western town playscapes), it appears in simulated games of city design (Cohen, McManus, Fox, & Kastelnik, 1973), and in students' perceptions of what kind of city layout they are likely to find when traveling abroad (Wood, 1973). Why is Main Street, or its equivalent, so important? In providing the essence of Main Street, a schema affording predictability, we support human well-being. In creating images, order, and identifiable elements, we support inhabitants (Brochmann, 1970; Crosby, 1965). A schema provides expectations about a town and its functions.

We all have memories of Main Streets from our youth. Mine center on our annual visit to Marietta, Ohio, a river town. These communities were distinctive. "River towns had a quality all their own. You first saw them from the dock at the river's edge. The busy strip along the waterfront was called Wharf or Front Street, sometimes simply First Street" (Kostof, 1987, p. 140). Marietta, Ohio, is at the confluence of two mighty rivers, the Muskingum and the Ohio. For a time my maternal grandmother lived on Second Street, parallel to the river; then she moved to Sacra Via, which ran perpendicular to the river. We used to walk along Front Street, parallel to the river, to the *W. P. Snyder*, at one time the sole-surviving coal-fired, steam-powered sternwheel towboat in the United States. Although I have not been there for over 30 years, I have no doubt that I could draw a reasonable map of Marietta, based on my experience and the schema I have of river towns.

The path, in its quintessential form, Main Street, is the primary ordering element in our mental schema of the city and our understanding of its spatial order.

THE PRINCIPLES OF CHRISTOPHER ALEXANDER

Another theorist who links cognition and urban planning is Christopher Alexander. Like Lynch, Alexander (1964, 1965, 1979; Alexander, Ishikawa, & Silverstein, 1977) is interested in creating pleasingly built environments. His emphasis tends to be more philosophical than pragmatic, and there are fewer comprehensive design guidelines to follow. In *The Timeless Way of Building* (1979), Alexander promotes the creation of environments that are "timeless." The words he uses to describe this timelessness are *alive, whole, comfortable, free, egoless*, and *eternal*. How does one achieve these qualities? The emphasis in on patterns in that particular place; these patterns are themselves defined by smaller patterns. What he gives us, and essentially he defines in the book *A Pattern Language* (Alexander et al., 1977), is a plethora of patterns that can be used in combinations to create this timeless way, this timeless language. There are patterns, hundreds of them, for such features as town main gateways, T-junctions, looped local roads, and building height limitations. Similar kinds of patterns have been offered in a book by Cullen (1961), who emphasizes vision as the primary sense in knowing the environment. Cullen stresses the cognitive principle of contrast between Here and There; This and That; the Existing View and the Emerging View. Only through contrast is the deeper sense of the environment revealed. Cullen's book describes the way space can be modulated to create this necessary contrast. Rapoport (1990) also describes a series of elements that reflect the kinds of streets pedestrians have preferred over time.

Alexander's patterns do not emerge all at once, and again we see the importance of a town or environment that emerges slowly, through accretion. This accretion is important because the timeless way of building stresses differentiation, marked by a balance between order and disorder. "These patterns can never be 'designed' or 'built' in one fell swoop—but patient piecemeal growth, designed in such a way that every individual act is always helping to create or generate these larger global patterns, will, slowly and surely, over the years, make a community that has these global patterns in it" (Alexander et al., 1977, p. 3). Master plans will not produce these patterns, according to Alexander, but organic growth, and cities that avoid a homogeneous and undifferentiated character.

Variety is fundamental to the timeless way and is the core of the pattern language. As with Lynch, we again see the importance of hierarchical differentiation. Alexander encourages what he calls a mosaic of subcultures, each of which is differentiable and with its own spatial territory. Not surprisingly, given its importance for other theorists, one of the spatial components that Alexander endorses is the neighborhood. It is an identifiable and important unit to which people belong. These neighborhoods have 400–500 residents, part of a downtown serving 300,000 people, and with a height limit of four stories imposed.

For Alexander (as for many others), Manhattan provides a good example of this kind of hierarchical differentiation he encourages. It works (is legible) in his view, because of the clear differentiation of districts, beneath which is the clear differentiation of avenues, beneath which is the clear differentiation of streets. While the foundation of this legibility may be the grid, it is supported by a hierarchy of buildings and natural forms (landscaping) within each component.

Theoretically, the dissatisfaction many of us feel about new towns or planned communities (those that obviously have not *grown* in the sense Alexander promotes), is related to Christopher Alexander's (1965) distinction between a semi-lattice and a tree. In a seminal article titled "The City Is Not a Tree," Alexander discussed the cognitive limitations that prevent us from simultaneously conceptualizing multiple categories—planners end up being "trapped in a tree," which means that the developments and towns they plan have little diversity, or at best a "planned diversity" most of us find unstimulating and dissatisfying. In many respects what we seek is an earlier form of development, common to Chicago, Boston, St. Louis, and many other cities across the country. In this form of development, cities, towns, and communities grew over time, enabling overlap or a semi-lattice to emerge, where the overlap creates functions that could not have been envisioned in the original plan. Planners today find themselves on the horns of a dilemma, of course, because they are forced into "planning" the functions of a community all at one time. The idea of development on a large scale that occurs in a more natural way, gradually, is in most instances an impossibility today.

A number of people echo Alexander's emphasis on the city as an organic entity. "A city is a natural phenomenon as well as a work of art in the environment. Form in nature is not a result of preconceived order. It evolves as it grows or happens, as mountains develop by upthrusting, boulders by glacial dropping" (Halprin, 1972, p. 220). Essentially Halprin is making the same case for semi-lattices emerging out of natural growth that Alexander endorses.

THE PERSPECTIVE OF DONALD APPLEYARD

Like Lynch and Alexander, Appleyard has provided us with an understanding of what aspects of the physical environment shape its legibility, but he typically has done so from a more research-based approach (1969, 1970, 1976, 1979). Using a variety of techniques including structured and free recall maps and interviews, Appleyard studied the perception of residents of a new industrial city, Ciudad Guayana, in Venezuela (1976). People perceived the city differently depending on a number of factors, including education and transportation mode. Referring to Lynch's five elements, Appleyard notes that cities can be structured or perceived with a combination of both sequential (paths and nodes) and spatial (landmarks, districts, and edges) elements.

Appleyard outlines a pattern of "knowing" the environment that we have seen previously. New residents first concentrate on the big picture before mastering the details. Like the conclusions drawn by DeJonge (1962), areas with a simple street pattern where there was a focus, perhaps consisting of landmarks or nodes such as plazas, were recalled with greater frequency than areas that were structurally confusing (Appleyard, 1976). As with Lynch, the road system again emerges as central to understanding the city. A road system with a single activity center (e.g., an open market) and a variety of establishments at a high density together lead to a clear identity, according to Appleyard's research.

Decision points are also critical. Travelers need to know that they are, in fact, at a decision point. Visibility at intersections is therefore critical. "The travelers' need to identify decision points or to describe them to others when giving directions appeared to be so strong that they were forced to search for distinctive features, even when there were no obvious ones" (Appleyard, 1976, p. 78).

Appleyard's (1976) research also revealed the relationship between knowledge level and environmental cognition. In that regard, his research provides a developmental sequence. Familiarity played a significant role in residents' knowledge level of the city, although the progression was not a simple one. The unfamiliar seemed to depend on visibility, or what they could actually see of the environment. Appleyard describes these unfamiliar "with a mental set searching for the significant, selecting only from the visible, and attracted to the unique and distinctive" (p. 86). What Appleyard is describing is the notion of a cognitive schema of a city, one that people unfamiliar with a *particular* environment, but familiar with the concept of a town or city, will employ. A useful concept here is Ulric Neisser's (1976) perceptual schema. The information in the environment modifies a schema, which in turn directs exploration to resample the environment, and so on, cyclically. Past experience with similar kinds of stimuli will lead us to predict outcomes based on that experience, but we are still very much responsive to the information that the stimulus provides. The environment is not, therefore, in the head; rather, our experience of the environment is the product of an interaction between stimulus information and an activated schema. In essence, when Appleyard talks about these unfamiliar residents "with a mental set searching for the significant," he is describing this process of using past experience to guide future action.

In residents' perception of the city, Appleyard judges the most important finding to be the role of visibility. In describing an ideal relationship of visibility to structure, he says, "Visibility would be highest around decision points on the main transportation system and at major activity centers, next highest along the edges and on the axes of the traveler's vision, down to the sites visible only from the secondary and tertiary system, or invisible from any circulation flow" (1976, p. 89).

Like Lynch and Alexander, Appleyard recognizes the role that environmental form can play in keeping residents informed as the city increases in complexity. An ideal layout, according to Appleyard, would incorporate a rectilinear structure, because rectilinearity facilitates inference. What comes to mind is something like a grid structure. Also in this ideal layout, the "elements should be scaled to some regular module, with high levels of intervisibility and simple rectilinear joints between the parts. The whole should be clearly related to the points of the compass and to a public map" (1976, p. 181). However, as we have seen before, Appleyard argues that order and predictability can be overdone, "a city that is too clearly defined and well connected becomes so predictable that it loses interest, invites no exploration, and becomes regimented" (p. 184). Appleyard argues that cities that facilitate making associations will have their parts differentiated in a systematic way, whether by physical, social, or functional aspects. Pointing to this idea of a perceptual cycle, he says, "It can be more easily structured if the pattern conforms to that of other known and structured cities" (p. 172).

In early work on legibility and imageability, Appleyard and Lynch worked collaboratively (Appleyard, Lynch, & Myer, 1964) on a book that explored "the view from the road." The highway was of particular importance in this project because it was a central feature in metropolitan areas that had such potential for helping to structure our image of the city. The focus of their study was the views that were available from the highway; these views had the potential to structure an individual's comprehension of the city. Long vistas from something like an elevated highway could facilitate city comprehension: "the driver would see how the city is organized, what it symbolizes, how people use it, how it relates to him. To our way of thinking, the highway is the great neglected opportunity in city design" (p. 3). Interestingly, some progressive urban design of the 1980s and 1990s has also stressed the highway and transportation as vehicles for transforming what have become less than ideal city movement patterns in and around cities (Smith, 1994). One prominent example is Playa Vista, in Los Angeles. Using neotraditional planning principles and a pedestrian orientation, the physical structure of the neighborhoods is being shaped by a hierarchical organization of streets and open space.

In the process of orienting themselves, the driver and his/her passengers search for primary features and relate themselves to those features. Appleyard and colleagues point to the cognitive demands that such orientation requires and state that "one cannot depend entirely upon such conventional aids as directional signs" (1964, p. 16). Mistakes and stress are likely to occur when the driver cannot orient him/herself to the city's environmental form. For these authors, the highway would be rich, coherent, and in sequential form. Terms like continuity, rhythm, and development are used to describe this environmental goal. The reader may be reminded of Lynch's (1981) view that environmental form, rather than ancillary sources of information like maps, should communicate structure. On a smaller scale, the importance of environmental form is also related to Weisman's (1981) work on how an understandable floor plan enhances legibility and way finding.

Like Appleyard and colleagues, Carr and Schissler (1969) have also considered how we experience the approach to the city on an elevated expressway. In their research, which involved having subjects wear headgear that recorded their directional gaze, they describe what it is that people remember from a trip. What influences their recollections: expectations? prominent features? Interestingly, independent of familiarity, people tended to report much the same things. Reflecting a position most commonly identified with the direct realism of J. J. Gibson (1966), the authors argue that it is the *form* of the environment that fundamentally determines the way people scan and the elements they select for scrutiny. Gibson's point is that we tune in or resonate to features in the environment (the "direct" realism), rather than constructing the environment "in our heads."

THE RECTILINEARITY OF LE CORBUSIER

Given Le Corbusier's role in building a theory of modern city planning (Gurlitt, 1975; Serenyi, 1975; Waldemar, 1975), it seems important to examine some of his fundamental principles. In *The City of To-morrow and Its Planning* (1929/1971), Le Corbusier provides the foundation of his work. He has little but disdain for continental cities because he views them as being guided by the "pack-donkey." Le Corbusier sees a match between rectilinear design and man's "straight-ahead" goals. Le Corbusier argues that the meandering kind of design, perhaps most typical of the Middle Ages, is a poor match for the pressures of growth in the modern city. Rectilinearity is therefore the answer. "The circulation of traffic demands the straight line; it is the proper thing for the heart of a city. The curve is ruinous, difficult and dangerous; it is a paralyzing thing" (p. 16). In Le Corbusier's mind, the right angle, a component of rectilinearity, provides a kind of security. Le Corbusier's guiding principles are four: decongesting the center of the city, increasing the city's density, improving the circulation paths, and adding parks and open spaces. Le Corbusier champions geometry, standardization, and speed.

Are there any clues about legibility in Le Corbusier's principles? He remarks ". . . the straight road gives a good sense of direction, owing to its regular transversals. The winding road destroys all sense of direction" (LeCorbusier, 1929/1971, p. 208). He also states that the straight line is architectural, and the right angle superior in creating an equilibrium of forces.

If we measure Le Corbusier's impact on the legibility of the city by such projects as Chandigarh and indirectly, Brasilia, we can conclude that his principles do not promote legibility at a practical level. This is what Barnett (1986) has to say about Le Corbusier and his influence: "The tall building and the expressway, as Le Corbusier foresaw, are the two most significant elements of the modern city. But rather than acting as design determinants, they have usually been constructed without any controlling concept of city design whatever" (p. 135). The judgment of Le Corbusier's contribution to the skyline is echoed by Fishman: "The symmetrically organized skyscrapers represent Le Corbusier's most daring and original contribution to urbanism" (1977, p. 191). Others, such as Safdie (1982), challenged Le Corbusier through their own designs and their own views of the city. Safdie's designs stress an integration with the surrounding environment. He sees city squares as the "living rooms of the city" (p. 43) and emphasizes the city's interconnectedness. Ironically, this brings us back to the fundamental element of urban planning: the street. Unless care is given to human scale and the relationship of the pedestrian to the street, the city has little to offer.

NEW TOWNS

This chapter devotes a good deal of attention to new towns as an environmental form because they present the opportunity to evaluate the application of design principles and the resulting impact on spatial cognition. New towns are planned, almost in every aspect. As such, we can at least see what it is that the designer was trying to achieve. We often have access to the very plans that guided development. This section surveys a variety of new towns, beginning with the impact of the garden city movement, and including international examples such as Brasilia and Chandigarh as well as American models such as Levittown, Roosevelt Island, Seaside, and Disney's contribution to new towns, Celebration.

To be successful, new towns must ultimately meet the same criteria as existing cities in affording both order and diversity. Speaking about the need for clarity, order, and activity in a new city such as Ciudad Guayana, Moltke says, "Above all, it must create order, a sense of unity, and a memorable image" (1967, p. 281). Planners of new towns are thus faced with a significant challenge: How to make environments that are legible, on the one hand, and diverse, on the other.

I remember visiting a former college roommate who, after graduation, moved to Columbia, Maryland, a planned community of 22 square miles situated between Baltimore and Washington, D.C. What struck me most about this environment, long before I became formally interested in the topic of environmental design, was its "planned heterogeneity." What I mean is that the environment looked as if there had been a conscious attempt to include different house styles in different colors; you knew that none of this had happened by chance, by accretion, or "naturally." My friend explained that regulations limited modifications to the environment, including the kinds of trees one could plant. Clearly the planners had a vision of how the environment was to appear.

Columbia, developed by Rouse in the 1960s, as well as Reston, Virginia, were forerunners of new town patterns in the sense that enough residences were planned to support a town center. Columbia was planned as nine villages to support about 30,000 residences (Garvin, 1996). Columbia embodied a hierarchical plan, with neighborhoods of 1,200–2,000 forming villages of 6,000–10,000 residents.

Critics of new town design such as Columbia are numerous (Moholy-Nagy, 1968), but the goal that new town design was trying to achieve, solving the problems of urbanization (Evans, 1972), was laudatory. When new town design is criticized, what is held up as a model is the older European city (Crosby, 1965; Lynch, 1981).

New towns, because of their newness, and their separation of functions, lack identifiable elements. Old cities are all mixed up; housing, shopping, offices, workshops are all in the same street, often in the same building. This makes for that unity in diversity, the complexity which is the essence of living in cities. Once functions are separated, the city goes to pieces. (Crosby, 1965, p. 17)

In speaking about classical European cities, Lynch says, "We have a great affection for these towns. They seem secure, legible, proportioned to the human scale, and charged with life, even if at times a little oppressive" (1981, p. 407). He goes on to inform us that as the whole of the city is lost through the impact of modern traffic and building styles, we ultimately come to depend on different aspects, including topographical features, street activities, and signs and names that comprise symbolic connections to make the city legible.

Halpern (1978) explains why we seem to turn to European cities as models. Think of the great enclosed galleria in Milan. Places like this, which may be considered structural elements, also provide the very important opportunity for interaction, the social environment that American cities, and new towns in particular, seem to lack.

The Garden City Movement

The Garden City Movement is closely identified with the development of new towns. Ebenezer Howard, who had no formal design training, is closely identified with this movement. Howard's ideas for a satellite garden city, outlined in the book *Garden Cities of To-morrow* (1898/1945), were developed to address the problems of English cities; they had nowhere to grow: ". . . the population of Great Britain increased enough between 1898 and 1945 to have created three hundred garden cities without changing the population of the cities that already existed" (Barnett, 1986, p. 86). The idea of planned growth also appealed to some as a way to address poor decision rules such as expediency and materialism (Kaiser, 1978; Kouwenhoven, 1961). Some even point to city pride as a reason to create new towns (Appleyard, 1976, p. 16): "New cities like Brasilia, Chandigarh, or Ciudad Guayana capture the imaginations of the citizens of their countries. . . . New cities have a raw, chunky quality."

One of the great successes of the garden city, according to Barnett (1986), is in showing that large developments can demonstrate a sympathetic relationship to the countryside or natural environment. Pressure on the town center was often relieved by the use of ring roads, perimeter roads for vehicular traffic (Llewelyn-Davies, 1972). We all recognize this legacy as it is manifested in suburban developments: "The suburb of curving streets and cul-de-sacs, where houses are built in a lawn-and-garden setting" (Barnett, 1986, p. 88); although some have found the concept of the garden city confusing (Creese, 1966).

Brasilia, Brazil

One of the new city developments that has been written about extensively is Brasilia, Brazil's modern capital city (Epstein, 1973; Galantay, 1975; Holston, 1989; Staubli, 1966). In Holston's (1989) case study, he argues that Brasilia had as its goal a kind of social transformation, embodying the philosophies of the Congrès Internationaux d'Architecture Moderne (CIAM). CIAM's premise was that "modern architecture and planning are the means to create new forms of collective association, personal habit, and daily life" (p. 31). According to Holston, Brasilia did not achieve these goals. At the same time, others (e.g., Bacon, 1976) view Brasilia more favorably. Bacon lauds what we will see as a challenge to legibility: "The gift of Brasilia is not primarily the form of its structures or the formal symmetry of its composition, but rather the reformulation of the vision of the city as a totality" (Bacon, 1976, p. 241).

Brasilia is a modern capital established 75 miles inland from the coast. Actual construction began in 1958, based on the design of Lucio Costa, who, in response to a planning competition, submitted a minimal plan, really just a concept, for this new capital (see Figure 5.5). Despite its lack of detail, Costa's plan was selected from among 26 entries. In the history of contemporary architecture, Brasilia has been called "the most significant example of a city designed as a whole" (Bacon, 1976, p. 235). However, it has been unsympathetically received by others: "The plan was obviously dictated by a vision of a formalistic pattern, possibly a bird or an airplane, rather than by a deep and intense study of human needs and requirements or by topographic and natural conditions" (Gruen, 1964, p. 110).

What do new cities such as Brasilia tell as about the principles of legibility and spatial cognition? Brasilia is organized around a monumental east–west axis, with wings like an eagle spreading out on either side of this, reminiscent of the daVinci sketches of flying machines or even of modern space stations, like the Russian *Mir*. The north and south wings of this creature contain the ministries, cultural sectors, banking, public service, hotel, commercial, medical, media, and sports facilities. Each superquadra is about 844,000 square feet and includes its own kindergarten and elementary school as well as about 3,000 residents. The maximum height allowed for residential sectors is six stories (Epstein, 1973).

Does this plan result in a legible environment? No, according to Holston (1989). He discusses the disorientation that results from a lack of street corners, for example. Brasilia has traffic circles rather than street corners. "In place of the street, Brasilia substitutes high-speed avenues and residential cul-de-sacs; in place of the pedestrian, the automobile; and in place of the system of public spaces that streets traditionally support, the vision of a modern and messianic urbanism" (p. 101). Holston argues that Brasilia lacks warmth because there are no crowds; the social life of the city vanished with the street corner (a comment made recently by architectural critic Paul Goldberger, 1999). Another aspect of design that may contribute to the city's illegibility is the dominance of voids as opposed to solids (Holston, 1989). The proliferation of empty space (the voids) may create a more difficult imaging process and relates to principles of Gestalt psychology in terms of figure–ground differentiation. The voids may also create an absence of contiguity, which in turn may impede the creation of a spatial representation.

In a fascinating comparison of great urban streets, Jacobs (1993), who had earlier collaborated with Appleyard, provides a sense of the essential dullness of Brasilia. He compares the number of intersections (choice points) available in city plans, and notes that for the same area, "there are over 1,500 points of choice available in a square mile of Venice, and fewer than 100 in Brasilia" (p. 202). His book includes 50 plans of central square miles of cities from Ahmedabad, India, to Zurich, Switzerland, from old cities like Venice to new ones like Irvine, California, and Brasilia. His visual comparison of Venice with Brasilia or Irvine is extremely instructive in

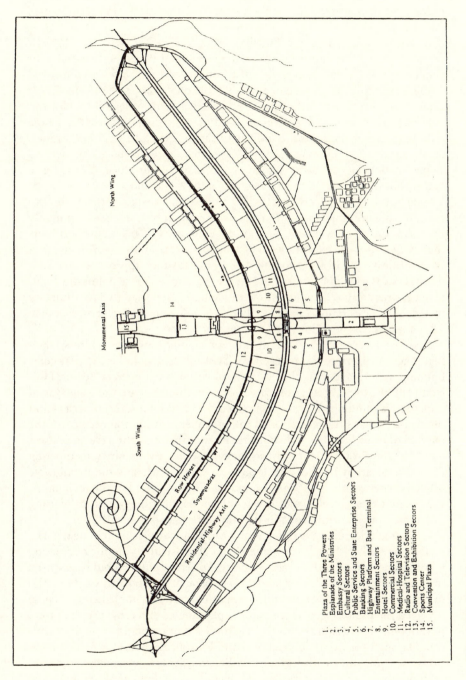

North Wing

Monumental Axis

15

14

13

H

12 10 9 8 6 4 5

11 10 9 8 6 4 5 3

11 8 6 4

2

South Wing

Row Houses

Superquadras

Residential-Highway Axis

1. Plaza of the Three Powers
2. Esplanade of the Ministries
3. Embassy Sectors
4. Cultural Sectors
5. Public Service and State Enterprise Sectors
6. Banking Sectors
7. Highway Platform and Bus Terminal
8. Entertainment Sectors
9. Hotel Sectors
10. Commercial Sectors
11. Medical-Hospital Sectors
12. Radio and Television Sectors
13. Convention and Exhibition Sectors
14. Sports Center
15. Municipal Plaza

Figure 5.5. Brasilia plan.

providing a sense of the intricacy of many older cities and the essential barrenness of newer ones, simply in terms of the street plan (see Figures 5.6 and 5.7).

In terms of the plan for Brasilia, order was to be achieved through types—"by typologizing social functions, building types, and spatial conventions, and by subsuming the distribution of social and architectural typologies into a single urban form" (Holston, 1989, pp. 148–149). Although supporters claim that this kind of order leads to legibility, Holston concludes that it creates a different kind of difficulty—because the whole may be clear but the parts are indistinguishable. As Holston (1989) argues, most cities we could image are not characterized by a particular defined shape. In Brasilia, the total shape may be easy to reproduce, but one gets lost within the whole. In most cities we know, "The idiosyncrasies of place are memorable and therefore crucial in one's knowledge of them. In contrast, Brasilienses understand Brasilia as a single, legible image—commonly read as a cross, an airplane, or a bird—composed of neighborhood units that with very few exceptions they find uniform, undistinguishable, and landmarkless" (p. 149). In giving directions, abstract approaches are activated, because, as Holston points out, few unique reference points are available for orientation. Even long-time residents are reported to have difficulty in reaching destinations because there are few singular reference points. They may grasp the whole, but not the parts.

Another aspect of Brasilia that hinders legibility involves address labeling. The word *street* is not used to label addresses; rather, a particular building might have a numbered location within a commercial sector. Holston (1989) provides other examples of how this ultimate ordering system impedes way finding. The address system is based on a series of letters and numbers, perhaps the hardest way to remember information because of the overlap of cues. Nothing is distinctive. An apartment might have an address like TPT 203-E-607. "Not only do Brasilienses have difficulty remembering the exact location of shops in look-alike blocks (what is the memorable difference between CLS 403-A-33 and CLS 405-A-33?) but the merchants, too, exhibit their ambivalence toward the system by idiosyncratically using different versions of the code in their advertisements" (p. 149).

Is Brasilia a legible environment? Not in a practical sense it appears. The sectors created within the airplane shape are essentially uniform, creating a homogeneity that undermines legibility. Differentiation would be essential in creating identifiable superquadras. Unfortunately, some of Costa's original suggestions for fostering differentiation were not implemented. These involved the use of green space and the planting of different species of trees in different superquadras and the use of different colors in each city quadrant. Though providing less detail than Holston, Epstein (1973) also mentions the difficulties with legibility in Brasilia, where newcomers complain that buildings are "all alike" and, "People complain of never knowing

BRASILIA
(city center)

BRAZIL

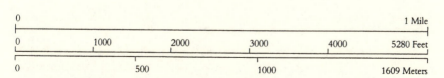

Figure 5.6. Brasilia city center illustrating voids.

VENICE
———————
ITALY

0					1 Mile
0	1000	2000	3000	4000	5280 Feet
0		500		1000	1609 Meters

Figure 5.7. Venice, Italy, covering the same area.

where they are" (p. 102). Regarding the lack of diversity in Brasilia, Gruen (1964) reports, "Tourists who have been to Brasilia have told me that in order to escape its sterility, people visit the more populous shantytown" (p. 111). Recently, Goldberger (1999) says that the excitement of city life takes place not within the city itself, but around its edges, where simple towns have developed. He comments, "Brasilia proves, better than any other place, what we have known all along: that modern architecture can't make cities, although it can make some wonderful buildings" (p. 67).

Chandigarh, India

Like Brasilia, Chandigarh was designed to be a new capital city, in this case, for East Punjab (Evenson, 1966; Fishman, 1977; Kalia, 1987; Sarin, 1977; Walden, 1977; Yoshizaka, 1974). American architect Albert Mayer (1956, 1967a, 1967b, 1971), who had considerable experience in urban planning, was the developer (with Matthew Nowicki, who tragically died in a plane crash during the project) of the initial plan for Nehru. However, a lack of funds to pay Mayer according to the terms of the original agreement led to the involvement of Charles-Edouard Jeanneret (Le Corbusier), who was the lead member of a team (including Mayer, Maxwell Fry, Pierre Jeanneret, and Jane Drew) that put the final plan in place in 1951. The initial plan (1949–1950) was to serve 150,000 residents, and used the concept of superblocks of four neighborhoods, surrounded and connected by a grid of roads to handle traffic (Koenigsberger, 1952).

Located 241 miles north of New Delhi, this new capital of East Punjab was to meet the needs of urban growth brought about with India's independence in 1947, with Hindus and Sikhs gravitating to India and Muslims to Pakistan. Much like Brasilia, Chandigarh was to exemplify a new social order for this new capital. With Le Corbusier involved, the application of principles from CIAM could be expected.

At its heart, Chandigarh was to have an administrative center with a population of about 100,000. Mayer's original plan was to address four problems he saw in American cities at mid-century: land crowding, few places for people to gather (lack of social spaces), the dominance of the automobile and the subservience of the pedestrian, and lack of conditions to support the neighborhood (need for nearby shopping service, recreation) (Kalia, 1987). The neighborhood unit was the fundamental planning element in the design, but site, topography, and regional location were also important. The basic form of the final design was a square with a cross axis, with the capitol structures situated at the end of the northeastern axis at the foot of the mountains.

While in some ways the plan, fan-shaped in nature, seems more imaginative than the plan for Brasilia, and was "meant to avoid the monotony often sensed in planned cities" (Kalia, 1987, p. 53), monotony was not completely avoided. The plan, in terms of the use of superblocks, is reminiscent of Brasilia, and with repetition typically comes some sterility and monotony. While Holston (1989, p. 125) has argued that architecture always manifests a "constructed logic" and that no such thing as an organic or spontaneous city really exists, most of us perceive a difference between cities that have had the opportunity to grow and change over time, to create "semi-lattices" in Christopher Alexander's terms, and those that are fully ordered from the beginning.

Thus we return to the designer's dilemma: How can you "plan" with the sense of order that planning presumably produces, on the one hand, and yet create a sense of variety, interest, and vitality, on the other? Perhaps this can't be done. Ironically, legible environments, by their very nature, must contain variety. We need only return to our example of Manhattan to see how diversity within predictability can be achieved.

Mayer had been influenced by the Garden City Movement and his original plan for Chandigarh was not grid-like in nature. However, the original plan was modified because "the variation in sizes and shapes of the superblocks" was found unacceptable, "a result of the irregularity of street patterns in the Mayer plan" (Kalia, 1987, p. 67).

Kalia argues that Mayer's plan looked to India's past in terms of its villages and bazaars whereas Le Corbusier's plan looked to the industrialized future.

Preferring the rigor of geometric forms, the axis, Le Corbusier argued that "man walks in a straight line because he had a goal and knows where he is going; he has made up his mind to reach some particular place and he goes straight to it. The pack-donkey meanders along, mediates a little in his scatter-brained and distracted fashion, he zig-zags.' " (pp. 88–89)

Using the sector as the basic planning unit, Le Corbusier's plan for Chandigarh possesses organization and rigidity. It is certainly characterized by a separation of functions, particularly transportation modes (automobile and pedestrian), with the use of his seven divisions of traffic separation comprising a hierarchy of circulation.

And what do we know of the legibility of Chandigarh? Kalia writes, "the sectors, which make up the residential section, are marked by a sameness that leaves a visitor lost, without landmarks. Each sector is self-contained, providing essential services within walking distance of every dwelling" (1987, p. 152). "Chandigarh was meant to be something beyond a new state capital. But it lacks culture. It lacks the excitement of Indian streets. It lacks bustling, colorful bazaars. It lacks the noise and din of Lahore. It lacks the intimacy of Delhi. It is a stay-at-home city. It is not Indian. It is the anticity" (p. 152). The problems with legibility in Chandigarh sound surprisingly like those in Brasilia. While there may be comprehension of an overall order, it is within the residential sectors where a lack of visual interest and spatial variety leads to difficulty.

Can we avoid this outcome of undifferentiated order in cities that are planned all at one time? Throughout the history of planning, we have had repetition of units in a given area. However, earlier developments were simply smaller, an area of a few city blocks, for example. Cognitively, we can tolerate that much uniformity. Think of George Miller's (1956) description of the limitations on our information processing. Humans are limited in the amount of information they can process in immediate memory, and when components (such as housing units) are not differentiable and when the goal is to separate rather than group them, the coding is more difficult.

In developing the overall street plan, Mayer had stressed that he was not attempting to produce a specifically picturesque layout, but rather was seeking to modify the rigor of the geometric grid into a pattern of sweeping curves (Evenson, 1966, p. 18). Contrasting Mayer and Nowicki's plans with Le Corbusier's, Evenson (1966) states, "The most striking difference between the two plans is in the rectilinearity of Le Corbusier's design, a characteristic not unexpected in view of his predilection for formal, somewhat classical urbanity" (p. 30). Commenting on the limitations of planning evident in Chandigarh, Evenson thinks the mismatch occurs from an application of Western urban planning to an Indian locale, resulting in a city that "lacks not only the spatial variety and visual interest, but the functional viability of a traditional Indian town" (1975, p. 152). With its courtyards, narrow streets, and inward-oriented courtyards, Indian vernacular design did a far better job of meeting the needs of the climate, the pedestrian emphasis, and requirements for privacy than is apparent in "the misplaced Garden City ambiance of Chandigarh" (Evenson, 1975, p. 152).

Levittown, New Jersey

Levittown has played a central role in the history of new towns. A number of Levittowns were built, with the most widely known the one about which Herbert Gans wrote in his book entitled *The Levittowners: Ways of Life and Politics in a New Suburban Community* (1969). Built in New Jersey about 17 miles from Philadelphia, this Levittown was opened to potential purchasers in 1958, which essentially makes it a contemporary of Brasilia and Chandigarh. Gans lived in Levittown as a resident observer for about two years, and followed the formation of community in the development. Levittown was planned as a development of about 12,000 homes, with three basic house types, priced at between $11,500–$14,500. The organizational concept was the neighborhood, with each one to contain about 1,200 homes, with an elementary school and recreational facilities. There would thus be a total of about 10–12 such neighborhood units, joined by community-side facilities: shops, high schools, a library, and parks. Each street was to have a mixture of three house designs (Cape Cod, ranch, and Colonial). The same floor plan, with two different elevations possible, was used for each house type, and additional variety was achieved by varying the external color of the houses. In this new Levittown, only every 150th house was alike, the result of a highly differentiated color scheme. These steps toward diversity were apparently appreciated by those who moved from Levittown, Pennsylvania, where the blocks were architecturally homogeneous, but the new residents apparently did not have much concern about the architectural uniformity (Gans, 1969). However, the homogeneity seemed to bother critics. "During the 1950s, when attacks on the physical and demographic homogeneity of the postwar suburban subdivisions began, Levittown was frequently mentioned as the prototype" (Gans, 1969, p. 8). From a design and legibility perspective, we might have the same criticisms of Levittown as we do of the typical new town.

Regarding the creation of a sense of community, Gans (1969) recommended a "selective homogeneity at the block level and heterogeneity at the community level" (p. 172). What Gans has to say about Levittown's critics and its implications for legibility is quite revealing. These critics

also look at suburbia as outsiders, who approach the community with a "tourist" perspective. The tourist wants visual interest, cultural diversity, entertainment, esthetic pleasure, variety (preferably exotic), and emotional stimulation. The resident, on the other hand, wants a comfortable, convenient, and socially satisfying place to live—esthetically pleasing, to be sure, but first and foremost functional for his daily needs. Much of the critique of suburbia as community reflects the critics' disappointment that the new suburbs do not satisfy their particular tourist requirements; that they are not places for wandering, that they lack the charm of a medieval village, the excitement of a metropolis, or the architectural variety of an upper-income suburb. (p. 186)

In other words, you can't have it all.

Roosevelt Island, New York

Based on a 1969 plan by Philip Johnson and John Burgee during the Lindsay administration, Roosevelt Island, New York, originally known as Blackwell's Island, was planned as a mixed-income residential community for 20,000. With its hospitals, it was known as Welfare Island in this century, so called in 1931, for the "sick, the lame, the mad and the bad" (Bailey, 1974 p. 32). In the East River off Manhattan, this two-mile long island is a visual disappointment. Visiting there for the first time in about 15 years, I was struck by how little its appearance had changed, especially along the "main street" or corridor that defines what there is of a town

Figure 5.8. Roosevelt Island, Main Street, 1978.

(see Figures 5.8 and 5.9). Since its construction, I have been struck by the monotony of the signage used to label what few businesses there are along the main corridor. This kind of uniformity creates monotony and, if applied on a larger scale, illegibility. The Roosevelt Island logo is easily identified by the red background and white lettering of its tramway to and from Manhattan. Unfortunately, the uniform colors and lettering are repeated on business fronts instead of providing spaces to create much-needed diversity. While important historic landmarks such as the Chapel of the Good Shepard (built in the late 1800s), and the 1789 Blackwell family's farmhouse (the island was sold by the family to the city for $52,000 in 1828) have been maintained, they do not offset the uniformity in design that characterizes the commercial and residential structures.

While Roosevelt Island may succeed in a number of ways, such as providing safe housing, it fails to provide a diverse visual environment. As has happened with other projects such as Chandigarh, the original plan and the final plan differed. In the case of Roosevelt Island, Johnson and Burgee had developed the original plan, but other architects were brought in to develop some of the specific housing units. In the process, the central elements defining the "main street" of the island were sacrificed.

At the core of this new-town-in-town Johnson planned an exciting town center with two large public spaces, a glass-roofed retail arcade, a 300-room hotel, and at least 200,000 square feet of office space. Altogether, there were to be 5000

Figure 5.9. Roosevelt Island, Main Street, 1991.

apartments divided into two neighborhoods that would be built on either side of the town center. The master plan organized these elements along a central "Main Street" spine in a unique manner intended to maximize proximity to both river-fronts. (Garvin, 1996, p. 300)

But the new architects, according to Garvin, failed to understand the pri-mary elements in the plan and eliminated the town center. Where is the lively city street that was envisioned in the original master plan?

Seaside, Florida

Seaside does not constitute a large urban area, but the principles involved are those that are central to legibility: the importance of the street and the importance of diversity (Katz, 1994; Krieger & Lennertz, 1991; LaFrank, 1997; Mohney & Easterling, 1991). Architects Andres Duany and Eliza-beth Plater-Zyberk and developer Robert Davis are primarily responsible for Seaside, a town (although not a formal municipality) of about 80 acres where the buzzwords are *small-scale, mixed use, pro-pedestrian*, and *streetscape*. Ultimately, 350 houses will be built, but the growth of con-struction is purposely slow. Along with Peter Calthorpe (1992), champion of the pedestrian pocket that links housing, retail, and work space within a quarter-mile walking distance of a light rail system, architects such as Duany and Plater-Zyberk are developing communities in what has been called a neotraditional style. Plater-Zyberk has been quoted as saying, "We should not be doing anything but building new towns" (Gruss, 1996).

For readers who saw the movie *The Truman Show* starring Jim Carey, Seaside was the physical stage for this story about Truman Burbank, who was trapped in a perfectly predictable world. Given the kudos it has received in some planning circles, some might find it ironic that Seaside was depicted somewhat negatively as a perfect, predictable environment. Consider this praise for Seaside: "it is the master planners' subtler urban traditionalism—the town center, the civic buildings, the street grid and narrow streets, the lot sizes, alleys and setbacks—that distinguishes Seaside from scores of instantly erected ersatz-old-fashioned places" (Andersen, 1991, p. 44).

The location of the town center at the intersection of the north–south axis with the highway emphasizes its prominence in the plan. What makes Seaside important from the standpoint of legibility is the role of the street and the emphasis on diversity within a housing vocabulary. Rather than bypass the east–west state highway, it was incorporated into the design, with development on both sides of the two-lane road. Somewhat reminiscent of Christopher Alexander (1965), Duany and Plater-Zyberk have developed a design code (a pattern language, if you will) to guide the final form of structures within the community. Duany and Plater-Zyberk are associated with a number of developments in the neotraditional mode, including Kentlands near Gaithersburg, Maryland, and they have also worked with communities nationwide in writing Traditional Neighborhood Development ordinances. According to Vincent Scully (1996), the plan of Seaside marks the revival of traditional American planning principles. It is the revival of the principles of planner John Nolen and of the vernacular and classical traditions of urbanism.

Celebration, Florida

Like Seaside, the media has highlighted Celebration, Disney's new planned community near Orlando (Flanagan, 1996). The development is just under 5,000 acres, formerly part of land in Walt Disney World. "New Urbanism advocates a return to walkable neighborhoods instead of far-flung subdivisions that can be reached only with a car. It champions mixed-use communities, where houses mingle with stores—instead of single-use developments such as office parks and shopping centers" (Flanagan, 1996, p. 54). Much of this is reminiscent of the mixed-use neighborhoods championed by Jane Jacobs (1961) over 30 years ago. Sense of community and social diversity are essential components of this design philosophy. A limited diversity of homes (six styles are defined in a pattern book) is intermingled (see Figure 5.10), and a "downtown" was built, quite close, with apartments stacked over amenities like restaurants and shops. In addition

Figure 5.10. Celebration, Florida, house types.

to the residential areas, people will also live in the commercial areas, with apartments above the stores, much like the communities Jane Jacobs described. No national chains are included in the retail area; the offerings are from local and regional stores and restaurants. The goal is to foster community, realizing that it cannot be manufactured. Parking is tucked into courtyards in these blocks downtown, and a number of features like arcades, terraces, and fountains invite leisurely strolls. The street or path is championed, a feature prominent in Lynch's writings, and helps organize our mental schema. The main street is called Market Street (see Figure 5.11), at the base of which is a small lake, bordered by a street called Front Street, reminiscent of the street naming in river towns described earlier in this chapter.

As part of a conference tour, I visited Celebration in June 1999, and was impressed with the civic structures designed by such architects as Philip Johnson (the town hall), Michael Graves (the post office), Cesar Pelli (the cinema), and Venturi and Scott-Brown (the bank). There is no doubt that Celebration has popular appeal, and the original homeowners were chosen by lottery, given the interest that had been created in settling there. In June 1999, about 2,000 residents resided there; the community is ultimately to house about 20,000 residents in 8,000 homes. The downtown area is legible; it could hardly be otherwise because of its limited scope. The placement of certain civic structures throughout the community (the school, golf course, parks, boardwalks over natural areas) creates landmarks that also

Figure 5.11. Market Street in Celebration, Florida.

contribute to the community's legibility. But while the architectural styles were pleasing, the overall effect produced a certain artificiality. The artifice of Celebration has been applied to other issues on the American scene, including politics. In describing problems with Al Gore's 2000 presidential campaign, Tomasky (1999) writes, "It's the Celebration, Florida of political campaigns, simulated with precision on the advice of the greatest minds in America down to the last (supposedly) randomly placed cobblestone but recognizable as false goods in an instant, evanescent, forgettable, even rather embarrassing" (p. 26). However, some teenagers to whom our group spoke were pleased with the proximity of their friends who were just a walk or a bicycle ride away, just as they might have been at one time in small-town America. Only time will tell whether this kind of new town achieves the sense of community it purports to offer. It remains to be seen whether Disney's seal of approval will result in widespread acceptance of the neotraditionalist form, as some suggest (Flanagan, 1996).

Summary

Consistent with principles from cognitive psychology, the legible city is one based on hierarchical principles where order is complemented by diversity. The grid pattern is a useful planning principle in this regard, but it must permit the kind of differentiation, through the development of districts of different character, that promotes legibility. That is, the city is legible when people are able to recognize where they are and predict what will happen next, as Kaplan (1973) argues.

One of the primary culprits in undermining legibility is the need to plan at one time, just as Christopher Alexander (1965) lamented in his description of the difference between a city that embodies a tree structure and one that emerges over time as a semi-lattice. The accretion that is characteristic of a semi-lattice pattern produces a dense, layered, and embedded environment. Seaside, one of the neotraditionalist developments that has gained attention in planning and development circles, may help change the way planning occurs in its advocacy of slow growth. Although it is unrealistic to imagine that this process could be used in central urban areas, it may influence the appearance of the environment as portions of urban areas are renovated and as the fringes of cities are developed.

CONCLUSION

Humans are spatial animals, from infants who grasp that an object is near or far to adults who travel error free to a destination in a complex urban environment. Humans have evolved to carry out the fundamental task of way finding in a manner that reflects brain architecture and cognitive abilities. Characteristics of development, neuroscience, and gender have created the spatial tools with which humans interact with the environment. Drawing heavily on research, this book has created links between these typically independent avenues of inquiry.

A fuller appreciation of cognitive preferences may help the designers of small-scale tools (i.e., maps) and large-scale environments (i.e., new towns, urban developments) better match the cognitive tendencies that humans possess. Fundamentally, tools and environments that facilitate understanding are those that reflect cognitive principles—that are clear about the whereness and whatness of objects, that punctuate order with diversity. Tools and environments with these principles work because they reflect our biological tendencies.

References

Acredolo, L. P. (1977). Developmental changes in the ability to coordinate perspectives of a large-scale space. *Developmental Psychology, 13,* 1–8.

Acredolo, L. P., Pick, H. L., Jr., & Olsen, M. G. (1975). Environmental differentiation and familiarity as determinants of children's memory for spatial location. *Developmental Psychology, 11,* 495–501.

Ahrentzen, S., & Groat, L. N. (1992). Rethinking architectural education: Patriarchal conventions and alternative visions from the perspectives of women faculty. *Journal of Architectural and Planning Research, 9,* 95–111.

Alexander, C. (1964). *Notes on the synthesis of form.* Cambridge, MA: Harvard University Press.

Alexander, C. (1965, April, May). A city is not a tree. *Architectural Forum, 1,* 58–62; 2, 58–62.

Alexander, C. (1979). *The timeless way of building.* New York: Oxford University Press.

Alexander, C., Ishikawa, S., & Silverstein, M. (1977). *A pattern language: Towns, buildings, construction.* New York: Oxford University Press.

Allen, G. L. (1981). A developmental perspective on the effects of "subdividing" macrospatial experience. *Journal of Experimental Psychology: Human Learning and Memory, 7,* 120–132.

Allen, G. L., & Kirasic, K. C. (1985). Effects of the cognitive organization of route knowledge on judgments of macrospatial distance. *Memory and Cognition, 13,* 218–227.

Allen, G. L., Kirasic, K. C., Siegel, A. W., & Herman, J. F. (1979). Developmental issues in cognitive mapping: The selection and utilization of environmental landmarks. *Child Development, 50,* 1062–1070.

Alvarez, P., Zola-Morgan, S., & Squire, L. R. (1995). Damage limited to the hippocampal region produces long-lasting memory impairment in monkeys. *The Journal of Neuroscience, 15*, 3796–3807.

Andersen, K. (1991). Is Seaside too good to be true? In D. Mohney & K. Easterling (Eds.), *Seaside: Making a town in America* (pp. 42–47). Princeton, NJ: Princeton Architectural Press.

Andersen, R. (1988). The neurobiological basis of spatial cognition: Role of the parietal lobe. In J. Stiles-Davis, M. Kritchevsky, & U. Bellugi (Eds.), *Spatial cognition: Brain bases and development* (pp. 57–80). Hillsdale, NJ: Erlbaum.

Anderson, J. (2000). *Cognitive psychology and its implications* (5th ed.) New York: Worth.

Andrews, S. K. (1983). Spatial cognition through tactual maps. In J. W. Wiedel (Ed.), *Proceedings of the first international symposium on maps and graphics for the visually handicapped* (pp. 30–40). Washington, DC: Association of American Geographers.

Annett, M. (1980). Sex differences in laterality—meaningfulness versus reliability. *The Behavioral and Brain Sciences, 3*, 227.

Annett, M. (1985). *Left, right, hand and brain: The right shift theory*. Hillsdale, NJ: Erlbaum.

Annett, M. (1995). The fertility of the right shift theory. *Current Psychology of Cognition, 14*, 623–650.

Anooshian, L. J., & Nelson, S. K. (1987). Children's knowledge of directional relationships within their neighborhood. *Cognitive Development, 2*, 113–126.

Anooshian, L. J., & Wilson, K. L. (1977). Distance distortions in memory for spatial locations. *Child Development, 48*, 1704–1707.

Anooshian, L. J., & Young, D. (1981). Developmental changes in cognitive maps of a familiar neighborhood. *Child Development, 52*, 341–348.

Appleton, J. (1975). *The experience of landscape*. New York: Wiley.

Appleyard, D. (1969). Why buildings are known. *Environment and Behavior, 1*, 131–156.

Appleyard, D. (1970). Styles and methods of structuring a city. *Environment and Behavior, 2*, 100–117.

Appleyard, D. (1976). *Planning a pluralistic city*. Cambridge, MA: MIT Press.

Appleyard, D. (Ed.). (1979). *The conservation of European cities*. Cambridge, MA: MIT Press.

Appleyard, D., Lynch, K., & Myer, J. R. (1964). *The view from the road*. Cambridge, MA: MIT Press.

Arnheim, R. (1966). *Toward a psychology of art: Collected essays*. Berkeley: University of California Press.

Arnheim, R. (1976). The perception of maps. *American Cartographer, 3*, 5–10.

Atkinson, J. (1993). A neurological approach to the development of "where" and "what" systems for spatial representation in human infants. In N. Eilan, R. McCarthy, & B. Brewer (Eds.), *Spatial representation: Problems in philosophy and psychology* (pp. 325–339). Cambridge, MA: Blackwell.

Aubrey, J. B., & Dobbs, A. R. (1990). Age and sex differences in the mental realignment of maps. *Experimental Aging Research, 16*, 133–139.

Bacon, E. N. (1976). *Design of cities*. New York: Penguin.

Bailey, A. (1974, December 1). Manhattan's other island. *New York Times Magazine*, pp. 32–36, 38, 40, 42, 44, 47, 49, 52, 56.

Baillargeon, R. (1993). The object concept revisited: New directions in the investigation of infants' physical knowledge. In C. Granrud (Ed.), *Visual perception and cognition in infancy* (pp. 265–315). Hillsdale, NJ: Erlbaum.

Banaji, M. R., & Crowder, R. G. (1989). The bankruptcy of everyday memory. *American Psychologist, 44*, 1185–1193.

Banerjee, T., & Southworth, M. (Eds.). (1990). *City sense and city design: Writings and projects of Kevin Lynch.* Cambridge, MA: MIT Press.

Barber, P. O., & Lederman, S. J. (1988). Encoding direction in manipulatory space and the role of visual experience. *Journal of Visual Impairment and Blindness, 82*, 99–106.

Barnett, J. (1986). *The elusive city: Five centuries of design, ambition and miscalculation.* New York: Harper & Row.

Bartz, B. S. (1970). An analysis of the topographic legibility literature. *The Cartographic Journal, 7*, 10–16.

Beatty, W. W. (1984). Hormonal organization of sex differences in play fighting and spatial behavior. In G. J. DeVries, J. P. C. DeBruin, H. B. M. Uylings, & M. A. Corner (Eds.), *Progress in brain research, Vol. 61* (pp. 315–330). New York: Elsevier.

Beatty, W. W. (1988). The Fargo Map Test: A standardized method for assessing remote memory for visuospatial information. *Journal of Clinical Psychology, 44*, 61–67.

Beatty, W. W., & Troster, A. I. (1987). Gender differences in geographical knowledge. *Sex Roles, 16*, 565–590.

Begley, S. (1995, March 27). Gray matters. *Newsweek, 125* (13), 48–54.

Benbow, C. P., & Benbow, R. M. (1984). Biological correlates of high mathematical reasoning ability. In G. J. DeVries, J. P. C. DeBruin, H. B. M. Uylings, & M. A. Corner (Eds.), *Progress in brain research, Vol. 61* (pp. 469–490). New York: Elsevier.

Benevolo, L. (1981). *The history of the city.* Cambridge, MA: MIT Press.

Berenbaum, S. A., & Hines, M. (1992). Early androgens are related to childhood sex-typed toy preferences. *Psychological Science, 3*, 203–206.

Berg, C., Hertzog, C., & Hunt, E. (1982). Age differences in the speed of mental rotation. *Developmental Psychology, 18*, 95–107.

Berkeley, E. P. (1973). More than you may want to know about the Boston City Hall. *Architecture Plus, 1*, 72–77, 98.

Bertin, J. (1983). *Semiology of graphics: Diagrams, networks, maps* (W. J. Berg, Trans.). Madison: University of Wisconsin Press.

Biel, A. (1982). Children's spatial representation of their neighborhood: A step towards a general spatial competence. *Journal of Environmental Psychology, 2*, 193–200.

Birenbaum, M., Kelly, A. E., & Levi-Keren, M. (1994). Stimulus features and sex difference in mental rotation test performance. *Intelligence, 19*, 51–64.

Blades, M., & Cooke, Z. (1994). Young children's ability to understand a model as a spatial representation. *Journal of Genetic Psychology, 155*, 201–218.

Blades, M., & Spencer, C. (1986). The implications of psychological theory and methodology for cognitive cartography. *Cartographica, 23*, 1–13.

Blades, M., & Spencer, C. (1987a). The use of maps by 4–6-year old children in a large scale maze. *British Journal of Developmental Psychology, 16,* 197–218.

Blades, M., & Spencer, C. (1987b). Young children's strategies when using maps with landmarks. *Journal of Environmental Psychology, 7,* 201–217.

Blades, M., & Spencer, C. (1989). Young children's ability to use coordinate references. *Journal of Genetic Psychology, 150,* 5–18.

Blades, M., & Spencer, C. (1990). The development of 3- to 6-year-olds' map using ability: The relative importance of landmarks and map alignment. *Journal of Genetic Psychology, 151,* 181–194.

Blades, M., & Spencer, C. (1994). The development of children's ability to use spatial representations. In H. W. Reese (Ed.), *Advances in child development and behavior* (pp. 157–199). New York: Academic Press.

Blaut, J. M., & Stea, D. (1974). Mapping at the age of three. *Journal of Geography, 73,* 5–9.

Blough, P. M., & Slavin, L. K. (1987). Reaction time assessments of gender differences in visual-spatial performance. *Perception and Psychophysics, 41,* 276–281.

Bluestein, N., & Acredolo, L. (1979). Developmental changes in map-reading skills. *Child Development, 50,* 691–697.

Bockemuehl, H. W., & Wilson, P. B. (1976). Minimum letter size for visual aids. *The Professional Geographer, 28,* 185–189.

Borke, H. (1975). Piaget's mountains revisited: Changes in the egocentric landscape. *Developmental Psychology, 11,* 240–243.

Bower, G. H., Clark, M. C., Lesgold, A. M., & Winzenz, D. (1969). Hierarchical retrieval schemes in recall of categorical word lists. *Journal of Verbal Learning and Verbal Behavior, 8,* 323–343.

Boynton, R. M., Fargo, L., Olson, C. X, & Smallman, H. S. (1989). Category effects in color memory. *Color Research and Application, 14,* 229–234.

Brambring, M. (1982). Language and geographic orientation in the blind. In R. J. Jarvella & W. Klein (Eds.), *Speech, place, and action: Studies in deixis and related topics* (pp. 203–218). New York: Wiley.

Breines, S., & Dean, W. J. (1974). *The pedestrian revolution: Streets without cars.* New York: Vintage.

Bremner, J. G. (1978). Egocentric versus allocentric spatial coding in nine-month-old infants: Factors influencing the choice of code. *Developmental Psychology, 14,* 346–355.

Bremner, J. G., & Andreasen, G. (1998). Young children's ability to use maps and models to find ways in novel spaces. *British Journal of Developmental Psychology, 16,* 197–218.

Bremner, J. G., & Bryant, P. E. (1977). Place versus response as the basis of spatial errors made by young infants. *Journal of Experimental Child Psychology, 23,* 162–171.

Brett, L. (1970). *Architecture in a crowded world: Vision and reality in planning.* New York: Schocken.

Brochmann, O. (1970). *Good or bad design?* New York: Van Nostrand Reinhold.

Brodzinsky, D. M. (1980). Cognitive style differences in children's spatial perspective taking. *Developmental Psychology, 16,* 151–152.

Brodzinsky, D. M. (1982). Relationship between cognitive style and cognitive development: A 2-year longitudinal study. *Developmental Psychology, 18,* 617–626.

Bronzaft, A. L., Dobrow, S. B., & O'Hanlon, T. J. (1976). Spatial orientation in a subway system. *Environment and Behavior, 8,* 575–594.

Brown, H. D., & Kosslyn, S. M. (1995). Hemispheric differences in visual object processing: Structural versus allocation theories. In R. J. Davidson & K. Hugdahl (Eds.), *Brain asymmetry* (pp. 77–97). Cambridge, MA: MIT Press.

Brown, R., & Kulik, J. (1977). Flashbulb memories. *Cognition, 5,* 73–99.

Brown, R. M., Hall, L. R., Holtzer, R., Brown, S. L., & Brown, N. L. (1997). Gender and video game performance. *Sex Roles, 36,* 793–812.

Bruce, C., Desimone, R., & Gross, C. G. (1981). Visual properties of neurons in a polysensory area in superior temporal sulcus of the macaque. *Neurophysiology, 46,* 369–384.

Bryden, M. P. (1980). Sex differences in brain organization: Different brains or different strategies? *Behavioral and Brain Sciences, 3,* 230–231.

Bryden, M. P. (1982). *Laterality: Functional asymmetry in the intact brain.* New York: Academic Press.

Bryden, M. P., George, J., & Inch, R. (1990). Sex differences and the role of figural complexity in determining the rate of mental rotation. *Perceptual and Motor Skills, 70,* 467–477.

Buffery, A. W. H., & Gray, J. A. (1972). Sex differences in the development of spatial and linguistic skills. In C. Ounsted & D. C. Taylor (Eds.), *Gender differences: Their ontogeny and significance* (pp. 123–157). Edinburgh: Churchill Livingstone.

Burgess, N., Recce, M., & O'Keefe, J. (1994). A model of hippocampal function. *Neural Networks, 7,* 1065–1081.

Burke, B., Chrisler, J. C., & Devlin, A. S. (1989). The creative thinking, environmental frustration, and self-concept of left- and right-handers. *Creativity Research Journal, 2,* 279–285.

Burns, P. C. (1998). Wayfinding errors while driving. *Journal of Environmental Psychology, 18,* 209–217.

Buss, D. M. (1995). Psychological sex differences: Origins through sexual selection. *American Psychologist, 50,* 164–168.

Butters, N., & Barton, M. (1970). Effect of parietal lobe damage on the performance of reversible operations in space. *Neuropsychologia, 8,* 205–214.

Byrne, R. W. (1979). Memory for urban geography. *Quarterly Journal of Experimental Psychology, 31,* 147–154.

Byrne, R. W., & Salter, E. (1983). Distances and directions in the cognitive maps of the blind. *Canadian Journal of Psychology, 37,* 293–299.

Cacioppo, J. T., & Petty, R. E. (1982). The need for cognition. *Journal of Personality and Social Psychology, 42,* 116–131.

Cahill, M. C., & Carter, R. C., Jr. (1976). Color code size for searching displays of different density. *Human Factors, 18,* 273–280.

Calthorpe, P. (1992). The pedestrian pocket: New strategies for suburban growth. In B. Walter, L. Arkin, & R. Crenshaw (Eds.), *Sustainable cities: Concepts and strategies for eco-city development* (pp. 27–35). Los Angeles, CA: Eco-Home Media.

Calvin, W. (1990). *The cerebral symphony.* New York: Bantam.

Canter, D. (1974). *Psychology for architects.* New York: Wiley.

Canter, D., & Tagg, S. K. (1975). Distance estimation in cities. *Environment and Behavior, 7,* 59–80.

Caplan, P. J., MacPherson, G. M., & Tobin, P. (1985). Do sex-related differences in spatial abilities exist? A multi-level critique with new data. *American Psychologist, 40,* 786–799.

Carpman, J. R., Grant, M. A., & Simmons, D. A. (1986). *Design that cares: Planning health facilities for patients and visitors.* Chicago: American Hospital Publishing.

Carr, S., & Schissler, D. (1969). The city as a trip: Perceptual selection and memory in the view from the road. *Environment and Behavior, 1,* 7–35.

Carreiras, M., & Garling, T. (1990). Discrimination of cardinal compass direction. *Acta Psychologica, 73,* 3–11.

Carswell, C. M. (1992). Choosing specifiers: An evaluation of the basic tasks model of graphical perception. *Human Factors, 34,* 535–554.

Carter, L. F. (1947). An experiment on the design of tables and graphs used for presenting numerical data. *Journal of Applied Psychology, 31,* 640–650.

Carter, R. C. (1982). Visual search with color. *Journal of Experimental Psychology: Human Perception and Performance, 8,* 127–136.

Casali, J. G., & Gaylin, K. B. (1988). Selected graph design variables in four interpretation tasks: A microcomputer-based pilot study. *Behavior and Information Technology, 7,* 31–49.

Casey, M. B., & Brabeck, M. M. (1989). Exceptions to the male advantage on a spatial task: Family handedness and college major as factors identifying women who excel. *Neuropsychologia, 27,* 689–696.

Casey, M. B., & Brabeck, M. M. (1990). Women who excel on a spatial task: Proposed genetic and environmental factors. *Brain and Cognition, 12,* 73–84.

Casey, M. B., Colon, D., & Goris, Y. (1992). Family handedness as a predictor of mental rotation ability among minority girls in a math-science training program. *Brain and Cognition, 18,* 88–96.

Casey, S. M. (1978). Cognitive mapping by the blind. *Journal of Visual Impairment and Blindness, 72,* 297–301.

Cassell, J., & Jenkins, H. (Eds.). (1998). *From Barbie to Mortal Kombat: Gender and computer games.* Cambridge, MA: MIT Press.

Cassidy, R. (1980). *Livable cities: A grass-roots guide to rebuilding urban America.* New York: Holt, Rinehart, and Winston.

Chabris, C. F., & Kosslyn, S. M. (1998). How do the cerebral hemispheres contribute to encoding spatial relations? *Current Directions in Psychological Science, 7,* 8–14.

Chambers, J. M., Cleveland, W. S., Kleiner, B., & Tukey, P. A. (1983). *Graphical methods for data analysis.* Boston: Duxbury Press.

Chen, L. (1982). Topological structure in visual perception. *Science, 218,* 699–700.

Christ, R. E. (1975). Review and analysis of color coding research for visual displays. *Human Factors, 17*, 542–570.

Churchill, H. S. (1962). *The city is the people.* New York: W.W. Norton.

Clear, S.-J. (1978). Sex differences in spatial ability: A critique. *International Journal of Behavioral Development, 1*, 241–246.

Cleveland, W. S., & McGill, R. (1984). Graphical perception: Theory, experimentation, and application to the development of graphical methods. *Journal of the American Statistical Association, 79*, 531–554.

Cleveland, W. S., & McGill, R. (1985). Graphical perception and graphical methods for analyzing scientific data. *Science, 229*, 828–833.

Cleveland, W. S., & McGill, R. (1986). An experiment in graphical perception. *International Journal of Man-Machine Studies, 25*, 491–500.

Cleveland, W. S., & McGill, R. (1987). Graphical perception: The visual decoding of quantitative information on graphical displays of data. *Journal of the Royal Statistical Society, 150* (Series A, Pt. 3), 192–229.

Cochran, K. F., & Wheatley, G. H. (1989). Ability and sex-related differences in cognitive strategies on spatial tasks. *Journal of General Psychology, 116*, 43–55.

Cohen, R., Baldwin, L. M., & Sherman, R. C. (1978). Cognitive maps of a naturalistic setting. *Child Development, 49*, 1216–1218.

Cohen, R., McManus, J., Fox, D., & Kastelnik, C. (1973). *Psych city: A simulated community.* New York: Pergamon Press.

Cohen, R., Weatherford, D. L., Lomenick, T., & Koeller, K. (1979). Development of spatial representations: Role of task demands and familiarity with the environment. *Child Development, 50*, 1257–1260.

Collins, A. M., & Quillian, M. R. (1969). Retrieval time from semantic memory. *Journal of Verbal Learning and Verbal Behavior, 8*, 240–247.

Conning, A. M., & Byrne, R. W. (1984). Pointing to preschool children's spatial competence: A study in natural settings. *Journal of Environmental Psychology, 4*, 165–175.

Connor, J. M., & Serbin, L. A. (1977). Behaviorally based masculine-and feminine-activity-preference scales for preschoolers: Correlates with other classroom behaviors and cognitive tests. *Child Development, 48*, 1411–1416.

Constantinidis, C., & Steinmetz, M. A. (1996). Neuronal activity in posterior parietal area 7a during the delay periods of a spatial memory task. *Journal of Neurophysiology, 76*, 1352–1355.

Corballis, M. C. (1980). Is left-handedness genetically determined? In J. Herron (Ed.), *Neuropsychology of left-handedness* (pp. 159–176). New York: Academic Press.

Corballis, M. C. (1982). Mental rotation: Anatomy of a paradigm. In M. Potegal (Ed.), *Spatial abilities: Development and physiological foundations* (pp. 173–198). New York: Academic Press.

Corballis, M. C. (1988). Recognition of disoriented shapes. *Psychological Review, 95*, 115–123.

Corballis, M. C. (1991). *The lop-sided ape: Evolution of the generative mind.* New York: Oxford University Press.

Corballis, M. C. (1994). The generation of generativity: A response to Bloom. *Cognition, 51*, 191–198.

Corballis, M. C. (1995a). Evolving theories of handedness. *Current Psychology of Cognition, 14*, 529–536.

Corballis, M. C. (1995b). Visual integration in the split brain. *Neuropsychologia, 33*, 937–959.

Corballis, M. C. (1996). Hemispheric interactions in temporal judgments about spatially separated stimuli. *Neuropsychology, 10*, 42–50.

Corballis, M. C., & Beale, I. L. (1983). *The ambivalent mind: The neuropsychology of left and right.* Chicago: Nelson-Hall.

Corballis, M. C., & Manalo, R. (1993). Effect of spatial attention on mental rotation. *Neuropsychologia, 31*, 199–205.

Corballis, M. C., & Sergent, J. (1988). Imagery in a commissurotomized patient. *Neuropsychologia, 26*, 13–26.

Corballis, M. C., & Sergent, J. (1989a). Hemispheric specialization for mental rotation. *Cortex, 25*, 15–25.

Corballis, M. C., & Sergent, J. (1989b). Mental rotation in a commissurotomized subject. *Neuropsychologia, 27*, 585–597.

Corballis, M. C., & Sidney, S. (1993). Effects of concurrent memory load on visual-field differences in mental rotation. *Neuropsychologia, 31*, 183–197.

Corballis, M. C., & Trudel, C. I. (1993). Role of the forebrain commissures in interhemispheric integration. *Neuropsychology, 7*, 306–324.

Coren, S., & Girgus, J. S. (1980). Principles of perceptual organization and spatial distortion: The Gestalt illusions. *Journal of Experimental Psychology: Human Perception and Performance, 6*, 404–412.

Cornell, E. H., & Hay, D. H. (1984). Children's acquisition of a route via different media. *Environment and Behavior, 16*, 627–641.

Cornell, E. H., Heth, C. D., & Broda, L. S. (1989). Children's wayfinding: Response to instructions to use environmental landmarks. *Developmental Psychology, 25*, 755–764.

Cornell, E. H., Heth, C. D., & Rowat, W. L. (1992). Wayfinding by children and adults: Response to instructions to use look-back and retrace strategies. *Developmental Psychology, 28*, 328–336.

Cosmides, L., & Tooby, J. (1995). From function to structure: The role of evolutionary biology and computational theories in cognitive neuroscience. In M. S. Gazzaniga (Ed.), *The cognitive neurosciences* (pp. 1199–1210). Cambridge, MA: MIT Press.

Couclelis, H., Golledge, R. G., Gale, N., & Tobler, W. (1987). Exploring the anchor-point hypothesis of spatial cognition. *Journal of Environmental Psychology, 7*, 99–122.

Cousins, J. H., Siegel, A. W., & Maxwell, S. E. (1983). Way finding and cognitive mapping in large-scale environments: A test of a developmental model. *Journal of Experimental Child Psychology, 35*, 1–20.

Creese, W. L. (1966). *The search for environment: The garden city: Before and after.* New Haven, CT: Yale University Press.

Crook, T. H., Youngjohn, J. R., & Larrabee, G. J. (1993). The influence of age, gender, and cues on computer-simulated topographic memory. *Developmental Neuropsychology, 9*, 41–53.

Crosby, T. (1965). *Architecture: City sense.* New York: Van Nostrand Reinhold.

Crosby, T. (1973). *How to play the environment game.* Baltimore: Penguin.

Crowe, N. (1995). *Nature and the idea of a man-made world: An investigation into the evolutionary roots of form and order in the built environment.* Cambridge, MA: MIT Press.

Cuff, D. J. (1973). Colour on temperature maps. *Cartographic Journal, 10,* 17–21.

Cullen, G. (1961). *Townscape.* London: Architectural Press.

Curran, R. J. (1983). *Architecture and the urban experience.* New York: Van Nostrand Reinhold.

Dandonoli, P., Demick, J., & Wapner, S. (1990). Physical arrangement and age as determinants of environmental representation. *Children's Environments Quarterly, 7,* 26–36.

Daniel, M-P., Carite, L., & Denis, M. (1996). Modes of linearization in the description of spatial configurations. In J. Portugali (Ed.), *The construction of cognitive maps* (pp. 297–318). Boston: Kluwer Academic.

Darvizeh, Z., & Spencer, C. P. (1984). How do young children learn novel routes? The importance of landmarks in the child's retracing routes through the large scale environment. *Environmental Education and Information, 3,* 97–105.

Deasy, C. M. (1985). *Designing places for people: A handbook on human behavior for architects, designers, and facility managers.* New York: Whitney Library of Design.

DeGroot, A. D. (1965). *Thought and choice in chess.* The Hague, Netherlands: Mouton.

DeJonge, D. (1962). Images of urban areas: Their structure and psychological foundations. *Journal of the American Institute of Planners, 28,* 266–276.

DeLucia, A. A., & Hiller, D. W. (1982). Natural legend design for thematic maps. *Cartographic Journal, 19,* 46–52.

Denis, M., Goncalves, M.-R., & Memmi, D. (1995). Mental scanning of visual images generated from verbal descriptions: Towards a model of image accuracy. *Neuropsychologia, 33,* 511–530.

Dent, B. D. (1972). Visual organization and thematic map communication. *Annals of the Association of American Geographers, 62,* 25–38.

Dent, B. D. (1985). *Principles of thematic map design.* Reading, MA: Addison-Wesley.

DeRenzi, E., Faglioni, P., & Villa, P. (1977). Topographical amnesia. *Journal of Neurology, Neurosurgery, and Psychiatry, 40,* 498–505.

DeValois, R. L., & DeValois, K. K. (1988). *Spatial vision.* New York: Oxford University Press.

DeVega, M., Marschark, M., Intons-Peterson, M. J., Johnson-Laird, P. N., & Denis, M. (1996). Representations of visuospatial cognition: A discussion. In M. DeVega, M. J. Intons-Peterson, P. N. Johnson-Laird, M. Denis, & M. Marschark (Eds.), *Models of visuospatial cognition* (pp. 198–226). New York: Oxford University Press.

Devlin, A. S. (1973). Some factors in enhancing knowledge of a natural area. In W. F. E. Preiser (Ed.), *Environmental design research: Symposia and workshops* (Vol. 2; pp. 200–206). Stroudsburg, PA: Dowden, Hutchinson, & Ross.

Devlin, A. S. (1976). The "small town" cognitive map: Adjusting to a new environment. In G. T. Moore & R. G. Golledge (Eds.), *Environmental knowing:*

Theories, research, and methods (pp. 58–66). Stroudsburg, PA: Dowden, Hutchinson, & Ross.

Devlin, A. S. (1980). Housing for the elderly: Cognitive considerations. *Environment and Behavior, 12,* 451–466.

Devlin, A. S. (1997). Architects: Gender-role and hiring decisions. *Psychological Reports, 81,* 667–676.

Devlin, A. S. (1999). *Gender differences in wayfinding preferences and skill.* Unpublished manuscript.

Devlin, A. S., & Bernstein, J. (1995). Interactive wayfinding: Use of cues by men and women. *Journal of Environmental Psychology, 15,* 23–38.

Devlin, A. S., & Bernstein, J. (1997). Interactive wayfinding: Map style and effectiveness. *Journal of Environmental Psychology, 17,* 99–110.

DeVries, G. J., DeBruin, J. P. C., Uylings, H. B. M., & Corner, M. A. (1984). *Progress in brain research. Vol. 61: Sex differences in the brain.* New York: Elsevier.

Dimond, S. J., & Beaumont, J. G. (1974). *Hemisphere function in the human brain.* London: Elek Science.

Dobson, M. W. (1979). Visual information processing during cartographic communication. *Cartographic Journal, 16,* 14–20.

Dodds, A. G., Howarth, C. I., & Carter, D. C. (1982). The mental maps of the blind: The role of previous visual experience. *Journal of Visual Impairment and Blindness, 76,* 5–12.

Dodwell, P. C. (1963). Children's understanding of spatial concepts. *Canadian Journal of Psychology, 17,* 141–161.

Doherty, S., Gale, N., Pellegrino, J. W., & Golledge, R. (1989). Children's versus adults' knowledge of places and distances in a familiar neighborhood environment. *Children's Environments Quarterly, 6,* 65–71.

Doherty, S., & Pellegrino, J. W. (1985). Developmental changes in neighborhood scene recognition. *Children's Environments Quarterly, 2,* 38–43.

Dorner, G. (1977). Hormone dependent differentiation, maturation and function of the brain and sexual behavior. In R. Gemme & C. C. Wheeler (Eds.), *Progress in sexology: Selected papers for the proceedings of the 1976 International Congress of Sexology* (pp. 21–42). New York: Plenum Press.

Doss, E. (1997). Making imagination safe in the 1950s: Disneyland's fantasy art and architecture. In K. A. Marling (Ed.), *Designing Disney's theme parks: The architecture of reassurance* (pp. 178–189). New York: Flammarion.

Downs, R. (1979). Mazes, minds, and maps. In D. Pollet & P. C. Haskell (Eds.), *Sign systems for libraries: Solving the wayfinding problem* (pp. 17–32). New York: Bowker.

Doxiadis, C. A. (1963). *Architecture in transition.* New York: Oxford University Press.

Dunlap, D. W. (1999, July 11). Developing an Illinois suburb, with principles. *New York Times,* Sec. 11, p. 7.

Dunlop, B. (1996). *Building a dream: The art of Disney architecture.* New York: Abrams.

Eagly, A. H. (1994). On comparing women and men. *Feminism and Psychology, 4,* 513–522.

Eagly, A. H. (1995). The science and politics of comparing women and men. *American Psychologist, 50*, 145–158.

Eals, M., & Silverman, I. (1994). The hunter-gatherer theory of spatial sex differences: Proximate factors mediating the female advantage in recall of object arrays. *Ethology and Sociobiology, 15*, 95–105.

Eastman, J. R. (1985). Graphic organization and memory structures for map learning. *Cartographica, 22*, 1–20.

Eells, W. C. (1926). The relative merits of circles and bars for representing component parts. *Journal of the American Statistical Association, 21*, 119–132.

Egan, D. E., & Schwartz, B. J. (1979). Chunking in recall of symbolic drawings. *Memory and Cognition, 7*, 149–158.

Ekstrom, R. B., French, J. W., & Harman, H. H. (1976). *Manual for Kit of Factor Reference Cognitive Tests*. Princeton, NJ: Educational Testing Service.

Ellis, A. W., & Young, A. W. (1988). *Human cognitive neuropsychology*. Hillsdale, NJ: Erlbaum.

Emmorey, K., Kosslyn, S. M., & Bellugi, U. (1993). Visual imagery and visual-spatial language: Enhanced imagery abilities in deaf and learning ASL signers. *Cognition, 46*, 139–181.

Epstein, D. G. (1973). *Brasilia, planning and reality: A study of planned and spontaneous urban development*. Berkeley: University of California Press.

Evans, G. W., Brennan, P. L., Skorpanich, M. A., & Held, D. (1984). Cognitive mapping and elderly adults: Verbal and location memory for urban landmarks. *Journal of Gerontology, 39*, 452–457.

Evans, H. (Ed.). (1972). *New towns: The British experience*. New York: Wiley.

Evenson, N. (1966). *Chandigarh*. Berkeley: University of California Press.

Evenson, N. (1975). Chandigarh. In P. Serenyi (Ed.), *Le Corbusier in perspective* (pp. 144–153). Englewood Cliffs, NJ: Prentice-Hall.

Fairweather, H. (1976). Sex differences in cognition. *Cognition, 4*, 231–280.

Farah, M. J. (1984). The neurological basis of mental imagery: A componential analysis. *Cognition, 18*, 245–272.

Farah, M. J. (1988a). Is visual imagery really visual? Overlooked evidence from neuropsychology. *Psychological Review, 95*, 307–317.

Farah, M. J. (1988b). The neuropsychology of mental imagery. In J. Stiles-Davis, M. Kritchevsky, & U. Bellugi (Eds.), *Spatial cognition: Brain bases and development* (pp. 33–56). Hillsdale, NJ: Erlbaum.

Farah, M. J. (1991). *Visual agnosia: Disorders of object recognition and what they tell us about normal vision*. Cambridge, MA: MIT Press.

Farah, M. J. (1994). Neuropsychological inference with an interactive brain: A critique of the "locality" assumption. *Behavioral and Brain Sciences, 17*, 43–104.

Farah, M. J. (1995). The neural bases of mental imagery. In M. S. Gazzaniga (Ed.), *The cognitive neurosciences* (pp. 963–976). Cambridge, MA: MIT Press.

Farah, M. J., Gazzaniga, M. S., Holtzman, J. D., & Kosslyn, S. M. (1985). Note: A left hemisphere basis for visual mental imagery? *Neuropsychologia, 23*, 115–118.

Feingold, A. (1988). Cognitive gender differences are disappearing. *American Psychologist, 43*, 95–103.

Ferguson, E. L., & Hegarty, M. (1994). Properties of cognitive maps constructed from texts. *Memory and Cognition, 22,* 455–473.

Findlay, R., Ashton, R., & McFarland, K. (1994). Hemispheric differences in image generation and use in the haptic modality. *Brain and Cognition, 25,* 67–78.

Fischer, S. C., & Pellegrino, J. W. (1988). Hemisphere differences for components of mental rotation. *Brain and Cognition, 7,* 1–15.

Fisher, H. T. (1982). *Mapping information: The graphic display of quantitative information.* Cambridge, MA: Abt Books.

Fishman, R. (1977). *Urban utopias in the twentieth century. Ebenezer Howard, Frank Lloyd Wright, and Le Corbusier.* New York: Basic Books.

Flanagan, B. (1996, September /October). Cause to celebrate? *Metropolitan Home,* pp. 54, 56.

Fleming, D. K. (1984). Cartographic strategies for airline advertising. *Geographical Review, 74,* 76–93.

Fletcher, J. F. (1980). Spatial representation in the blind 1: Development compared to sighted children. *Journal of Visual Impairment and Blindness, 74,* 318–385.

Fodor, J. A. (1983). *Modularity of mind: An essay on faculty psychology.* Cambridge, MA: MIT Press.

Ford, M. E. (1979). The construct validity of egocentrism. *Psychological Bulletin, 86,* 1169–1188.

Ford, M. E. (1985). Two perspectives on the validation of developmental constructs: Psychometric and theoretical limitations in research on egocentrism. *Psychological Bulletin, 97,* 497–501.

Fotheringham, A. S., & Curtis, A. (1992). Encoding spatial information: The evidence for hierarchical processing. In A. U. Frank, I. Campari, & U. Formentini (Eds.), *Theories and methods of spatio-temporal reasoning in geographic space* (pp. 269–287). New York: Springer-Verlag.

Francaviglia, R. V. (1977, Spring-Summer). Main Street USA: The creation of a popular image. *Landscape,* pp. 18–22.

Franklin, N. (1992). Spatial representation for described environments. *Geoforum, 23,* 165–174.

Franklin, N., Tversky, B., & Coon, V. (1992). Switching points of view in spatial mental models. *Memory and Cognition, 20,* 507–518.

Freedman, R. J., & Rovegno, L. (1981). Ocular dominance, cognitive strategy, and sex differences in spatial ability. *Perceptual and Motor Skills, 52,* 651–654.

Freksa, C. (1992). Using orientation information for qualitative spatial reasoning. In A. U. Frank, I. Campari, & U. Formentini (Eds.), *Theories and methods of spatio-temporal reasoning in geographic space* (pp. 162–178). New York: Springer-Verlag.

French, J. W. (1951). The description of aptitude and achievement tests in terms of rotated factors. *Psychometric Monograph,* No 5. Chicago: University of Chicago Press.

Freundschuh, S. M. (1992). Is there a relationship between spatial cognition and environmental patterns? In A. U. Frank, I. Campari, & U. Formentini (Eds.), *Theories and methods of spatio-temporal reasoning in geographic space* (pp. 288–304). New York: Springer-Verlag.

Frye, C. A. (1995). Estrus-associated decrements in a water maze task are limited to acquisition. *Physiology and Behavior, 57,* 5–14.

Galantay, E. Y. (1975). *New towns: Antiquity to the present.* New York: George Braziller.

Galea, L. A., & Kimura, D. (1993). Sex differences in route-learning. *Personality and Individual Differences, 14,* 53–65.

Gallion, A. B., & Eisner, S. (1950). *The urban pattern: City planning and design.* New York: D. Van Nostrand.

Gans, H. J. (1969). *The Levittowners: Ways of life and politics in a new suburban community.* New York: Vintage.

Garland, H. C., Haynes, J. J., & Grubb, G. C. (1979). Transit map color coding and street detail effects on trip planning performance. *Environment and Behavior, 11,* 162–184.

Garling, T., Book, A., & Lindberg, E. (1984). Cognitive mapping of large-scale environments: The interrelationship of action plans, acquisition, and orientation. *Environment and Behavior, 16,* 3–34.

Garling, T., Book, A., & Lindberg, E. (1986). Spatial orientation and wayfinding in the designed environment. *Journal of Architectural Planning Research, 3,* 55–64.

Garling, T., Lindberg, E., & Mantyla, T. (1983). Orientation in buildings: Effects of familiarity, visual access, and orientation aids. *Journal of Applied Psychology, 68,* 177–186.

Garvin, A. (1996). *The American city: What works, what doesn't?* New York: McGraw-Hill.

Gaulin, S. J. C. (1995). Does evolutionary theory predict sex differences in the brain? In M. S. Gazzaniga (Ed.), *The cognitive neurosciences* (pp. 1211–1226). Cambridge, MA: MIT Press.

Gazzaniga, M. (1983). Right hemisphere language following brain bisection. *American Psychologist, 38,* 525–537.

Gazzaniga, M. S. (1989). Organization of the human brain. *Science, 245,* 947–952.

Gazzaniga, M. S., & Miller, G. A. (1989). The recognition of antonymy by a language-enriched right hemisphere. *Journal of Cognitive Neuroscience, 12,* 187–193.

Georgopoulos, A. P., Lurito, J. T., Petrides, M., Schwartz, A. B., & Massey, J. T. (1989, January 13). Mental rotation of the neuronal population vector. *Science, 243,* 234–236.

Geschwind, N. (1974). The anatomical basis of hemispheric differentiation. In S. J. Dimond & J. G. Beaumont (Eds.), *Hemisphere function in the human brain* (pp. 7–24). London: Elek Science.

Geschwind, N. L. (1980). Neurological knowledge and complex behaviors. *Cognitive Science, 4,* 185–194.

Geschwind, N., & Galaburda, A. M. (1985). Cerebral lateralization: Biological mechanisms, associations, and pathology: I. A hypothesis and a program for research. *Archives of Neurology, 42,* 428–459.

Geschwind, N., & Galaburda, A. M. (1987). *Cerebral lateralization: Biological mechanisms, associations, and pathology.* Cambridge, MA: MIT Press.

Ghaem, O., Mellet, E., Crivello, F., Tzourio, N., Mazoyer, B., Berthoz, A., & Denis, M. (1997). Mental navigation along memorized routes activates the hippocampus, precuneus, and insula. *Cognitive Neuroscience and Neuropsychology, 8,* 739–744.

Ghiselli-Crippa, T., Hirtle, S. C., & Munro, P. (1996). Connectionist models in spatial cognition. In J. Portugali (Ed.), *The construction of cognitive maps* (pp. 87–104). Boston: Kluwer Academic.

Gibson, B., & Werner, C. (1994). Airport waiting areas as behavior settings: The role of legibility cues in communicating the setting program. *Journal of Personality and Social Psychology, 66,* 1049–1060.

Gibson, J. J. (1950). *The perception of the visual world.* Boston: Houghton Mifflin.

Gibson, J. J. (1966). *The senses considered as perceptual systems.* Boston: Houghton Mifflin.

Gibson, J. J. (1979). *The ecological approach to visual perception.* Boston: Houghton Mifflin.

Gladue, B. A., Beatty, W. W., Larson, J., & Staton, R. D. (1990). Sexual orientation and spatial ability in men and women. *Psychobiology, 18,* 101–108.

Golbeck, S. L. (1983). Reconstructing a large-scale spatial arrangement: Effects of environmental organization and operativity. *Developmental Psychology, 19,* 644–653.

Gold, J. R. (1992). Image and environment: The decline of cognitive-behaviouralism in human geography and grounds for regeneration. *Geoforum, 23,* 239–247.

Goldberg, E., & Costa, L. D. (1981). Hemisphere differences in the acquisition and use of descriptive systems. *Brain and Language, 14,* 144–173.

Goldberg, E., Podell, K., Harner, R., Lovell, M., & Riggio, S. (1994). Cognitive bias, functional cortical geometry, and the frontal lobes: Laterality, sex and handedness. *Journal of Cognitive Neuroscience, 6,* 276–296.

Goldberger, P. (1999, March 8). The skyline: Far out. *The New Yorker,* pp. 62–67.

Goldman-Rakic, P. S. (1988). Topography of cognition: Parallel distributed networks in primate association cortex. *Annual Review of Neuroscience, 11,* 137–156.

Goldman-Rakic, P. S. (1992, September). Working memory and the mind. *Scientific American,* pp. 111–117.

Goldstein, D., Haldane, D., & Mitchell, C. (1990). Sex differences in visual-ability: The role of performance factors. *Memory and Cognition, 18,* 546–550.

Golledge, R. G. (1991a). Cognition of physical and built environments. In T. Garling & G. W. Evans (Eds.), *Environment, cognition, and action: An integrated approach* (pp. 35–62). New York: Oxford University Press.

Golledge, R. G. (1991b). Tactual strip maps as navigational aids. *Journal of Visual Impairment and Blindness, 85,* 296–301.

Golledge, R. G. (1992a). Place recognition and wayfinding: Making sense of space. *Geoforum, 23,* 199–214.

Golledge, R. G. (1992b). The case of first-order primitives. In A. U. Frank, I. Campari, & U. Formentini (Eds.), *Theories and methods of spatio-temporal reasoning in geographic space* (pp. 1–21). New York: Springer-Verlag.

Golledge, R., Parkes, D., & Dear, R. (1989). *NOMAD: An auditory-tactile information system for blind or vision-impaired travellers* (NSF-Australian Cooperative Science Program, Final Report). Santa Barbara Department of Geography, University of California, Santa Barbara.

Golledge, R. G., Smith, T. R., Pellegrino, J. W., Doherty, S., & Marshall, S. P. (1985). A conceptual model and empirical analysis of children's acquisition of spatial knowledge. *Journal of Environmental Psychology, 5*, 125–152.

Golledge, R. G., & Stimson, R. J. (1997). *Spatial behavior: A geographic perspective.* New York: Guilford Press.

Goodman, R. (1971). *After the planners.* New York: Simon and Schuster.

Gopal, S. Klatzky, R. L., & Smith, T. R. (1989). Navigator: A psychologically based model of environmental learning through navigation. *Journal of Environmental Psychology, 9*, 309–331.

Gopal, S., & Smith, T. R. (1990). Human way-finding in an urban environment: A performance analysis of a computational process model. *Environment and Planning A, 22*, 169–191.

Gordon, D. A., & Wood, H. C. (1970). How drivers locate unfamiliar addresses— an experiment in route finding. *Public Roads, 26*, 44–47.

Gorski, R. A. (1984). Critical role for the medial preoptic area in the sexual differentiation of the brain. In G. J. DeVries, J. P. C. DeBruin, H. B. M. Uylings, & M. A. Corner (Eds.), *Progress in Brain Research, Vol. 61* (pp. 129–146). New York: Elsevier.

Gouchie, C., & Kimura, D. (1991). The relationship between testosterone levels and cognitive ability patterns. *Psychoneuroendocrinology, 16*, 323–334.

Green, B. F., & Anderson, L. K. (1956). Color coding with a visual search task. *Journal of Experimental Psychology, 51*, 19–24.

Groth, P. (1981, Spring). Streetgrids as frameworks for urban variety. *Harvard Architectural Review, 2*, 68–75.

Gruen, V. (1964). *The heart of our cities. The urban crisis: Diagnosis and cure.* New York: Simon and Schuster.

Gruss, J. (1996, July 29). A moving celebration. *Tampa Tribune,* p. 8.

Gurlitt, C. (1975). Le Corbusier and the "pack-donkey's way" (1929). In P. Serenyi (Ed.), *Le Corbusier in perspective* (pp. 121–124). Englewood Cliffs, NJ: Prentice-Hall, Inc.

Gzesh, S. M., & Surber, C. F. (1985). Visual perspective-taking skills in children. *Child Development, 56*, 1204–1213.

Haavind, R. C. (1985). Etak: Navigating cars with video maps. *High Technology, 5*, 10–11.

Haber, L., Haber, R. N., Penningroth, S., Novak, K., & Radgowski, H. (1993). Comparison of nine methods of indicating the direction to objects: Data from blind adults. *Perception, 22*, 35–47.

Hakstian, A. R., & Cattell, R. B. (1975). *The Comprehensive Ability Battery.* Champaign, IL: Institute for Personality and Ability Testing.

Hall, R. H., & Sidio-Hall, M. A. (1994). The effect of color enhancement on knowledge map processing. *Journal of Experimental Education, 62*, 209–217.

Halpern, D. F. (1986). *Sex differences in cognitive abilities.* Hillsdale, NJ: Erlbaum.

Halpern, D. F. (1994). Stereotypes, science, censorship, and the study of sex differences. *Feminism and Psychology, 4*, 523–530.

Halpern, K. (1978). *Downtown USA: Urban design in nine American cities.* New York: Whitney Library of Design.

Halprin, L. (1972). *Cities* (Rev. ed.). Cambridge, MA: MIT Press.

Hardwick, D. A., McIntyre, C. W., & Pick, H. L., Jr. (1976). The content and manipulation of cognitive maps in children and adults. *Monographs of the Society for Research in Child Development, 41* (3), 1–55.

Hardwick, D. A., Woolridge, S. C., & Rinalducci, E. J. (1983). Selection of landmarks as a correlate of cognitive map organization. *psychological Reports, 53,* 807–813.

Hare-Mustin, R. T., & Marecek, J. (1988). The meaning of difference: Gender theory, postmodernism, and psychology. *American Psychologist, 43,* 455–464.

Hare-Mustin, R. T., & Marecek, J. (1994). Asking the right questions: Feminist psychology and sex differences. *Feminism and Psychology, 4,* 531–537.

Harris, L. J. (1978). Sex differences in spatial ability: Possible environmental, genetic, and neurological factors. In M. Kinsbourne (Ed.), *Asymmetrical functions of the brain* (pp. 405–522). Cambridge, UK: Cambridge University Press.

Harris, L. J. (1981). Sex-related variations in spatial skill. In L. S. Liben, A. H. Patterson, & N. Newcombe (Eds.), *Spatial representation and behavior across the life span* (pp. 83–125). New York: Academic Press.

Harshman, R. A., Hampson, E., & Berenbaum, S. A. (1983). Individual differences in cognitive abilities and brain organization, Part I: Sex and handedness differences in ability. *Canadian Journal of Psychology, 37,* 144–192.

Hart, R. A., & Moore, G. T. (1973). The development of spatial cognition: A review. In R. Downs & D. Stea (Eds.), *Image and environment* (pp. 246–288). Chicago: Aldine.

Hassler, M. (1993). Anomalous dominance, immune parameters, and spatial ability. *International Journal of Neuroscience, 68,* 145–156.

Hastie, R., Hammerle, O., Kerwin, J., Croner, C. M., & Hermann, D. J. (1996). Human performance reading statistical maps. *Journal of Experimental Psychology: Applied, 2,* 3–16.

Hayward, W. G., & Tarr, M. J. (1995). Spatial language and spatial representation. *Cognition, 55,* 39–84.

Hazen, N. L., Lockman, J. J., & Pick, H. L., Jr. (1978). The development of children's representations of large-scale environments. *Child Development, 44,* 623–636.

Hecaen, H., Tzortzis, C., & Rondot, P. (1980). Loss of topographic memory with learning deficits. *Cortex, 16,* 525–542.

Hellige, J. B., & Michimota, C. (1989). Categorization versus distance: Hemispheric differences for processing spatial information. *Memory and Cognition, 17,* 770–776.

Herman, J. F., & Bruce, P. R. (1983). Adults' mental rotation of spatial information: Effects of age, sex, and cerebral laterality. *Experimental Aging Research, 9,* 83–85.

Herman, J. F., Kail, R. V., & Siegel, A. W. (1979). Cognitive maps of a college campus: A new look at freshman orientation. *Bulletin of the Psychonomic Society, 13,* 183–186.

Herman, J. F., Kolker, R. G., & Shaw, M. L. (1982). Effects of motor activity on children's intentional and incidental memory for spatial locations. *Child Development, 53,* 239–244.

Herman, J. F., Norton, L. M., & Klein, C. A. (1986). Children's distance estimates in a large-scale environment: A search for the route angularity effect. *Environment and Behavior, 18,* 533–558.

Herman, J. F., & Siegel, A. W. (1978). The development of cognitive mapping of the large-scale environment. *Journal of Experimental Child Psychology, 26,* 389–406.

Hier, D. B., & Crowley, W. F. (1982, May 20). Spatial ability in androgen-deficient men. *New England Journal of Medicine, 306,* 1202–1205.

Hier, D. B., & Kaplan, J. (1980). Are sex differences in cerebral organization clinically significant? *Behavioral and Brain Sciences, 3,* 238–239.

Hilgard, E. R. (1951). The role of learning in perception. In R. R. Blacke & G. Ramsey (Eds.), *Perception: An approach to personality* (pp. 95–120). New York: Roland Press.

Hill, K., & Hurtado, A. M. (1989). Hunter-gatherers of the new world. *American Scientist, 77,* 436–443.

Hill, M. R. (1987). "Asking directions" and pedestrian wayfinding. *Man-Environment Systems, 17,* 113–120.

Hirtle, S. C., & Jonides, J. (1985). Evidence of hierarchies in cognitive maps. *Memory and Cognition, 13,* 208–217.

Holding, C. S. (1992). Clusters and reference points in cognitive representations of the environment. *Journal of Environmental Psychology, 12,* 45–55.

Holding, C. S., & Holding, D. H. (1989). Acquisition of route network knowledge by males and females. *Journal of General Psychology, 116,* 29–41.

Holmes, N. (1984). *Designer's guide to creating charts and diagrams.* New York: Watson-Guptill.

Holston, J. (1989). *The modernist city: An anthropological critique of Brasilia.* Chicago: University of Chicago Press.

Holtzman, J. D., & Kosslyn, S. M. (1990). Image generation in the cerebral hemispheres. In A. Caramazza (Ed.), *Cognitive neuropsychology and neurolinguistics: Advances in models of cognitive function and impairment* (pp. 169–186). Hillsdale, NJ: Erlbaum.

Holyoak, K. J., & Mah, W. A. (1982). Cognitive reference points in judgments of symbol magnitude. *Cognitive Psychology, 14,* 328–352.

Horan, P. F., & Rosser, R. A. (1984). A multivariable analysis of spatial abilities by sex. *Developmental Review, 4,* 387–411.

Howard, E. (1945). *Garden cities of to-morrow.* London: Faber and Faber. (Original work published 1898).

Hunt, M. E. (1985). Enhancing a building's imageability. *Journal of Architectural Planning Research, 2,* 151–168.

Huttenlocher, J., & Newcombe, N. (1984). The child's representation of information about location. In C. Sophian (Ed.), *Origins of cognitive skills* (pp. 81–111). Hillsdale, NJ: Erlbaum.

Hyde, J. S. (1981). How large are cognitive gender differences? *American Psychologist, 36,* 892–901.

Hyde, J. S. (1990). Meta-analysis and the psychology of gender differences. *Signs, 16,* 55–73.

Hyde, J. S. (1994). Should psychologists study gender differences? Yes, with some guidelines. *Feminism and Psychology, 4,* 507–512.

Hyde, J. S., Geiringer, E. R., & Yen, W. M. (1975, July). On the empirical relation between spatial ability and sex differences in other aspects of cognitive performance. *Multivariate Behavioral Research, 10,* 289–309.

Hyde, J. S., & Plant, E. A. (1995). Magnitude of psychological gender differences: Another side to the story. *American Psychologist, 50,* 159–161.

Imhof, E. (1975). Positioning names on maps. *American Cartographer, 2,* 128–144.

Jacobs, A. B. (1993). *Great streets.* Cambridge, MA: MIT Press.

Jacobs, J. (1961). *The death and life of great American cities.* New York: Random House.

Jacobs, R. A., & Kosslyn, S. M. (1994). Encoding shape and spatial relations: The role of receptive field size in coordinating complementary representations. *Cognitive Science, 18,* 361–386.

James, T. W., & Kimura, D. (1997). Sex differences in remembering the locations of objects in an array: Location-shifts versus location exchanges. *Evolution and Human Behavior, 18,* 155–163.

Janowsky, J. S. (1989). Sexual dimorphism in the human brain: Dispelling the myths. *Developmental Medicine and Child Neurology, 31,* 255–263.

Johnson, E. S., & Meade, A. C. (1987). Developmental patterns of spatial ability: An early sex difference. *Child Development, 58,* 725–740.

Johnston, A. L., & File, S. E. (1991). Sex differences in animal tests of anxiety. *Physiology and Behavior, 49,* 245–250.

Jones, B., & Anuza, T. (1982). Effects of sex, handedness, stimulus and visual field in "mental rotation." *Cortex, 18,* 501–514.

Juraska, J. M. (1984). Sex differences in developmental plasticity in the visual cortex and hippocampal dentate gyrus. In G. J. DeVries, J. P. C. DeBruin, H. B. M. Uylings, & M. A. Corner (Eds.), *Progress in Brain Research, Vol. 61* (pp. 205–214). New York: Elsevier.

Just, M. A., & Carpenter, P. A. (1985). Cognitive coordinate systems: Accounts of mental rotation and individual differences in spatial ability. *Psychological Review, 92,* 137–172.

Juurmaa, J. (1973). Transposition in mental spatial manipulation: A theoretical analysis. *American Foundation for the Blind Research Bulletin, 26,* 87–134.

Kahl, H. B., Herman, J. F., & Klein, C. A. (1984). Distance distortions in children's cognitive maps: An examination of the information storage model. *Journal of Experimental Child Psychology, 38,* 124–146.

Kahneman, D., & Tversky, A. (1983). On the psychology of prediction. *Psychological Review, 80,* 237–251.

Kahneman, D., & Tversky, A. (1984). Choices, values, and frames. *American Psychologist, 39,* 341–350.

Kail, R., Carter, P., & Pellegrino, J. (1979). The locus of sex differences in spatial ability. *Perception and Psychophysics, 26,* 182–186.

Kaiser, H. H. (1978). *The building of cities: Development and conflict.* Ithaca, NY: Cornell University Press.

Kalia, R. (1987). *Chandigarh: In search of an identity.* Carbondale: Southern Illinois University Press.

Kaplan, K. (1997, March 20). Experts: Theme park visitors no boon for tourism industry. *New London Day, 116,* (262), A.1, A.2.

Kaplan, R., Kaplan, S., & Deardorff, H. L. (1974). The perception and evaluation of a simulated environment. *Man-Environment Systems, 4,* 191–192.

Kaplan, S. (1973). Cognitive maps in perception and thought. In R. Downs & D. Stea (Eds.), *Image and environment* (pp. 63–78). Chicago: Aldine.

Katz, P. (1994). *The new urbanism: Toward an architecture of community.* New York: McGraw-Hill.

Kemmis, D. (1995). *The good city and the good life: Renewing the sense of community.* Boston: Houghton Mifflin.

Kennedy, J. (1983). Pictorial displays and the blind: Elements, patterns, and metaphors. In J. W. Wiedel (Ed.), *Proceedings of the First International Symposium on Maps and Graphics for the Visually Handicapped* (pp. 75–86). Washington, DC: Association of American Geographers.

Kennedy, J. M., Gabias, P., & Heller, M. A. (1992). Space, haptics and the blind. *Geoforum, 23,* 175–189.

Kerns, K. A., & Berenbaum, S. A. (1991). Sex differences in spatial ability in children. *Behavior Genetics, 21,* 383–396.

Kimura, D. (1983). Sex differences in cerebral organization for speech and praxic functions. *Canadian Journal of Psychology, 37,* 19–35.

Kimura, D. (1987). Are men's and women's brains really different? *Canadian Psychology, 28,* 133–147.

Kimura, D. (1992). Sex differences in the brain. *Scientific American, 267,* 118–125.

Kimura, D., & Durnford, M. (1974). Normal studies on the function of the right hemisphere in vision. In S. J. Dimond & J. G. Beaumont (Eds.), *Hemisphere function in the human brain* (pp. 25–47). London: Elek Science.

Kimura, D., & Hampson, E. (1993). Neural and hormonal mechanisms mediating sex differences in cognition. In P. A. Vernon (Ed.), *Biological approaches to the study of human intelligence* (pp. 375–397). Norwood, NJ: Ablex.

Kimura, D., & Harshman, R. A. (1984). Sex differences in brain organization for verbal and non-verbal functions. In G. J. DeVries, J. P. C. DeBruin, H. B. M. Uylings, & M. A. Corner (Eds.), *Progress in brain research, Vol. 61* (pp. 423–441). New York: Elsevier.

Kingsberg, S. A., LaBarba, R. C., & Bowers, C. A. (1987). Sex differences in lateralization for spatial abilities. *Bulletin of the Psychonomic Society, 25,* 247–250.

Kingstone, A., Enns, J. T., Mangun, G. R., & Gazzaniga, M. S. (1995). Guided visual search is a left-hemisphere process in split-brain patients. *Psychological Science, 6,* 118–121.

Kirasic, K. C. (1985). A road map to research for spatial cognition in the elderly adult. In R. Cohen (Ed.), *The development of spatial cognition* (pp. 185–198). Hillsdale, NJ: Erlbaum.

Kirasic, K. C., Allen, G. L., & Haggerty, D. (1992). Age-related differences in adults' macrospatial cognitive processes. *Experimental Aging Research, 18,* 33–39.

Kirasic, K. C., Allen, G. L., & Siegel, A. W. (1984). Expression of configurational knowledge of large-scale environments: Students' performance of cognitive tasks. *Environment and Behavior, 16,* 687–712.

Kirasic, K. C., & Mathes, E. A. (1990). Effects of different means for conveying environmental information in elderly adults' spatial cognition and behavior. *Environment and Behavior, 22,* 591–607.

Klatzky, R. L., Golledge, R. G., Loomis, J. M., Cicinelli, J. G., & Pellegrino, J. W. (1995). Performance of blind and sighted persons on spatial tasks. *Journal of Visual Impairment and Blindness, 89,* 70–82.

Koenig, O., Reiss, L. P., & Kosslyn, S. M. (1990). The development of spatial relation representations: Evidence from studies of cerebral lateralization. *Journal of Experimental Child Psychology, 50,* 119–130.

Koenigsberger, O. H. (1952). New towns in India. *Town Planning Review, 23,* 92–132.

Kohler, W. (1947). *Gestalt psychology: An introduction to new concepts in modern psychology.* New York: Liveright.

Kosslyn, S. M. (1985). Graphics and human information processing: A review of five books. *Journal of the American Statistical Association, 80,* 499–512.

Kosslyn, S. M. (1987). Seeing and imagining in the cerebral hemispheres: A computational approach. *Psychological Review, 94,* 148–175.

Kosslyn, S. M. (1989). Understanding charts and graphs. *Applied Cognitive Psychology, 3,* 185–226.

Kosslyn, S. M. (1991). A cognitive neuroscience of visual cognition: Further developments. In R. H. Logie & M. Denis (Eds.), *Mental images in human cognition* (pp. 351–381). New York: North-Holland.

Kosslyn, S. M. (1994a). *Elements of graph design.* New York: W. H. Freeman.

Kosslyn, S. M. (1994b). *Image and brain: The resolution of the imagery debate.* Cambridge, MA: MIT Press.

Kosslyn, S. M., Alpert, N. M., Thompson, W. L., Chabris, C. F., Rauch, S. L., & Anderson, A. K. (1994). Identifying objects seen from different viewpoints: A PET investigation. *Brain, 117,* 1055–1071.

Kosslyn, S. M., Alpert, N. M., Thompson, W. L., Maljkovic, V., Weise, S. B., Chabris, C. F., Hamilton, S. E., Rauch, S. L., & Buonanno, F. S. (1993). Visual mental imagery activates topographically organized visual cortex: PET investigations. *Journal of Cognitive Neuroscience, 5,* 263–287.

Kosslyn, S. M., Anderson, A. K., Hillger, L. A., & Hamilton, S. E. (1994). Hemispheric differences in sizes of receptive fields or attentional biases? *Neuropsychology, 8,* 139–147.

Kosslyn, S. M., Ball, T. M., & Reiser, B. J. (1978). Visual images preserve metric spatial information: Evidence from studies of image scanning. *Journal of Experimental Psychology: Human Perception and Performance, 4,* 47–60.

Kosslyn, S. M., Chabris, C. F., Marsolek, C. J., & Koenig, O. (1992). Categorical versus coordinate spatial relations: Computational analyses and computer simulation. *Journal of Experimental Psychology: Human Perception and Performance, 18,* 562–577.

Kosslyn, S. M., Flynn, R. A., Amsterdam, J. B., & Wang, G. (1990). Components of high-level vision: A cognitive neuroscience analysis and accounts of neurological syndromes. *Cognition, 34,* 203–277.

Kosslyn, S. M., Holtzman, J. D., Farah, M. J., & Gazzaniga, M. S. (1985). A computational analysis of mental image generation: Evidence from functional dissociations in split-brain patients. *Journal of Experimental Psychology: General, 114,* 311–341.

Kosslyn, S. M., Koenig, O., Barrett, A., Cave, C. B., Tang, J., & Gabrieli, J. D. E. (1989). Evidence for two types of spatial representations: Hemispheric specialization for categorical and coordinate relations. *Journal of Experimental Psychology: Human Perception and Performance, 15*, 723–735.

Kosslyn, S. M., Maljkovic, V., Hamilton, S. E., Horwitz, G., & Thompson, W. L. (1995). Two types of image generation: Evidence for left and right hemispheric processes. *Neuropsychologia, 33*, 1485–1510.

Kosslyn, S. M., & Ochsner, K. N. (1994). In search of occipital activation during visual mental imagery. *Trends in Neurosciences, 17*, 290–292.

Kosslyn, S. M., Pick, H. L., & Fariello, G. R. (1974). Cognitive maps in children and men. *Cognitive Development, 45*, 707–716.

Kosslyn, S. M., & Shin, L. M. (1994). Visual mental images in the brain: Current issues. In M. J. Farah & G. Ratcliff (Eds.), *The neuropsychology of high-level vision* (pp. 269–296). Hillsdale, NJ: Erlbaum.

Kosslyn, S. M., Sokolov, M. A., & Chen, J. C. (1989). The lateralization of BRIAN: A computational theory and model of visual hemispheric specialization. In D. Klahr & K. Kotovsky (Eds.), *Complex information processing: The impact of Herbert A. Simon* (pp. 3–29). Hillsdale, NJ: Erlbaum.

Kostof, S. (1987). *America by design*. New York: Oxford University Press.

Kouwenhoven, J. A. (1961). *The beer can by the highway: Essays on what's "American" about America*. Baltimore: Johns Hopkins University Press.

Kovach, R. C., Jr., Surrette, M. A., & Aamodt, M. G. (1988). Following informal street maps: Effects of map design. *Environment and Behavior, 20*, 683–699.

Kozlowski, L. T., & Bryant, K. J. (1977). Sense of direction, spatial orientation, and cognitive maps. *Journal of Experimental Psychology: Human Perception and Performance, 3*, 590–598.

Krasnoff, A. C., Walker, J. T., & Howard, M. (1989). Early sex-linked activities and interests related to spatial abilities. *Personality and Individual Differences, 10*, 81–85.

Krieger, A., & Lennertz, W. (Eds.). (1991). *Andres Duany and Elizabeth Plater-Zyberk: Towns and town-making principles*. New York: Rizzoli.

Kritchevsky, M. (1988). The elementary spatial functions of the brain. In J. Stiles-Davis, M. Kritchevsky, & U. Bellugi (Eds.), *Spatial cognition: Brain bases and development* (pp. 111–140). Hillsdale, NJ: Erlbaum.

Kulhavy, R. W., Caterino, L. C., & Melchiori, F. (1989). Spatially cued retrieval of sentences. *Journal of General Psychology, 116*, 297–304.

Kulhavy, R. W., Stock, W. A., Verdi, M. P., & Rittschof, K. A. (1993). Why maps improve memory for text: The influence of structural information on working memory operation. *European Journal of Cognitive Psychology, 5*, 375–392.

Kulhavy, R. W., Stock, W. A., Woodard, K. A., & Haygood, R. C. (1993). Comparing elaboration and dual coding theories: The case of maps and text. *American Journal of Psychology, 106*, 483–498.

Kuo, F. (1996). The visual design of maps: Facilitating spatial learning through simple format changes [Abstract]. In J. L. Nasar & B. B. Brown (Eds.), *Public and private places: Proceedings of the 27th Environmental Design Re-*

search Association (p. 233). Edmond, OK: Environmental Design Research Association.

Laeng, B. (1994). Lateralization of categorical and coordinate spatial functions: A study of unilateral stroke patients. *Journal of Cognitive Neuroscience, 6,* 189–203.

Laeng, B., Shah, J., & Kosslyn, S. (1999). Identifying objects in conventional and contorted poses: Contributions of hemisphere-specific mechanisms. *Cognition, 70,* 53–85.

LaFrank, K. (1997). Seaside, Florida: "The new town—the old ways." In C. L. Hudgins, & E. C. Cromley (Eds.), *Shaping communities: Perspectives in vernacular architecture, VI* (pp. 111–121). Knoxville, TN: University of Tennessee Press.

Lambert, L. M., & Lederman, S. J. (1989). An evaluation of the legibility and meaningfulness of potential map symbols. *Journal of Visual Impairment and Blindness, 83,* 397–401.

Landau, B., & Jackendoff, R. (1993). "What" and "where" in spatial language and spatial cognition. *Behavioral and Brain Sciences, 16,* 217–265.

Landau, B., Spelke, E., & Gleitman, H. (1984). Spatial knowledge in a young blind child. *Cognition, 16,* 225–260.

Lavoie, T., & Demick, J. (1995, March). *Young, middle-aged, and older adults' cognitive representations of the city of Boston.* Poster session presented at the Environmental Design Research Association Conference, Boston.

Law, D. J., Pellegrino, J. W., & Hunt, E. B. (1993). Comparing the tortoise and the hare: Gender differences and experience in dynamic spatial reasoning tasks. *American Psychological Society, 4,* 35–40.

Lawton, C. A. (1994). Gender differences in way-finding strategies: Relationship to spatial ability and spatial anxiety. *Sex Roles, 30,* 765–779.

Lawton, C. A. (1996). Strategies for indoor wayfinding: The role of orientation. *Journal of Environmental Psychology, 16,* 137–145.

Lawton, C. A., Charleston, S. I., & Zieles, A. S. (1996). Individual-and gender-related differences in indoor wayfinding. *Environment and Behavior, 28,* 204–219.

Le Corbusier (1971). *The city of to-morrow and its planning.* Cambridge, MA: MIT Press. (Original work published 1929)

Leiser, D., & Zilbershatz, A. (1989). The traveller: A computational model of spatial network learning. *Environment and Behavior, 21,* 435–463.

Levine, M. (1982). You-are-here maps: Psychological considerations. *Environment and Behavior, 14,* 221–237.

Levine, M., Marchon, I., & Hanley, G. (1984). The placement and misplacement of you-are-here maps. *Environment and Behavior, 16,* 139–157.

Levy, J. (1969). Possible bases for the evolution of lateral specialization of the human brain. *Nature, 224,* 614–615.

Levy, J. (1976). Cerebral lateralization and spatial ability. *Behavior Genetics, 6,* 171–188.

Levy, J., & Reid, M. (1978). Variations in cerebral organization as a function of handedness, hand posture in writing, and sex. *Journal of Experimental Psychology: General, 107,* 119–144.

Lewandowsky, S., & Spence, I. (1989). Discriminating strata in scatterplots. *Journal of the American Statistical Association, 84,* 682–688.

Liben, L. S. (1991). Environmental cognition through direct and representational experiences: A life-span perspective. In T. Garling & G. W. Evans (Eds.), *Environment, cognition, and action: An integrated approach* (pp. 245–276). New York: Oxford University Press.

Liben, L. S., & Downs, R. M. (1989). Understanding maps as symbols: The development of map concepts in children. In H. W. Reese (Ed.), *Advances in child development and behavior, Vol. 22* (pp. 145–201). New York: Academic Press.

Liben, L. S., & Golbeck, S. L. (1980). Sex differences in performance on Piagetian spatial tasks: Differences in competence or performance? *Child Development, 51,* 594–597.

Lieblich, I., & Arbib, M. A. (1982). Multiple representations of space underlying behavior. *Behavioral and Brain Sciences, 5,* 627–659.

Liebowitz, B., Lawton, M. P., & Waldman, A. (1979, February). Designing for confused elderly people: Lessons from the Weiss Institute. *AIA Journal, 68,* 59–61.

Linn, M. C., & Petersen, A. C. (1985). Emergence and characterization of sex differences in spatial ability: A meta-analysis. *Child Development, 56,* 1479–1498.

Linn, M. C., & Petersen, A. C. (1986). A meta-analysis of gender differences in spatial ability: Implications for mathematics and science achievement. In J. S. Hyde & M. C. Linn (Eds.), *The psychology of gender: Advances through meta-analysis* (pp. 67–101). Baltimore: Johns Hopkins University Press.

Llewelyn-Davies, L. (1972). Changing goals in design: The Milton Keynes example. In H. Evans (Eds.), *New towns: The British experience* (pp. 102–116). New York: Wiley.

Lohman, D. F. (1986). The effect of speed-accuracy tradeoff on sex differences in mental rotation. *Perception and Psychophysics, 39,* 427–436.

Loomis, J. M., Klatzky, R. L., Golledge, R. G., Cicinelli, J. G., Pellegrino, J. W., & Fry, P. A. (1993). Nonvisual navigation by blind and sighted: Assessment of path integration ability. *Journal of Experimental Psychology: General, 122,* 73–91.

Loomis, R. J., & Parsons, M. B. (1979). Orientation needs and the library setting. In D. Pollet & P. C. Haskell (Eds.), *Sign systems for libraries: Solving the wayfinding problem* (pp. 3–15). New York: Bowker.

Loring-Meier, S., & Halpern, D. F. (1999). Sex differences in visuospatial working memory: Components of cognitive processing. *Psychonomic Bulletin and Review, 6,* 464–471.

Lynch, K. (1960). *The image of the city.* Cambridge, MA: MIT Press.

Lynch, K. (1976). *Managing the sense of a region.* Cambridge, MA: MIT Press.

Lynch, K. (1981). *A theory of good city form.* Cambridge, MA: MIT Press.

Lynch, K. (1990a). The city as environment. In T. Banerjee & M. Southworth (Eds.), *City sense and city design: Writings and projects of Kevin Lynch* (pp. 87–95). Cambridge, MA: MIT Press. (Original work published 1965)

Lynch, K. (1990b). The form of cities. In T. Banerjee & M. Southworth (Eds.),

City sense and city design: Writings and projects of Kevin Lynch (pp. 35–46). Cambridge, MA: MIT Press. (Original work published 1954)

Lynch, K. (1990c). The pattern of the metropolis. In T. Banerjee & M. Southworth (Eds.), *City sense and city design: Writings and projects of Kevin Lynch* (pp. 47–64). Cambridge, MA: MIT Press. (Original work published 1961)

Lynch, K. (1990d). The visual shape of the shapeless metropolis. In T. Banerjee & M. Southworth (Eds.), *City sense and city design: Writings and projects of Kevin Lynch* (pp. 65–86). Cambridge, MA: MIT Press.

Lynch, K., & Hack, G. (1984). *Site planning* (3rd ed.). Cambridge, MA: MIT Press.

Lynch, K., & Rodwin, L. (1958). A theory of urban form. *Journal of the American Institute of Planners, 24*, 204–214.

Maccoby, E. E., & Jacklin, C. N. (1974). *The psychology of sex differences.* Stanford, CA: Stanford University Press.

MacEachern, A. M. (1980). Travel time as the basis of cognitive distance. *Professional Geographer, 32*, 30–36.

MacKay, D. B., Olshavsky, R. W., & Sentell, G. (1975). Cognitive maps and spatial behavior of consumers. *Geographical Analysis, 3*, 19–34.

Magliano, J. P., Cohen, R., Allen, G. L., & Rodrigue, J. R. (1995). The impact of a wayfinder's goal on learning a new environment: Different types of spatial knowledge as goals. *Journal of Environmental Psychology, 15*, 65–75.

Maguire, E. (1997). Hippocampal involvement in human topographical memory: Evidence from functional imaging. *Philosophical Transactions of the Royal Society of London, B, 352*, 1475–1480.

Maguire, E. A., Burgess, N., Donnett, J. G., Frackowiak, R. S. J., Frith, C. D., & O'Keefe, J. (1998). Knowing where and getting there: A human navigation network. *Science, 280*, 921–924.

Maguire, E. A., Frackowiak, R. S. J., & Frith, C. D. (1996). Learning to find your way: A role for the human hippocampal formation. *Proceedings of the Royal Society of London, B, 263*, 1745–1750.

Maguire, E. A., Frackowiak, R. S. J., & Frith, C. D. (1997). Recalling routes around London: Activation of the right hippocampus in taxi drivers. *Journal of Neuroscience, 17*, 7103–7110.

Mann, V. A., Sasanuma, S., Sakuma, N., & Masaki, S. (1990). Sex differences in cognitive abilities: A cross-cultural perspective. *Neuropsychologia, 28*, 1063–1077.

Marling, K. A. (1997). Imagineering the Disney theme parks. In K. A. Marling (Ed.), *Designing Disney's theme parks: The architecture of reassurance* (pp. 28–177). New York: Flammarion.

Marr, D. (1982). *Vision: A computational investigation into the human representation and processing of visual information.* New York: W. H. Freeman.

Marr, D., & Nishihara, H. K. (1978). Representation and recognition of the spatial organization of three-dimensional shapes. *Proceedings of the Royal Society of London, B, 200*, 269–294.

Masters, M. S., & Sanders, B. (1993). Is the gender difference in mental rotation disappearing? *Behavior Genetics, 23*, 337–341.

Matthews, M. H. (1987). Sex differences in spatial competence: The ability of young children to map "primed" unfamiliar environments. *Educational Psychology, 7,* 77–90.

Mayer, A. (1956, May). New way of life in Britain's new towns. *Town and Country Planning: The Quarterly Review of the Town and Country Planning Association, 24,* 238–242.

Mayer, A. (1967a). Greenbelt towns revisited: In search of new directions for new towns for America. *Journal of Housing, 24,* 12–26.

Mayer, A. (1967b). *The urgent future: People, housing, city, region.* New York: McGraw-Hill.

Mayer, A. (1971, November). Architecture with inner meaning: Notes toward a definition of urban design. *Forum,* pp. 60–63.

Mayes, J. T. (1982). Hemisphere function and spatial ability: An exploratory study of sex and cultural differences. *International Journal of Psychology, 17,* 65–80.

McClurg, P. A., & Chaille, C. (1987). Computer games: Environments for developing spatial cognition? *Journal of Educational Computing Research, 3,* 95–111.

McCormack, P. D. (1982). Coding of spatial information by young and elderly adults. *Journal of Gerontology, 37,* 80–86.

McDermott, P. D. (1969). Cartography in advertising. *Canadian Cartographer, 6,* 149–155.

McGee, M. G. (1979a). Human spatial abilities: Psychometric studies and environmental, genetic, hormonal, and neurological influences. *Psychological Bulletin, 86,* 889–918.

McGee, M. G. (1979b). *Human spatial abilities: Sources of sex differences.* New York: Praeger.

McGee, M. G. (1982). Spatial abilities: The influence of genetic factors. In M. Potegal (Ed.), *Spatial abilities: Development and physiological foundations* (pp. 199–222). New York: Academic Press.

McGee, S. H. (1996, April 3). Parents can help children, especially daughters, succeed at math. *New London Day,* p. C7.

McGuinness, D., & Sparks, J. (1983). Cognitive style and cognitive maps: Sex differences in representations of a familiar terrain. *Journal of Mental Imagery, 7,* 91–100.

McManus, I. C., & Bryden, M. P. (1991). Geschwind's theory of cerebral lateralization: Developing a formal, causal model. *Psychological Bulletin, 110,* 237–253.

McNamara, T. P. (1986). Mental representations of spatial relations. *Cognitive Psychology, 18,* 87–121.

McNamara, T. P. (1992). Spatial representation. *Geoforum, 23,* 139–150.

McNamara, T. P., Ratcliff, R., & McKoon, G. (1984). The mental representation of knowledge acquired from maps. *Journal of Experimental Psychology: Learning, Memory, and Cognition, 10,* 723–732.

Medyckyj-Scott, D., & Blades, M. (1992). Human spatial cognition: Its relevance to the design and use of spatial information systems. *Geoforum, 23,* 215–226.

Mehta, Z., & Newcombe, F. (1991). A role for the left hemisphere in spatial processing. *Cortex, 27,* 153–167.

Mehta, Z., Newcombe, F., & Damasio, H. (1987). A left hemisphere contribution to visuospatial processing. *Cortex, 23*, 447–461.

Merriman, W. E., Keating, D. P., & List, J. A. (1985). Mental rotation of facial profiles: Age-, sex-, and ability-related differences. *Developmental Psychology, 21*, 888–900.

Metcalfe, J., Funnell, M., & Gazzaniga, M. S. (1995). Right-hemisphere memory superiority: Studies of a split-brain patient. *Psychological Science, 6*, 157–164.

Milgram, S. (1976). Psychological maps of Paris. In H. M. Proshansky, W. H. Ittelson, & L. G. Rivlin (Eds.), *Environmental psychology: People and their physical settings* (pp. 104–124). New York: Holt, Rinehart, & Winston.

Miller, G. A. (1956). The magical number seven, plus or minus two: Some limits on our capacity for processing information. *Psychological Review, 63*, 81–97.

Miller, L. K., & Santoni, V. (1986). Sex differences in spatial abilities: Strategic and experimental correlates. *Acta Psychologica, 62*, 225–235.

Milner, B. (1965). Visually-guided maze learning in man: Effects of bilateral hippocampal, bilateral frontal, and unilateral cerebral lesions. *Neuropsychologia, 3*, 317–338.

Milroy, R., & Poulton, E. C. (1978). Labelling graphs for improved reading speed. *Ergonomics, 21*, 55–61.

Moar, I., & Bower, G. H. (1983). Inconsistency in spatial knowledge. *Memory and Cognition, 11*, 107–113.

Moeser, S. D. (1988). Cognitive mapping in a complex building. *Environment and Behavior, 20*, 21–49.

Mohney, D., & Easterling, K. (Eds.). (1991). *Seaside: Making a town in America.* Princeton, NJ: Princeton Architectural Press.

Moholy-Nagy, S. (1968). *Matrix of man: An illustrated history of the urban environment.* New York: Praeger.

Moltke, W. (1967). The visual development of Ciudad Guayana. In W. Eldridge (Ed.), *Taming megalopolis: Vol. 1. What is and what could be* (pp. 274–286). Garden City, NY: Anchor.

Money, J., Alexander, D., & Walker, H. T. (1965). *A standardized road-map test of direction sense.* Baltimore: Johns Hopkins University Press.

Monmonier, M. (1996). *How to lie with maps* (2nd ed.). Chicago: University of Chicago Press.

Monmonier, M., & Schnell, G. A. (1988). *Map appreciation.* Englewood Cliffs, NJ: Prentice-Hall.

Moore, G. T. (1976). Theory and research in the development of environmental knowing. In G. T. Moore & R. G. Golledge (Eds.), *Environmental knowing: Theories, research and methods* (pp. 138–164). Stroudsburg, PA: Dowden, Hutchinson & Ross.

Moraglia, G., Maloney, K. P., Fekete, E. M., & Al-Basi, K. (1989). Visual search along the colour dimension. *Canadian Journal of Psychology, 43*, 1–12.

Morrow, L., & Ratcliff, G. (1988). Neuropsychology of spatial cognition: Evidence from cerebral lesions. In J. Stiles-Davis, M. Kritchevsky, & U. Bellugi (Eds.), *Spatial cognition: Brain bases and development* (pp. 5–32). Hillsdale, NJ: Erlbaum.

Muehrcke, P. C. (1982). An integrated approach to map design and production. *American Cartographer, 9,* 109–122.

Muehrcke, P. C. (1986). *Map use: Reading, analysis, and interpretation* (2nd ed). Madison, WI: J.P. Publications.

Muller, R. U., Kubie, J. L., Bostock, E. M., Taube, J. S., & Quirk, G. J. (1991). Spatial firing correlates of neurons in the hippocampal formation of freely moving rats. In J. Paillard (Ed.), *Brain and space* (pp. 296–333). New York: Oxford University Press.

Mumford, L. (1961). *The city in history: Its origins, its transformations, and its prospects.* New York: Harcourt, Brace & World.

Nadel, L. (1990). Varieties of spatial cognition: Psychological considerations. In A. Diamond (Ed.), *The development and neural bases of higher cognitive functions* (pp. 613–636). New York: Annals of the New York Academy of Sciences.

Nadelson, C. C. (1989). Professional issues for women. *Psychiatric Clinics of North America, 12,* 25–33.

Neisser, U. (1976). *Cognition and reality: Principles and implications of cognitive psychology.* New York: W. H. Freeman.

Neisser, U. (1982a). *Memory observed: Remembering in natural contexts.* San Francisco: W. H. Freeman.

Neisser, U. (1982b). Snapshots or benchmarks. In U. Neisser (Ed.), *Memory observed: Remembering in natural contexts* (pp. 43–49). San Francisco: W. H. Freeman.

Neisser, U., Boodoo, G., Bouchard, T. J., Jr., Boykin, A. W., Brody, N., Ceci, S. J., Halpern, D. F., Loehlin, J. C., Perloff, R., Sternberg, R., & Urbina, S. (1996). Intelligence: Knowns and unknowns. *American Psychologist, 51,* 77–101.

Nelson, T. O., & Chaiklin, S. (1980). Immediate memory for spatial location. *Journal of Experimental Psychology: Human Learning and Memory, 6,* 529–545.

Newcombe, N. (1982). Sex-related differences in spatial ability: Problems and gaps in current approaches. In M. Potegal (Ed.), *Spatial abilities: Development and physiological foundations* (pp. 223–250). New York: Academic Press.

Newcombe, N. (1989). The development of spatial perspective taking. In H. W. Reese (Ed.), *Advances in child development and behavior* (pp. 203–247). New York: Academic Press.

Newcombe, N., Bandura, M. M., & Taylor, D. G. (1983). Differences in spatial ability and spatial activities. *Sex Roles, 9,* 377–386.

Newland, G. A. (1981). Differences between left and right-handers on a measure of creativity. *Perceptual and Motor Skills, 53,* 787–792.

Newman, O. (1973). *Defensible space: Crime prevention through urban design.* New York: Collier.

Nothdurft, H. C. (1991). Texture segmentation and pop-out from orientation contrast. *Vision Research, 31,* 1073–1078.

O'Brian, B. (1995, March 28). Signs and blunders: Airport travelers share graphic tales. *Wall Street Journal,* pp. A1, A5.

Ohta, R. J., & Kirasic, K. C. (1983). The investigation of environmental learning in the elderly. In G. D. Rowles & R. J. Ohta (Eds.), *Aging and milieu: Environmental perspectives on growing old* (pp. 83–95). New York: Academic Press.

O'Keefe, J. (1991). The hippocampal cognitive map and navigational strategies. In J. Paillard (Ed.), *Brain and space* (pp. 273–295). New York: Oxford University Press.

O'Keefe, J. (1993). Kant and the sea-horse: An essay in the neurophilosophy of space. In N. Eilan, R. McCarthy, & B. Brewer (Eds.), *Spatial representation: Problems in philosophy and psychology* (pp. 43–64). Cambridge, MA: Basil Blackwell.

O'Keefe, J., & Nadel, L. (1978). *The hippocampus as a cognitive map*. Oxford, UK: Clarendon Press.

Olson, J. M. (1987). Color and the computer in cartography. In H. J. Durrett (Ed.), *Color and the computer* (pp. 205–220). New York: Academic Press.

O'Neill, M. J. (1986). Effects of computer simulated environmental variables on wayfinding accuracy. In J. Wineman, R. Barnes, & C. Zimring (Eds.), *Proceedings of the 17th Annual Conference of the Environmental Design Research Association* (pp. 55–63). Atlanta, GA: Environmental Design Research Association.

O'Neill, M. J. (1991a). A biologically based model of spatial cognition and wayfinding. *Journal of Environmental Psychology, 11*, 299–320.

O'Neill, M. J. (1991b). Effects of signage and floor plan configuration on wayfinding accuracy. *Environment and Behavior, 23*, 553–574.

O'Neill, M. J. (1991c). Evaluation of a conceptual model of architectural legibility. *Environment and Behavior, 23*, 259–284.

O'Neill, M. J. (1992). Effects of familiarity and plan complexity on wayfinding in simulated buildings. *Journal of Environmental Psychology, 12*, 319–327.

Orleans, P. (1973). Differential cognition of urban residents: Effects of social scale on mapping. In R. M. Downs & D. Stea (Eds.), *Image and environment* (pp. 115–130). Chicago: Aldine.

Ornstein, R., Johnstone, J., Herron, J., & Swencionis, C. (1980). Differential right hemisphere engagement in visuospatial tasks. *Neuropsychologia, 18*, 49–64.

Ozer, D. J. (1987). Personality, intelligence, and spatial visualization: Correlates of mental rotations test performance. *Journal of Personality and Social Psychology, 53*, 129–134.

Paivio, A. (1971). *Imagery and verbal processes*. New York: Holt, Rinehart, and Winston.

Paivio, A. (1986). *Mental representations: A dual coding approach*. New York: Oxford University Press.

Passig, D., & Levin, H. (1999). Gender interest differences with multimedia learning. *Computers in Human Behavior, 15*, 173–183.

Passini, R. (1984). Spatial representations, a wayfinding perspective. *Journal of Environmental Psychology, 4*, 153–164.

Passini, R., Dupre, A., & Langlois, C. (1986). Spatial mobility of the visually handicapped active person: A descriptive study. *Journal of Visual Impairment and Blindness, 80*, 904–907.

Passini, R., Proulx, G., & Rainville, C. (1990). The spatio-cognitive abilities of the visually impaired population. *Environment and Behavior, 22*, 91–118.

Pearson, J. L., & Ferguson, L. R. (1989). Gender differences in patterns of spatial ability, environmental cognition, and math and English achievement in late adolescence. *Adolescence, 24*, 421–431.

Peponis, J., Zimring, C., & Choi, Y. K. (1990). Finding the building in wayfinding. *Environment and Behavior, 22,* 555–590.

Perin, C. (1970). *With man in mind: An interdisciplinary prospectus for environmental design.* Cambridge, MA: MIT Press.

Peruch, P., Girando, M. D., & Garling, T. (1989). Distance cognition by taxi drivers and the general public. *Journal of Environmental Psychology, 9,* 233–239.

Peruch, P., & Savoyant, A. (1991). Conflicting spatial frames of reference in locating a task. In R. H. Logie & M. Denis (Eds.), *Mental images in human cognition* (pp. 49–55). New York: North-Holland.

Petersen, A. C. (1976). Physical androgyny and cognitive functioning in adolescence. *Developmental Psychology, 12,* 524–533.

Petersen, A. C., & Crockett, L. (1985, August). Factors influencing sex differences in spatial ability during adolescence. In S. L. Willis (Chair), *Sex differences in spatial ability across the lifespan.* Symposium conducted at the 93rd annual convention of the American Psychological Association, Los Angeles, CA.

Peterson, J. M., & Lansky, L. M. (1977). Left-handedness among architects: Partial replication and some new data. *Perceptual and Motor Skills, 45,* 1216–1218.

Pezaris, E., & Casey, M. B. (1991). Girls who use "masculine" problem-solving strategies on a spatial task: Proposed genetic and environmental factors. *Brain and Cognition, 17,* 1–22.

Phelps, E. A., & Gazzaniga, M. S. (1992). Hemispheric differences in mnemonic processing: The effects of left hemisphere interpretation. *Neuropsychologia, 30,* 293–297.

Phillips, R. J. (1979). Making maps easy to read: A summary of research. In P. A. Kolers, M. E. Wrolstad, & H. Bouma (Eds.), *Processing of visible language, Vol. 1* (pp. 165–174). New York: Plenum Press.

Phillips, R. J., Coe, B., Kono, E., Knapp, J., Barrett, S., Wiseman, G., & Eveleigh, P. (1990). An experimental approach to the design of cartographic symbols. *Applied Cognitive Psychology, 4,* 485–497.

Phillips, R. J., Noyes, E., & Audley, R. J. (1978). Searching for names on maps. *Cartographic Journal, 15,* 72–77.

Piaget, J., & Inhelder, B. (1956). *The child's conception of space.* New York: W. W. Norton. (Original work published 1948).

Plaut, D. C., & Farah, M. J. (1990). Visual object representation: Interpreting neurophysiological data within a computational framework. *Journal of Cognitive Neuroscience, 2,* 320–393.

Poizner, H., Klima, E. S., & Bellugi, U. (1987). *What the hands reveal about the brain.* Cambridge, MA: MIT Press.

Pollet, D., & Haskell, P. C. (1979). *Sign systems for libraries: Solving the wayfinding problem.* New York: Bowker.

Portugali, J. (1996). Inter-representation networks and cognitive maps. In J. Portugali (Ed.), *The construction of cognitive maps* (pp. 11–43). Boston: Kluwer Academic.

Portugali, J., & Haken, H. (1992). Synergetics and cognitive maps. *Geoforum, 23,* 111–130.

Posner, M. I., Peterson, S. E., Fox, P. T., & Raichle, M. E. (1988). Localization of cognitive operations in the human brain. *Science, 240,* 1627–1631.

Poulton, E. C. (1972). Size, style, and vertical spacing in the legibility of small typefaces. *Journal of Applied Psychology, 56,* 156–161.

Poulton, E. C. (1985). Geometric illusions in reading graphs. *Perception and Psychophysics, 37,* 543–548.

Prak, N. L. (1968). *The language of architecture: A contribution to architectural theory.* The Hague, Netherlands: Montouido.

Premack, D., & Premack, A. J. (1983). *The mind of an ape.* New York: W. W. Norton.

Presson, C. C. (1982). The development of map-reading skills. *Child Development, 53,* 196–199.

Presson, C. C., DeLange, N., & Hazelrigg, M. D. (1989). Orientation specificity in spatial memory: What makes a path different from a map of the path? *Journal of Experimental Psychology: Learning, Memory, and Cognition, 15,* 887–897.

Presson, C. C., & Ihrig, L. H. (1982). Using mother as a spatial landmark: Evidence against egocentric coding in infancy. *Developmental Psychology, 18,* 699–703.

Purcell, A. T. (1987). The relationship between buildings and behaviour. *Building and Environment, 22,* 215–232.

Pylyshyn, Z. (1973). What the mind's eye tells the mind's brain: A critique of mental imagery. *Psychological Bulletin, 80,* 1–24.

Rand, G. (1969, September). Pre-Copernican views of the city. *Forum,* pp. 77–81.

Rapoport, A. (1990). *History and precedent in environmental design.* New York: Plenum Press.

Ratcliff, G. (1979). Spatial Thought, Mental Rotation and the Right Cerebral Hemisphere. *Neuropsychologia, 17,* 49–54.

Ratcliff, G. (1991). Brain and space: Some deductions from the clinical evidence. In J. Paillard (Ed.), *Brain and space* (pp. 237–250). New York: Oxford University Press.

Ratcliff, G., & Newcombe, F. (1973). Spatial orientation in man: Effects of left, right, and bilateral posterior cerebral lesions. *Journal of Neurology, Neurosurgery, and Psychiatry, 36,* 448–454.

Raven, J. C. (1960). *Guide to the Standard Progressive Matrices.* London: H. K. Lewis.

Reinisch, J. (1981). Prenatal exposure to synthetic progestins increases potential for aggression in humans. *Science, 211,* 1171–1173.

Resnick, S. M. (1993). Sex differences in mental rotations: An effect of time limits? *Brain and Cognition, 21,* 71–79.

Resnick, S. M., Berenbaum, S. A., Gottesman, I. I., & Bouchard, T. J., Jr. (1986). Early hormonal influences on cognitive functioning in congenital adrenal hyperplasia. *Developmental Psychology, 22,* 191–198.

Richardson, J. T. E. (1991). Gender differences in imagery, cognition, and memory. In R. H. Logie & M. Denis (Eds.), *Mental images in human cognition* (pp. 271–303). New York: North-Holland Elsevier.

Richardson, J. T. E. (1994). Gender differences in mental rotation. *Perceptual and Motor Skills, 78,* 435–448.

Rieser, J. (1979). Spatial orientation of six-month-old infants. *Child Development, 50,* 1078–1087.

Rieser, J. J., Guth, D. A., & Hill, E. W. (1982). Mental processes mediating independent travel: Implications for orientation and mobility. *Journal of Visual Impairment and Blindness, 76*, 213–218.

Rieser, J. J., Guth, D. A., & Hill, E. W. (1986). Sensitivity to perspective structure while walking without vision. *Perception, 15*, 173–188.

Rieser, J. J., Hill, E. W., Talor, C. R., Bradfield, A., & Rosen, S. (1992). Visual experience, visual field size, and the development of nonvisual sensitivity to the spatial structure of outdoor neighborhoods explored by walking. *Journal of Experimental Psychology: General, 121*, 210–221.

Rifkind, C. (1977). *Main Street: The face of urban America.* New York: Harper Colophon.

Robinson, A. H. (1952). *The look of maps: An examination of cartographic design.* Madison: University of Wisconsin Press.

Robinson, A. H. (1982). A program of research to aid cartographic design. *American Cartographer, 9*, 25–29.

Robinson, A. H., Morrison, J. L., Muehrcke, P. C., Kimerling, A. J., & Guptell, S. C. (1995). *Elements of cartography.* New York: Wiley.

Robinson, A. H., Sale, R. D., Morrison, J. L., & Muehrcke, P. C. (1984). *Elements of cartography.* (5th ed.) New York: Wiley.

Roland, P. E., & Friberg, L. (1985). Localization of cortical areas activated by thinking. *Journal of Neurophysiology, 53*, 1219–1243.

Roland, P. E., & Gulyas, B. (1994). Visual representations of scenes and objects: Retinotopical or non-retinotopical. *Trends in Neurosciences, 17*, 294–297.

Roof, R. L. (1993). Neonatal exogenous testosterone modifies sex difference in radial arm and Morris water maze performance in prepubescent and adult rats. *Behavioral Brain Research, 53*, 1–10.

Rossano, M. J., & Warren, D. H. (1989). Misaligned maps lead to predictable errors. *Perception, 18*, 215–229.

Rosser, R. (1994). The developmental course of spatial cognition: Evidence for domain multidimensionality. *Child Study Journal, 24*, 255–280.

Rouw, R., Kosslyn, S. M., & Hamel, R. (1998). Aspects of mental images: Is it possible to get the picture? *Cognition, 66*, 103–107.

Rueckl, J. G., Cave, K. R., & Kosslyn, S. M. (1989). Why are "what" and "where" processed by separate cortical visual systems? A computational investigation. *Journal of Cognitive Neuroscience, 1*, 171–186.

Rybash, J. M., & Hoyer, W. J. (1992). Hemispheric specialization for categorical and coordinate spatial representations: A reappraisal. *Memory and Cognition, 20*, 271–276.

Rybczynski, W. (1996, July 22). Tomorrowland: Living in a community planned by Disney has to be a nightmare, doesn't it? *The New Yorker*, pp. 36–39.

Sadalla, E. K., Burroughs, W. J., & Staplin, L. J. (1980). Reference points in spatial cognition. *Journal of Experimental Psychology: Human Learning and Memory, 6*, 516–528.

Sadalla, E. K., & Montello, D. R. (1989). Remembering changes in direction. *Environment and Behavior, 21*, 346–363.

Safdie, M. (1982). *Form and purpose.* Boston: Houghton Mifflin.

Saisa, J., & Garling, R. (1987). Sequential spatial choices in the large-scale environment. *Environment and Behavior, 14*, 614–635.

Salthouse, T. A. (1991). *Theoretical perspectives on cognitive aging.* Hillsdale, NJ: Erlbaum.

Sanders, B., & Soares, M. P. (1986). Sexual maturation and spatial ability in college students. *Developmental Psychology, 22,* 199–203.

Sanders, B., Soares, M. P., & D'Aquila, J. M. (1982). The sex difference on one test of spatial visualization: A nontrivial difference. *Child Development, 53,* 1106–1110.

Sanders, G., & Ross-Field, L. (1986). Sexual orientation and visuo-spatial ability. *Brain and Cognition, 5,* 280–290.

Sarin, M. (1977). Chandigarh as a place to live in. In R. Walden (Ed.), *The open hand: Essays on Le Corbusier* (pp. 374–411). Cambridge, MA: MIT Press.

Schaie, K. W., & Willis, S. L. (1986). Can decline in adult intellectual functioning be reversed? *Developmental Psychology, 22,* 223–232.

Schiano, D. J., & Tversky, B. (1992). Structure and strategy in encoding simplified graphs. *Memory and Cognition, 20,* 12–20.

Schlichtmann, H. (1991). Plan information and its retrieval in map interpretation: The view from semiotics. In D. M. Mark & A. U. Frank (Eds.), *Cognitive and linguistic aspects of geographic space* (pp. 263–284). Cambridge, MA: MIT Press.

Schluntz, R. L., Erickson, D., Blackwell, J., Shneider, J., & Peterson, S. (1973). *Design for downtown.* Lincoln: Urban Research and Development Center, University of Nebraska.

Schoenstein, R. (1995, June 11). East Is: (a) West (b) North (c) I Don't Know. *New York Times,* p. 39.

Scholnick, E. K., Fein, G. G., & Campbell, P. F. (1990). Changing predictors of map use in wayfinding. *Developmental Psychology, 26,* 188–193.

Schouela, D. A., Steinberg, L. M., Leveton, L. B., & Wapner, S. (1980). Development of the cognitive organization of an environment. *Canadian Journal of Behavioural Science, 12,* 1–16.

Schuyler, D. (1986). *The new urban landscape: The redefinition of city form in nineteenth-century America.* Baltimore: Johns Hopkins University Press.

Schwartz, M. L., & Goldman-Rukic, P. S. (1982, September). Single cortical neurons have axon collaterals to ipsilateral and contralateral cortex in fetal and adult primates. *Nature, 299,* 154–155.

Schwartz, N. H., & Kulhavy, R. W. (1981). Map features and the recall of discourse. *Contemporary Educational Psychology, 6,* 151–158.

Scott Brown, D. (1989). Room at the top? Sexism and the star system in architecture. In E. P. Berkeley (Ed.), *Architecture: A place for women* (pp. 237–246). Washington, DC: Smithsonian Institution Press.

Scully, V. (1996). *The architecture of community.* Ann Arbor: College of Architecture and Urban Planning, University of Michigan.

Self, C. M., & Golledge, R. G. (1994). Sex-related differences in spatial ability: What every geography educator should know. *Journal of Geography, 43,* 234–243.

Selfridge, K. M. (1979). Planning library signage systems. In D. Pollet & P. C. Haskell (Eds.), *Sign systems for libraries: Solving the wayfinding problem* (pp. 49–67). New York: Bowker.

Selkoe, D. J. (1992, September). Aging brain, aging mind. *Scientific American*, pp. 135–142.

Semmes, J. (1968). Hemispheric specialization: A possible clue to mechanism. *Neuropsychologia, 6*, 11–26.

Serbin, L. A., & Connor, J. M. (1979). Sex-typing of children's play preferences and patterns of cognitive performance. *Journal of Genetic Psychology, 134*, 315–316.

Serenyi, P. (Ed.). (1975). *Le Corbusier in perspective*. Englewood Cliffs, NJ: Prentice-Hall.

Sergent, J., & Corballis, M. C. (1989). Categorization of disoriented faces in the cerebral hemispheres of normal and commissurotomized subjects. *Journal of Experimental Psychology: Human Perception and Performance, 15*, 701–710.

Sharps, M. J., Welton, A. L., & Price, J. L. (1993). Gender and task in the determination of spatial cognitive performance. *Psychology of Women Quarterly, 17*, 71–83.

Shepard, R. N. (1988). The role of transformations in spatial cognition. In J. Stiles-Davis, M. Kritchevsky, & U. Bellugi (Eds.), *Spatial cognition: Brain bases and development* (pp. 81–110). Hillsdale, NJ: Erlbaum.

Shepard, R. N., & Cooper, L. A. (1982). *Mental images and their transformations*. Cambridge, MA: MIT Press.

Shepard, R. N., & Metzler, J. (1971). Mental rotation of three-dimensional objects. *Science, 171*, 701–703.

Sherman, J. (1967). Problems of sex differences in space perception and aspects of intellectual functioning. *Psychological Review, 74*, 290–299.

Sherman, J. A. (1978). *Sex-related cognitive differences: An essay on theory and evidence*. Springfield, IL: Charles C. Thomas.

Sherman, J. A., & Denmark, F. L. (1978). *The psychology of women: Future directions in research*. New York: Psychological Dimensions.

Sherry, D. F., Forbes, M. R. L., Khurgel, M., & Ivy, G. O. (1993). Females have a larger hippocampus than males in the brood-parasitic brown-headed cowbird. *Proceedings of the National Academy of Sciences of the United States of America, 90*, 7839–7843.

Sherry, D. F., Jacobs, L. F., & Gaulin, S. J. (1992). Spatial memory and adaptive specialization of the hippocampus. *Trends in Neuroscience, 15*, 298–303.

Sherry, D., & Healy, S. (1998). Neural mechanisms of spatial representation. In S. Healy (Ed.), *Spatial representation in animals* (pp. 133–157). New York: Oxford University Press.

Sholl, M. J. (1992). Landmarks, places, environments: Multiple mind-brain systems for spatial orientation. *Geoforum, 23*, 151–164.

Shontz, W. D., Trumm, G. A., & Williams, L. G. (1971). Color coding for information location. *Human Factors, 13*, 237–246.

Shortridge, B. G. (1979). Map reader discrimination of lettering size. *American Cartographer, 6*, 13–20.

Shuttleworth, S. (1980). The use of photographs as an environment presentation medium in landscape studies. *Journal of Environmental Management, 11*, 61–76.

Siegel, A. W., Allen, G. L., & Kirasic, K. C. (1979). Children's ability to make distance comparisons: The advantage of thinking ahead. *Developmental Psychology, 15*, 656–657.

Siegel, A. W., & Schadler, M. (1977). The development of young children's spatial representations of their classroom. *Child Development, 48*, 388–394.

Siegel, A. W., & White, S. H. (1975). The development of spatial representations of large-scale environments. In H. W. Reese (Ed.), *Advances in child development and behavior, Vol. 10* (pp. 9–55). New York: Academic Press.

Siegler, R. S. (1996). *Emerging minds: The process of change in children's thinking.* New York: Oxford University Press.

Silverman, I., & Eals, M. (1992). Sex differences in spatial abilities: Evolutionary theory and data. In J. H. Barkow, L. Cosmides, & J. Tooby (Eds.), *The adapted mind* (pp. 533–549). New York: Oxford.

Simcox, W. A. (1984). A method for pragmatic communication in graphic displays. *Human Factors, 26*, 483–487.

Simkin, D., & Hastie, R. (1987). An information-processing analysis of graph perception. *Journal of American Statistical Association, 82*, 454–465.

Simon, H. A., & Gilmartin, K. (1973). A simulation of memory for chess positions. *Cognitive Psychology, 5*, 29–46.

Sloan, G. (1997, January 16). Steering drivers to restaurants, hotels by satellite. *USA Today*, p. D1.

Smallman, H. S., & Boynton, R. M. (1990). Segregation of basic colors in an information display. *Journal of the Optical Society of America, Part A, 7*, 1985–1994.

Smith, E. A. T. (1994). Urban revisions: Current projects for the public realm. In R. Ferguson (Ed.), *Urban revisions: Current projects for the public realm* (pp. 2–15). Cambridge, MA: MIT Press.

Smith, E. E., Jonides, J., Koeppe, R. A., Awh, E., Schumacher, E. H., & Minoshima, S. (1995). Spatial versus object working memory: PET investigations. *Journal of Cognitive Neuroscience, 7*, 337–356.

Smith, S. L. (1962). Color coding and visual search. *Journal of Experimental Psychology, 64*, 434–440.

Smith, S. L. (1978). The limited readability of Lansdell numerals. *Human Factors, 20*, 57–64.

Smith, S. L. (1979). Letter size and legibility. *Human Factors, 21*, 661–670.

Smith, T. R., Pellegrino, J. W., & Golledge, R. G. (1982). Computational process modeling of spatial cognition and behavior. *Geographical Analysis, 14*, 305–325.

Snow, J. H., & Strope, E. E. (1990). Development of mental rotation matching abilities with children. *Developmental Neuropsychology, 6*, 207–214.

Somerville, S. C., & Bryant, P. E. (1985). Young children's use of spatial coordinates. *Child Development, 56*, 604–613.

Southworth, M., & Southworth, S. (1982). *Maps: A visual survey and design guide.* Boston: Little, Brown.

Spence, I. (1990). Visual psychophysics of simple graphical elements. *Journal of Experimental Psychology: Human Perception and Performance, 16*, 683–692.

Spence, I., & Lewandowsky, S. (1991). Displaying proportions and percentages. *Applied Cognitive Psychology, 5,* 61–77.

Spencer, C., Blades, M., & Morsely, K. (1989). *The child in the physical environment: The development of spatial knowledge and cognition.* New York: Wiley.

Spencer, C., & Darvizeh, A. (1981). The case for developing a cognitive environmental psychology that does not underestimate the abilities of young children. *Journal of Environmental Psychology, 1,* 21–31.

Spencer, C., Morsley, K., Ungar, S., Pike, E., & Blades, M. (1992). Developing the blind child's cognition of the environment: The role of direct and map-given experience. *Geoforum, 23,* 191–197.

Spreen, O., Tupper, D., Risser, A., Tuokko, H., & Edgell, D. (1984). *Human developmental neuropsychology.* New York: Oxford University Press.

Spreiregen, P. D. (Ed.). (1967). *The modern metropolis: Its origins, growth, characteristics, and planning.* Cambridge, MA: MIT Press.

Squire, L. R. (1987). *Memory and brain.* New York: Oxford University Press.

Squire, L. R. (1992). Memory and the hippocampus: A synthesis from findings with rats, monkeys, and humans. *Psychological Review, 99,* 195–231.

Squire, L. R. (1993). The hippocampus and spatial memory. *Trends in Neuroscience, 16,* 56–57.

Squire, L. R., & Knowlton, B. J. (1995). Memory, hippocampus, and brain systems. In M. S. Gazzaniga (Ed.), *The cognitive neurosciences* (pp. 825–837). Cambridge, MA: MIT Press.

Staubli, W. (1966). *Brasilia.* London: Leonard Hill.

Stevens, A., & Coupe, P. (1978). Distortions in judged spatial relations. *Cognitive Psychology, 10,* 422–437.

Stewart, C. A., & Clayson, D. (1980). A note on change in creativity by handedness over a maturational time period. *Journal of Psychology, 104,* 39–42.

Streeter, L. A., & Vitello, D. (1986). A profile of drivers' map-reading abilities. *Human Factors, 28,* 223–239.

Strelow, E. R. (1985). What is needed for a theory of mobility: Direct perception and cognitive maps—lessons from the blind. *Psychological Review, 92,* 226–248.

Sullivan, J. (1996, July 7). Signs of change: Corporate names on public spaces. *New York Times, Metro Section,* p. 19.

Suzuki, W. A., Zola-Morgan, S., Squire, L. R., & Amaral, D. G. (1993). Lesions of the perirhinal and parahippocampal cortices in the monkey produce long-lasting memory impairment in the visual and tactual modalities. *Journal of Neuroscience, 13,* 2430–2451.

Tanaka, J. S., Panter, A. T., & Winborne, W. C. (1988). Dimensions of the need for cognition: Subscales and gender differences. *Multivariate Behavioral Research, 23,* 35–50.

Tapley, S. M., & Bryden, M. P. (1977). An investigation of sex differences in spatial ability: Mental rotation of three-dimensional objects. *Canadian Journal of Psychology, 31,* 122–130.

Taylor, H. A., & Tversky, B. (1992a). Descriptions and depictions of environments. *Memory and Cognition, 20,* 483–496.

Taylor, H. A., & Tversky, B. (1992b). Spatial mental models derived from survey and route descriptions. *Journal of Memory and Language, 31*, 261–292.

Teng, E. L., & Lee, A. L. (1982). Right–left discrimination: No sex difference among normals on the hand test and the route test. *Perceptual and Motor Skills, 55*, 299–302.

Thinus-Blanc, C., Save, E., Buhot, M. C., & Poucet, B. (1991). The hippocampus, exploratory activity, and spatial memory. In J. Paillard (Ed.), *Brain and space* (pp. 334–352). New York: Oxford University Press.

Thomas, H., & Kail, R. (1991). Sex differences in speed of mental rotation and the X-linked genetic hypothesis. *Intelligence, 15*, 17–32.

Thomas, H., & Lohaus, A. (1993). Modeling growth and individual differences in spatial tasks. *Monographs of the Society for Research in Child Development, 58*, (9) v-169.

Thorndike, E. L. (1940). *144 smaller cities.* New York: Harcourt, Brace.

Thorndyke, P. W., & Hayes-Roth, B. (1982). Differences in spatial knowledge acquired from maps and navigation. *Cognitive Psychology, 14*, 560–589.

Thurstone, L. (1938). Primary mental abilities. *Psychometric Monograph*, No. 1. Chicago: University of Chicago Press.

Thurstone, L. L. (1950). *Some primary abilities in visual thinking.* Chicago: [Report No. 59] University of Chicago Psychometric Laboratory.

Tlauka, M., & Wilson, P. N. (1996). Orientation-free representations from navigation through a computer-simulated environment. *Environment and Behavior, 28*, 647–664.

Tolman, E. C. (1948). Cognitive maps in rats and men. *Psychological Review, 55*, 189–208.

Tomasky, M. (1999, November 8). The wrong stuff. *New York Magazine*, p. 26.

Tracy, D. M. (1987). Toys, spatial ability, and science and mathematics achievement: Are they related? *Sex Roles, 17*, 115–138.

Tracy, D. M. (1990). Toy-playing behavior, sex-role orientation, spatial ability, and science achievement. *Journal of Research in Science Teaching, 27*, 637–649.

Travis, D. (1991). *Effective color displays: Theory and practice.* New York: Academic Press.

Trillin, C. (1977, May 16). U.S. Journal: New England. Thoughts brought on by prolonged exposure to exposed brick. *The New Yorker*, pp. 101–102, 104–107.

Trumbo, B. E. (1981). A theory for coloring bivariate statistical maps. *American Statistician, 35*, 220–226.

Tuan, Y. (1974). *Topophilia: A study of environmental perception, attitudes, and values.* Ithaca, NY: Cornell University Press.

Tuddenham, R. D. (1970). A 'Piagetian' test of cognitive development. In W. B. Dockrell (Ed.), *On intelligence* (pp. 49–70). London: Methuen.

Tufte, E. R. (1983). *The visual display of quantitative information.* Cheshire, CT: Graphics Press.

Tufte, E. R. (1990). *Envisioning information.* Cheshire, CT: Graphics Press.

Tullis, T. S. (1981). An evaluation of alphanumeric, graphic, and color information displays. *Human Factors, 23*, 541–550.

Tunnard, C. (1951, Summer). Cities by design. *Journal of the American Institute of Planners, 17*, 142–150.

Tunnard, C., & Pushkarev, B. (1963). *Man-made America: Chaos or control?* New Haven, CT: Yale University Press.

Tversky, B. (1981). Distortions in memory for maps. *Cognitive Psychology, 13,* 407–433.

Tversky, B. (1992). Distortions in cognitive maps. *Geoforum, 23,* 131–138.

Tversky, B., & Schiano, D. J. (1989). Perceptual and conceptual factors in distortions in memory for graphs and maps. *Journal of Experimental Psychology: General, 118,* 387–398.

Tye, M. (1991). *The imagery debate.* Cambridge, MA: MIT Press.

Uecker, A., & Obrzut, J. E. (1993). Hemisphere and gender differences in mental rotation. *Brain and Cognition, 22,* 42–50.

Ulrich, R., Simons, R. F., Losito, B. D., Fiorito, E., Miles, M. A., & Zelson, M. (1991). Stress recovery during exposure to natural and urban environments. *Journal of Environmental Psychology, 11,* 201–230.

Ungar, S., Blades, M., Spencer, C., & Morsley, K. (1994, May/June). Can visually impaired children use tactile maps to estimate directions? *Journal of Visual Impairment and Blindness,* 221–233.

Unger, R., & Crawford, M. (1992). *Women and gender: A feminist psychology.* New York: McGraw-Hill.

Ungerleider, L. G., & Mishkin, M. (1982). Two cortical visual systems. In D. J. Ingle, M. A. Goodale, & R. J. W. Mansfield (Eds.), *Analyses of visual behavior* (pp. 549–586). Cambridge, MA: MIT Press.

Updike, J. (1997, March 10). My father on the verge of disgrace. *The New Yorker, 73(3),* 80–85.

Vandenberg, S., & Kuse, A. (1978). Mental rotation: A group test of three dimensional spatial visualization. *Perceptual and Motor Skills, 47,* 599–604.

VanKleeck, M. H., & Kosslyn, S. M. (1989). Gestalt laws of perceptual organization in an embedded figures task: Evidence for hemispheric specialization. *Neuropsychologia, 27,* 1179–1186.

VanPraag, H., Dreyfus, C. F., & Black, I. B. (1994). Dissociation of motor hyperactivity and spatial memory deficits by selective hippocampal lesions in the neonatal rat. *Journal of Cognitive Neuroscience, 6,* 321–331.

Van Strien, J. W., & Bouma, A. (1990). Mental rotation of laterally presented random shapes in males and females. *Brain and Cognition, 12,* 297–303.

Van Vliet, W. (1983). Exploring the fourth environment: An examination of the home range of city and suburban teenagers. *Environment and Behavior, 15,* 567–588.

Von Senden, M. (1960). *Space and sight.* London: Methuen. (Original work published 1932)

Voyer, D., & Bryden, M. P. (1990). Gender, level of spatial ability, and lateralization of mental rotation. *Brain and Cognition, 13,* 18–29.

Waber, D. P. (1976). Sex differences in cognition: A function of maturation rate? *Science, 192,* 572–574.

Waber, D. P. (1977). Sex differences in mental abilities, hemispheric lateralization, and rate of physical growth at adolescence. *Developmental Psychology, 13,* 29–38.

Waber, D. P., Carlson, D., & Mann, M. (1982). Developmental and differential aspects of mental rotation in early adolescence. *Child Development, 53,* 1614–1621.

Wainer, H., & Francollini, C. M. (1980). An empirical inquiry concerning human understanding of two-variable color maps. *American Statistician, 34,* 81–93.

Waldemar, G. (1975). A plan for a contemporary city (1922). In P. Serenyi (Ed.), *Le Corbusier in perspective* (pp. 117–120). Englewood Cliffs, NJ: Prentice-Hall.

Walden, R. (1977). *The open hand: Essays on Le Corbusier.* Cambridge, MA: MIT Press.

Wall, H. M., Karl, K., & Smigiel, J. (1986). Use of contextual information in the formation of cognitive maps. *American Journal of Psychology, 99,* 547–558.

Waller, G., & Harris, P. L. (1988). Who's going where?: Children's route descriptions for peers and younger children. *British Journal of Developmental Psychology, 6,* 137–143.

Walter, E. V. (1988). *Placeways: A theory of the human environment.* Chapel Hill: University of North Carolina Press.

Ward, S. L., Newcombe, N., & Overton, W. F. (1986). Turn left at the church, or three miles north: A study of direction giving and sex differences. *Environment and Behavior, 13,* 189–204.

Warren, D. H. (1994). Self-localization on plan and oblique maps. *Environment and Behavior, 26,* 71–98.

Warren, D. H., Rossano, M. J., & Wear, T. D. (1990). Perception of map-environment correspondence: The roles of features and alignment. *Ecological Psychology, 2,* 131–150.

Warren, D. H., & Scott, T. E. (1993). Map alignment in traveling multisegment routes. *Environment and Behavior, 25,* 643–666.

Warren, D. H., Scott, T. E., & Medley, C. (1992). Finding locations in the environment: The map as mediator. *Perception, 21,* 671–689.

Waters, H. S., & Tinsley, V. S. (1985). Evaluating the discriminant and convergent validity of developmental constructs: Another look at the concept of egocentrism. *Psychological Bulletin, 97,* 483–496.

Watson, N. V., & Kimura, D. (1989). Right-hand superiority for throwing but not for intercepting. *Neuropsychologia, 27,* 1399–1414.

Webb, J. M., Saltz, E. D., McCarthy, M. T., & Kealy, W. A. (1994). Conjoint influence of maps and auded prose on children's retrieval of instruction. *Journal of Experimental Education, 62,* 195–208.

Weber, R. J., Brown, L. T., & Weldon, J. K. (1978). Cognitive maps of environmental knowledge and preference in nursing home patients. *Experimental Aging Research, 4,* 157–174.

Webley, P. (1981). Sex differences in home range and cognitive maps in eight-year old children. *Journal of Environmental Psychology, 1,* 293–302.

Webley, P., & Whalley, A. (1987). Sex differences in children's environmental cognition. *Journal of Social Psychology, 127,* 223–225.

Weekes, N. Y. (1994). Sex differences in the brain. In D. W. Zaidel (Ed.), *Neuropsychology* (pp. 293–315). New York: Academic Press.

Weisman, G. D. (1981). Evaluating architectural legibility: Way-finding in the built environment. *Environment and Behavior, 13,* 189–204.

Weisman, G. D. (1987). Improving wayfinding and architectural legibility in housing for the elderly. In V. Regnier & J. Pynoos (Eds.), *Housing the aged: Design directives and policy considerations* (pp. 441–464). New York: Elsevier.

Weisman, G. D., O'Neill, M. J., & Doll, C. (1987). Computer graphic simulation of wayfinding in a public environment: A validation study. In J. Harvey & D. Henning (Eds.), *Proceedings of the 18th Annual Conference of the Environmental Design Research Association* (pp. 74–80). Ottawa, Canada: Environmental Design Research Association.

Wellman, H. M., Fabricius, W. V., & Sophian, C. (1985). The early development of planning. In H. M. Wellman (Ed.), *Children's searching: The development of search skill and spatial representation* (pp. 123–149). Hillsdale, NJ: Erlbaum.

Wendt, P. E., & Risberg, J. (1994). Cortical activation during visual spatial processing: Relation between hemispheric asymmetry of bloodflow and performance. *Brain and Cognition, 24,* 87–103.

Whyte, W. (1979). *The social life of small urban spaces.* [Film]. New York: The Municipal Art Society of New York.

Wiegmann, D. A., Dansereau, D. F., McCagg, E. C., Rewey, K. L., & Pitre, U. (1992). Effects of knowledge map characteristics on information processing. *Contemporary Educational Psychology, 17,* 136–155.

Williams, C. L., Barnett, A. M., & Meck, W. H. (1990). Organizational effects of early gonadal secretions on sexual differentiation in spatial memory. *Behavioral Neuroscience, 104,* 84–97.

Willis, S. L., & Schaie, K. W. (1988). Gender differences in spatial ability in old age: Longitudinal and intervention findings. *Sex Roles, 18,* 189–203.

Wilson, J. R., & Vandenberg, S. Q. (1978). Sex differences in cognition: Evidence from the Hawaii family study. In T. E. McGill, D. A. Dewsbury, & B. D. Sachs (Eds.), *Sex and behavior: Status and prospectus* (pp. 317–335). New York: Plenum Press.

Wilt, L. J. M., & Maienschein, J. (1979). Symbol signs for libraries. In D. Pollet & P. C. Haskell (Eds.), *Sign systems for libraries: Solving the wayfinding problem* (pp. 105–113). New York: Bowker.

Windley, P. G., & Vandeventer, W. H. (1982). Environmental cognition of small rural towns: The case of older residents. *Journal of Environmental Psychology, 2,* 285–294.

Witelson, S. F. (1974). Hemispheric specialization for linguistic and nonlinguistic tactual perception using a dichotomous stimulation technique. *Cortex, 10,* 3–17.

Witelson, S. F. (1985). The brain connection: The corpus callosum is larger in left-handers. *Science, 229,* 665–668.

Witelson, S. F. (1991). Neural sexual mosaicism: Sexual differentiation of the human temporo-parietal region for functional asymmetry. *Psychoneuroendocrinology, 16,* 131–153.

Witelson, S. F., & Goldsmith, C. H. (1991). The relationship of hand preference to anatomy of the corpus callosum in men. *Brain Research, 545,* 175–182.

Witelson, S. F., Kigar, D. L., & McKanna, J. A. (1992). A computer-assisted direct imaging system to obtain numerical densities of neurons in human cortex. *Brain Research Bulletin, 29,* 441–447.

Witkin, H. A., Dyk, R. B., Faterson, H. F., Goodenough, D. R., & Karp, S. A. (1962). *Psychological differentiation.* New York: Wiley.

Witkin, H., Oltman, P., Raskin, E., & Karp, S. (1971). *A manual for the Embedded Figures Test.* Palo Alto, CA: Consulting Psychologists Press.

Wittig, M. A., & Petersen, A. C. (1979). *Sex-related differences in cognitive functioning: Developmental issues.* New York: Academic Press.

Wong, K. W., & Yacoumelos, N. G. (1973). Identification of cartographic symbols from TV displays. *Human Factors, 15,* 21–31.

Wood, D. (1973). *I don't want to, but I will: The genesis of geographic knowledge: A real-time developmental study of adolescent images of novel environments, Vols. I & II.* Worcester, MA: Clark University Cartographic Laboratory.

Wood, M. (1968). Visual perception and map design. *Cartographic Journal, 5,* 54–64.

Wright, J. K. (1942). Map makers are human: Comments on the subjective in maps. *Geographical Review, 32,* 527–544.

Yoshizaka, T. (1974). *Le Corbusier: Chandigarh: The new capital of Punjab, India.* Tokyo: A.D.A. Edita.

Young, A. W. (Ed.). (1983). *Functions of the right cerebral hemisphere.* New York: Academic Press.

Young, A. W., & Ratcliff, G. (1983). Visuospatial abilities of the right hemisphere. In A. W. Young (Ed.), *Functions of the right cerebral hemisphere* (pp. 1–32). New York: Academic Press.

Yuille, A. L., & Ullman, S. (1990). Computational theories of low-level vision. In D. N. Osherson, S. M. Kosslyn, & J. M. Hollerbach (Eds.), *Visual cognition and action: An invitation to cognitive science* (pp. 5–39). Cambridge, MA: MIT Press.

Zola-Morgan, S., & Squire, L. R. (1990). The primate hippocampal formation: Evidence for a time-limited role in memory storage. *Science, 250,* 288–290.

Zola-Morgan, S., Squire, L. R., & Ramus, S. J. (1994). Severity of memory impairment in monkeys as a function of locus and extent of damage within the medial temporal lobe memory system. *Hippocampus, 4,* 483–495.

Zucker, P. (1959). *Town and square: From the agora to the village green.* New York: Columbia University Press.

Index

Acquired hypergonadotropic hypogon-
adism, 134
Acredolo, Linda, 18–19, 22–23
Adaptation, 64–69
Alexander, Christopher, 29, 31, 146,
208, 210–211, 213, 224, 229, 232.
Works: *A Pattern Language*, 210;
The Timeless Way of Building, 210
Allen, Gary, 20–21, 23, 75–76, 152
Anchor point theory, 9, 24–27
Anderson, John, 25, 98–99
Annett, Marian, 122–123, 126, 135–
136
Anomalous dominance, 122
Anooshian, Linda, 17, 21–23, 75, 82
Appleton, Jay, 192
Appleyard, Donald, 146, 211–214,
217–218
Arnheim, Rudolf, 148–149, 175, 197
Aubrey, Jocelyn, 42, 72, 87

Bacon, Edmund, 194, 217–218
Banerjee, Tridib, 146
Barnett, Jonathan, 195, 215, 217

Beatty, William, 72, 73, 124
Benevolo, Leonardo, 196
Bent Twig theory, 92, 126
Berg, Cynthia, 48, 56–57
Bertin, Jacques, 149, 168
Birenbaum, Menucha, 48, 64
Blades, Mark, 5–6, 10, 16, 18–19, 79–
80, 148
Blaut, James, 17–18
Blindness, spatial cognition and, 30, 35–
39
Blough, Patricia, 48, 50
Bluestein, Neil, 18–19
Borke, Helene, 5–6, 17
Brain lesions, 105–118
Brasilia, Brazil, 215, 217–223; com-
pared to Venice, 218, 221–222; legi-
bility of, 218–223
Bremner, J. Gavin, 13–15
Bronzaft, Arline, 162
Bryden, M.P., 48, 64, 123, 135
Buss, David, 47, 64
Butters, Nelson, 115–116
Byrne, R.W., 37, 153

Calthorpe, Peter, 228
Canter, David, 197, 207
Caplan, Paula, 88–90
Carpman, Janet, 177–178
Casey, M. Beth, 91–92, 126, 136
Categorical judgments, brain and, 103
Celebration, Florida, 195, 215, 229–231
Cerebral lateralization, 122–134; Geschwind and Galaburda's theory of, 122–123; hemisphere, right, lesions and, 105–118; hormonal effects and, 123–128; sex differences in, 123–128
Chabris, Christopher, 102–103
Chandigarh, India, 215, 223–225, 227
Christ, Richard, 169, 171
Churchill, Henry, 193–195
Ciudad Guayana, Venezuela, 212–213, 215
Cleveland, William, 151
Cognitive bias task, 137–138
Cognitive map: development of, 8–11; interrepresentation network as, 29; linguistic structure as, 29–30; representation as, 142. See also Spatial cognition
Cohen, Robert, 18, 22, 79, 209
Color, 167–171
Columbia, Maryland, 216
Comprehensive ability battery, 48
Computational process models, 28–30
Congenital adrenal hyperplasia, 129–130, 133
Congrès Internationaux d'Architecture Moderne (CIAM), 217, 223
Conning, Alison, 21–23
Coordinate judgments, brain and, 103
Corballis, Michael, 47, 49, 99–100, 102, 105, 114, 135, 137, 142
Cornell, Edward, 21, 75, 77
Cosmides, Leda, 140
Couclelis, Helen, 1–2, 9, 24–25, 58
Cousins, Jennifer, 21–23, 42, 75, 79
Crosby, Theo, 193, 209, 216
Cullen, Gordon, 210

Daniel, Marie-Paule, 29
Darvizeh, Zhra, 5, 12, 29
DeGroot, Adrianus, 156
DeJonge, Derk, 206–207, 212
Dent, Borden, 149–151, 158
DeRenzi, Ennio, 106–107
Developmental theory of spatial cognition: Moore's, 8; Piaget's, 2–10; Siegel and White's, 9–11, 67
Devlin, Ann S., 25–27, 31, 61, 68–69, 71–72, 77, 94–95, 149, 159, 164, 171–172, 177, 188, 191, 200
Differential aptitude test, 46, 50, 69, 134
Disney theme parks, 201–202, 208
Districts, 201
Doherty, Sally, 15, 21–23, 75–76, 82–83
Doss, Erik, 201–202
Downs, Roger, 16–17, 42, 181
Duany, Andres, 228–229
Dunlop, Beth, 208

Eagly, Alice, 88–89, 94
Eals, Marion, 65–66, 69
Ecological validity, of spatial tasks, 17–21
Edelman, Gerald, 29
Edges, 201
Egocentrism, child and, 4–8, 13
Embedded Figures Test, 43, 69, 134
Epstein, David, 217–218, 220, 223
Euclidean relationships, 3, 9–10, 155, 164
Evans, Gary, 34, 86
Evenson, Norma, 223, 225
Evolutionary psychology, spatial cognition and, 64–69

Farah, Martha, 98, 102, 110, 112, 141, 143
Fargo map test, 73–74
Fischer, Susan, 113–114
Fisher, Howard, 149–150
Fishman, Robert, 215, 223
Flavell, John, 7
Fodor, Jerry, 102
Form qualities, Lynch and, 203–207

Francaviglia, Richard, 208
French, John, 43–44

Galea, Liisa, 42, 63–64, 68–69, 72
Gans, Herbert, 225–226. Works: *The Levittowners*, 225
Garden city movement, 217, 224
Garland, Howard, 171
Garling, Tommy, 1, 9, 24, 27–28, 189
Garvin, Alexander, 216, 228
Gaulin, Steven, 125–126
Gazzaniga, Michael, 100–102, 113
Gender differences in spatial cognition, 88–95; arguments against, 88–89; genetic explanations of, 89–90; hormonal influences on, 90-91; neurological explanations of, 91–92; psychosocial explanations of, 92–95
Geographical information systems (GIS), 28
Geography: ability in, 41–42; cognitive-behavioral approach to, 24
Geschwind, Norman, 47, 90–91, 122, 135
Gestalt principles, 157–158
Gibson, James J., 11, 23, 35, 141–142, 157–158, 214
Golbeck, Susan, 18–19
Goldberg, Elkhonon, 99, 104–105, 137–138
Goldberger, Paul, 218, 223
Goldman-Rakic, Patricia, 100–101, 104
Golledge, Reginald, 1, 15, 24–28, 30, 38–39, 41, 164
Gopal, Sucharita, 28, 164
Gouchie, Catherine, 132–133
Grid, history in city design, 193–197
Gruen, Victor, 192, 218, 223

Halpern, Diane, 47, 89–91
Handedness, 126, 135–139; Annett's theory of, 135
Hardwick, Douglas, 5, 167
Hare-Mustin, Rachel, 88–89, 94–95
Harris, Lauren, 47, 89, 124
Hart, Roger, 2, 25
Hassler, Marianne, 47, 90

Hastie, Reid, 170–171
Hazen, Nancy, 18–19, 80
Hemisphere, dissociations of, 102–104
Hemisphere, right: cerebral blood flow studies of, 108–110; lesions and, 105–118; vis-à-vis left, 110–118
Hemisphere, structure of, 98. *See also* Cerebral lateralization
Herman, James, 18–19, 22, 47, 56–57, 68–69, 78–79, 92
Hill, Michael, 165–166
Hippocampus, 118–122
Hirtle, Stephen, 152, 162
Holding, Carol, 42, 58, 62, 70–72
Holmes, Nigel, 149–150
Holston, James, 217–218, 220, 224
Horan, Patricia, 46, 53, 88
Howard, Ebenezer, 217. Works: *Garden Cities of To-morrow*, 217
Hunt, Michael, 187–188
Huttenlocher, Janellen, 11–12
Hyde, Janet, 42, 45–47, 52, 72, 88–89, 94, 123

Idiopathic hypergonadotropic hypogonadism, 134
Imageability, 141, 192–193
Imagery, 142–146
Imhof, Eduard, 151, 157–158, 174, 177
InterConnection density, 189

Jacobs, Allan, 200, 218
Jacobs, Jane, 196, 208, 229–230
James, Thomas, 65–67, 69
Johnson, Edward, 55–56

Kahneman, Daniel, 20
Kail, Robert, 49–50, 54
Kalia, Ravi, 223–224
Kaplan, Stephen, 9, 24–25, 27, 142, 174–175, 188, 192, 232
Kennedy, John M., 37–38
Kimura, Doreen, 42, 63–69, 72, 105, 123–125, 129, 132, 136
Kingsberg, Sheryl, 126–128
Kirasic, Kathleen, 3, 33–34, 42, 60, 69, 85, 87

Klatzky, Roberta, 35, 38
Knowledge. *See* Spatial cognition
Kosslyn, Stephen, 18–19, 97, 102–104,
    112, 140, 143–145, 149–150, 167
Kostof, Spiro, 194, 203, 208–209
Kozlowski, Lynn, 72, 77, 167
Kritchevsky, Mark, 104, 110
Kulhavy, Raymond, 176–177

Laeng, Bruno, 101–103
Landau, Barbara, 29–30, 35
Landmarks: children's use of, 23; evo-
    lutionary theory and, 64–69; infant's
    use of, 5; knowledge of, 9–11, 13;
    Lynch and, 201
Lateralization. *See* Cerebral lateraliza-
    tion; hemisphere, dissociations of
Lawton, Carol, 59, 70, 72–73, 77
LeCorbusier, 214–215. Works: *The
    City of To-morrow and Its Planning*,
    214
Legibility, 141, 192–193
Lesions, 105–118
Levine, Marvin, 142, 159–161, 164,
    187
Levittown, New Jersey, 215, 225–226
Levy, Jerre, 91, 99, 105, 135
Lewandowsky, Stephan, 156, 169–170
Liben, Lynn, 16–17, 42–46, 53
Linn, Marcia, 43, 45–47, 90, 123
Location coding, theory of, 11–12
Location memory, 65–67
Lynch, Kevin, 1, 8, 10, 23, 26, 141,
    145, 148, 187, 192, 196, 198, 207,
    210–214, 216, 230; structural ele-
    ments of, 198–202. Works: *A
    Theory of Good City Form*, 206;
    The Image of the City, 197–203,
    205

Maguire, Eleanor, 120–121
Main Street, 207–210
Mapping Project at Penn State
    (MAPPS), 16–17
Maps, 148–153; distortions in, 153–
    155; hierarchies in, 151–153; way-
    finding aids as, 148–151. *See also*
    Cognitive map

Marr, David, 28, 30, 102–103, 140–
    142, 144, 158
Masters, Mary, 42, 46, 72
Matthews, M. H., 7, 78, 83
Mayer, Albert, 223
McClurg, Patricia, 81, 93
McGee, Mark, 44–48, 90
McGuinness, Diane, 42, 62, 68–69,
    72, 78
McNamara, Timothy, 27, 154–155
Mehta, Ziyah, 101, 111, 113
Mental imagery, 142–146
Mental model. *See* Cognitive map
Mental rotation task. *See* Vandenberg
    and Kuse mental rotation test
Milgram, Stanley, 153, 206
Miller, George, 58, 183, 200, 203, 225
Miller, Leon, 42, 64, 72
Milner, Brenda, 118
Moeser, Shannon, 153, 155–156, 184,
    187, 189
Monmonier, Mark, 148–149, 167
Moore, Gary, 1–2, 8–9, 167
Morrow, Lisa, 102–103, 105, 110–111
Muehrcke, Phillip, 148–149
Mumford, Lewis, 195

Nadel, Lynn, 14, 118–119
NAVIGATOR, 28–29
Neisser, Ulric, 10, 18, 48, 61, 212
Newcombe, Nora, 3, 6–7, 11–12, 89,
    93
Newcomers, way-finding behavior in,
    9, 26
Newman, Oscar, 3
NOMAD, 39
"Now Print!" mechanism, 10–11

Ohta, Russell, 3, 33–34
O'Keefe, John, 14, 118–119, 144.
    Works: *The Hippocampus as a Cog-
    nitive Map*, 118
Olson, Judy, 167–168
O'Neill, Michael, 98, 164, 188–189
Orientation, guidance, and place the-
    ory, 14, 119–120
Orleans, Peter, 206
Ornstein, Robert, 116–117

Paivio, Allan, 143, 176
Paper Folding Test, 43, 132
Passini, Romedi, 9, 35, 39
Paths, 199–201
Perspective-taking, 4–8, 13
Peruch, Patrick, 142, 156
Petersen, Anne, 90, 132
Phillips, Richard, 156, 161
Piaget, Jean, 2–10, 43–44
Plater-Zyberk, Elizabeth, 228–229
Plaut, David, 98, 141
Plot and choice points, 25
Porteus maze test, 131
Portugali, Juval, 29
Poulton, E. Christopher, 153, 175
Presson, Clark, 5, 12, 18, 27
Primary Mental Abilities Test, 43, 50, 54, 113
Projective relations, 3
Purdue Spatial Visualization Test, 50
Pylyshyn, Zenon, 143

Ratcliff, Graham, 51, 102, 107
Reinisch, June, 90, 134
Resnick, Susan, 49, 133
Richardson, John T. E., 48, 51
Rieser, John, 13–14, 36, 38
Robinson, Arthur, 149–151, 167
Rod and Frame Test, 44, 45
Roland, P. E, 108–109, 143
Roof, Robin, 131–132
Roosevelt Island, New York, 215, 226–228

Sadalla, Edward, 42, 153
Safdie, Moshe, 215
Salthouse, Timothy, 32
Sanders, Barbara, 47
Scale, and spatial tasks: large, 20–21, 75–78; mid-range, 18–20, 78–81; small, 12–18
Schaie, K. Warner, 32–33, 56, 93
Scott Brown, Denise, 94
Scully, Vincent, 229
Seaside, Florida, 195, 215, 228–229
Selfridge, Katherine, 172–173, 181
Shepard, Roger, 42, 52, 54–55, 109, 115–116, 142–143

Sherman, Julia, 123, 126
Sherry, David, 120, 125
Siegel, Alexander, 1, 8–11, 15, 21, 23, 25, 67, 75, 84–85
Silverman, Irwin, 65–66, 69
Simulation studies, 69–72
Smallman, Harvey, 168–169
Smith, Sidney, 168–169, 175
SoHo, 202–205
Southworth, Michael, 146, 148–150, 167
Space syntax theory, 189
Spatial ability, factors of, 43–47; age and, 52–57; real-world and, 57–61; traditional tasks of, 47–52
Spatial anxiety, 72–73
Spatial cognition: child and infant development of, 1–2, 9; computational theories of, 24–30; computer use and, 81–82; design implications for, 38–39; elderly and, 31–35; gender and age differences in, 52–57; Piaget and child's conception of, 2–8; visually impaired and, 30, 35–39
Spencer, Christopher, 5–6, 10, 12, 38–39, 79–80
Squire, Larry, 118–120
Streeter, Lynn, 72, 157

Taylor, Holly, 9, 42
Three mountains task, 4
Thurstone, Louis L., 43–44
Topographic memory failure, 86, 106–107
Topological relations, 3
Toy play, 93, 133
Tracy, Dyanne, 93, 123
Travel plan, spatial behavior as, 9, 27–28
Travis, David, 167–168
Trillin, Calvin, 196–197
Tufte, Edward, 149, 170–171, 175
Tullis, Thomas, 170–171
Tversky, Barbara, 9, 27, 151, 153–155

Ulrich, Roger, 69
Unger, Rhoda, 41, 89, 92–94, 123

Ungerleider, Leslie, 30, 102
Updike, John, 207

Vandenberg and Kuse mental rotation test, 43–44, 49, 51, 69, 81, 90, 94, 126, 132
Van Vliet, Willem, 78, 84
Venturi, Robert, 94
Visual field crossover, 100

Waber, Deborah, 52, 54, 90, 123
Ward, Shawn, 42, 61, 69, 72, 166
Water Level Test, 44, 53
Way-finding aids: buildings as, 177–183; color-coding in, 167–171; computer-based, 164–165; detail in, 174–175; directions as, 165–167; familiarity and, 156–157; format in, 173; Gestalt principles and, 157–158; label placement and, 175–177; signs as, 177–183; typeface in, 175–177
Webley, Paul, 75, 78, 83–84, 87
Weisman, Gerald, 130, 163–164, 172, 182, 188, 214
Wendt, Peter, 109–110
What and where visual systems, 30, 103–104
Whyte, William, 195
Williams, Christina, 129–130
Willis, Sherry, 56–57, 93
Witelson, Sandra, 104–105, 128, 138–139
Witkin, Herman, 43–44
Wood, Denis, 209

You-are-here maps, 159–161
Young, Andrew W., 101–102

Zola-Morgan, Stuart, 118
Zucker, Paul, 194

About the Author

ANN SLOAN DEVLIN received her Ph.D. in the area of environmental psychology at the University of Michigan. She is currently a professor of Psychology at Connecticut College in New London, CT, where she teaches and does research in the areas of spatial cognition and environment-behavior issues. She is on the board of directors of the Environmental Design Research Association (EDRA) and serves on the Editorial Review Board for the journal *Environment and Behavior*.